Data Structures and Algorithms with the C++ STL

A guide for modern C++ practitioners

John Farrier

Data Structures and Algorithms with the C++ STL

Group Product Manager: Kunal Sawant
Publishing Product Manager: Samriddhi Murarka
Book Project Manager: Manisha Singh
Senior Editor: Aditi Chatterjee
Technical Editor: Jubit Pincy
Copy Editor: Safis Editing
Indexer: Hemanigini Bari
Production Designer: Gokul Raj S.T
DevRel Marketing Coordinator: Shrinidhi Manoharan

First published: February 2024

Production reference: 1160224

Published by
Packt Publishing Ltd.
Grosvenor House
11 St Paul's Square
Birmingham
B3 1RB, UK.

ISBN 978-1-83546-855-5

www.packtpub.com

To my parents, John and Sharon, who ignited the spark of curiosity within me by introducing me to the world of computers and not being too upset when I broke them—thank you for setting me on this path. To my wife, Lisa, whose unwavering support has been my cornerstone throughout this journey. And to my children, Corbin and Regan, who give every day a purpose and every challenge a reward—this book is for you. Your love and belief in me make every endeavor worthwhile.

Contributors

About the author

John Farrier has over 25 years of experience as a successful founder and software engineering leader, particularly noted for delivering high-value projects to the U.S. Air Force clients.

Under his leadership as Co-Founder and CEO, his first company, Hellebore, saw remarkable growth and was pivotal in the defense sector, particularly in designing advanced mission systems architectures for next-generation aircraft.

In his expansive technical repertoire, John commands expertise in Design Patterns, C++, Python, DevOps, AI, Game Engine Design, Large-Scale Agile Project Management, and Modeling & Simulation. Leveraging Agile principles and stream-aligned teams, he constantly explores the outer reaches of software engineering possibilities. John's credentials are reinforced by numerous publications in the realm of Modeling and Simulation.

John's commitment extends beyond mere technical excellence. He's an unwavering advocate for fostering strong software cultures, emphasizing collaboration and career evolution. He operates with a strong ethos of principle-based decision-making and hyper-transparency, fostering both trust and clarity in professional relationships.

At present, John leads Polyrhythm Software, one of a new generation of software companies focused on delivering high-value software to the Department of Defense and commercial clients.

About the reviewer

Kevin Carpenter, an experienced Software Engineer, excels in crafting high-availability C++ solutions for Linux and Windows, with expertise in transaction software, financial modeling, and system integration. As a Lead Project Engineer, he ensures secure, high-speed credit card transactions. In his prior position, he played a lead role in developing an interest rate risk model for large credit unions, enhancing legacy code, and optimizing ERP data integration.

Kevin actively engages in the C++ community, volunteering at conferences such as CppCon, C++ on Sea, and C++Now, where he holds key positions of Speaker Liaison and Volunteer Coordinator/Chair. His diverse contributions to the C++ community showcase his commitment to excellence and drive for collaborative growth, leaving a lasting impact on the tech world.

Table of Contents

Part 1: Mastering std::vector

1

3

Mastering Memory and Allocators with std::vector   51

4

Mastering Algorithms with std::vector   71

Part 2: Understanding STL Data Structures

6

7

Advanced Ordered Associative Container Usage   141

8

Advanced Unordered Associative Container Usage   165

9

Advanced Container Adaptor Usage   191

10

Advanced Container View Usage   223

Part 3: Mastering STL Algorithms

11

12

13

Part 4: Creating STL-Compatible Types and Algorithms

16

Creating STL-Types Containers   303

17

18

Part 5: STL Data Structures and Algorithms: Under the Hood

19

20

21

STL Interaction with Concepts and Coroutines   389

22

Parallel Algorithms with the STL   401

Preface

Welcome to *Data Structures and Algorithms with the C++ STL*, a resource that aims to deepen your understanding of data structures and algorithms using the robust tools provided by the C++ **Standard Template Library (STL)**. Within these pages, you will explore `std::vector`, advanced usage of sequence and associative containers, in-depth discussions on STL algorithms and their enhancements with modern C++ features, and a penetrating look at creating STL-compatible types and algorithms.

The book is structured into five parts, each focusing on a different aspect of STL. *Part 1, Mastering std::vector*, details the fundamental usage of vectors and their manipulation with STL algorithms. *Part 2, Understanding STL Data Structures*, expands your repertoire with sequence, ordered and unordered associative containers, and container adaptors. *Part 3, Mastering STL Algorithms*, provides comprehensive coverage of fundamental, numeric, and range-based algorithms, focusing on best practices. *Part 4, Creating STL-Compatible Types & Algorithms*, guides you through developing your own types and algorithms that integrate seamlessly with STL. Lastly, *Part 5, STL Data Structures and Algorithms: Under the Hood*, offers advanced insights into exception safety, thread safety, concurrency, and the interactions of STL with the latest C++ features such as concepts and coroutines.

Each chapter is structured to build on previously introduced concepts, ensuring a cohesive learning experience. By the end of this book, you should be proficient in the practical application of the STL, equipped to tackle modern software challenges with confidence and expertise. Let us embark on this journey not only to understand the mechanics of the STL but also to appreciate its elegance and power in crafting exceptional C++ software.

Who this book is for

This book is crafted for intermediate-level C++ developers who wish to refine their skills and knowledge in applying STL components to solve complex problems efficiently.

What this book covers

Chapter 1, The Basics of std::vector, introduces `std::vector`, comparing it with C-style arrays, and demonstrates its declaration, initialization, and element manipulation.

Chapter 2, Mastering Iterators with std::vector, explores the different types of iterators in the STL and their application within `std::vector` contexts, including custom iterator creation.

Chapter 3, Mastering Memory and Allocators with std::vector, discusses vector capacity versus size, memory optimization techniques, and the design of custom allocators for enhanced performance.

Chapter 4, Mastering Algorithms with std::vector, delves into algorithmic operations on vectors, such as sorting and searching, and the importance of understanding iterator invalidation.

Chapter 5, Making the Case for std::vector, examines the performance aspects, practical applications, and versatility of `std::vector` as a go-to STL container.

Chapter 6, Advanced Sequence Container Usage, analyzes advanced usage scenarios and best practices for sequence containers like `std::array`, `std::deque`, and others.

Chapter 7, Advanced Ordered Associative Container Usage, explores the intricacies of ordered associative containers such as `std::set` and `std::map` and their unique performance considerations.

Chapter 8, Advanced Unordered Associative Container Usage, investigates unordered associative containers, highlighting their internal workings and use cases.

Chapter 9, Advanced Container Adaptor Usage, focuses on container adaptors like `std::stack` and `std::queue`, discussing their implementation and when to use them effectively.

Chapter 10, Advanced Container View Usage, introduces container views such as `std::span` and `std::mdspan`, providing insights into their utility and performance benefits.

Chapter 11, Fundamental Algorithms and Searching, Covers the foundational algorithms for sorting and searching within STL and their practical applications.

Chapter 12, Manipulation and Transformation, Details the techniques for transforming data within STL containers, including the nuances of copying, moving, and removing elements.

Chapter 13, Numeric and Range-Based Operations, Explores numeric operations and their applications on ranges, demonstrating how they can optimize algorithmic complexity.

Chapter 14, Permutations, Partitions, and Heaps, Provides an in-depth look at data organization algorithms, such as partitioning and heap operations, within the STL.

Chapter 15, Modern STL with Ranges, Discusses the modern approach to STL with ranges, enhancing the composability and efficiency of algorithms.

Chapter 16, Creating STL-Types Containers, Guides through the creation of custom containers that are compatible with STL algorithms and the essential components required for full integration.

Chapter 17, Creating STL-Compatible Algorithms, Details the development of custom algorithms that work seamlessly with STL containers and adhere to STL principles.

Chapter 18, Type Traits and Policies, Delves into the advanced topics of type traits and policies, key in crafting adaptable and efficient template code.

Chapter 19, Exception Safety, Examines the levels of exception safety guaranteed by STL and how to write robust STL-compatible code with noexcept.

Chapter 20, Thread Safety and Concurrency with the STL, Discusses the concurrency and thread safety features of STL containers, the prevention of race conditions, and best practices for multithreaded programming.

Chapter 21, STL Interaction with Concepts and Coroutines, Explores the interaction between STL and the latest C++ features like concepts and coroutines, showcasing their synergy.

Chapter 22, Parallel Algorithms with the STL, Introduces execution policies for parallel algorithms in STL, the role of constexpr, and the considerations for performance and efficiency.

To get the most out of this book

Before embarking on this book, readers should have a firm grasp of fundamental C++ programming concepts, such as syntax, control structures, and basic object-oriented principles. An understanding of pointers, memory management, and template basics is also assumed, as these are foundational to effectively utilizing the STL. The book presumes familiarity with C++11 standard features, as many examples and explanations rely on this version of the language or newer. Moreover, a basic knowledge of data structures such as arrays and linked lists, as well as classic algorithms, will be beneficial for following the advanced topics discussed within.

Software/hardware covered in the book	Operating system requirements
C++	Windows, macOS, or Linux
C++ STL	

If you are using the digital version of this book, we advise you to type the code yourself or access the code from the book's GitHub repository (a link is available in the next section). Doing so will help you avoid any potential errors related to the copying and pasting of code.

Download the example code files

You can download the example code files for this book from GitHub at `https://github.com/PacktPublishing/Data-Structures-and-Algorithms-with-the-CPP-STL`. If there's an update to the code, it will be updated in the GitHub repository.

We also have other code bundles from our rich catalog of books and videos available at `https://github.com/PacktPublishing/`. Check them out!

Conventions used

There are a number of text conventions used throughout this book.

`Code in text`: Indicates code words in text, database table names, folder names, filenames, file extensions, pathnames, dummy URLs, user input, and Twitter handles. Here is an example: "This is where the genius of std::vector shines; over-allocating reduces the need for frequent and, potentially, computationally costly reallocations."

A block of code is set as follows:

```
template <typename T,
          typename AllocatorPolicy = std::allocator<T>>
class CustomVector {
  // Implementation using AllocatorPolicy for memory
  // allocation
};
```

Any command-line input or output is written as follows:

```
Time without reserve: 0.01195 seconds
Time with reserve:     0.003685 seconds
```

> Tips or important notes
> Appear like this.

Get in touch

Feedback from our readers is always welcome.

General feedback: If you have questions about any aspect of this book, email us at customercare@packtpub.com and mention the book title in the subject of your message.

Errata: Although we have taken every care to ensure the accuracy of our content, mistakes do happen. If you have found a mistake in this book, we would be grateful if you would report this to us. Please visit www.packtpub.com/support/errata and fill in the form.

Piracy: If you come across any illegal copies of our works in any form on the internet, we would be grateful if you would provide us with the location address or website name. Please contact us at copyright@packt.com with a link to the material.

If you are interested in becoming an author: If there is a topic that you have expertise in and you are interested in either writing or contributing to a book, please visit authors.packtpub.com

Share Your Thoughts

Once you've read *Data Structures and Algorithms with the C++ STL*, we'd love to hear your thoughts! Scan the QR code below to go straight to the Amazon review page for this book and share your feedback.

https://packt.link/r/1835468551

Your review is important to us and the tech community and will help us make sure we're delivering excellent quality content.

Download a free PDF copy of this book

Thanks for purchasing this book!

Do you like to read on the go but are unable to carry your print books everywhere?

Is your eBook purchase not compatible with the device of your choice?

Don't worry, now with every Packt book you get a DRM-free PDF version of that book at no cost.

Read anywhere, any place, on any device. Search, copy, and paste code from your favorite technical books directly into your application.

The perks don't stop there, you can get exclusive access to discounts, newsletters, and great free content in your inbox daily

Follow these simple steps to get the benefits:

1. Scan the QR code or visit the link below

https://packt.link/free-ebook/978-1-83546-855-5

2. Submit your proof of purchase
3. That's it! We'll send your free PDF and other benefits to your email directly

Part 1:
Mastering std::vector

In this Part, we will build our knowledge of C++ **Standard Template (STL)** Library containers and algorithms on a foundation of a comprehensive examination of `std::vector`. We will start with introducing `std::vector`, contrasting it with traditional C-style arrays, and covering essential operations such as initializing, accessing, and modifying elements. We then advance to the intricacies of iterators, revealing their types and uses in `std::vector` operations and the elegance of range-based for loops. Memory management is demystified by constructing an understanding of optimizing the allocation and deallocation of resources, including an introduction to creating custom allocators. The section then builds into applying algorithms to sort, search, and manipulate vector contents efficiently, emphasizing the role of custom comparators and the importance of understanding iterator invalidation. The final chapter encapsulates the performance considerations and practical applications of `std::vector`, cementing its status as the default container choice for C++ developers.

This part has the following chapters:

- *Chapter 1: The Basics of std::vector*

- *Chapter 2: Mastering Iterators with std::vector*

- *Chapter 3: Mastering Memory and Allocators with std::vector*

- *Chapter 4: Mastering Algorithms with std::vector*

- *Chapter 5: Making a Case for std::vector*

1

The Basics of std::vector

`std::vector` is a fundamental component of C++ programming. This chapter will explore `std::vector` as a dynamic array, discussing its utility in various programming contexts. By the end of the chapter, you should be adept at declaring, initializing, and manipulating vectors. These skills will enable you to utilize `std::vector` effectively in diverse applications. It will provide a solid foundation for understanding the broader set of data structures and algorithms of the **Standard Template Library** (**STL**).

In this chapter, we're going to cover the following main topics:

- The significance of `std::vector`
- Declaring and initializing `std::vector`
- Accessing elements
- Adding and removing elements

Technical requirements

The code in this chapter can be found on GitHub:

```
https://github.com/PacktPublishing/Data-Structures-and-Algorithms-
with-the-CPP-STL
```

The significance of std::vector

In C++, `std::vector` is a frequently chosen data structure. While beginners might initially see parallels between it and the basic arrays in C, the advantages of `std::vector` become evident with deeper exploration. Additionally, a solid grasp of `std::vector` facilitates a smoother transition to understanding other components of STL.

Both vectors and arrays function as containers for collections of elements. The critical distinction between them lies in their flexibility and capabilities. Arrays are static in size, set at declaration time, and cannot be altered afterward.

In contrast, vectors are dynamic. They can expand or contract based on the operations performed on them. Unlike arrays, which commit to a fixed memory block upon declaration, vectors dynamically manage memory. They frequently allocate extra memory to anticipate future growth, optimizing efficiency and flexibility. While arrays offer simple index-based element access and modification, vectors provide a broader set of functions, including methods for inserting, deleting, and locating elements.

The primary advantage of `std::vector` is its combination of dynamic resizing and optimized performance. Traditional C++ arrays have their size set at compile time. If an array is declared to hold 10 elements, it's constrained to that capacity. However, in many real-world scenarios, the volume of data isn't determined until runtime. This is where `std::vector` shines.

A basic comparison of C-style arrays and std::vector

Acting as a dynamic array, `std::vector` can adjust its size during program execution. It efficiently manages its memory, reallocating not for each new addition, but in larger chunks to maintain a balance between performance and adaptability. Thus, rather than pre-committing to a specific size and risking either memory waste or a shortage, `std::vector` dynamically responds to varying data demands.

Here are two code examples that demonstrate the contrast between using a C-style array and `std::vector`.

The following code demonstrates the use of a C-style array:

```
#include <iostream>

int main() {
  int *cArray = new int[5];

  for (int i = 0; i < 5; ++i) { cArray[i] = i + 1; }

  for (int i = 0; i < 5; ++i) {
    std::cout << cArray[i] << " ";
  }
  std::cout << "\n";

  const int newSize = 7;
  int *newCArray = new int[newSize];

  for (int i = 0; i < 5; ++i) { newCArray[i] = cArray[i]; }

  delete[] cArray;

  cArray = newCArray;
```

```
  for (int i = 0; i < newSize; ++i) {
    std::cout << cArray[i] << " ";
  }
  std::cout << "\n";

  int arraySize = newSize;
  std::cout << "Size of cArray: " << arraySize << "\n";

  delete[] cArray;

  return 0;
}
```

Here is the example output:

```
1 2 3 4 5
1 2 3 4 5 0 0
Size of cArray: 7
```

In this example, we do the following:

1.   Declare a C-style dynamic array with a size of 5.

2.   Initialize the dynamic array.

3.   Print the contents of the array.

4.   Resize the array to a new size (e.g., 7).

5.   Copy the elements from the old array to the new one.

6.   Deallocate the old array.

7.   Update the pointer to the new array.

8.   Print the contents of the resized array.

9.   Get the size of the resized array.

10. Deallocate the resized array when done.

In contrast, the following code demonstrates the use of std::vector:

```
#include <iostream>
#include <vector>

int main() {
  std::vector<int> stlVector = {1, 2, 3, 4, 5};

  for (const int val : stlVector) {
```

```
      std::cout << val << " ";
   }
   std::cout << "\n";

   stlVector.resize(7);

   for (const int val : stlVector) {
     std::cout << val << " ";
   }
   std::cout << "\n";

   std::cout << "Size of stlVector: " << stlVector.size()
             << "\n";

   return 0;
}
```

Here is the example output:

```
1 2 3 4 5
1 2 3 4 5 0 0
Size of stlVector: 7
```

By way of contrast with the C-style version, in this example, we do the following:

1. Declare `std::vector` with initial values.

2. Print the contents of the vector.

3. Resize. This operation is easy with `std::vector`.

4. Print again to see the change.

5. Get the size. This operation is simple with the `size()` member function.

In the initial example, the C-style array is constrained by its fixed size. Modifying its size typically requires a non-trivial procedure. Conversely, `std::vector` can adjust its size effortlessly and provides a `size()` method to determine the number of elements it holds.

Beyond its dynamic resizing capability, `std::vector` further simplifies memory management compared to traditional arrays. With `std::vector`, there's no need for explicit memory allocations or deallocations as it internally handles these tasks. This approach minimizes the risk of memory leaks and streamlines the development process. As a result, many C++ developers, regardless of their experience level, prefer using `std::vector` over raw arrays for convenience and safety.

Let's look at an example that contrasts how a legacy C-style array manages memory and how `std::vector` makes this easier and safer.

Comparison of C-style arrays and std::vector for memory management

First, let us consider an example of a C-style array with manual memory management.

In this example, we'll use dynamic memory allocation (`new` and `delete`) to simulate some of the resizing capabilities of `std::vector`:

```
#include <iostream>

int main() {
  int *cArray = new int[5];

  for (int i = 0; i < 5; ++i) { cArray[i] = i + 1; }

  int *temp = new int[10];
  for (int i = 0; i < 5; ++i) { temp[i] = cArray[i]; }
  delete[] cArray; // Important: free the old memory
  cArray = temp;

  for (int i = 5; i < 10; ++i) { cArray[i] = i + 1; }

  for (int i = 0; i < 10; ++i) {
    std::cout << cArray[i] << " ";
  }
  std::cout << "\n";

  delete[] cArray;

  return 0;
}
```

Here is the example output:

```
1 2 3 4 5 6 7 8 9 10
```

In this example, we do the following:

1. Dynamically allocate a C-style array with a size of 5.

2. Populate the array.

3. Simulate a resize: allocate a larger array and copy the data.

4. Populate the rest of the new array.

5. Print the array's content.

6. Clean up the allocated memory.

Now, let us consider an example of `std::vector` with built-in memory management.

Using `std::vector`, you don't have to allocate or deallocate memory manually; it is managed internally:

```cpp
#include <iostream>
#include <vector>

int main() {
  std::vector<int> myVector(5);

  for (int i = 0; i < 5; ++i) { myVector[i] = i + 1; }

  for (int i = 5; i < 10; ++i) {
    myVector.push_back(i + 1);
  }

  for (int val : myVector) { std::cout << val << " "; }
  std::cout << "\n";

  return 0;
}
```

Here is the example output:

```
1 2 3 4 5 6 7 8 9 10
```

The steps in this example include the following:

1. Create `std::vector` with a size of 5.

2. Populate the vector.

3. Resizing is straightforward with `push_back()` or `resize()`.

4. Print the vector's contents.

    There's no need for explicit memory deallocation.

In the first example, the challenges of manual memory management are evident. Failing to use `delete` appropriately can result in memory leaks. On the other hand, the second example highlights the efficiency of `std::vector`, which internally manages memory, eliminating the need for manual resizing and memory operations and enhancing the development process.

Traditional arrays come with a basic set of operations. In contrast, `std::vector` offers various member functions that provide advanced data manipulation and retrieval capabilities. These functions will be explored in subsequent sections.

In C++ development, `std::vector` is a fundamental tool. Its flexibility makes it a go-to choice for various applications, from game development to complex software projects. The built-in safety mechanisms against common memory issues underscore its value. As an STL component, `std::vector` encourages consistent and optimal coding practices by integrating well with other STL elements.

This section explored the fundamental differences between C-style arrays and `std::vector`. Unlike static C-style arrays, we learned that `std::vector` offers dynamic resizing and robust memory management, which are critical for developing flexible and efficient applications. The comparison detailed how `std::vector` abstracts away low-level memory handling, thus minimizing common errors associated with manual memory management.

Understanding `std::vector` is beneficial because it is one of the most widely used sequence containers in C++ programming. `std::vector` supports dynamic growth in contiguously allocated memory and random access iteration and is compatible with a range of algorithms in the STL. We also discussed how `std::vector` provides a safer and more intuitive interface for managing collections of objects.

The following section will build upon this foundational knowledge. We will learn the syntax for declaring `std::vector` and the various methods available for initializing it. This will include an examination of default, copy, and move semantics as they pertain to vectors.

Declaring and initializing std::vector

Having established the foundational knowledge of `std::vector` in C++ development, it's time to delve into its practical applications—expressly, how to declare and initialize vectors.

The essence of `std::vector` lies in its dynamic nature. Unlike traditional arrays with fixed sizes, vectors can grow or shrink as necessary, making them a versatile tool for developers.

Declaring a vector

The performance of `std::vector` stems from its design, which combines the benefits of a contiguous memory layout (such as arrays) with the flexibility of dynamic resizing. It reserves memory to hold that many elements when initialized with a specified size. But if the vector fills up and more capacity is needed, it allocates a larger memory block, transfers the existing elements, and deallocates the old memory. This dynamic resizing process is optimized to reduce overhead, ensuring that vectors remain efficient. The fusion of contiguous storage and automated memory management distinguishes `std::vector` as an essential component in the C++ ecosystem.

To declare a basic `std::vector`, use the following:

```
std::vector<int> vec;
```

This line of code initializes an empty `std::vector` named `vec` specifically designed to hold values of type `int`. (`int` is the template parameter inside the `<>` for `std::vector`'s type.) `std::vector` is a dynamic array, which means that even though `vec` begins with a size of 0, its capacity can grow as needed. As you insert integers into `vec`, the container will automatically allocate memory to accommodate the increasing number of elements. This dynamic resizing makes `std::vector` a versatile and widely used container in C++ for situations where the number of elements isn't known in advance or might change over time.

When creating `std::vector`, it's possible to specify its initial size. This can be beneficial if you have prior knowledge about the number of elements you'll need to store:

```
std::vector<int> vec(10);
```

In the preceding code, `std::vector` named `vec` is initialized with space for 10 integers. By default, these integers will be value-initialized, which means they will be set to 0 for fundamental data types such as `int`.

If you wish to initialize the elements with a specific value, you can provide a second argument during the vector's construction:

```
std::vector<int> vec(10, 5);
```

Here, `std::vector` is declared with 10 integers, and each of those 10 integers is initialized to the value of 5. This approach ensures efficient memory allocation and desired value initialization in a single step.

Initializing a vector

In C++11 and later versions, `std::vector` initialization became more straightforward with the introduction of initializer lists. This allows developers to specify the initial values of the vector directly within curly braces:

```
std::vector<int> vec = {1, 2, 3, 4, 5};
```

The preceding statement creates an instance of `std::vector` named `vec` and initializes it with five integers. This method provides a concise way to declare and populate a vector simultaneously. This is just one way to initialize `std::vector`. Depending on your needs, there are many ways this can be done:

```
// Method 1: Declare a vector and then add elements using
// push_back (Add integers from 0 to 4)
std::vector<int> vec1;
```

```
for (int i = 0; i < 5; ++i) { vec1.push_back(i); }

// Method 2: Initialize a vector with a specific size and
// default value (5 elements with the value 10)
std::vector<int> vec2(5, 10);

// Method 3: List initialization with braced initializers
// Initialize with a list of integers
std::vector<int> vec3 = {1, 2, 3, 4, 5};

// Method 4: Initialize a vector using the fill
// constructor Default-initializes the five elements (with
// zeros)
std::vector<int> vec4(5);

// Method 5: Using std::generate with a lambda function
std::vector<int> vec5(5);
int value = 0;
std::generate(vec5.begin(), vec5.end(),
              [&value]() { return value++; });
```

`std::vector` is a versatile templated container capable of storing various data types, not just primitives such as `int`. You can store objects of custom classes, other standard library types, and pointers. This adaptability makes `std::vector` suitable for a wide range of applications and scenarios.

Furthermore, vectors provide a straightforward mechanism for copying the contents of one vector to another. This is known as **copy initialization**. The following code demonstrates this:

```
std::vector<int> vec1 = {1, 2, 3, 4, 5};
std::vector<int> vec2(vec1);
```

In this example, `vec2` is initialized as an exact copy of `vec1`, meaning `vec2` will contain the same elements as `vec1`. This copy initialization ensures that the original vector (`vec1`) remains unchanged and that the new vector (`vec2`) is provided with a separate copy of the data.

One of the true strengths of STL containers is their ability to handle user-defined types seamlessly, extending beyond primitive data types such as `int` or `double`. This flexibility is a testament to its templated design, which allows it to adapt to various data types while maintaining type safety. In the upcoming example, we illustrate this versatility by utilizing `std::vector` with a custom class:

```
#include <iostream>
#include <string>
#include <vector>

class Person {
```

```cpp
public:
  Person() = default;
  Person(std::string_view n, int a) : name(n), age(a) {}

  void display() const {
    std::cout << "Name: " << name << ", Age: " << age
              << "\n";
  }

private:
  std::string name;
  int age{0};
};

int main() {
  std::vector<Person> people;
  people.push_back(Person("Lisa", 30));
  people.push_back(Person("Corbin", 25));

  people.resize(3);
  people[2] = Person("Aaron", 28);

  for (const auto &person : people) { person.display(); }

  return 0;
}
```

Here is the example output:

```
Name: Lisa, Age: 30
Name: Corbin, Age: 25
Name: Aaron, Age: 28
```

In this example, `std::vector` is first used to manage objects of the custom `Person` class. It demonstrates the ease with which `std::vector` accommodates and manages memory for built-in and user-defined types.

In C++, while static arrays have their utility, they come with fixed sizes that can sometimes be limiting. On the other hand, `std::vector` provides a dynamic and flexible alternative.

Understanding the declaration and initialization of vectors is essential for effective C++ programming. `std::vector` is a versatile tool suitable for various tasks, from implementing complex algorithms to developing large-scale applications. Incorporating `std::vector` into your programming practices can enhance the efficiency and maintainability of your code.

In this section, we covered the syntactical aspects of working with `std::vector`. Specifically, we delved into the proper techniques for declaring `std::vector` of various types and the diverse strategies for initializing these vectors to suit different programming scenarios.

We learned that declaring `std::vector` involves specifying the type of elements it will contain and, optionally, the initial size and default value for the elements. We discovered multiple methods regarding initialization, including direct-list initialization and initializing with a specific range of values. This section underscored the flexibility of `std::vector`, showing how it can be tailored to start with a predefined set of elements or be constructed from existing collections.

This information is crucial for practical C++ development as it provides a foundation for using `std::vector` effectively. Proper initialization can lead to performance optimizations and ensure the vector is in a valid state appropriate for its intended use. The ability to declare and initialize vectors succinctly and correctly is a foundational skill for leveraging the power of the STL in real-world C++ applications.

In the next section, *Accessing elements*, we will focus on the operations that allow us to retrieve and modify the contents of a `std::vector`. We will learn about random access, which allows for the efficient retrieval and modification of elements at any position within the vector. Additionally, we will explore how to access the first and last elements, and the importance of understanding and managing vector size to ensure robust and error-free code.

Accessing elements

Having discussed the declaration and initialization of `std::vector`, our focus now shifts to accessing and manipulating the contained data. Multiple methods in C++ allow you to access vector elements with both speed and safety.

Random access

The subscript `[]` operator allows direct element access via indices, similar to arrays. In the following example, given a vector, the expression `numbers[1]` returns the value `20`. However, using this operator doesn't involve boundary checks. An index that is out of range, such as `numbers[10]`, results in undefined behavior, leading to unpredictable outcomes.

This is shown in the following example:

```
#include <iostream>
#include <vector>

int main() {
  std::vector<int> numbers = {10, 20, 30, 40, 50};

  const auto secondElement = numbers[1];
  std::cout << "The second element is: " << secondElement
```

```
        << "\n";

    // Beware: The following line can cause undefined
    // behavior!
    const auto outOfBoundsElement = numbers[10];
    std::cout << "Accessing an out-of-bounds index: "
              << outOfBoundsElement << "\n";

    return 0;
}
```

Here is the example output:

The second element is: 20
Accessing an out-of-bounds index: 0

For safer index-based access, std::vector offers the at() member function. It performs an index boundary check and throws an out_of_range exception for invalid indices.

Here is an example of this:

```
#include <iostream>
#include <vector>

int main() {
    std::vector<int> numbers = {10, 20, 30, 40, 50};

    try {
        const auto secondElement = numbers.at(1);
        std::cout << "The second element is: " << secondElement
                  << "\n";
    } catch (const std::out_of_range &e) {
        std::cerr << "Error: " << e.what() << "\n";
    }

    try {
        const auto outOfBoundsElement = numbers.at(10);
        std::cout << "Accessing an out-of-bounds index: "
                  << outOfBoundsElement << "\n";
    } catch (const std::out_of_range &e) {
        std::cerr << "Error: " << e.what() << "\n";
    }

    return 0;
}
```

Caution is paramount when accessing vector elements. While C++ favors performance, it often sidesteps safety checks, as evident with the subscript operator. Hence, developers must ensure valid access through careful index management or by employing safer methods such as `at()`.

Accessing the first and last elements

The first and last elements can be accessed with `front()` and `back()`, respectively.

This is shown in the following example:

```
#include <iostream>
#include <vector>

int main() {
  std::vector<int> numbers = {10, 20, 30, 40, 50};

  const auto firstElement = numbers.front();
  std::cout << "The first element is: " << firstElement
            << "\n";

  const auto lastElement = numbers.back();
  std::cout << "The last element is: " << lastElement
            << "\n";

  return 0;
}
```

The example output is as follows:

```
The first element is: 10
The last element is: 50
```

Vector size

With `std::vector`, understanding the structure and the amount of data it contains is essential. The `size()` member function provides the current count of elements stored within the vector. Invoking this function on an instance of `std::vector` will return the number of elements it holds. This count represents the active elements and can be used to determine the range for valid indexing. The returned value is of type `size_t`, an unsigned integer type suitable for representing sizes and counts. It's beneficial when iterating through a vector, performing size comparisons, or allocating space based on the number of vector elements.

Let us look at the following code:

```cpp
#include <iostream>
#include <vector>

int main() {
  std::vector<int> data = {1, 2, 3, 4, 5};

  const auto elementCount = data.size();
  std::cout << "Vector contains " << elementCount
            << " elements.\n";

  return 0;
}
```

In the preceding code, the size() function is called on the data vector to retrieve and display the number of elements it contains. The result, as expected, indicates that there are five elements in the vector.

In summary, std::vector offers a suite of tools, ranging from the efficient subscript operator to the safer at() method, and the convenient front() and back() methods. Understanding these tools is vital to efficiently and safely access and manipulate data within a vector.

In this section, we concentrated on the methodologies for retrieving and inspecting the contents of std::vector. We learned about the capabilities of std::vector to provide random access to its elements, enabling direct access to any element using its index with constant time complexity. This section also detailed the methods to access a vector's first and last elements through the front() and back() member functions, respectively.

Moreover, we discussed the importance of understanding and utilizing the size() member function to determine the number of elements currently stored in std::vector. This understanding is instrumental in ensuring that our access patterns remain within the bounds of the vector, thereby preventing out-of-range errors and undefined behavior.

The skills acquired from this section are essential, as they form the basis of interacting with std::vector's contents. These access patterns are core to using vectors effectively in C++ applications, whether for reading or modifying elements. The ability to directly access elements in a vector leads to efficient algorithms and supports a wide range of everyday programming tasks.

The following section will advance our knowledge further by addressing how to modify the size and contents of std::vector. We will explore how to add elements to a vector and the various methods available to remove them. This will include understanding how vectors manage their capacity and its implications on performance. We will learn why and how to use .empty() as a more performant alternative to checking whether the size is 0, and we will delve into clearing all elements from a vector.

Adding and removing elements

One of the advantages of `std::vector` over traditional arrays is its ability to resize dynamically. As applications evolve, so do data requirements; static data structures do not cut it. In this section, we will explore dynamic data management with `std::vector`, learning to seamlessly add to and remove from vectors while making sure we are staying safe.

Adding elements

Let's start with adding elements. The `push_back()` member function is possibly the most straightforward way to add an element to the end of a vector. Suppose you have `std::vector<int> scores;` and wish to append a new score, say `95`. You would simply invoke `scores.push_back(95);`, and voilà, your score is added.

Here's a simple illustrative code example:

```cpp
#include <iostream>
#include <vector>

int main() {
  std::vector<int> scores;

  std::cout << "Initial size of scores: " << scores.size()
            << "\n";

  scores.push_back(95);

  std::cout << "Size after adding one score:"
            << scores.size() << "\n";
  std::cout << "Recently added score: " << scores[0]
            << "\n";

  return 0;
}
```

When run, this program will display the vector's size before and after adding a score and the score itself, demonstrating the `push_back()` function in action.

What if you need to insert a score at a specific position, not just at the end? The `insert()` function becomes your best ally. If you wanted to insert a score of `85` at the third position, you'd use an iterator to specify the location:

```cpp
scores.insert(scores.begin() + 2, 85);
```

Remember that vector indexing starts at `0`; the `+ 2` is for the third position.

Let's expand on the previous example by incorporating the use of the insert() function in the following:

```cpp
#include <iostream>
#include <vector>

int main() {
  std::vector<int> scores = {90, 92, 97};

  std::cout << "Initial scores: ";
  for (int score : scores) { std::cout << " " << score; }
  std::cout << "\n";

  scores.push_back(95);

  std::cout << "Scores after adding 95 to the end: ";
  for (int score : scores) { std::cout << " " << score; }
  std::cout << "\n";

  scores.insert(scores.begin() + 2, 85);

  std::cout << "Scores after inserting 85 at the third "
               "position:";
  for (int score : scores) { std::cout << " " << score; }
  std::cout << "\n";

  return 0;
}
```

This program will showcase the original scores, display the scores after appending one to the end, and inserting one in the third position. It illustrates the push_back() and insert() functions in action.

And vectors don't stop there. The emplace_back() and emplace() functions allow for constructing elements directly inside the vector. This means fewer temporary objects and a potential boost in performance, especially with complex data types.

Let's consider a Person class that has a few data members. To create a new Person object, a string concatenation operation is performed. Using emplace_back() and emplace() will avoid extra temporary objects and copy/move operations that push_back() might cause, offering a performance boost. The following code demonstrates this:

```cpp
#include <iostream>
#include <string>
#include <vector>
```

```cpp
class Person {
public:
  Person(const std::string &firstName,
         const std::string &lastName)
      : fullName(firstName + " " + lastName) {}

  const std::string &getName() const { return fullName; }

private:
  std::string fullName;
};

int main() {
  std::vector<Person> people;
  people.emplace_back("John", "Doe");
  people.emplace(people.begin(), "Jane", "Doe");

  for (const auto &person : people) {
    std::cout << person.getName() << "\n";
  }

  return 0;
}
```

This example clarifies how `emplace_back()` and `emplace()` allow for the direct construction of objects inside the vector. Using `push_back()` might create temporary `Person` objects. Using `emplace_back()` directly constructs the object in place, potentially avoiding temporary object creation. Using `insert()` might create temporary `Person` objects. Using `emplace()` directly constructs the object in place at the specified location. This is particularly beneficial with types such as `Person`, where the constructor might involve resource-intensive operations (such as string concatenation). In such scenarios, the performance advantage of `emplace` methods over their push counterparts becomes evident.

Removing elements

But life isn't just about adding. Sometimes, we need to remove data. The `pop_back()` function removes the last element of a vector, reducing its size by one. If, however, you're looking to remove from a specific position or even a range of positions, the `erase()` function will be your go-to.

The erase-remove idiom

In C++ and its STL, there are established coding patterns that experienced developers often use. One notable pattern is the **erase-remove** idiom, which facilitates the removal of specific elements from a container based on defined criteria. This section will detail the functionality of this idiom and discuss newer alternatives introduced in C++20.

STL containers, especially `std::vector`, do not provide a straightforward method to remove elements based on a predicate. Instead, they provide separate methods: one to rearrange elements (using `std::remove` and `std::remove_if`) and another to erase them.

Here's how the erase-remove idiom works:

1. `std::remove` or `std::remove_if` is used to reorder elements of the container. Elements that need to be removed are moved to the end.
2. These algorithms return an iterator pointing to the start of the removed elements.
3. The container's `erase` method is then used to remove the elements from the container physically.

A classic example removes all instances of 0 from `std::vector<int>`:

```
std::vector<int> numbers = {1, 0, 3, 0, 5};
auto end = std::remove(numbers.begin(), numbers.end(), 0);
numbers.erase(end, numbers.end());
```

Modernizing with std::erase and std::erase_if

Recognizing the ubiquity and somewhat counterintuitive nature of the erase-remove idiom, C++20 introduced direct utility functions to simplify this operation: `std::erase` and `std::erase_if`. These functions merge the two-step process into one, offering a more intuitive and less error-prone approach.

Using the previous example, removing all instances of 0 with C++20 becomes:

```
std::vector<int> numbers = {1, 0, 3, 0, 5};
std::erase(numbers, 0);
```

No longer does one have to invoke separate algorithms and remember to handle both stages of the process. Similarly, to remove elements based on a predicate, you would do the following:

```
std::vector<int> numbers = {1, 2, 3, 4, 5};
std::erase_if(numbers, [](int x){ return x % 2 == 0; });
```

While the erase-remove idiom has been a cornerstone of STL-based C++ programming for years, modern C++ continues to evolve and simplify common patterns. With `std::erase` and `std::erase_if`, developers now have more straightforward tools to remove container elements, leading to cleaner and more readable code. It's a testament to the ongoing commitment of the C++ community to enhance the language's user-friendliness while retaining its power and expressiveness.

Note that `std::vector` has been ingeniously designed to optimize memory operations. While one might intuitively expect the underlying array to resize every time an element is added or removed, that isn't the case. Instead, when a vector grows, it often allocates more memory than immediately necessary, anticipating future additions. This strategy minimizes the frequent memory reallocations, which could be computationally expensive. Conversely, when elements are removed, the vector doesn't always shrink its allocated memory immediately. This behavior provides a balance between memory usage and performance. However, it is worth noting that the specifics of these memory management decisions can vary by the C++ library implementation. As such, while the behavior is consistent across implementations in terms of the interface, the internal memory management nuances might differ.

Capacity

You can use the capacity() member function to know how much memory has been allocated. The std::vector::capacity() member function returns the amount of memory allocated for the vector, which may be greater than its actual size. This value represents the maximum number of elements the vector can hold before reallocating memory, ensuring efficient growth patterns without frequent memory operations.

This can be seen in the following:

```cpp
#include <iostream>
#include <vector>

int main() {
  std::vector<int> numbers;

  std::cout << "Initial size: " << numbers.size() << "\n";
  std::cout << "Initial capacity: " << numbers.capacity()
            << "\n";

  for (auto i = 1; i <= 10; ++i) { numbers.push_back(i); }

  std::cout << "Size after adding 10 elements: "
            << numbers.size() << "\n";
  std::cout << "Capacity after adding 10 elements: "
            << numbers.capacity() << "\n";

  for (auto i = 11; i <= 20; ++i) { numbers.push_back(i); }

  std::cout << "Size after adding 20 elements: "
            << numbers.size() << "\n";
  std::cout << "Capacity after adding 20 elements: "
            << numbers.capacity() << "\n";

  for (auto i = 0; i < 5; ++i) { numbers.pop_back(); }

  std::cout << "Size after removing 5 elements: "
```

```
                << numbers.size() << "\n";
    std::cout << "Capacity after removing 5 elements: "
                << numbers.capacity() << "\n";

    return 0;
}
```

The exact output may be different for your compiler, but here is an example output:

```
Initial size: 0
Initial capacity: 0
Size after adding 10 elements: 10
Capacity after adding 10 elements: 16
Size after adding 20 elements: 20
Capacity after adding 20 elements: 32
Size after removing 5 elements: 15
Capacity after removing 5 elements: 32
```

This example illustrates how the size and capacity of a std::vector instance change as elements are added and removed. Examining the outputs shows that the capacity often doesn't correspond directly with the size, highlighting the memory optimization techniques.

Prefer using empty() when possible

In C++, when the primary intention is to check whether a container is devoid of elements, it's recommended to use the .empty() member function instead of comparing .size() or .capacity() with 0. The .empty() function provides a direct way to ascertain whether a container has any elements, and in many implementations, it can offer a performance advantage. Specifically, .empty() typically has a constant time complexity of O(1), whereas .size() might have a linear time complexity of O(n) for some container types, making .empty() a more efficient choice for mere emptiness checks. Using .empty() can lead to more concise and potentially faster code, especially in performance-critical sections.

Clearing all elements

The clear() function of std::vector is a powerful utility that swiftly erases all elements within the container. After invoking this function, the size() of the vector will return 0, indicating its now-empty state. However, a crucial aspect to be aware of is that any references, pointers, or iterators that previously pointed to the elements within the vector are invalidated by this operation. This also holds for any past-the-end iterators. Interestingly, while clear() purges all the elements, it doesn't alter the capacity of the vector. This means that the memory allocated for the vector remains unchanged, allowing for efficient subsequent insertions without immediate reallocation.

The clear() member function of std::vector removes all elements from the vector, effectively reducing its size to 0. Here's a simple example to demonstrate its usage:

```cpp
#include <iostream>
#include <vector>

int main() {
  std::vector<int> numbers = {1, 2, 3, 4, 5};

  std::cout << "Original numbers: ";
  for (const auto num : numbers) {
    std::cout << num << " ";
  }
  std::cout << "\n";

  numbers.clear();

  std::cout << "After using clear(): ";

  // This loop will produce no output.
  for (const auto num : numbers) {
    std::cout << num << " ";
  }
  std::cout << "\n";

  std::cout << "Size of vector after clear(): "
            << numbers.size() << "\n";

  return 0;
}
```

Here is the example output:

```
Original numbers: 1 2 3 4 5
After using clear():
Size of vector after clear(): 0
```

This example underscores the efficiency of std::vector in handling bulk deletions with a single function call, making data management even more straightforward.

Dynamic resizing is a prominent feature of std::vector, but it requires careful management to maintain efficiency. When a vector's contents exceed its capacity, it necessitates memory reallocation, which involves allocating a new memory block, copying the existing elements, and deallocating the old memory. This process can introduce performance overheads, mainly if the vector grows by small amounts repeatedly. If you can anticipate the maximum size, use the `reserve()` function to pre-allocate memory to mitigate such inefficiencies.

For example, invoking `scores.reserve(100);` allocates memory for 100 elements, reducing the need for frequent reallocations up to that limit.

`std::vector` offers a comprehensive set of functions tailored for dynamic data management. It facilitates quickly adding elements, inserting them in between, or removing them from various positions. Coupled with its efficient memory management, `std::vector` stands out as both a flexible and performance-oriented container. As you delve deeper into C++, the utility of `std::vector` will become increasingly apparent, as it addresses a wide range of programming scenarios effectively.

In this section, we explored the dynamic nature of `std::vector`, which allows us to modify its content and size. We learned how to add elements to a vector using methods such as `push_back`, `emplace_back`, and insertion at a specific position using iterators. We also examined the process of removing elements, whether a single element at a particular position, a range of elements, or removing elements by value.

We discussed the concept of capacity, the amount of pre-allocated space for elements in a vector, and how it differs from size, which is the actual number of elements currently in the vector. Understanding this distinction is critical for writing memory- and performance-efficient programs.

The use of `empty()` as a preferred method for checking whether a vector contains any elements was also highlighted. We discussed the advantages of `empty()` over checking whether `size()` returns 0, particularly regarding clarity and potential performance benefits.

Additionally, we covered the importance of the `clear()` function, which removes all elements from a vector, effectively resetting its size to 0 without necessarily changing its capacity.

This section's information is handy because it allows us to manage `std::vector`'s contents actively and efficiently. Knowledge of adding and removing elements is vital for implementing algorithms that require dynamic data manipulation, which is a common scenario in software development.

Summary

In this chapter, you have learned the foundational aspects of `std::vector` in C++ STL. The chapter began by explaining the significance of `std::vector`, highlighting its advantages over C-style arrays, particularly regarding memory management and ease of use. The chapter thoroughly compared C-style arrays and `std::vector`, demonstrating how `std::vector` facilitates dynamic size adjustment and safer memory operations.

Next, you were guided through the processes of declaring and initializing vectors. You learned how to declare `std::vector` and initialize these instances using different methods. The chapter then explored the myriad ways of accessing elements within `std::vector`, from random access to accessing the first and last elements, and underscored the importance of understanding vector size.

Further, the chapter delved into the intricacies of adding and removing elements. This section illuminated the best practices for modifying the contents of a vector, including when to use `empty()` instead of checking for a size of `0` and the significance of understanding a vector's capacity.

The information presented in this chapter is invaluable as it builds the foundational knowledge required to effectively utilize `std::vector` (and many other STL data types) in various programming scenarios. Mastery of `std::vector` allows for writing more efficient and maintainable code, enabling C++ developers to leverage STL's full potential for dynamic array manipulation.

In the next chapter, you will elevate your understanding of `std::vector` by learning about iterators, central to navigating through elements in STL containers.

2

Mastering Iterators with std::vector

In this chapter, we will gain a deeper exploration of `std::vector`, focusing on the intricacies of iteration. This chapter equips us with the knowledge to handle the ins and outs of vector traversal. Mastering these core areas bolsters the efficiency and reliability of one's C++ code and provides insights into the underpinnings of dynamic array behavior, which is critical for effective C++.

In this chapter, we're going to cover the following main topics:

- Types of iterators in the STL
- Basic iteration techniques with `std::vector`
- Using `std::begin` and `std::end`
- Understanding iterator requirements
- Range-based `for` loops
- Creating a custom iterator

Technical requirements

The code in this chapter can be found on GitHub:

`https://github.com/PacktPublishing/Data-Structures-and-Algorithms-with-the-CPP-STL`

Types of iterators in the STL

In the **Standard Template Library** (**STL**), iterators play a pivotal role by connecting algorithms to containers. They provide a means for developers to traverse, access, and potentially modify the elements of a container. Iterators are essential tools for efficient data manipulation in the STL. However, they aren't uniform in their functionalities. The STL delineates iterators into five primary types, each offering varying access and control over the elements. This section will get into these iterator types, elaborating on their distinct capabilities and uses.

Input iterators

Input iterators (*LegacyInputIterator*) are the starting point in exploring iterator types. They represent the foundational category of iterators. As their name implies, input iterators focus on reading and progressing through elements. They enable developers to advance to the subsequent element in the container and retrieve its value. It's crucial to note that revisiting the prior element is impossible after moving an input iterator forward, and modifying the present element is not permitted. This iterator category is often employed in algorithms that require data processing without modification.

The following is a simple example using `std::vector` and its input iterator:

```cpp
#include <iostream>
#include <vector>

int main() {
  std::vector<int> numbers = {10, 20, 30, 40, 50};

  for (auto it = numbers.begin(); it != numbers.end();
       ++it) {
    std::cout << *it << " ";
  }
  std::cout << "\n";

  return 0;
}
```

In this example, we use `std::vector<int>::const_iterator` as the input iterator to traverse the vector and print its elements. We're following the principles of the input iterator by not modifying the elements or moving the iterator backward. It is important to note that we cannot change the element or go back to the previous element with the input iterator.

Output iterators

Next, we will look into output iterators (*LegacyOutputIterator*). Although they bear similarities to input iterators, they serve a different primary function: writing to elements. Output iterators facilitate assignment to the elements they reference. However, directly reading these elements through the iterator is not supported. They are commonly utilized in algorithms designed to produce and populate a sequence of values within a container.

Here's an example demonstrating the use of output iterators with `std::vector`:

```
#include <algorithm>
#include <iostream>
#include <iterator>
#include <vector>

int main() {
  std::vector<int> numbers;

  std::generate_n(std::back_inserter(numbers), 10,
                  [n = 0]() mutable { return ++n; });

  for (auto num : numbers) { std::cout << num << " "; }
  std::cout << "\n";

  return 0;
}
```

In the preceding code, `std::back_inserter` is an output iterator adapter designed to work with containers like `std::vector`. It allows you to *write* or push new values to the back of the vector. We use the `std::generate_n` algorithm to generate and insert the numbers. This pattern perfectly encapsulates the *write-only* characteristic of output iterators. We don't use the output iterator to read. For reading, we use a regular iterator.

Forward iterators

With the basics behind us, let's move on to the forward iterators (*LegacyForwardIterator*). Forward iterators combine the capabilities of both input iterators and output iterators. Thus, they support reading, writing, and—as the name implies—always moving forward. Forward iterators never reverse their direction. Their versatility makes them well-suited for many algorithms that operate on singly linked lists (i.e., `std::forward_list`).

`std::forward_list` is explicitly designed for singly linked lists, making it the ideal candidate for illustrating forward iterators.

Here's a simple code example to illustrate their use:

```
#include <forward_list>
#include <iostream>

int main() {
  std::forward_list<int> flist = {10, 20, 30, 40, 50};

  std::cout << "Original list: ";
```

```
    for (auto it = flist.begin(); it != flist.end(); ++it) {
      std::cout << *it << " ";
    }
    std::cout << "\n";

    for (auto it = flist.begin(); it != flist.end(); ++it) {
      (*it)++;
    }

    std::cout << "Modified list: ";
    for (auto it = flist.begin(); it != flist.end(); ++it) {
      std::cout << *it << " ";
    }
    std::cout << "\n";

    return 0;
}
```

Here is the example output:

```
Original list: 10 20 30 40 50
Modified list: 11 21 31 41 51
```

This code initializes a `std::forward_list`, uses a forward iterator to traverse and display its elements, and then increments each element by 1, demonstrating the reading and writing capabilities of the forward iterator.

Reverse iterators

Sometimes, you might find the need to traverse the vector in reverse. Enter `rbegin()` and `rend()`. These functions return reverse iterators that start at the end of the vector and conclude at the beginning. Such backward traversal can be handy in specific algorithms and data-processing tasks.

Note the reverse iterator is technically an iterator adaptor. `std::reverse_iterator` is classified as an iterator adaptor. It takes a given iterator, which should either be a *LegacyBidirectionalIterator,* or comply with the `bidirectional_iterator` criteria introduced from C++20 onwards, and reverses its direction. When given a bidirectional iterator, `std::reverse_iterator` yields a new iterator that traverses the sequence in the opposite direction—from the end to the beginning.

Bidirectional iterators

Continuing, we address bidirectional iterators (*LegacyBidirectionalIterator*). These iterators permit traversal in both forward and backward directions within a container. Inheriting all functionalities of forward iterators, they introduce the ability to move in the reverse direction. Their design is particularly beneficial for data structures such as doubly linked lists, where bidirectional traversal is frequently required.

Here's an example using `std::list` and its bidirectional iterators:

```cpp
#include <iostream>
#include <list>

int main() {
    std::list<int> numbers = {1, 2, 3, 4, 5};

    std::cout << "Traversing the list forwards:\n";
    for (std::list<int>::iterator it = numbers.begin();
            it != numbers.end(); ++it) {
        std::cout << *it << " ";
    }
    std::cout << "\n";

    std::cout << "Traversing the list backwards:\n";
    for (std::list<int>::reverse_iterator rit =
                numbers.rbegin();
            rit != numbers.rend(); ++rit) {
        std::cout << *rit << " ";
    }
    std::cout << "\n";

    return 0;
}
```

Here is the example output:

```
Traversing the list forwards:
1 2 3 4 5
Traversing the list backward:
5 4 3 2 1
```

In this example, we create a `std::list` of integers. We then demonstrate bidirectional iteration by first traversing the list in a forward direction using a regular iterator and then in reverse using a reverse iterator.

Random access iterators

Concluding our iterator categorization, we introduce the random access iterators (*LegacyRandomAccessIterator* and *LegacyContiguousIterator*). These iterators represent the highest versatility, enabling more than just sequential access. With random access iterators, developers can move forward by multiple steps, retreat backward, or access elements directly without sequential traversal. Such capabilities make them highly suitable for data structures such as arrays or vectors, which allow direct element access.

Here's an example showcasing the flexibility and capabilities of random access iterators with `std::vector`:

```cpp
#include <chrono>
#include <iostream>
#include <mutex>
#include <thread>
#include <vector>

std::mutex vecMutex;

void add_to_vector(std::vector<int> &numbers, int value) {
  std::lock_guard<std::mutex> guard(vecMutex);
  numbers.push_back(value);
}

void print_vector(const std::vector<int> &numbers) {
  std::lock_guard<std::mutex> guard(vecMutex);
  for (int num : numbers) { std::cout << num << " "; }
  std::cout << "\n";
}

int main() {
  std::vector<int> numbers;
  std::thread t1(add_to_vector, std::ref(numbers), 1);
  std::thread t2(add_to_vector, std::ref(numbers), 2);
  t1.join();
  t2.join();
  std::thread t3(print_vector, std::ref(numbers));
  t3.join();
  return 0;
}
```

This example demonstrates the various capabilities of random access iterators. We start with direct access, then jump positions, leap back, calculate distances, and even access elements in a non-linear manner.

It is vital to understand that the choice of iterator type is not arbitrary. Each one is designed with specific use cases in mind, and choosing the right one can significantly enhance the efficiency and elegance of your C++ code. When working with STL algorithms and containers, having a solid grasp of the different iterator types and their functionalities is paramount. This knowledge not only streamlines the coding process but also aids in debugging and optimizing the performance of your applications.

In exploring the STL's iterators, we've learned the six core types: input, output, forward, reverse, bidirectional, and random access. Recognizing each type's unique functions is vital for efficient C++ programming, as it affects how we traverse and interact with STL containers. Grasping these differences is not just academic; it's practical. It enables us to choose the right iterator for tasks, such as using random access iterators with `std::vector` for their rapid element access capability.

In the next section, we'll apply this knowledge, where we'll see iteration in action, emphasize the use of constant iterators for read-only purposes, and underscore the adaptability of iterators across various containers, setting the stage for robust and versatile code development.

Basic iteration techniques with std::vector

Now that we understand the different types of iterators available, let's explore the essential concept of iterating over data structures. Iteration is a fundamental technique in programming that allows developers to access and manipulate each element in a data structure efficiently. Specifically for `std::vector`, iteration is crucial due to its dynamic nature and widespread use in C++ applications. By mastering iteration, you can harness the full potential of `std::vector`, enabling operations such as searching, sorting, and modifying elements with precision and ease. This section aims to deepen your understanding of why iteration is a crucial skill in managing and utilizing data structures effectively, setting the stage for more advanced applications in your programs.

Iterating over std::vector

One of the powerful features of `std::vector` is its ability to allow seamless traversal of its elements. Whether you're accessing individual elements or looping through each one, understanding the iterative capabilities of `std::vector` is crucial. Iteration is fundamental to numerous operations in programming, from data processing to algorithmic transformations. As you journey through this section, you'll become well acquainted with how to traverse vectors in C++ efficiently and effectively.

At the heart of iteration in the C++ STL is the concept of iterators. Think of iterators as sophisticated pointers, guiding you through each element in a container, such as our beloved `std::vector`. Armed with iterators, one can move forward, backward, jump to the start or the end, and access the content they point to, making them indispensable tools in your C++ toolkit.

Basic iteration using iterators

Every `std::vector` provides a set of member functions that return iterators. The two primary ones are `begin()` and `end()`. While we'll dive deeper into these functions in the next section, understand that `begin()` returns an iterator pointing to the first element, and `end()` returns an iterator pointing just *past* the last element.

For instance, to traverse a vector named `values`, you would typically use a loop, as shown in the following code:

```
for(auto it = values.begin(); it != values.end(); ++it) {
    std::cout << *it << "\n";
}
```

In this code example, `it` is an iterator that moves through each element in values. The loop continues until `it` reaches the position indicated by `values.end()`.

Using constant iterators

When you're sure you won't modify the elements during iteration, it is good practice to use constant iterators. They ensure that the elements remain immutable during traversal.

Imagine you're a museum guide showing visitors the precious artifacts. You want them to appreciate and understand the history, but you wouldn't want them to touch or modify these delicate items. Similarly, in programming, there are scenarios where you'd like to traverse a collection, showcasing (or reading) its contents but not altering them. This is where constant iterators come into play.

To employ a constant iterator, `std::vector` provides the `cbegin()` and `cend()` member functions:

```
for(auto cit = values.cbegin(); cit != values.cend(); ++cit) {
    std::cout << *cit << "\n";
}
```

Benefits of iteration

Why is iteration so pivotal? By effectively iterating over vectors, you can do the following:

- **Process data**: Whether normalizing data, filtering it, or performing any transformation, iteration is at the core of these operations.
- **Search operations**: Looking for a particular element? Iteration allows you to comb through each item, checking against a condition or a value.
- **Algorithm application**: Many algorithms in the C++ STL, such as `sort`, `find`, and `transform`, require iterators to specify the range they operate on.

The versatility and efficiency of `std::vector` iteration make it a prime choice for developers. While arrays also allow for traversal, vectors offer dynamic size, robustness against overflows, and integration with the rest of the C++ STL, making them a preferred choice in many scenarios.

In conclusion, mastering iteration with `std::vector` is foundational to becoming proficient in C++. By understanding how to traverse this dynamic array, you unlock a wide range of capabilities, enabling you to harness the power of algorithms, efficiently process data, and craft robust, performant software. You'll build a deeper understanding of other vector utilities as we progress, solidifying your knowledge and skills in this vibrant language.

In this section, we've navigated `std::vector` traversal with iterators, learning to access elements sequentially and utilize constant iterators for read-only operations. Understanding these techniques is critical for crafting flexible and optimized C++ code compatible with various container types. Iteration is a cornerstone of data manipulation in the STL; mastering it is essential for harnessing the library's full potential.

Next, we turn to the *Using std::begin and std::end* section to further our iterator knowledge. We'll uncover how these functions standardize the initiation and conclusion of iterations across different containers, paving the way for more versatile and decoupled code.

Using std::begin and std::end

As you discover more use cases for `std::vector`, you'll encounter situations where it is advantageous, or even necessary, to venture beyond member functions. Here's where non-member functions, specifically `std::begin` and `std::end`, step into the spotlight. These two functions are handy and offer a more generic way to access the beginning and end of a container, including but not limited to `std::vector`.

Why the distinction, you might ask? Aren't there member functions such as `vector::begin()` and `vector::end()`? Indeed, there are. However, the beauty of the non-member `std::begin` and `std::end` is their broader applicability across different container types, making your code more flexible and adaptable.

Vectors in C++ offer a potent blend of dynamic memory and continuous storage, making them indispensable in many coding scenarios. But to truly leverage their potential, understanding their interaction with iterators is crucial. While the spotlight often shines on the `begin()` and `end()` member functions, there are two versatile actors behind the curtains: `std::begin` and `std::end`.

When working with C++ containers, the `std::begin` function might seem like another way to start iterating through a container. However, it comes with its own set of marvels. While it primarily fetches an iterator pointing to the first element of a container, its application isn't limited to vectors alone.

When you pass `std::vector` to `std::begin`, it is like having a backstage pass. Behind the scenes, the function smoothly delegates the task by calling the vector's `begin()` member function. This intuitive behavior ensures that the transition remains seamless even as you venture into generic programming.

Mirroring its counterpart, `std::end` is more than just a function that returns an iterator pointing past the last element. It's a testament to C++'s commitment to consistency. Just as `std::begin` relies on `begin()`, when you engage with `std::end`, it subtly and efficiently calls upon the container's `end()` member function.

And here's the true magic: while these non-member functions shine with std::vector, they are not constrained by it. Their generic nature means they play well with various containers, from traditional arrays to lists, making them indispensable tools for those seeking adaptability in their code.

Let's look at an example that demonstrates the utility of the std::begin and std::end non-member functions in contrast to their member counterparts:

```cpp
#include <array>
#include <iostream>
#include <list>
#include <vector>

template <typename Container>
void displayElements(const Container &c) {
  for (auto it = std::begin(c); it != std::end(c); ++it) {
    std::cout << *it << " ";
  }
  std::cout << "\n";
}

int main() {
  std::vector<int> vec = {1, 2, 3, 4, 5};
  std::list<int> lst = {6, 7, 8, 9, 10};
  std::array<int, 5> arr = {11, 12, 13, 14, 15};

  std::cout << "Elements in vector: ";
  displayElements(vec);

  std::cout << "Elements in list: ";
  displayElements(lst);

  std::cout << "Elements in array: ";
  displayElements(arr);

  return 0;
}
```

In this preceding example, we notice the following:

- We have a displayElements generic function that takes any container and uses the std::begin and std::end non-member functions to iterate over its elements.

- We then create three containers: a std::vector, a std::list, and a std::array.

- We call displayElements for each container to display its elements.

Using `std::begin` and `std::end`, our `displayElements` function is versatile and works across different container types. This would not have been as straightforward if we relied solely on member functions such as `vector::begin()` and `vector::end()`, emphasizing the power and flexibility of non-member functions.

Imagine being handed a toolkit that promises not just efficiency but also adaptability. That's what `std::vector` offers, complemented beautifully by functions such as `std::begin` and `std::end`. They're not just functions but gateways to more type-agnostic memory management and iteration.

We've seen how `std::begin` and `std::end` elevate our code by extending iteration capabilities to all STL containers, not just `std::vector`. Embracing these non-member functions is key to crafting container-independent, reusable code—a pillar for versatile algorithm implementation in C++. Understanding this distinction is fundamental for employing iterators effectively across the STL.

Looking ahead, the next section will guide us through the nuances of iterator categories and their essentials. This insight is pivotal for aligning algorithms with appropriate iterator capabilities, reflecting the depth of C++'s type system and its close ties with pointer semantics.

Understanding iterator requirements

Iterators in C++ serve as a consistent interface to various data structures, such as containers and, since C++20, ranges. The iterator library supplies definitions for iterators and associated traits, adaptors, and utility functions.

Given that iterators extend the idea of pointers, they inherently adopt many pointer semantics in C++. Consequently, any function template accepting iterators can also seamlessly work with regular pointers.

Iterators are categorized into six types: *LegacyInputIterator*, *LegacyOutputIterator*, *LegacyForwardIterator*, *LegacyBidirectionalIterator*, *LegacyRandomAccessIterator*, and *LegacyContiguousIterator*. Instead of being determined by their intrinsic types, these categories are distinguished by the operations they support. As an illustration, pointers accommodate all the operations defined for *LegacyRandomAccessIterator*, allowing them to be utilized wherever a *LegacyRandomAccessIterator* is required.

These iterator categories, except for *LegacyOutputIterator*, can be arranged hierarchically. More versatile iterator categories, such as *LegacyRandomAccessIterator*, encompass the capabilities of the less powerful ones, such as *LegacyInputIterator*. If an iterator conforms to any of these categories and also meets the criteria for *LegacyOutputIterator*, it's termed a mutable iterator, capable of input and output functions. Iterators that aren't mutable are referred to as constant iterators.

In this section, we discovered the critical role of iterators as the unifying interface for C++ data structures, including containers and ranges. We examined how the iterator library in C++ defines iterator types, associated traits, adaptors, and utility functions, providing a standardized way to traverse these structures.

We learned that iterators extend pointer semantics, allowing any function template that accepts iterators to work seamlessly with pointers. We further explored the hierarchy of iterator categories—*LegacyInputIterator*, *LegacyOutputIterator*, *LegacyForwardIterator*, *LegacyBidirectionalIterator*, *LegacyRandomAccessIterator*, and *LegacyContiguousIterator*. These categories are defined not by their types but by the operations they support, with more advanced iterators inheriting the capabilities of the simpler ones.

This knowledge is crucial for us as it informs our choice of iterator based on the operations we need to perform. Understanding the requirements and capabilities of each iterator category enables us to write more efficient and robust code, as we can choose the least powerful iterator that satisfies our needs, thereby avoiding unnecessary performance overhead.

In the next section, titled *Range-based for loops in C++*, we will transition from the theoretical underpinnings of iterators to practical application by learning how to use range-based `for` loops to iterate over `std::vector`. We will understand how these loops utilize `std::begin` and `std::end` under the hood, providing a more intuitive and error-resistant method for element access and modification.

Range-based for loops

In C++, range-based `for` loops provide a concise and practical mechanism for iterating over containers such as `std::vector`. Armed with knowledge about `std::vector` operations and the `std::begin` and `std::end` functions, it's evident that range-based `for` loops offer a streamlined traversal technique.

Traditional iteration over a vector necessitates declaring an iterator, initializing it to the container's start, and updating it to progress to the end. Although this method works, it requires careful management and is prone to errors. Range-based `for` loops present a more efficient solution.

Overview of range-based for loops

The following code demonstrates the basic structure of a range-based `for` loop:

```
std::vector<int> numbers = {1, 2, 3, 4, 5};
for (int num : numbers) {
  std::cout << num << " ";
}
```

In this example, every integer within the `numbers` vector is printed. This approach eliminates the need for explicit iterators and manual loop boundary definitions.

Underlying mechanism

Internally, the range-based `for` loop leverages the `begin()` and `end()` functions to navigate the container. The loop successively retrieves each item from the container, assigning it to the loop variable (num in this case).

This approach simplifies the iteration process, allowing developers to concentrate on operations to perform on each element rather than the retrieval process.

When to use range-based for loops

Range-based `for` loops are particularly beneficial in the following situations:

- **Accessing every element is required**: Range-based `for` loops are optimal for complete vector traversal.

- **Direct iterator access isn't necessary**: These loops are excellent for displaying or altering elements. However, traditional loops are more appropriate if access to the iterator itself is required (e.g., for mid-traversal element insertion or deletion).

- **Code clarity is paramount**: For enhancing code legibility, range-based `for` loops succinctly express the intention to operate on every container element.

Modifying elements during iteration

For scenarios where vector element modification is needed during iteration, it's essential to use a reference as the loop variable, which is shown in the following code:

```
for (auto &num : numbers) {
  num *= 2;
}
```

In this case, each integer within the numbers vector is multiplied by two. Without the reference (`&`), the loop would alter a copied element, leaving the original vector untouched.

Range-based `for` loops are a testament to C++'s ongoing development, striking a balance between performance and readability. They grant developers a direct way to navigate containers, enhancing code clarity and minimizing potential mistakes. As you progress in C++, it's crucial to understand the available tools and select the most fitting ones for your tasks. A thorough grasp of `std::vector` functions and capabilities ensures effective utilization in diverse situations.

This section highlighted range-based for loops' advantages in iterating through STL containers, emphasizing their readability and minimized error potential compared to traditional `for` loops. Utilizing `std::begin` and `std::end`, these loops streamline the iteration process, letting us concentrate on the element-level logic. They are optimal when direct iterator control isn't needed, exemplifying modern C++'s emphasis on high-level abstractions for efficiency and clarity.

Moving forward, the *Creating a custom iterator* section will utilize our iterators for advanced abstraction, data transformation, or filtered data views. We'll explore the technical requirements and how to align our custom iterators with the STL's categorization.

Creating a custom iterator

One of the beauties of C++ is its flexibility, empowering developers to mold the language to suit their needs. This flexibility doesn't stop with built-in functionality for container iteration. While `std::vector` comes with its set of built-in iterators, nothing is stopping us from creating our own. But why might we want to?

The appeal of custom iterators

Let's examine the reasons you'd want to implement a custom iterator:

- **Enhanced abstraction**: Consider a vector storing a matrix in a flat format. Wouldn't it be more intuitive to iterate through rows or columns rather than individual elements? Custom iterators can facilitate this.

- **Data transformation**: Perhaps you wish to iterate through the vector but retrieve transformed data, like the squared values of each element. Instead of changing the data before or during retrieval, a custom iterator can abstract this.

- **Filtered views**: Imagine skipping over certain elements based on a condition, presenting a filtered view of your `std::vector`.

Creating a custom STL iterator might seem like an arduous task, but with the proper guidance, it is a breeze! At its core, an iterator is a fancy pointer—a guide that escorts you through the elements of a container. To make your iterator play well with the STL, there are certain member functions you'll need to implement.

Core requirements

The exact set of these functions varies based on the type of iterator you're creating, but some are common across the board.

1. **Type aliases**:

   - `value_type`: Denotes the type of the element the iterator points to.

   - `difference_type`: Represents the distance between two iterators.

- `pointer` and `reference`: Define the iterator's pointer and reference types.

- `iterator_category`: Classifies the iterator into categories such as input, output, forward, bidirectional, or random access. Each category has its unique characteristics, making iterators versatile and fun!

2. **Operators**:

    - `operator*`: The dereference operator, granting access to the element your iterator points to.

    - `operator++`: The increment operators! These move your iterator forward (either in pre-increment or post-increment style).

    - `operator==` and `operator!=`: Equipped with these, your iterators can be compared, letting algorithms know if they've reached the end or need to keep going.

Iterator categories and their specialties

Iterators come in different flavors; each flavor (or category) has unique requirements:

- **Input iterators**: These iterators are read-only. They can move forward and read elements.

  - **Essential**: `operator*`, `operator++`, `operator==`, and `operator!=`

- **Output iterators**: These iterators are write-only. They can move forward and write elements.

  - **Essential**: `operator*` and `operator++`

- **Forward iterators**: They combine input and output iterators—reading, writing, and always moving forward.

  - **Essential**: All the core requirements

- **Bidirectional iterators**: They can move both forwards and backward, reading and writing.

  - **Additional**: `operator--` to step back

- **Random access iterators**: As the name implies, they can leap to any position. They can read from and write to any position, making them perfect for random access data structures such as `std::vector`.

  - **Additional**: `operator+`, `operator-`, `operator+=`, `operator-=`, `operator[]`, and relational operators such as `operator<`, `operator<=`, `operator>`, and `operator>=`

  A random access iterator in C++ is one of the most potent iterator categories and requires several functions and operators to be fully compatible with STL algorithms and containers.

Here's a list of functions and operators you'd typically implement for a random access iterator:

- **Type aliases**:
  - `iterator_category` (should be set to `std::random_access_iterator_tag`)
  - `value_type`
  - `difference_type`
  - `pointer`
  - `reference`

- **Dereference**:
  - `operator*()` (dereference operator)
  - `operator->()` (arrow operator)

- **Increment and decrement**:
  - `operator++()` (prefix increment)
  - `operator++(int)` (postfix increment)
  - `operator--()` (prefix decrement)
  - `operator--(int)` (postfix decrement)

- **Arithmetic operations** (with a difference type, often `ptrdiff_t`):
  - `operator+(difference_type)` (move iterator forward by some amount)
  - `operator-(difference_type)` (move iterator backward by some amount)
  - `operator+=(difference_type)` (increment iterator by some amount)
  - `operator-=(difference_type)` (decrement iterator by some amount)

- **Difference between two iterators**:
  - `operator-(const RandomAccessIteratorType&)`

- **Subscript operator**:
  - `operator[](difference_type)`

- **Relational operators**:
  - `operator==` (equality)
  - `operator!=` (inequality)

- operator< (less than)

  - operator<= (less than or equal to)

  - operator> (greater than)

  - operator>= (greater than or equal to)

- **Swap** (sometimes useful, though not strictly required for the iterator itself):

  - A swap function to swap two iterators

Not all of these will always be applicable, especially if the underlying data structure has limitations or the iterator's specific usage case doesn't require all these operations. However, for full compatibility with STL's random access iterators, this is the complete set of functions and operators you'd want to consider implementing.

A custom iterator example

Let's create a custom iterator for std::vector<int> that, when dereferenced, returns the square of the value in the vector:

```
#include <iostream>
#include <iterator>
#include <vector>

class SquareIterator {
public:
  using iterator_category =
      std::random_access_iterator_tag;
  using value_type = int;
  using difference_type = std::ptrdiff_t;
  using pointer = int *;
  using reference = int &;

  explicit SquareIterator(pointer ptr) : ptr(ptr) {}

  value_type operator*() const { return (*ptr) * (*ptr); }
  pointer operator->() { return ptr; }

  SquareIterator &operator++() {
    ++ptr;
    return *this;
  }

  SquareIterator operator++(int) {
```

```cpp
    SquareIterator tmp = *this;
    ++ptr;
    return tmp;
  }

  SquareIterator &operator+=(difference_type diff) {
    ptr += diff;
    return *this;
  }
  SquareIterator operator+(difference_type diff) const {
    return SquareIterator(ptr + diff);
  }

  value_type operator[](difference_type diff) const {
    return *(ptr + diff) * *(ptr + diff);
  }

  bool operator!=(const SquareIterator &other) const {
    return ptr != other.ptr;
  }

private:
  pointer ptr;
};

int main() {
  std::vector<int> vec = {1, 2, 3, 4, 5};
  SquareIterator begin(vec.data());
  SquareIterator end(vec.data() + vec.size());

  for (auto it = begin; it != end; ++it) {
    std::cout << *it << ' ';
  }

  SquareIterator it = begin + 2;
  std::cout << "\nValue at position 2: " << *it;
  std::cout
      << "\nValue at position 3 using subscript operator: "
      << it[1];

  return 0;
}
```

When run, this code will output the following:

```
1 4 9 16 25
Value at position 2: 9
Value at position 3 using subscript operator: 16
```

The iterators in the code can be used very similarly to a built-in array or `std::vector` iterators but with the unique functionality of squaring values when dereferenced.

Custom iterator challenges and use cases

Creating a custom iterator isn't just about understanding your data or use case; it is also about grappling with some challenges:

- **Complexity**: Crafting an iterator requires adherence to certain iterator concepts. Different requirements must be met whether it is an input, forward, bidirectional, or random access iterator.

- **Maintaining validity**: Iterators can be invalidated with operations such as `push_back` or `erase`. Ensuring the custom iterator remains valid is essential for safe and predictable behavior.

- **Performance overhead**: With added functionality can come extra computation. Ensuring that the iterator's overhead doesn't negate its benefits is crucial.

Illustrative use cases of custom iterators

To wrap our minds around the idea, let's briefly look at a couple of scenarios where custom iterators shine:

- **Image data processing**: A `std::vector` might store pixel data linearly for an image. A custom iterator could facilitate iteration by rows, channels, or even regions of interest.

- **Text parsing**: For text stored in a `std::vector<char>`, an iterator could be designed to jump from word to word or sentence to sentence, ignoring whitespace and punctuation.

- **Statistical sampling**: An iterator might sample every *n*th element for large datasets stored in vectors, providing a quick overview without traversing each element.

Creating a custom iterator involves adhering to specific conventions and defining a set of required operators to give it the behavior of an iterator.

The following code shows us how to create a custom iterator for extracting the alpha channel from a bitmap stored in std::vector:

```cpp
#include <iostream>
#include <iterator>
#include <vector>

struct RGBA {
  uint8_t r, g, b, a;
};

class AlphaIterator {
public:
  using iterator_category = std::input_iterator_tag;
  using value_type = uint8_t;
  using difference_type = std::ptrdiff_t;
  using pointer = uint8_t *;
  using reference = uint8_t &;

  explicit AlphaIterator(std::vector<RGBA>::iterator itr)
      : itr_(itr) {}

  reference operator*() { return itr_->a; }

  AlphaIterator &operator++() {
    ++itr_;
    return *this;
  }

  AlphaIterator operator++(int) {
    AlphaIterator tmp(*this);
    ++itr_;
    return tmp;
  }

  bool operator==(const AlphaIterator &other) const {
    return itr_ == other.itr_;
  }

  bool operator!=(const AlphaIterator &other) const {
    return itr_ != other.itr_;
  }

private:
```

```
    std::vector<RGBA>::iterator itr_;
};

int main() {
  std::vector<RGBA> bitmap = {
      {255, 0, 0, 128}, {0, 255, 0, 200}, {0, 0, 255, 255},
      // ... add more colors
  };

  std::cout << "Alpha values:\n";

  for (AlphaIterator it = AlphaIterator(bitmap.begin());
       it != AlphaIterator(bitmap.end()); ++it) {
    std::cout << static_cast<int>(*it) << " ";
  }
  std::cout << "\n";

  return 0;
}
```

We've defined an `RGBA` struct in this example to represent the color. We then create a custom `AlphaIterator` iterator to navigate the alpha channel. Next, the iterator uses the underlying `std::vector<RGBA>::iterator`, but exposes only the alpha channel when dereferenced. Finally, the `main` function demonstrates using this iterator to print alpha values.

This custom iterator adheres to the conventions of a C++ input iterator, making it usable with various algorithms and range-based `for` loops. The `AlphaIterator` class in the example demonstrates a custom input iterator's basic structure and behavior in C++. Here's a breakdown of the key member functions and their significance for STL compatibility:

- **Type aliases**:

  - `iterator_category`: Defines the type/category of the iterator. It helps algorithms determine the operations supported by the iterator. Here, it is defined as `std::input_iterator_tag`, indicating it is an input iterator.

  - `value_type`: The data type that can be read from the underlying container. Here, it is `uint8_t` representing the alpha channel.

  - `difference_type`: Used to represent the result of subtracting two iterators. Commonly used in random access iterators.

  - `pointer` and `reference`: The pointer and reference types to `value_type`. They give direct access to the value.

- **Constructor**:

  - `explicit AlphaIterator(std::vector<RGBA>::iterator itr):` This constructor is essential to initialize the iterator with an instance of the underlying `std::vector` iterator.

- **Dereference operator (operator*)**:

  - `reference operator*():` The dereference operator returns a reference to the current item in the sequence. For this iterator, it returns a reference to the alpha channel of the RGBA value.

- **Increment operators**:

  - `AlphaIterator& operator++():` The pre-increment operator advances the iterator to the next element.

  - `AlphaIterator operator++(int):` The post-increment operator advances the iterator to the next element but returns an iterator to the current element before the increment. This behavior is needed for constructs such as `it++`.

- **Equality and inequality operators**:

  - `bool operator==(const AlphaIterator& other) const:` Checks whether two iterators point to the same position. This is crucial for comparison and to determine the end of a sequence.

  - `bool operator!=(const AlphaIterator& other) const:` The opposite of the previous one: this checks whether two iterators are not equal.

These member functions and type aliases are essential to make the iterator compatible with the STL and enable its seamless use with various STL algorithms and constructs. They define the fundamental interface and semantics required for a functioning input iterator.

Additional operations would be required for iterators with more capabilities (such as bidirectional or random access). But for the input iterator demonstrated in the `AlphaIterator`, the preceding are the core components.

This section covered custom iterators and understanding their creation for specific needs such as data abstraction, transformation, and filtering. Learning to define essential type aliases and implement key operators is crucial in extending the functionality of `std::vector`. This knowledge lets us customize data interaction, ensuring our code meets the unique domain requirements with precision.

Summary

In this chapter, we have comprehensively explored the role and usage of iterators as they apply to one of the most versatile containers in the C++ STL. We started by discussing the various types of iterators available in the STL—input, output, forward, reverse, bidirectional, and random access—and their specific applications and support operations.

We then moved on to practical iteration techniques, detailing how to traverse `std::vector` effectively using standard and constant iterators. We underscored the importance of choosing the correct type of iterator for the task at hand to write clean, efficient, and error-resistant code.

The section on using `std::begin` and `std::end` expanded our toolkit, showing how these non-member functions can make our code more flexible by not being tightly bound to container types. We also covered the requirements and categorization of iterators, essential knowledge for understanding the STL's inner workings, and implementing custom iterators.

Range-based `for` loops were introduced as a modern C++ feature that simplifies iteration by abstracting the details of iterator management. We learned when and how to use these loops to their fullest potential, particularly noting the ease with which they allow the modification of elements during iteration.

Finally, we tackled the advanced topic of creating custom iterators. We discovered the motivations behind this, such as providing more intuitive navigation or presenting a filtered data view. We examined the core requirements, challenges, and use cases for custom iterators, rounding out our understanding of how they can be tailored to fit specialized needs.

While the standard iterators provided with `std::vector` cover many use cases, they're not the end of the story. Custom iterators offer an avenue to stretch the boundaries of what's possible with iteration, tailor-fitting traversal logic to specific needs. The complexity of crafting reliable custom iterators is not to be underestimated. As we close this chapter, remember that custom iterators can be powerful tools in the right hands. You can make informed decisions about when and how to wield them with a solid understanding of their workings.

The knowledge gained in this chapter is beneficial as it enables the creation of more sophisticated, robust, and performant C++ applications. Understanding and utilizing iterators effectively allows us to harness the full power of `std::vector` and write container-agnostic and highly optimized algorithms.

The upcoming chapter, *Mastering Memory and Allocators with std::vector*, builds upon our existing knowledge and directs our focus toward memory efficiency, a critical aspect of high-performance C++ programming. We will continue to emphasize the practical, real-world applications of these concepts, ensuring that the content remains valuable and directly applicable to our work as intermediate-level C++ developers.

3

Mastering Memory and Allocators with std::vector

This chapter dives into the critical memory management concepts in modern C++ programming. We begin by distinguishing between the capacity and size of `std::vector`, which is fundamental to writing efficient code. As we progress, we'll understand the mechanics of memory reservation and optimization, and why these actions matter in real-world applications. The chapter culminates with thoroughly exploring custom allocators, including when to use them and their impact on container performance. It equips us with the expertise to fine-tune memory usage for their programs.

In this chapter, we are going to cover the following main topics:

- Understanding capacity versus size
- Resizing and reserving memory
- Custom allocator basics
- Creating a custom allocator
- Allocators and container performance

Technical requirements

The code in this chapter can be found on GitHub:

`https://github.com/PacktPublishing/Data-Structures-and-Algorithms-with-the-CPP-STL`

Understanding capacity versus size

As you venture deeper into the art of C++ programming with `std::vector`, it becomes crucial to grasp the distinctions between a vector's size and capacity. While closely related, these terms serve different roles in managing and optimizing dynamic arrays, and understanding them will dramatically enhance both the efficiency and clarity of your code.

Revisiting the basics

Recall from the previous chapter that the size of a vector denotes the number of elements it currently holds. When you add or remove elements, this size adjusts accordingly. So, if you have a vector containing five integers, its size is 5. Remove an integer, and the size becomes 4.

But herein lies a compelling facet of `std::vector`: while its size changes based on its elements, the memory it allocates doesn't always follow suit immediately. To understand this thoroughly, we need to explore the concept of capacity. Let us do that in the next section.

What exactly is capacity?

Capacity, in the context of `std::vector`, pertains to the amount of memory the vector has reserved for itself – the number of elements it can hold before reallocating memory. This doesn't always equal the number of elements it currently holds (its size). `std::vector` often allocates more memory than is required, a preemptive strategy to accommodate future elements. This is where the genius of `std::vector` shines; over-allocating reduces the need for frequent and, potentially, computationally costly reallocations.

Let's use an analogy to make this more straightforward. Think of a vector as a train with compartments (memory blocks). When the train (vector) starts its journey, it might only have a few passengers (elements). However, anticipating more passengers at upcoming stations, the train starts with some empty compartments. The train's capacity is the total number of compartments, while its size is the number of compartments with passengers.

Why this distinction matters

You might wonder why we don't just expand the memory each time a new element is added. The answer lies in computational efficiency. Memory operations, especially reallocations, can be time-consuming. The vector minimizes these operations by allocating more memory than is immediately needed, ensuring that adding elements remains a fast operation in most scenarios. This optimization is one reason why `std::vector` has become a staple in C++ programming.

However, there's a flip side. Over-allocation means that some memory might go unused, at least temporarily. Understanding and managing capacity becomes paramount if memory usage is a critical concern. In some extreme cases, a vector might have a size of 10 but a capacity of 1000!

Looking under the hood

One must occasionally peek under the hood to appreciate the nuances of size and capacity. Consider a newly initiated `std::vector<int> numbers;`. If you push 10 integers into it one by one and periodically check its capacity, you might notice something interesting: the capacity doesn't increase by one for each integer! Instead, it might jump from 1 to 2, then to 4, then to 8, and so on. This exponential growth strategy is a typical implementation approach, ensuring that the vector's capacity doubles whenever it runs out of space.

Let's look at a code example that showcases the difference between size and capacity in `std::vector`:

```cpp
#include <iostream>
#include <vector>

int main() {
  std::vector<int> myVec;

  std::cout << "Initial size: " << myVec.size()
            << ", capacity: " << myVec.capacity() << "\n";

  for (auto i = 0; i < 10; ++i) {
    myVec.push_back(i);

    std::cout << "After adding " << i + 1
              << " integers, size: " << myVec.size()
              << ", capacity: " << myVec.capacity()
              << "\n";
  }

  myVec.resize(5);
  std::cout << "After resizing to 5 elements, size: "
            << myVec.size()
            << ", capacity: " << myVec.capacity() << "\n";

  myVec.shrink_to_fit();
  std::cout << "After shrinking to fit, size: "
            << myVec.size()
            << ", capacity: " << myVec.capacity() << "\n";

  myVec.push_back(5);
  std::cout << "After adding one more integer, size: "
            << myVec.size()
            << ", capacity: " << myVec.capacity() << "\n";
```

```
    return 0;
}
```

Here is the example output:

```
Initial size: 0, capacity: 0
After adding 1 integers, size: 1, capacity: 1
After adding 2 integers, size: 2, capacity: 2
After adding 3 integers, size: 3, capacity: 3
After adding 4 integers, size: 4, capacity: 4
After adding 5 integers, size: 5, capacity: 6
After adding 6 integers, size: 6, capacity: 6
After adding 7 integers, size: 7, capacity: 9
After adding 8 integers, size: 8, capacity: 9
After adding 9 integers, size: 9, capacity: 9
After adding 10 integers, size: 10, capacity: 13
After resizing to 5 elements, size: 5, capacity: 13
After shrinking to fit, size: 5, capacity: 5
After adding one more integer, size: 6, capacity: 7
```

Here is the explanation of this code block:

- We start by creating an empty `std::vector<int>` named `myVec`.

- We then print out the initial `size` and `capacity`. Since it is empty, the `size` value will be 0. The initial `capacity` value might vary depending on the C++ **Standard Template Library (STL)** implementation, but it is often 0 as well.

- We can see how size and capacity change as we push integers into the vector individually. The `size` value will always increase by one for each added element. However, the `capacity` value might remain unchanged or increase, often doubling, depending on when the underlying memory needs reallocation.

- Resizing the vector down to five elements demonstrates that while `size` decreases, `capacity` remains unchanged. This ensures that previously allocated memory remains reserved for potential future elements.

- `shrink_to_fit()` reduces the vector's `capacity` to match its `size`, thus releasing unused memory.

- We can observe how the capacity behaves again by adding one more element after the shrink.

When you run this example, you'll see firsthand the differences between size and capacity and how `std::vector` manages memory in the background.

By understanding the relationship between size and capacity, you optimize memory usage and preempt potential performance pitfalls. It lays the foundation for the upcoming sections, where we'll discuss manual memory management with vectors and understand how to iterate over them efficiently.

This section deepened our understanding of `std::vector`'s size and capacity. We compared these concepts to a train's compartments, emphasizing how capacity planning can prevent frequent, costly reallocations and lead to more memory-efficient programs. Grasping this is crucial for performance-sensitive and memory-constrained environments.

Building on this, we'll next look at `resize()`, `reserve()`, and `shrink_to_fit()`, learning to manage `std::vector`'s memory footprint proactively for optimal performance and memory usage.

Resizing and reserving memory

In our exploration of `std::vector`, understanding how to manage its memory effectively is essential. A vector's beauty is in its dynamism; it can grow and shrink, adapting to the ever-changing requirements of our applications. Yet, with this flexibility comes the responsibility to ensure efficient memory utilization. This section digs into the operations that let us manipulate vector sizes and their preallocated memory: `resize`, `reserve`, and `shrink_to_fit`.

When working with vectors, we've seen how their capacity (preallocated memory) might differ from their actual size (number of elements). The methods to manage these aspects can significantly affect your programs' performance and memory footprint.

The power of resize()

Imagine you have `std::vector` holding five elements. If you suddenly need it to keep eight elements, or perhaps only three, how would you make this adjustment? The `resize()` function is your answer.

`resize()` is used to change the size of a vector. If you increase its size, the new elements will be default-initialized. For instance, for `std::vector<int>`, the new elements will have a value of `0`. Conversely, the extra elements will be discarded if you reduce its size.

But remember, resizing doesn't always influence the capacity. If you expand a vector beyond its current capacity, the capacity will grow (often more than the size to accommodate future growth). However, shrinking a vector's size doesn't reduce its capacity.

Let's look at an example that demonstrates manually resizing the capacity of a `std::vector` instance:

```
#include <iostream>
#include <vector>

int main() {
  std::vector<int> numbers = {1, 2, 3, 4, 5};

  auto printVectorDetails = [&]() {
    std::cout << "Vector elements: ";
    for (auto num : numbers) { std::cout << num << " "; }
    std::cout << "\nSize: " << numbers.size() << "\n";
```

```
        std::cout << "Capacity: " << numbers.capacity()
                  << "\n";
    };

    std::cout << "Initial vector:\n";
    printVectorDetails();

    numbers.resize(8);
    std::cout << "After resizing to 8 elements:\n";
    printVectorDetails();

    numbers.resize(3);
    std::cout << "After resizing to 3 elements:\n";
    printVectorDetails();

    std::cout << "Reducing size doesn't affect capacity:\n";
    std::cout << "Capacity after resize: "
              << numbers.capacity() << "\n";

    return 0;
}
```

Here is the example output:

```
Initial vector:
Vector elements: 1 2 3 4 5
Size: 5
Capacity: 5
After resizing to 8 elements:
Vector elements: 1 2 3 4 5 0 0 0
Size: 8
Capacity: 10
After resizing to 3 elements:
Vector elements: 1 2 3
Size: 3
Capacity: 10
Reducing size doesn't affect capacity:
Capacity after resize: 10
```

In this example, we saw the following:

- We start with std::vector<int> containing five elements.

- A print utility printVectorDetails lambda function displays the vector's elements, size, and capacity.

- We resize the vector to hold eight elements and observe the changes.

- We then resize the vector to hold only three elements and see how the size decreases, but the capacity remains unchanged.

This demonstrates the power of the `resize()` function and how it affects the size but not always the capacity of `std::vector`.

Enter reserve()

Sometimes, we have foreknowledge about the data. Say you know you'll insert 100 elements into a vector. Letting the vector adjust its capacity incrementally as elements are added would be inefficient. Here's where `reserve()` comes into play.

By calling `reserve()`, you can set aside a specific amount of memory for the vector upfront. It's like booking seats in advance. The size remains unchanged, but the capacity is adjusted to at least the specified value. If you reserve less memory than the current capacity, the call has no effect; you cannot decrease capacity with `reserve()`.

Let's look at an example that demonstrates the utility of the `reserve()` function:

```
#include <chrono>
#include <iostream>
#include <vector>

int main() {
  constexpr size_t numberOfElements = 100'000;

  std::vector<int> numbers1;
  auto start1 = std::chrono::high_resolution_clock::now();
  for (auto i = 0; i < numberOfElements; ++i) {
    numbers1.push_back(i);
  }
  auto end1 = std::chrono::high_resolution_clock::now();

  std::chrono::duration<double> elapsed1 = end1 - start1;
  std::cout << "Time without reserve: " << elapsed1.count()
            << " seconds\n";

  std::vector<int> numbers2;
  numbers2.reserve(
      numberOfElements); // Reserve memory upfront.

  auto start2 = std::chrono::high_resolution_clock::now();
  for (auto i = 0; i < numberOfElements; ++i) {
```

```
    numbers2.push_back(i);
}
auto end2 = std::chrono::high_resolution_clock::now();

std::chrono::duration<double> elapsed2 = end2 - start2;
std::cout << "Time with reserve:     " << elapsed2.count()
          << " seconds\n";

return 0;
}
```

Here is the example output:

```
Time without reserve: 0.01195 seconds
Time with reserve:     0.003685 seconds
```

We learn the following from the preceding example:

- We intend to insert many elements (`numberOfElements`) into two vectors.

- In the first vector (`numbers1`), we directly insert the elements without reserving any memory upfront.

- In the second vector (`numbers2`), we use the `reserve()` function to preallocate memory for the elements before inserting them.

- We measure and compare the time taken to insert elements in both scenarios.

When you run the code, you'll likely notice that the insertion time is shorter (often significantly) with `reserve()` since it reduces the number of memory reallocations. This example effectively demonstrates the performance benefit of using `reserve()` judiciously. In this example, using `reserve()` was more than 3x faster than not calling `reserve()`.

Using `reserve()` judiciously can significantly boost performance, especially when dealing with large datasets. Preallocating memory means fewer memory reallocations, leading to faster insertions.

Optimizing with shrink_to_fit()

While `reserve()` lets you expand the preallocated memory, what if you want to do the opposite? What if, after numerous operations, you find a vector with a size of 10 but a capacity of 1000? Holding onto that extra memory can be wasteful.

The `shrink_to_fit()` function allows you to request the vector to reduce its capacity to match its size. Notice the word *request*. Implementations might not always guarantee the reduction, but in most cases, they'll comply. Reclaiming memory after bulk deletions or when a vector's growth phase has ended is an excellent way to reduce a vector's capacity.

Let's illustrate the usage of `shrink_to_fit()` with the following simple code example:

```cpp
#include <iostream>
#include <vector>

int main() {
  std::vector<int> numbers;
  numbers.reserve(1000);
  std::cout << "Initial capacity: " << numbers.capacity()
            << "\n";

  for (auto i = 0; i < 10; ++i) { numbers.push_back(i); }

  std::cout << "Size after adding 10 elements: "
            << numbers.size() << "\n";
  std::cout << "Capacity after adding 10 elements: "
            << numbers.capacity() << "\n";

  numbers.shrink_to_fit();

  std::cout << "Size after shrink_to_fit: "
            << numbers.size() << "\n";
  std::cout << "Capacity after shrink_to_fit: "
            << numbers.capacity() << "\n";

  return 0;
}
```

Here is the example output:

```
Initial capacity: 1000
Size after adding 10 elements: 10
Capacity after adding 10 elements: 1000
Size after shrink_to_fit: 10
Capacity after shrink_to_fit: 10
```

The following are the key takeaways from the preceding example:

- We start with `std::vector<int>` and reserve memory for 1000 elements.
- We only add 10 elements to the vector.
- At this point, the size of the vector is 10, but its capacity is 1000.
- We then call `shrink_to_fit()` to reduce the vector's capacity to match its size perfectly.
- We display the size and capacity after calling `shrink_to_fit()`.

Upon running the code, you should observe that the vector's capacity has been reduced closer to its size, illustrating the function's utility in reclaiming memory.

Real-world relevance

Understanding the distinction between size and capacity and knowing how to manipulate them has profound implications. Managing memory effectively is critical for applications where performance is paramount, such as real-time systems or high-frequency trading platforms. Similarly, ensuring that every byte is efficiently used in embedded systems or devices with limited memory is crucial.

While `std::vector` provides a dynamic and efficient approach to handling arrays, wielding it with mastery requires a deep understanding of its memory behavior. By effectively using `resize`, `reserve`, and `shrink_to_fit`, developers can tailor memory usage to the exact requirements of their applications, achieving an optimal balance between performance and resource consumption.

To master the art of C++, one must be more than just a coder; one must think like an architect, understanding the materials at hand and building structures that stand the test of time and load. As we move forward, we will dive deeper into iteration methods, bringing us closer to mastery of `std::vector`.

This section has honed our understanding of `std::vector`'s memory allocation techniques. We learned how `reserve()` strategically allocates memory to optimize performance, while `shrink_to_fit()` can minimize memory footprint by releasing unneeded space. These strategies are pivotal for developers to enhance application efficiency and manage resources wisely.

Next, we'll examine allocators' integral role in memory management. We'll dissect the allocator interface and the scenarios that may necessitate custom allocators, evaluating their impact on performance and memory usage compared to standard practices.

Custom allocator basics

The magic behind dynamic memory management in `std::vector` (and many other STL containers) lies in a component that might not immediately catch your attention: the allocator. At its core, an **allocator** serves as an interface, abstracting the memory source for the container. This abstraction ensures that the container, like our trusty `std::vector`, can function without being tethered to a specific memory source or allocation strategy.

The role and responsibility of an allocator

Allocators are the unsung heroes of memory management. They handle allocating and deallocating memory chunks, thus ensuring that our data structures grow and shrink gracefully. Beyond these tasks, allocators can also construct and destroy objects. They bridge the gap between raw memory operations and higher-level object management.

But why do we need such an abstraction? Why not simply use the new and delete operations? The answer lies in flexibility. The STL empowers developers to implement custom memory strategies by decoupling the container from specific memory operations. For performance-critical applications, this flexibility is a godsend.

Under the hood – the allocator interface

A default std::allocator provides member functions that align closely with its responsibilities. Let us take a brief look at the member functions:

- allocate(): Allocates a memory block suitable for holding a specified number of objects
- deallocate(): Returns a block of memory previously allocated by the allocator to the system
- construct(): Constructs an object in a given memory location
- destroy(): Calls the destructor on an object at a given memory location

Remember, while std::allocator uses the heap for memory operations by default, the true power of the allocator interface shines when custom allocators are in play.

To demonstrate the benefits of std::allocator, let's first illustrate how a simple custom allocator might look. This custom allocator will track and print its operations, allowing us to visualize its interactions.

We'll then use this custom allocator with std::vector in the following code block:

```
#include <iostream>
#include <memory>
#include <vector>

template <typename T> class CustomAllocator {
public:
  using value_type = T;

  CustomAllocator() noexcept {}

  template <typename U>
  CustomAllocator(const CustomAllocator<U> &) noexcept {}

  T *allocate(std::size_t n) {
    std::cout << "Allocating " << n << " objects of size "
              << sizeof(T) << " bytes.\n";
    return static_cast<T *>(::operator new(n * sizeof(T)));
  }

  void deallocate(T *p, std::size_t) noexcept {
```

```
    std::cout << "Deallocating memory.\n";
    ::operator delete(p);
  }

  template <typename U, typename... Args>
  void construct(U *p, Args &&...args) {
    std::cout << "Constructing object.\n";
    new (p) U(std::forward<Args>(args)...);
  }

  template <typename U> void destroy(U *p) {
    std::cout << "Destroying object.\n";
    p->~U();
  }
};

int main() {
  std::vector<int, CustomAllocator<int>> numbers;

  std::cout << "Pushing back numbers 1 to 5:\n";
  for (int i = 1; i <= 5; ++i) { numbers.push_back(i); }

  std::cout << "\nClearing the vector:\n";
  numbers.clear();

  return 0;
}
```

Here is the example output:

```
Pushing back numbers 1 to 5:
Allocating 1 objects of size 4 bytes.
Constructing object.
Allocating 2 objects of size 4 bytes.
Constructing object.
Constructing object.
Destroying object.
Deallocating memory.
Allocating 4 objects of size 4 bytes.
Constructing object.
Constructing object.
Constructing object.
Destroying object.
Destroying object.
```

```
Deallocating memory.
Constructing object.
Allocating 8 objects of size 4 bytes.
Constructing object.
Constructing object.
Constructing object.
Constructing object.
Constructing object.
Destroying object.
Destroying object.
Destroying object.
Destroying object.
Deallocating memory.

Clearing the vector:
Destroying object.
Destroying object.
Destroying object.
Destroying object.
Destroying object.
Deallocating memory.
```

The following are the key takeaways from the preceding example:

- We've created a simple `CustomAllocator` that prints messages when it performs specific operations such as allocation, deallocation, construction, and destruction. It uses global `new` and `delete` operators for memory operations.

- `std::vector` in the `main()` function uses our `CustomAllocator`.

- When we push elements into the vector, you'll notice the messages indicating memory allocation and object construction.

- Clearing the vector will trigger object destruction and memory deallocation messages.

Using our custom allocator, we've added custom behavior (printing in this case) to the memory management operations of `std::vector`. This showcases the flexibility allocators provide in STL and how they can be tailored for specific needs.

Trade-offs and the need for custom allocators

You might be wondering, if `std::allocator` works out of the box, why bother with custom allocators? As with many things in software development, the answer boils down to trade-offs.

The general-purpose nature of the default allocator ensures broad applicability. However, this jack-of-all-trades approach might not be optimal for specific scenarios. For instance, applications that frequently allocate and deallocate small chunks of memory might suffer from fragmentation if the default allocator is used.

Additionally, some contexts might have unique memory constraints, such as embedded systems with limited memory or real-time systems with stringent performance requirements. In these situations, the control and optimization offered by custom allocators become invaluable.

Choosing std::allocator over new, delete, and managed pointers

Regarding memory management in C++, several mechanisms are at a developer's disposal. While using raw pointers with `new` and `delete` or even smart pointers such as `std::shared_ptr` and `std::unique_ptr` might seem intuitive, there's a compelling case for relying on `std::allocator` when working with STL containers. Let's explore these advantages.

Consistency with STL containers

Containers in the STL have been designed with allocators in mind. Using `std::allocator` ensures a level of compatibility and consistency across the library. It ensures that your customization or optimization can be applied uniformly across various containers.

Memory abstraction and customization

Raw memory operations and even managed pointers do not provide an immediate path to customizing memory allocation strategies. On the other hand, `std::allocator` (and its customizable brethren) offers an abstraction layer, paving the way for tailored memory management approaches. This means you can implement strategies that combat fragmentation, use **memory pools**, or tap into specialized hardware.

Centralized memory operations

With raw pointers and manual memory management, allocation and deallocation operations are scattered throughout the code. This decentralization can lead to errors and inconsistencies. `std::allocator` encapsulates these operations, ensuring that memory management remains consistent and traceable.

Safety against common pitfalls

Manual memory management with `new` and `delete` is prone to issues such as memory leaks, double deletions, and undefined behaviors. Even with smart pointers, cyclic references can become a headache. When used with containers, allocators mitigate many of these concerns by automating the underlying memory processes.

Better synergy with advanced STL features

Certain advanced features and optimizations in the STL, such as allocator-aware containers, directly leverage the capabilities of allocators. Using `std::allocator` (or a custom allocator) ensures you're better positioned to harness these enhancements.

While `new`, `delete`, and managed pointers have their places in C++ programming, when it comes to container-based memory management, `std::allocator` stands out as a clear choice. It offers a blend of customization, safety, and efficiency that's hard to achieve with manual or semi-manual memory management techniques. As you navigate the rich landscape of C++ development, let the allocator be your steadfast companion in dynamic memory.

This section examined allocators and their role in managing memory for `std::vector`. We uncovered how allocators provide an abstraction for memory operations in STL containers and examined the allocator interface's workings. This understanding is essential for crafting memory management strategies that enhance application performance in various environments.

Next, we will explore implementing custom allocators, investigating memory pools, and guiding you through creating a custom allocator for `std::vector`, showcasing the benefits of personalized memory management.

Creating a custom allocator

Creating a custom allocator is a strategic decision to enhance memory management. This approach becomes particularly valuable when the default memory allocation strategies do not align with a specific application's unique performance requirements or memory usage patterns. By designing a custom allocator, developers can fine-tune memory allocation and deallocation processes, potentially improving efficiency, reducing overhead, and ensuring better control over how resources are managed within their applications. This level of customization is crucial for applications where standard allocation schemes may fall short in addressing specialized needs or optimizing performance.

Custom allocators – the heart of memory flexibility

When you think about how STL containers handle memory, there's a hidden power beneath the surface. Containers such as `std::vector` have memory needs that are met through allocators. By default, they use `std::allocator`, a general-purpose allocator suitable for most tasks. However, in some scenarios, you might need more control over memory allocation and deallocation strategies. That's where custom allocators come into play.

Understanding the motivation behind custom allocators

At first glance, one might wonder why there's a need for anything beyond the default allocator. After all, isn't that sufficient? While `std::allocator` is versatile, it is designed to cater to a broad range of use cases. Specific situations call for particular memory strategies. Here are a few motivators:

- **Performance optimizations**: Different applications have different memory access patterns. For instance, a graphics application might frequently allocate and deallocate small chunks of memory. A custom allocator can be optimized for such patterns.

- **Memory fragmentation mitigation**: Fragmentation can lead to inefficient memory usage, especially in long-running applications. Custom allocators can employ strategies to reduce or even prevent fragmentation.

- **Specialized hardware or memory regions**: Sometimes, applications might need to allocate memory from specific regions or even specialized hardware, such as **graphics processing unit (GPU)** memory. Custom allocators grant this flexibility.

Memory pools – a popular custom allocator strategy

One widely appreciated strategy in custom memory allocation is the concept of memory pools. Memory pools preallocate a chunk of memory and then distribute it in smaller blocks as needed by the application. The brilliance of memory pools lies in their simplicity and efficiency. Here's why they're beneficial:

- **Faster allocations and deallocation**: Handing out smaller blocks is quick since a large chunk is already preallocated.

- **Reduced fragmentation**: Memory pools naturally reduce fragmentation by controlling the memory layout and ensuring continuous blocks.

- **Predictable behavior**: Memory pools can offer a level of predictability, especially beneficial in real-time systems where consistent performance is paramount.

Unlocking the potential of custom allocators

While diving into custom allocators can seem daunting, their benefits are tangible. Whether for performance enhancements, memory optimization, or specific application needs, understanding the potential of custom allocators is a valuable asset in a C++ developer's toolkit. As you continue your journey with `std::vector`, remember that an allocator works diligently to manage memory efficiently beneath every element. With custom allocators, you can tailor this management to suit your application's needs.

This section introduced the design and use of custom allocators in `std::vector`, emphasizing how they allow for specialized memory management, which is crucial for optimizing applications with unique memory usage patterns. With this insight, developers can surpass STL's default mechanisms, enhancing performance through tailored allocation strategies such as memory pools.

We'll next examine allocators' effects on STL container performance, scrutinize `std::allocator`'s traits, identify scenarios for custom alternatives, and underline the role of **profiling** in informed allocator selection.

Allocators and container performance

At the heart of every container's efficiency lies its memory management strategy, and for `std::vector`, allocators play a crucial role. While memory allocation might seem straightforward, the nuances in allocator design can bring various performance implications.

Why allocators matter in performance

Before we can harness the potential of allocators, we need to understand why they matter. Memory allocation isn't a one-size-fits-all operation. Depending on the application's specific needs, the frequency of allocations, the size of memory blocks, and the lifetime of these allocations can vary drastically.

- **Speed of allocation and deallocation**: The time it takes to allocate and deallocate memory can be a significant factor. Some allocators might optimize for speed at the expense of memory overhead, while others might do the opposite.

- **Memory overhead**: The overhead involves the allocator's extra memory for bookkeeping or fragmentation. A low overhead might mean a faster allocator but could lead to higher fragmentation. Conversely, a higher overhead allocator might be slower but could result in lower fragmentation.

- **Memory access patterns**: How memory is accessed can influence cache performance. Allocators that ensure contiguous memory allocations can lead to better cache locality, boosting performance.

The performance characteristics of std::allocator

The default `std::allocator` aims to provide a balanced performance for the general case. It's a jack of all trades, but it might not always be the master for specific use cases. Here's what you can expect:

- **General purpose efficiency**: It performs decently across various scenarios, making it a reliable choice for many applications

- **Low overhead**: While the overhead is minimal, memory fragmentation is risky, especially in scenarios with frequent allocations and deallocations of varying sizes

- **Consistent behavior:** Since it is part of the standard library, its behavior and performance are consistent across different platforms and compilers

When to consider alternative allocators

Given that `std::allocator` is a solid general-purpose choice, when should one consider alternatives? A few scenarios stand out:

- **Specialized workloads**: If you know your application predominantly allocates small chunks of memory frequently, a memory-pool-based allocator might be more efficient

- **Real-time systems**: For systems with predictable performance, custom allocators tailored to the application's needs can make a difference

- **Hardware constraints**: Custom allocators can be designed to fit those constraints if you're working in an environment with limited or specialized memory

Profiling – the key to making informed decisions

While understanding the theoretical aspects of allocator performance is beneficial, there's no substitute for actual profiling. Measuring the performance of your application using different allocators is the most reliable way to determine the best fit. Tools such as Valgrind or platform-specific profilers can offer insights into memory usage patterns, allocation times, and fragmentation.

Though often behind the scenes, memory management is a cornerstone of efficient C++ programming. Allocators, serving as the unsung heroes, offer a means to tune this aspect finely. While `std::vector` provides incredible versatility and performance out of the box, understanding the role and potential of allocators allows developers to push their applications to new performance heights. As we wrap up this chapter, remember that while theory provides direction, profiling delivers clarity.

In this section, we examined how allocators influence `std::vector`'s performance. We discovered the significant impact of allocator choice on container efficiency and learned about the default `std::allocator` in the C++ STL, including scenarios where an alternative might be preferable.

This knowledge equips us to customize our container's memory management to specific performance needs, ensuring our applications run more efficiently.

Summary

In this chapter, we have thoroughly examined the relationship between memory management and the use of `std::vector`. We began by revisiting the fundamental concepts of capacity versus size, emphasizing their distinct roles and the importance of this distinction for efficient memory use. The mechanics underlying the `std::vector` container's memory allocation were then explored, clarifying what happens internally when vectors grow or shrink.

We discussed the nuances of resizing and reserving memory, where functions such as `reserve()` and `shrink_to_fit()` were introduced as tools for optimizing memory usage. The real-world relevance of these methods was underscored, highlighting their utility in high-performance applications.

The chapter introduced the basics of custom allocators, elaborating on their role and delving into the allocator interface. We addressed the trade-offs and illustrated why custom allocators can be preferable to directly using `new`, `delete`, and managed pointers. Creating and implementing a custom memory pool allocator for `std::vector` demonstrated how custom allocators unlock the potential for greater memory flexibility.

Finally, we analyzed the impact of allocators on container performance, detailing why allocators are a significant consideration for performance tuning. We covered the performance characteristics of `std::allocator` and discussed when alternative allocators should be considered. Profiling was presented as the key to making informed decisions about allocator use.

The insights from this chapter are invaluable, equipping us with sophisticated techniques for mastering memory management with `std::vector`. This knowledge enables us to write high-performance C++ applications as it allows for granular control over memory allocation, which is especially important in environments with tight memory constraints or those requiring quick allocation and deallocation cycles.

Next, we will focus on the algorithms operating on vectors. We will explore sorting techniques, search operations, and the manipulation of vector contents, emphasizing the importance of understanding the efficiency and versatility of these algorithms. We will discuss using custom comparators and predicates and how they can be leveraged to perform complex operations on user-defined data types. The next chapter will also provide guidance on maintaining container invariants and managing iterator invalidation, which is essential for ensuring robustness and correctness in multi-threaded scenarios.

4

Mastering Algorithms with std::vector

In this chapter, we will explore the interaction of `std::vector` with C++ **Standard Template Library** (**STL**) algorithms to unlock the potential of the C++ STL. This chapter delineates the process of efficiently sorting, searching, and manipulating vectors, leveraging the algorithms provided in the header. Moreover, focusing on lambda expressions, custom comparators, and predicates establishes a clear path to customizable, concise, and efficient vector operations.

In this chapter, we will cover the following topics:

- Sorting a vector
- Searching elements
- Manipulating vectors
- Custom comparators and predicates
- Understanding container invariants and iterator invalidation

Technical requirements

The code in this chapter can be found on GitHub:

```
https://github.com/PacktPublishing/Data-Structures-and-Algorithms-
with-the-CPP-STL
```

Sorting a vector

It's a common requirement in software: organizing data. In C++, `std::vector` is frequently the container of choice for many, and quite naturally, one would want to sort its elements. Enter the `std::sort` algorithm, a versatile tool from the `<algorithm>` header that elevates your `std::vector` game to the next level.

Getting started with std::sort

`std::sort` isn't just for vectors; it can sort any sequential container. However, its symbiotic relationship with `std::vector` is particularly noteworthy. At its simplest, using `std::sort` to sort a vector is a straightforward task, as shown in the following code:

```
std::vector<int> numbers = {5, 1, 2, 4, 3};
std::sort(std::begin(numbers), std::end(numbers));
```

After execution, `numbers` would store {1, 2, 3, 4, 5}. The beauty lies in simplicity: pass the start and end iterators of the vector to `std::sort`, and it takes care of the rest.

The engine under the hood – introsort

In the vast array of algorithms offered by the C++ STL, one that consistently stands out for its efficacy is `std::sort`. When paired with the dynamic nature of `std::vector`, it becomes an unstoppable force, propelling your code's efficiency to new heights. But what makes it tick?

To appreciate the genius behind `std::sort`, one must first get acquainted with the introsort algorithm. Introsort isn't just any ordinary sorting algorithm. It's a magnificent hybrid, artfully melding the strengths of three celebrated sorting algorithms: quicksort, heapsort, and insertion sort. This combination ensures that `std::sort` can adapt and perform optimally in myriad scenarios.

While we could plunge deep into algorithmic intricacies, what truly matters for everyday use is this: introsort ensures that `std::sort` remains blazingly fast. The underlying mechanics have been refined and optimized to suit various data patterns.

Efficiency unparalleled – O(n log n)

For those not deep into computer science jargon, time complexities might sound like arcane chants. However, there's a simple beauty to them. When we say that `std::sort` has an average time complexity of $O(n \log n)$, we express its commitment to speed.

Think of $O(n \log n)$ as a promise. Even as your vector grows, scaling to vast sizes, `std::sort` ensures that the number of operations doesn't explode uncontrollably. It strikes a balance, ensuring that the time taken to sort grows at a manageable rate, making it a reliable choice for even the largest vectors.

Sorting in descending order

While ascending order is the default behavior, there are scenarios where you'd want the largest values at the front. C++ has got you covered. With the aid of `std::greater<>()`, a predefined comparator from the `<functional>` header, you can sort your vector in descending order as shown in the following code:

```
std::sort(numbers.begin(), numbers.end(), std::greater<>());
```

After execution, if `numbers` originally had {1, 2, 3, 4, 5}, it would now store {5, 4, 3, 2, 1}.

Sorting custom data types

Vectors aren't limited to primitive types. You might have vectors of custom objects. To demonstrate this, we will use an example. We will use a `Person` class and a vector of `Person` objects. The goal is to sort the vector first by name (using an inline comparator) and then by age (using a lambda function object as a comparator).

Let's look at an example of a custom sort:

```cpp
#include <algorithm>
#include <iostream>
#include <string>
#include <vector>

struct Person {
  std::string name;
  int age{0};

  Person(std::string n, int a) : name(n), age(a) {}

  friend std::ostream &operator<<(std::ostream &os,
                                  const Person &p) {
    os << p.name << " (" << p.age << ")";
    return os;
  }
};

int main() {
  std::vector<Person> people = {Person("Regan", 30),
                                Person("Lisa", 40),
                                Person("Corbin", 45)};

  auto compareByName = [](const Person &a,
                          const Person &b) {
    return a.name < b.name;
  };

  std::sort(people.begin(), people.end(), compareByName);

  std::cout << "Sorted by name:\n";
  for (const auto &p : people) { std::cout << p << "\n"; }
```

```cpp
std::sort(people.begin(), people.end(),
          [](const Person &a, const Person &b) {
            return a.age < b.age;
          });

std::cout << "\nSorted by age:\n";
for (const auto &p : people) { std::cout << p << "\n"; }

return 0;
}
```

Here is the example output:

```
Sorted by name:
Corbin (45)
Lisa (40)
Regan (30)

Sorted by age:
Regan (30)
Lisa (40)
Corbin (45)
```

In this example, we do the following:

- We define a `Person` class with a name and age as attributes.
- We also provide an inline comparator function (`compareByName`) to sort `Person` objects by name.
- We then sort the `people` vector using the inline comparator.
- Afterward, we sort the `people` vector by age using a lambda function as a comparator.
- The results are displayed to verify that the sorting operations work as expected.

Pitfalls and precautions

There's a temptation to view `std::sort` as a magic wand, but remember that while it is powerful, it is not omniscient. The algorithm assumes that the range (`begin, end`) is valid; passing invalid iterators can lead to undefined behavior. Additionally, the comparator provided must establish a strict weak ordering; failing to do so might produce unexpected results.

Strict weak ordering

The term **strict weak ordering** is a critical concept, especially when dealing with sorting algorithms such as `std::sort`. This concept pertains to the comparison function that is used to order the elements in a collection. Let's break it down for clarity:

- **Strictness**: This means that for any two distinct elements *a* and *b*, the comparison function comp must not report both *comp(a, b)* and *comp(b, a)* as true. In simpler terms, if *a* is considered less than *b*, then *b* cannot be less than *a*. This ensures a consistent ordering.

- **Weakness**: The term *weak* in this context refers to the allowance of equivalence classes. In a strict ordering (such as a strict total ordering), two different elements cannot be equivalent. However, in a strict weak ordering, different elements can be considered equivalent. For example, if you have a list of people sorted by age, two people of the same age are in the same equivalence class even if they are different individuals.

- **Transitivity of comparison**: If *comp(a, b)* is true and *comp(b, c)* is true, then *comp(a, c)* must also be true. This ensures that the ordering is consistent across the entire set of elements.

- **Transitivity of equivalence**: If *a* is not less than *b* and *b* is not less than *a* (meaning they are equivalent in terms of the sorting criteria), and similarly *b* and *c* are equivalent, then *a* and *c* must also be considered equivalent.

A comparator providing a strict weak ordering allows `std::sort` to correctly and efficiently sort elements. It ensures that the order is consistent, allows for the grouping of equivalent elements, and respects the logical transitivity both in terms of comparison and equivalence. Failing to adhere to these rules can lead to unpredictable behavior in sorting algorithms.

Let's illustrate the concepts mentioned in the text with a code example. We will show what happens when an invalid range is provided to `std::sort`, and what can occur if the comparator doesn't establish a strict weak ordering:

```
#include <algorithm>
#include <iostream>
#include <vector>

int main() {
  std::vector<int> numbers = {3, 1, 4, 1, 5, 9};

  // Let's mistakenly provide an end iterator beyond the
  // actual end of the vector.
  std::vector<int>::iterator invalid = numbers.end() + 1;

  // Uncommenting the following line can lead to undefined
  // behavior due to the invalid range.
  // std::sort(numbers.begin(), invalidEnd);
```

```cpp
    // This comparator will return true even when both
    // elements are equal. This violates the strict weak
    // ordering.
    auto badComparator = [](int a, int b) { return a <= b; };

    // Using such a comparator can lead to unexpected
    // results.
    std::sort(numbers.begin(), numbers.end(), badComparator);

    // Displaying the sorted array (might be unexpectedly
    // sorted or cause other issues)
    for (int num : numbers) { std::cout << num << " "; }
    std::cout << "\n";

    return 0;
}
```

In this example, we do the following:

- We see how mistakenly providing an end iterator beyond the vector's end can lead to undefined behavior. (This portion is commented out for safety reasons.)

- We provide a comparator that does not maintain a strict weak ordering because it returns true even when two numbers are equal. Using such a comparator with `std::sort` can lead to unexpected results or other undefined behaviors.

With `std::sort` at your disposal, you have an efficient and adaptable tool. You can handle a broad spectrum of sorting tasks with confidence and finesse by understanding its default behaviors, harnessing the power of standard comparators, and crafting custom comparators for unique scenarios. As we proceed in this chapter, remember this foundational skill as we delve deeper into the vast landscape of STL algorithms and `std::vector`.

In this section, we optimized element sorting in `std::vector` with the `std::sort` algorithm, unpacking its introsort mechanism—a hybrid of quicksort, heapsort, and insertion sort—to ensure top performance, usually with $O(n \log n)$ complexity. This understanding is pivotal for data processing efficiency in algorithmic design and high-performance application development.

Next, we'll shift our focus from sorting to searching, contrasting the linear and binary search techniques to effectively find elements in `std::vector`, dissecting their efficiency in various use cases.

Searching elements

Finding elements in a collection is as crucial as storing them. In the C++ STL, there's a buffet of algorithms tailored for searching. Whether `std::vector` is sorted or unsorted, the STL provides an array of functions that'll lead you straight to your target using the classic linear or faster binary search. With `std::vector`, these techniques become indispensable in many scenarios.

Linear search with std::find

The most basic and intuitive searching algorithm is the **linear search**. If you're not sure about the order of your vector or it is simply unsorted, this method comes to the rescue.

Consider `std::vector<int> numbers = {21, 12, 46, 2};`. To find the position of the element 46, we will use the following code:

```
auto it = std::find(numbers.begin(), numbers.end(), 46);
```

If the element exists, it will point to its location; otherwise, it'll point to `numbers.end()`. It's a direct, no-frills approach, checking each element from the beginning to the end. However, the time it takes grows linearly with the size of the vector, making it less ideal for massive datasets.

Binary search techniques

Few algorithmic searching strategies stand out for their sheer elegance and efficiency, quite like the **binary search**. When integrated with the dynamic capabilities of `std::vector`, binary search offers a masterclass in how strategic thinking can transform how we tackle problems. Let's delve deeper into the world of halves to unearth the brilliance behind binary search.

Binary search operates on a beautifully simple principle: divide and conquer. Instead of tediously scanning each element one by one, binary search makes a beeline to the center of the dataset. A quick assessment determines whether the desired element lies in the dataset's first or second half. This insight allows it to dismiss half of the remaining elements, continually narrowing down the search field until the desired element emerges.

For the binary search to work its magic, there's one non-negotiable requirement: the dataset, or `std::vector`, must be sorted in our context. This precondition is vital because the efficiency of binary search hinges on predictability. Each decision to halve the search space is made with the confidence that elements are organized in a specific order. This structured arrangement allows the algorithm to confidently exclude large data portions, making the search incredibly efficient.

Using std::lower_bound and std::upper_bound

But what if you want more than just existence? Sometimes, the questions we seek to answer are more nuanced: If this element isn't in the vector, where would it fit best based on the current ordering? Or, given multiple occurrences of an element, where do they commence or conclude? The C++ STL offers two powerful tools to address these queries: `std::lower_bound` and `std::upper_bound`.

The `std::lower_bound` function plays a pivotal role in the realm of sorted vectors. When presented with a specific element, this function ventures to find the position where this element either first appears in the vector or where it would be rightly placed, ensuring the vector's order remains intact. It effectively returns an iterator pointing to the first element that is not less than (i.e., greater than or equal to) the specified value.

For instance, if our vector contains {1, 3, 3, 5, 7} and we're seeking 3 using `std::lower_bound`, the function would point to the first occurrence of 3. However, if we were searching for 4, the function would indicate the position right before 5, highlighting where 4 would fit best while preserving the vector's sorted nature.

On the other hand, `std::upper_bound` provides insight into the ending of a sequence. When given an element, it identifies the first position where an element greater than the specified value resides. Effectively, if you have multiple occurrences of an element, `std::upper_bound` will point just past the last occurrence.

Referring back to our vector {1, 3, 3, 5, 7}, if we employ `std::upper_bound` in search of 3, it would direct us to the position right before 5, showcasing the end of the 3 sequence.

Let's look at a complete example of using `std::upper_bound` and `std::lower_bound` with `std::vector` of integers.

```
#include <algorithm>
#include <iostream>
#include <vector>

int main() {
  std::vector<int> numbers = {1, 3, 3, 5, 7};

  int val1 = 3;
  auto low1 = std::lower_bound(numbers.begin(),
                               numbers.end(), val1);
  std::cout << "std::lower_bound for value " << val1
          << ": " << (low1 - numbers.begin()) << "\n";

  int val2 = 4;
  auto low2 = std::lower_bound(numbers.begin(),
                               numbers.end(), val2);
```

```
    std::cout << "std::lower_bound for value " << val2
              << ": " << (low2 - numbers.begin()) << "\n";

    int val3 = 3;
    auto up1 = std::upper_bound(numbers.begin(),
                                numbers.end(), val3);
    std::cout << "std::upper_bound for value " << val3
              << ": " << (up1 - numbers.begin()) << "\n";

    return 0;
}
```

When you run the preceding code, the following output will be generated for the specified values:

```
std::lower_bound for value 3: 1
std::lower_bound for value 4: 3
std::upper_bound for value 3: 3
```

The explanation of the code example is as follows:

- For `std::lower_bound` with 3, it returns an iterator pointing to the first occurrence of 3, which is at index 1.

- For `std::lower_bound` with 4, it indicates where 4 would fit best, right before 5 (i.e., at index 3).

- For `std::upper_bound` with 3, it points just past the last occurrence of 3, right before 5 (i.e., at index 3).

While confirming the existence of an element is undoubtedly essential, the actual depth of algorithmic exploration with `std::vector` comes when we pose more detailed questions. With the combined capabilities of `std::lower_bound` and `std::upper_bound`, we begin to appreciate the data analysis capabilities supported by the STL.

Binary search versus linear search – efficiency and versatility

Within the realm of algorithmic searching techniques, both binary and linear search emerge as fundamental strategies. Each has unique strengths and ideal use cases, mainly applied to the versatile `std::vector`. Let's delve deeper into understanding the nuances of these two approaches.

Binary search – the speedster with a condition

Binary search is a highly efficient method renowned for its logarithmic time complexity. This efficiency translates into significant speed, especially when dealing with large vectors. However, this swiftness has a caveat: `std::vector` must be sorted. The essence of binary search is its ability to eliminate half of the remaining elements with each step, making educated guesses based on the order of the elements.

But what happens if this order isn't maintained? Simply put, the results become unpredictable. If a vector isn't sorted, binary search might fail to locate an element even if it exists or return inconsistent results. Thus, it is imperative to ensure a sorted landscape before venturing into a binary search on `std::vector`.

Linear search – the reliable workhorse

Linear search, on the other hand, is characterized by its straightforward approach. It methodically checks each element in the vector until it finds the desired item or concludes it isn't present. This simplicity is its strength; the method doesn't require any prior conditions on the arrangement of elements, making it versatile and applicable to sorted and unsorted vectors.

However, this step-by-step examination comes at a cost: linear search has a linear time complexity. While it might be efficient for smaller vectors, its performance can be noticeably slower as the size of the vector increases, especially when compared to the swift binary search in sorted vectors.

Searching is fundamental, and mastering linear and binary techniques amplifies your proficiency with `std::vector`. Whether you're hunting down a single element, gauging the position of an item in a sorted sequence, or finding the range of an element's occurrences, the STL grants you robust and efficient tools to accomplish these tasks. As you venture further into `std::vector` and the STL, understanding these searching methods is a bedrock, ensuring that no element remains elusive in your C++ journey.

This section honed our skills in element discovery within `std::vector`, starting with `std::find` for linear searches and advancing to binary searches with `std::lower_bound` and `std::upper_bound` for sorted data. Unlike linear search, we recognized binary search's speed advantage, though it requires a pre-sorted vector. Choosing the correct search technique is crucial for performance optimization in various applications.

We'll next explore altering vector contents with methods such as `std::copy`, focusing on practical manipulation techniques and the key considerations for preserving data structure integrity and performance.

Manipulating vectors

Vectors in C++ are dynamic arrays that not only store data but offer a suite of operations to manipulate that data, especially when paired with the algorithms provided by the STL. These algorithms allow developers to optimize data movement and transformation tasks with elegance. Let's delve into the art of manipulating `std::vector` with some powerful algorithms.

Transforming with std::copy

Imagine you've got one vector and wish to copy its elements to another. Simple looping might come to mind, but there's a more efficient and expressive way: `std::copy`.

Consider two vectors as shown in the following code:

```
std::vector<int> source = {1, 2, 3, 4, 5};
std::vector<int> destination(5);
```

Copying the elements is as straightforward as shown in the following:

```
std::copy(source.begin(), source.end(), destination.begin());
```

`destination` holds {1, 2, 3, 4, 5}. It's worth noting that the `destination` vector should have enough space to accommodate the copied elements.

Reversing elements with std::reverse

Often, you might need to reverse the elements of a vector. Instead of manually swapping elements, `std::reverse` comes to the rescue, as shown in the following code:

```
std::vector<int> x = {1, 2, 3, 4, 5};
std::reverse(x.begin(), x.end());
```

The vector numbers now read {5, 4, 3, 2, 1}.

Rotating vectors with std::rotate

Another handy algorithm for manipulating vectors is `std::rotate`, which allows you to rotate elements. Let's say you have a vector as follows:

```
std::vector<int> values = {1, 2, 3, 4, 5};
```

If you want to rotate it so that 3 becomes the first element, you will do the following:

```
std::rotate(values.begin(), values.begin() + 2, values.end());
```

Your vector `values` now hold {3, 4, 5, 1, 2}. This shifts the elements, wrapping them around the vector.

Filling a vector with std::fill

There might be scenarios where you wish to reset or initialize all vector elements to a specific value. `std::fill` is the perfect tool for this:

```
std::vector<int> data(5);
std::fill(data.begin(), data.end(), 42);
```

Every element in the `data` is now `42`.

Putting manipulation to use

A music streaming service wants to allow users to manage their playlists in the following ways:

- At the end of the year, they have a unique feature: users can take their top 10 songs and move them to the beginning of the playlist as a *Year in Review*.

- Users can reverse their playlist to rediscover old songs they haven't listened to in a while for a specific promotion.

- Occasionally, when a user buys a new album, they like to insert its tracks in the middle of their current playlist and rotate the old favorites to the end to have a mix of new and old songs.

- For a fresh start in spring, users can fill their playlist with calm and refreshing spring-themed music.

The following code shows how users can manage their playlists:

```
#include <algorithm>
#include <iostream>
#include <vector>

int main() {
  std::vector<std::string> playlist = {
      "Song A", "Song B", "Song C", "Song D",
      "Song E", "Song F", "Song G", "Song H",
      "Song I", "Song J", "Song K", "Song L"};

  std::rotate(playlist.rbegin(), playlist.rbegin() + 10,
              playlist.rend());

  std::cout << "Year in Review playlist: ";

  for (const auto &song : playlist) {
    std::cout << song << ", ";
  }
  std::cout << "\n";
```

```cpp
std::reverse(playlist.begin(), playlist.end());
std::cout << "Rediscovery playlist: ";

for (const auto &song : playlist) {
  std::cout << song << ", ";
}
std::cout << "\n";

std::vector<std::string> newAlbum = {
    "New Song 1", "New Song 2", "New Song 3"};

playlist.insert(playlist.begin() + playlist.size() / 2,
                newAlbum.begin(), newAlbum.end());

std::rotate(playlist.begin() + playlist.size() / 2,
            playlist.end() - newAlbum.size(),
            playlist.end());

std::cout << "After new album purchase: ";

for (const auto &song : playlist) {
  std::cout << song << ", ";
}
std::cout << "\n";

std::vector<std::string> springSongs = {
    "Spring 1", "Spring 2", "Spring 3", "Spring 4"};

if (playlist.size() < springSongs.size()) {
  playlist.resize(springSongs.size());
}

std::fill(playlist.begin(),
          playlist.begin() + springSongs.size(),
          "Spring Song");

std::cout << "Spring Refresh: ";

for (const auto &song : playlist) {
  std::cout << song << ", ";
}
std::cout << "\n";
```

```
    return 0;
}
```

Here is the example output (truncated):

```
Year in Review playlist: Song C, Song D, Song E, Song F, Song G, Song
H, [...]
Rediscovery playlist: Song B, Song A, Song L, Song K, Song J, Song I,
[...]
After new album purchase: Song B, Song A, Song L, Song K, Song J, Song
I, [...]
Spring Refresh: Spring Song, Spring Song, Spring Song, Spring Song,
Song J, [...]
```

In this example, we do the following:

- The `std::rotate` function brings the user's top 10 songs to the beginning.

- The `std::reverse` function helps rediscover old songs.

- The user's new album purchase demonstrates a more practical use of `std::rotate`.

- The `std::fill` function fills the playlist with spring-themed songs for a fresh start.

Considerations in manipulation

While these functions provide a robust and efficient way to transform vectors, there are a few things to keep in mind:

- Ensure that the destination vectors, especially with functions such as `std::copy` have adequate space to accommodate the data. Using `std::back_inserter` can be helpful if you're unsure about the size.

- Algorithms such as `std::rotate` are highly efficient. They minimize the number of element moves. However, the order in which elements are shifted might not be apparent initially. Practicing with different scenarios will instill a more precise understanding.

- Functions such as `std::fill` and `std::reverse` work in place, transforming the original vector. Always ensure you won't need the original order or values before applying these functions or backing up.

Vectors paired with STL algorithms empower developers to create efficient, expressive, and concise manipulations. Whether you're copying, rotating, reversing, or filling, there's an algorithm tailored to the task. As you continue your journey with `std::vector`, embracing these tools ensures you handle data with finesse and speed, crafting efficient code that is a pleasure to read and write.

In this section, we've mastered modifying the contents of `std::vector` with STL algorithms, particularly `std::copy`, central to performing secure and efficient data operations. We've also covered critical considerations such as avoiding iterator invalidation to maintain data integrity and performance. This expertise is invaluable for C++ developers, as streamlining the execution of complex data manipulations is critical in practical applications.

Moving forward, we'll delve into customizing STL algorithm behavior using comparators and predicates, enabling the definition of bespoke sorting and searching criteria for user-defined data types.

Custom comparators and predicates

When working with `std::vector` and STL algorithms, you'll often encounter scenarios where the default behavior doesn't fit the bill. Sometimes, the way two elements are compared or the criteria for selecting elements must deviate from the norm. Here's where custom comparators and predicates come into play. They are a testament to the power and flexibility of the C++ STL, allowing you to inject your logic seamlessly into established algorithms.

Understanding comparators

A **comparator** is essentially a callable object that returns a `bool`. It's used to dictate the order of elements, especially in sorting or searching operations. By default, operations such as `std::sort` use the `(<)` operator to compare elements, but with a custom comparator, you can redefine this.

Imagine a `std::vector` of integers, and you want to sort them in descending order. Instead of writing another algorithm, you can use `std::sort` with a comparator:

```cpp
std::vector<int> numbers = {1, 3, 2, 5, 4};
std::sort(numbers.begin(), numbers.end(), [](int a, int b){
    return a > b;
});
```

In this example, the lambda expression acts as a comparator, reversing the usual less-than behavior.

The power of predicates

While comparators define ordering, predicates help in making decisions. A **predicate** is a callable object that returns a `bool` like a comparator. Predicates are commonly used with algorithms that need to make a selection or decision based on some criteria.

For instance, if you wanted to count how many numbers in a vector are even, you could employ `std::count_if` with a predicate as shown in the following code:

```cpp
std::vector<int> x = {1, 2, 3, 4, 5};
int evens = std::count_if(x.begin(), x.end(), [](int n){
```

```
        return n % 2 == 0;
    });
```

Here, the lambda predicate checks whether a number is even, allowing `std::count_if` to tally accordingly.

Crafting effective comparators and predicates

The following are the best practices to be kept in mind to craft effective comparators and predicates:

- **Clarity**: Ensure that the logic within is clear. The purpose of a comparator or predicate should be evident upon reading.

- **Statelessness**: A comparator or predicate should be stateless, meaning it should not have any side effects or change behavior between calls.

- **Efficiency**: Since comparators and predicates might be called repeatedly in algorithms, they should be efficient. Avoid unnecessary computations or calls within them.

User-defined structs and classes

While lambdas are concise and convenient, defining a struct or class allows us to define behavior that is more complex or better lends itself to reusability.

Consider a vector of students with names and grades. If you want to sort by grade and then by name, use the following code:

```
struct Student {
    std::string name;
    int grade;
};

std::vector<Student> students = { ... };

std::sort(students.begin(), students.end(), [](const Student& a, const
Student& b) {
    if(a.grade == b.grade){ return (a.name < b.name); }
    return (a.grade > b.grade);
});
```

While the lambda approach works, using a struct might be clearer for complex logic:

```
struct SortByGradeThenName {
  bool operator()(const Student &first,
                  const Student &second) const {
    if (first.grade == second.grade) {
```

```
      return (first.name < second.name);
    }
    return (first.grade > second.grade);
  }
};
std::sort(students.begin(), students.end(), SortByGradeThenName());
```

Custom comparators and predicates are like giving you the keys to the STL's engine room. They allow you to harness the raw power of the library but tailor it precisely to your needs. This fine-tuned control makes C++ a standout language for algorithmic tasks and data processing.

This section introduced us to custom comparators and predicates, enhancing our ability to sort and filter elements in `std::vector`. We learned how to define sorting criteria with comparators and set conditions with predicates, particularly for user-defined types, allowing for intricate data organization within algorithms. Understanding and utilizing these tools is crucial for developers to customize and optimize data operations in C++.

Next, we'll explore container invariants and iterator invalidation, learning to manage container stability and avoid the common issue of invalidation, which is essential for ensuring robustness, especially in multi-threaded contexts.

Understanding container invariants and iterator invalidation

Within the C++ STL, there lies a crucial consideration often overlooked by many: **container invariants**. These invariants are, essentially, a set of conditions that always hold for a container during its lifecycle. For example, in the case of `std::vector`, one such invariant might be that the elements are stored in contiguous memory locations. However, certain operations can disrupt these invariants, leading to potential pitfalls such as iterator invalidation. Armed with this knowledge, we can craft more resilient and efficient code.

Understanding iterator invalidation

A study of `std::vector` is incomplete without a grasp of **iterator invalidation**. Iterator invalidation is akin to trying to use a bookmark after someone's reshuffled the pages in your book. You think you're pointing to one location, but the data there might have changed or ceased to exist.

For instance, when we push an element to a vector (`push_back`), the element is added without any hitches if there's enough reserved memory (`capacity`). But, if the vector needs to allocate new memory due to space constraints, it may relocate all its elements to this new memory block. As a result, any iterator, pointer, or reference pointing to an element in the old memory block will now be invalidated.

Similarly, other operations, such as `insert`, `erase`, or `resize`, can also invalidate an iterator. The crux is to recognize when these operations might disrupt the vector's layout and be prepared to deal with the consequences.

The following is a code example that demonstrates iterator invalidation with `std::vector` and how certain operations might disrupt the container's layout:

```
#include <iostream>
#include <vector>

int main() {
  std::vector<int> numbers = {1, 2, 3, 4, 5};

  std::vector<int>::iterator it = numbers.begin() + 2;
  std::cout << "The element at the iterator before"
               "push_back: "
            << *it << "\n";

  for (int i = 6; i <= 1000; i++) { numbers.push_back(i); }

  std::cout << "The element at the iterator after"
               "push_back: "
            << *it << "\n";

  it = numbers.begin() + 2;
  numbers.insert(it, 99);

  it = numbers.begin() + 3;
  numbers.erase(it);

  return 0;
}
```

In the example, we do the following:

- We first set an iterator to point to the third element of the `numbers` vector.

- After pushing many elements to the vector, the original memory block might be reallocated to a new one, causing the iterator to become invalidated.

- We further demonstrate how the `insert` and `erase` operations can invalidate an iterator.

- It's emphasized that using an invalidated iterator can lead to undefined behavior, and therefore, one should always re-acquire iterators after modifying a vector.

Always be cautious after modifying operations on a vector, as they might invalidate your iterators. Re-acquire your iterators after such operations to ensure they're valid.

Strategies to counteract invalidation

Now that we have a clue about when our iterators might become invalidated, it is time to uncover ways to circumvent or handle these scenarios gracefully.

- **Reserve memory in advance**: If you have an estimate of the maximum number of elements your vector might hold, consider using the `reserve` method. This pre-allocates memory, reducing the need for reallocation and subsequent iterator invalidation during additions.

- **Prefer positions over iterators**: Consider storing positions (e.g., index values) instead of storing iterators. After an operation that may lead to iterator invalidation, you can easily recreate a valid iterator using the position.

- **Refresh iterators post-operation**: After any disruptive operation, avoid using any old iterators, pointers, or references. Instead, obtain fresh iterators to ensure they point to the correct elements.

- **Use algorithms that respect invariants**: The `<algorithm>` header offers many algorithms optimized for containers such as `std::vector`. These often handle potential invalidations internally, safeguarding your code against such pitfalls.

- **Caution with custom comparators and predicates**: When using algorithms that require comparators or predicates, ensure they don't internally modify the vector in a way that could cause invalidation. Maintain the principle of separation of concerns.

Let's look at an example that integrates key strategies to avoid iterator invalidation:

```
#include <algorithm>
#include <iostream>
#include <vector>

int main() {
  std::vector<int> numbers;
  numbers.reserve(1000);

  for (int i = 1; i <= 10; ++i) { numbers.push_back(i); }

  // 0-based index for number 5 in our vector
  size_t positionOfFive = 4;
  std::cout << "Fifth element: " << numbers[positionOfFive]
            << "\n";

  numbers.insert(numbers.begin() + 5, 99);
```

```
std::vector<int>::iterator it =
    numbers.begin() + positionOfFive;
std::cout << "Element at the earlier fifth position "
            "after insertion: "
        << *it << "\n";

// After inserting, refresh the iterator
it = numbers.begin() + 6;

std::sort(numbers.begin(), numbers.end());

// Caution with Custom Comparators and Predicates:
auto isOdd = [](int num) { return num % 2 != 0; };
auto countOdd =
    std::count_if(numbers.begin(), numbers.end(), isOdd);
std::cout << "Number of odd values: " << countOdd
        << "\n";

// Note: The lambda function 'isOdd' is just a read-only
// operation and doesn't modify the vector, ensuring we
// don't have to worry about invalidation.

return 0;
}
```

Here is the example output:

```
Fifth element: 5
Element at the earlier fifth position after insertion: 5
Number of odd values: 6
```

This example does the following:

- Demonstrates how to use `reserve` to pre-allocate memory, anticipating the size.

- Shows positions (index values) instead of iterators to handle potential invalidations.

- Refreshes iterators after a disruptive operation (`insert`).

- Uses the <algorithm> header (i.e., `std::sort` and `std::count_if`) that is optimized for containers and respect invariants.

- Emphasizes the importance of read-only operations (through the `isOdd` lambda) to avoid possible invalidations. (The `isOdd` lambda function is just a read-only operation and doesn't modify the vector, ensuring we don't have to worry about invalidation.)

Dealing with invalidation in multi-threaded scenarios

While iterator invalidation in a single-threaded application is easier to manage, things can get trickier in multi-threaded contexts. Imagine one thread modifying a vector while another attempts to read from it using an iterator. The chaos! The catastrophe! The following are the ways to tackle invalidation in multi-threaded scenarios:

- **Use mutexes and locks**: Safeguard sections of your code that modify the vector with **mutexes**. This ensures that only one thread can change the vector at a given time, preventing concurrent operations that might lead to unpredictable invalidations.

- **Use atomic operations**: Some operations might be made atomic, ensuring they're completed fully without interruption, reducing the chances of unsynchronized access and modification.

- **Consider thread-safe containers**: If multi-threading is central to your application, consider using **thread-safe containers** designed to handle concurrent accesses and modifications without compromising on invariants.

> Mutex
>
> A mutex, short for **mutual exclusion**, is a synchronization primitive used in concurrent programming to protect shared resources or critical sections of code from being accessed by multiple threads simultaneously. By locking a mutex before accessing a shared resource and unlocking it afterward, a thread ensures that no other thread can access the resource while it's being used, thus preventing race conditions and ensuring data consistency in multi-threaded applications.

> Thread-safe containers
>
> A thread-safe container refers to a data structure that allows multiple threads to access and modify its contents concurrently without causing data corruption or inconsistencies. This is achieved through internal mechanisms such as locking or atomic operations that ensure synchronization and mutual exclusion, thereby maintaining the integrity of the container's data even in a multi-threaded environment. Such containers are crucial in concurrent programming for safe and efficient data sharing between threads.

Let's look at a practical example of multi-threaded access to `std::vector`. This example will demonstrate the use of mutexes to prevent concurrent modifications, ensuring thread safety:

```cpp
#include <chrono>
#include <iostream>
#include <mutex>
#include <thread>
#include <vector>

std::mutex vecMutex;
```

```cpp
void add_to_vector(std::vector<int> &numbers, int value) {
  std::lock_guard<std::mutex> guard(vecMutex);
  numbers.push_back(value);
}

void print_vector(const std::vector<int> &numbers) {
  std::lock_guard<std::mutex> guard(vecMutex);

  for (int num : numbers) { std::cout << num << " "; }

  std::cout << "\n";
}

int main() {
  std::vector<int> numbers;

  std::thread t1(add_to_vector, std::ref(numbers), 1);
  std::thread t2(add_to_vector, std::ref(numbers), 2);

  t1.join();
  t2.join();

  std::thread t3(print_vector, std::ref(numbers));
  t3.join();

  return 0;
}
```

Here is the example output:

```
2 1
```

This example illustrates the following concepts:

- We use a mutex (vecMutex) to protect the shared std::vector from concurrent access and modification.

- The add_to_vector and print_vector functions lock the mutex using std::lock_guard, ensuring exclusive access to the vector during their scope.

- We use std::thread to run functions that concurrently modify or read from the vector. The use of mutexes ensures that these operations are thread-safe.

Remember, while mutexes safeguard against concurrent modifications, they can also introduce potential deadlocks and reduce parallelism. If multi-threading is deeply integrated into your application, you might consider other thread-safe containers or advanced synchronization techniques.

Understanding and respecting container invariants is paramount in harnessing the full power of STL containers and the `<algorithm>` header. Knowing when and why certain invariants might be disrupted allows for the creation of robust, efficient, and reliable code. As we continue our exploration of algorithms beyond `std::vector`, always keep these principles in mind.

In this section, we addressed the importance of preserving `std::vector` stability and the risks of iterator invalidation during container modification. We identified actions that cause invalidation and their potential to disrupt program integrity.

Understanding iterator behavior is vital for bug prevention and ensuring the robustness of our applications. We've also learned methods to mitigate invalidation risks, maintaining vector consistency throughout operations that might jeopardize it.

Summary

Throughout this chapter, we have deepened our understanding of the STL through the lens of `std::vector` and its interaction with various algorithms. We commenced with sorting vectors, where we explored the `std::sort` algorithm and its underlying engine, introsort, appreciating its *O(n log n)* efficiency. We progressed to searching within vectors, contrasting the conditions and efficiencies of linear and binary search techniques.

The chapter then guided us through effective vector manipulation, including transformation with `std::copy` and the considerations necessary to prevent performance degradation or logical errors. We learned to use custom comparators and predicates to extend the functionality of standard algorithms when working with user-defined structs and classes. Finally, we explored container invariants and iterator invalidation, acquiring strategies to maintain data integrity even in complex, multi-threaded environments.

Critically, this information provides us with practical and detailed insights into how to leverage `std::vector` effectively. Mastery of these algorithms allows developers to write efficient, robust, and adaptable code to various programming challenges.

Next, we will shift our focus from the technical intricacies of algorithms to a broader discussion on why `std::vector` should be our default container of choice. We will compare `std::vector` with other containers, dive into its memory advantages, and reflect on practical use cases, from data processing to game development. This will underscore the versatility and efficiency of `std::vector`, solidifying its status as a safe and powerful default choice, yet one among many tools available to the adept C++ programmer.

5
Making a Case for std::vector

This chapter discusses the reasons behind `std::vector`'s popularity by examining the performance metrics and real-world applications that make it a go-to container for many developers. By comparing `std::vector` against other containers, you will clearly understand its strengths and recognize scenarios where alternatives might be more suitable. Such insights will empower C++ developers to make informed container choices, leading to more efficient and effective code.

In this chapter, we will cover the following topics as they relate to `std::vector`:

- Performance considerations
- Practical use cases
- Versatility and efficiency

Performance considerations

When choosing a data container in C++, performance often ranks at the top of considerations. Naturally, the allure of `std::vector` doesn't solely rest on its ease of use, but mainly on its efficiency. In this section, we'll delve deep into the performance mechanics of `std::vector`, comparing it with other C++ containers and shedding light on where it truly shines.

At its core, `std::vector` is a dynamic array. This means that its elements are stored in contiguous memory locations. This adjacent nature gives `std::vector` a performance edge in many scenarios, such as the following:

- **Random access**: Accessing any element via its index, whether reading or writing, is an *O(1)* operation. This makes `std::vector` as fast as a raw array regarding direct element access.

- **Cache locality**: Modern CPUs have caches that temporarily store frequently accessed memory data. The contiguous memory storage of `std::vector` often results in better cache locality, making data access faster due to fewer cache misses.

- **Insertions at the end**: Appending an element to the end of a `std::vector` container is typically an *O(1)* operation. While occasional resizing may turn this into an *O(n)* operation, the amortized time remains constant.

  However, no container is universally the best, and `std::vector` has its limitations, too, which are as follows:

- **Insertions not at the end**: Inserting an element anywhere other than the end is an *O(n)* operation because it may require shifting the subsequent elements. However, this shift may still outperform purpose-built containers such as `std::list` because of the cache-friendliness of `std::vector`.

- **Deletions**: Similar to insertions, deleting an element from anywhere other than the end necessitates shifting, making it an *O(n)* operation.

Comparison with other containers

- `std::list`: This is a doubly linked list, which means that insertions and deletions at any position are *O(1)*. However, it lacks the cache locality of `std::vector`, making element access slower. Random access in a list is an *O(n)* operation, whereas it is *O(1)* in a vector.

- `std::deque`: A double-ended queue that supports efficient insertions and deletions at both ends. While it provides a similar random access time as `std::vector`, its non-contiguous nature might lead to more cache misses during certain operations.

- `std::array`: A static array with a fixed size. It offers similar performance characteristics as `std::vector` for direct access but lacks dynamic resizing.

So, when should you choose `std::vector` over these? If your primary operations are random access and insertion/removal at the end, `std::vector` is often the best choice due to its *O(1)* complexities and excellent cache performance. However, if you frequently insert into or delete from the middle, other containers such as `std::list` might be more efficient for large data. As always, measure performance in your specific use case to guide your decision.

The memory advantage

`std::vector` manages its memory efficiently. As you add elements, it intelligently resizes, often doubling its capacity to minimize the number of allocations. This dynamic resizing ensures that while the memory is used optimally, there's minimal overhead in allocations, leading to faster operations.

The takeaway

Performance isn't just about raw speed; it is about choosing the right tool for the right job. While `std::vector` offers outstanding performance in many scenarios, understanding its strengths and weaknesses is vital. When you match your problem's requirements with the intrinsic strengths of `std::vector`, you don't just write code—you craft optimized solutions ready to meet the demands of modern computing.

In the forthcoming sections, we'll explore the practicality of `std::vector` in real-world applications and dive deeper into its versatility, equipping you with the knowledge needed to harness its full power.

Practical use cases

While understanding the theoretical and performance advantages of `std::vector` is essential, it is often in real-world applications that the strength of a tool becomes evident. As we dive into practical use cases, you'll see why `std::vector` is frequently the container of choice for many developers and why, sometimes, other options might be more fitting.

A resizable dynamic array at heart

Imagine developing a simulation program that models the behavior of particles in a chamber. The number of particles can vary drastically as they split or merge. Here, using `std::vector` would be ideal due to its dynamic nature. The program would benefit from the constant-time direct access for particle updates, and its resizing capability would easily handle varying particle numbers.

Data processing and analytics

Data analytics often involves reading large datasets, processing them, and extracting information. Consider a scenario where you're tasked with reading sensor temperatures for an entire year. The data is vast, but once read, it is processed sequentially—calculating averages, detecting peaks, and so on. `std::vector`, with its contiguous memory and excellent cache locality, becomes a top pick, allowing for faster sequential processing of such vast datasets.

Graphics and game development

In game development, objects such as bullets, enemies, and items can be represented using `std::vector`. For instance, bullets fired in a shooter game can be stored in `std::vector`. As the bullets move or are destroyed, the vector resizes. The direct access capability of `std::vector` allows efficient updates to each bullet's position.

Beyond just containers

The choice of container also depends on the broader architecture of the application. For instance, in distributed systems, data might be better represented in structures optimized for serialization and deserialization, even if within a single node, `std::vector` might seem the best choice.

In conclusion, the utility of `std::vector` in real-world applications cannot be overstated. Its dynamic nature and the advantages of direct access and cache-friendly design make it a powerhouse. However, as with all tools, its effectiveness is best realized when matched with the right task. Knowing when to use `std::vector` and when to consider alternatives is a testament to a developer's understanding and adaptability. As we move on to explore the versatility and efficiency of `std::vector`, you'll gain even deeper insights into the world of this remarkable container.

Versatility and efficiency

The C++ **Standard Template Library** (**STL**) is a treasure trove of utilities, functions, and data structures. But amid this wealth of options, `std::vector` stands out, often serving as the default choice for many C++ developers. Its wide acceptance isn't a mere chance but a consequence of its versatility and efficiency.

A testament to versatility

The fundamental design of `std::vector` allows it to serve many programming needs. It's a dynamic array that can grow or shrink, offering the best of both worlds: the direct access of arrays and the flexibility of linked lists. This means that whether you're storing data temporarily, manipulating large datasets, or simply using it as a buffer, `std::vector` lends itself gracefully.

For many applications, especially those not bound by specific complexities, the first container that developers reach for is `std::vector`. It's not just because of tradition or familiarity; it is because, in a vast majority of cases, `std::vector` does the job, and it does it well.

Efficiency isn't just about speed

While we have delved into the performance aspects, it's worth noting that efficiency is not solely about raw speed. `std::vector`'s continuous memory layout offers cache-friendliness and simplifies memory management, reducing fragmentation. Its predictable behavior in terms of growth ensures minimal surprise overheads.

Moreover, its simple interface, mirrored by many other STL containers, reduces the learning curve. Developers can effortlessly switch to `std::vector` from other containers or even from arrays. The ease of use and its powerful capabilities make `std::vector` a tool that amplifies developer productivity.

A safe default, but not the only option

One of the hallmarks of a mature developer is knowing the tools at their disposal and choosing the right one for the job. `std::vector` is an incredible tool and it is versatile enough to be a safe default for many scenarios. Its direct access, dynamic sizing, and cache locality strengths make it a general-purpose powerhouse.

However, this does not mean it's always the right choice. There are situations where `std::deque`, `std::list`, or perhaps `std::set` might be more fitting. But what sets `std::vector` apart is that when you're unsure which container to start with, it is often a safe bet to begin with `std::vector`. As development progresses and needs become more apparent, transitioning to another, more specialized container, if required, becomes a strategic decision rather than a necessity.

Summary

`std::vector` embodies the spirit of C++ in many ways. It represents a balance of performance and flexibility, serving as a testament to the language's ethos of not sacrificing efficiency for high-level abstraction.

As we conclude this chapter, it's clear that `std::vector` is more than just another container in the STL. It's a cornerstone. By now, you should appreciate its significance in C++ and feel confident in harnessing its capabilities. As you venture further into C++ development, let the lessons of this part of the book guide your container choices, leaning on the strengths of `std::vector` when apt and branching out to other STL offerings when the situation demands it.

Part II of this book will look at all STL data structures. Armed with the knowledge you have gained in *Part I*, you can compare and contrast `std::vector` to its many alternatives.

Part 2:
Understanding STL
Data Structures

This part of the book is a detailed reference to the versatile world of STL data structures. We commence with the sequential containers—`std::array`, `std::vector`, `std::deque`, `std::list`, `std::forward_list`, and `std::string`—providing you with a granular understanding of their design, usage, and performance nuances. Each container's purpose and suitability are assessed, alongside discussions on their ideal use cases and performance characteristics. You will learn about the finer points of memory management and thread safety and how to interact with STL algorithms effectively.

We then focus on the ordered and unordered associative containers—`std::set`, `std::map`, `std::multiset`, `std::multimap`, and their unordered counterparts. The exploration continues with container adaptors such as `std::stack`, `std::queue`, and `std::priority_queue`, detailing their use cases and performance insights. We also introduce newer additions like `std::flat_set` and `std::flat_map`, which offer a balance between sequence and associative containers.

Concluding with container views like `std::span` and `std::mdspan`, this part equips you with the knowledge to select and manipulate the most fitting STL container for your data structure challenges while employing best practices and understanding exceptions and customization.

As the chapters in this part are a series of reference chapters, they are structured in a slightly different manner with no *Summary* section at the end.

By the end of this part, you will comprehend the full capabilities of STL containers and be proficient in applying them to create efficient and effective C++ applications.

This part has the following chapters:

- *Chapter 6: Advanced Sequence Container Usage*
- *Chapter 7: Advanced Ordered Associative Container Usage*
- *Chapter 8: Advanced Unordered Associative Container Usage*
- *Chapter 9: Container Adaptors*
- *Chapter 10: Container Views*

6

Advanced Sequence Container Usage

Sequence containers are at the core of C++ data handling, providing structures to hold data linearly. For intermediate developers, making the right choice from an array of sequence containers including vectors, arrays, deques, and lists can be pivotal. This chapter breaks down each container type, emphasizing their distinct advantages and ideal use cases. Furthermore, diving into best practices—from efficient resizing to iterator management—will ensure developers choose the right container and utilize it effectively. Grasping these nuances elevates code efficiency, readability, and maintainability in real-world applications.

In the sprawling expanse of the C++ **Standard Template Library** (**STL**), sequence containers hold a position of prominence. Not just because they're often the first choice of data structures for developers but also because of the unique and versatile solutions each offers. These containers, as their name implies, maintain elements sequentially. But as we dive deeper, you'll find that the similarities often end there. Each sequence container brings its strengths and is tailored for particular scenarios.

In this chapter, we're going to cover the following main topics:

- `std::array`
- `std::vector`
- `std::deque`
- `std::list`
- `std::forward_list`
- `std::string`

Technical requirements

The code in this chapter can be found on GitHub:

`https://github.com/PacktPublishing/Data-Structures-and-Algorithms-with-the-CPP-STL`

std::array

`std::array` is a fixed-size container that wraps around a traditional C-style array. If you're coming from a C background or even early C++, you'll be familiar with the headaches of raw arrays—the lack of bounds-checking, the cumbersome syntax, and more. With `std::array`, you get all the benefits of a traditional array, such as static memory allocation and constant-time access, while enjoying modern C++ amenities including range-based for-loops and member functions for size checking. Use `std::array` when you know the size of your dataset in advance, and it will not change. It's perfect for scenarios where performance is paramount and your memory needs are static.

> **Note**
>
> For more information on CPP core guidelines, please refer to *C++ Core Guidelines* `https://isocpp.github.io/CppCoreGuidelines/CppCoreGuidelines`

Purpose and suitability

`std::array` is a container that encapsulates fixed-size arrays. Its strengths are as follows:

- Predictable, fixed size
- Stack allocation, offering swift access and minimal overhead

It's best to choose `std::array` in the following situations:

- The array size is known at compile-time.
- Overhead minimization and performance predictability are crucial.

For dynamic sizing needs, consider `std::vector` instead.

Ideal use cases

The following are some of the ideal use cases of `std::array`:

- **Fixed size collections**: If you have a scenario where the size of your collection is known at compile-time and does not change, `std::array` is the go-to choice. This makes it apt for situations where dimension sizes are predefined, such as in certain mathematical operations or game board representations.

- **Performance-critical applications**: Due to its fixed-size nature, `std::array` does not involve dynamic memory allocations, which can benefit real-time or performance-critical applications.

- **Safe array manipulations**: `std::array` offers bounds-checking (with the `at()` member function), providing a safer alternative to C-style arrays, especially when dealing with potential out-of-bounds access.

- **Passing arrays to functions**: With C-style arrays, information about the size of the array is often lost when passed to a function. With `std::array`, size information is retained, making writing safer and more intuitive functions easier.

- **Interoperability with C and FORTRAN code**: `std::array` can seamlessly be used with C-style arrays, making it a great choice for projects with C and C++ integrations.

- **Stack-allocated data**: In situations where you prefer stack-allocated data over heap-allocated data for its deterministic allocation and deallocation, `std::array` is the best choice.

- **Cache-friendly iteration**: Like `std::vector`, `std::array` offers contiguous memory storage, making it cache-friendly for iterations.

- **Predictable memory patterns:** For applications where predictable memory patterns are essential, such as embedded systems or real-time simulations, the static nature of `std::array` ensures no surprise memory allocations.

- **Uniform data initialization:** If you need to initialize a fixed set of values in a structured manner, as in lookup tables or certain configuration values, `std::array` provides convenient initialization semantics.

However, while `std::array` offers several advantages over traditional arrays, it is essential to note that it doesn't fit situations where dynamic resizing is necessary. For those use cases, one might consider `std::vector` or other dynamic containers.

Performance

The algorithmic performance of `std::array` is characterized as follows:

- **Insertion**: Not applicable since the size is fixed

- **Deletion**: Not applicable

- **Access**: A constant *O(1)* for any position

- **Memory overhead**: Minimal, given stack allocation

- **Trade-off**: Fixed-size efficiency is at the cost of static sizing

Memory management

Unlike `std::vector`, `std::array` doesn't dynamically allocate memory. It is stack allocated, so there are no unexpected allocation behaviors or surprises.

Thread safety

Are you reading from multiple threads? Perfectly fine. However, writing concurrently to the same element demands synchronization.

Extensions and variants

For dynamic needs, `std::vector` serves as the STL's prime alternative. Other fixed-size array options include the plain old C-style arrays.

Sorting and searching complexity

- **Sorting**: *O(n log n)* using `std::sort()`
- **Searching**: *O(log n)* with a sorted array through `std::binary_search()`

Interface and member functions

Standard functions such as `begin()`, `end()`, and `size()` are present. Noteworthy member functions are as follows:

- `fill`: Sets all elements to a value
- `swap`: Swaps contents with another array of the same type and size

Comparisons

Compared to `std::vector`, `std::array` does not resize but offers predictable performance. When choosing, weigh the need for dynamic sizing against performance consistency.

Interactions with algorithms

STL algorithms play nicely with `std::array` due to random-access capabilities. However, those expecting dynamic sizing won't work with `std::array`.

Exceptions

With `std::array`, out-of-bounds access (such as using `at()`) can throw exceptions, primarily `std::out_of_range`.

Customization

While you cannot resize, you can integrate custom types. Given the container's stack-allocation nature, ensure they're efficiently movable/copyable.

Example

In this example, we will show the following best practices and use of `std::array`:

- Using `std::array` with a fixed size
- Using C++ structured bindings with `std::array` to destructure elements
- Implementing compile-time calculations with `std::array` (thanks to its constexpr nature)
- Using algorithms such as `std::sort` and `std::find` with `std::array`

> **Structured bindings**
>
> Structured bindings, introduced in C++17, allow for the convenient and readable unpacking of elements from tuples, pairs, or struct-like objects into separate named variables. This syntax simplifies accessing multiple elements returned from a function or decomposing the contents of complex data structures, enhancing code clarity and reducing verbosity.

Here is the code example discussing the above points:

```cpp
#include <algorithm>
#include <array>
#include <iostream>

struct Point {
  int x{0}, y{0};
};

constexpr int sumArray(const std::array<int, 5> &arr) {
  int sum = 0;
  for (const auto &val : arr) { sum += val; }
  return sum;
}

int main() {
  std::array<int, 5> numbers = {5, 3, 8, 1, 4};
  std::array<Point, 3> points = {{{1, 2}, {3, 4}, {5, 6}}};

  // Demonstrating structured bindings with &[x, y]
  for (const auto &[x, y] : points) {
```

```cpp
    std::cout << "(" << x << ", " << y << ")\n";
}

constexpr std::array<int, 5> constNumbers = {1, 2, 3, 4,
                                             5};

constexpr int totalSum = sumArray(constNumbers);

std::cout << "\nCompile-time sum of array elements: "
          << totalSum << "\n";

std::sort(numbers.begin(), numbers.end());

std::cout << "\nSorted numbers: ";
for (const auto &num : numbers) {
  std::cout << num << " ";
}
std::cout << "\n";

int searchFor = 3;

if (std::find(numbers.begin(), numbers.end(),
              searchFor) != numbers.end()) {
  std::cout << "\nFound " << searchFor
            << " in the array.\n";
} else {
  std::cout << "\nDidn't find " << searchFor
            << " in the array.\n";
}

return 0;
}
```

This example highlights the features and advantages of std::array, including its fixed-size nature, compatibility with modern C++ features like structured bindings, and its utility in compile-time computations. The preceding example also illustrates how STL algorithms can be seamlessly applied to std::array.

Best practices

Let us explore the best practices of using std::array:

- **Fixed-size with enhanced functionality**: `std::array` encapsulates the predictability of C-style arrays, enriching them with added utility. Its fixed size is particularly useful for situations with predetermined data sizes, making it a prime choice for such applications.

- **Modern array with usability**: C-style arrays have been a mainstay for years. However, `std::array` comes with a suite of member functions, elevating its capabilities. This makes it a compelling choice in contemporary C++ development over its traditional counterpart.

- **Access elements safely**: Square bracket notation is a quick means of accessing array elements, but it lacks boundary checks. To bolster safety, especially in unpredictable scenarios, the `.at()` member function is invaluable. It guards against out-of-bound accesses by throwing exceptions when boundaries are crossed.

- **Clarity on size is crucial**: The immutable size of `std::array` is both its strength and limitation. It promises constant time access but lacks flexibility in resizing. Therefore, it is essential to be precise about the desired size during its declaration to prevent potential issues.

- **Leverage range-based for-loops**: With the advent of C++11, range-based for-loops emerged as an efficient and readable means to iterate over arrays. When working with `std::array`, adopting this loop structure minimizes the chances of boundary errors, promoting code stability.

- **Efficient type containment**: While `std::array` can house diverse types, considering efficiency is pivotal. If the type, be it primitive or user-defined, is particularly large or intricate, ensure its move or copy operations are optimized to preserve performance during array operations.

- **Choosing the right container**: `std::array` excels in scenarios that demand a fixed-size container. However, for applications where dynamic resizing or extensive data is anticipated, alternatives such as `std::vector` may offer a more adaptive solution.

std::vector

`std::vector` is a dynamic array. It grows and shrinks as needed, offering an excellent balance between direct access performance and flexibility in size. `std::vector` has a cache-friendly contiguous memory layout and amortized constant-time insertions at the end, making it an excellent general-purpose container. It performs best when your primary operations are indexing and require dynamic resizing but without frequent insertions or deletions in the middle.

Purpose and suitability

`std::vector` is essentially a dynamic array within the STL. Its primary strength lies in the following:

- Offering constant-time random access
- Dynamically resizing as elements are inserted or removed

It's particularly suitable when the following is required:

- Random access is paramount.
- Insertions or deletions are primarily at the end of the sequence.
- Cache locality is essential.

Opt for `std::vector` when constant-time access, performance, or cache friendliness trump other concerns.

Ideal use cases

The following are some of the ideal use cases of `std::vector`:

- **Dynamic array replacement**: If you need an array that can grow or shrink in size, `std::vector` is your best choice. Unlike standard arrays, vectors automatically manage their size and handle memory allocation/deallocation seamlessly.
- **Random access**: `std::vector` offers constant-time access to any elements, making it suitable for frequently accessing or modifying data at specific indices.
- **Sequential data storage**: If the data to be stored has a natural sequence or order (such as time series data or a list of items), then `std::vector` provides a contiguous block of memory that's appropriate for this.
- **Frequent back insertions**: Since `std::vector` is optimized for insertions at its end, it is a good choice for applications such as log systems, where new entries are continuously added.
- **Low overhead data storage**: `std::vector` provides one of the most memory-efficient ways to store data because of its continuous memory block and lack of structural overhead, unlike linked-list-based containers.
- **Cache-friendly iteration**: Due to its contiguous memory storage, iterating over `std::vector` is cache-friendly, leading to faster performance in many scenarios compared to non-contiguous data structures.
- **Compactness and portability**: When serializing data for network transmission or file storage, the continuous memory block of `std::vector` can be easily streamed or written.

- **Implementing stacks**: Though there's `std::stack` for this purpose, `std::vector` can effectively implement a stack data structure where elements are added or removed only from the back.

- **Polymorphic data storage**: If storing pointers (such as raw pointers or smart pointers) to objects of polymorphic classes, `std::vector` provides an efficient and dynamic container for this.

However, there are a few caveats when using `std::vector`. If frequent insertions or deletions are needed in the middle, `std::vector` might not be the most efficient choice due to the need to shift elements. Also, if you're pushing elements frequently, using `reserve()` to preallocate memory and avoid frequent reallocations is a good practice.

Performance

The algorithmic performance of `std::vector` is characterized as follows:

- **Insertion:** *O(1)* average-case for the end, *O(n)* for elsewhere

- **Deletion:** *O(1)* at the end, *O(n)* for the middle

- **Access:** A swift *O(1)* for any position

- **Memory overhead:** Typically low, but can inflate if reserved capacity isn't managed

- **Trade-offs:** The convenience of *O(1)* access is counterbalanced by potential *O(n)* costs for insertion at the start or middle.

Memory management

`std::vector` automatically manages its memory. If its capacity is exhausted, it typically doubles its size, though this isn't strictly mandated. Allocators can influence this behavior, permitting fine-grained control.

Thread safety

Concurrent reads? No problem. But writes, or a mix of reads and writes, demand external synchronization. Consider mutexes or other concurrency tools.

Extensions and variants

While `std::vector` is a dynamic array, the STL offers other sequence containers such as `std::deque` that provide an API for fast insertions at both ends or `std::list`, possibly optimizing middle insertions and deletions.

Sorting and searching complexity

The sorting and search complexity is characterized as follows:

- **Sorting:** Typically *O(n log n)* with `std::sort()`
- **Searching:** *O(log n)* with a sorted vector using `std::binary_search()`

Special interface and member functions

Beyond the regulars (`push_back`, `pop_back`, `begin`, and `end`), acquaint yourself with the following:

- `emplace_back`: Constructs elements directly
- `resize`: Changes the number of elements
- `shrink_to_fit`: Reduces memory usage

Comparisons

Against `std::list` and `std::deque`, `std::vector` excels at random access, but may falter with frequent middle modifications of very large data types.

Interactions with algorithms

Many STL algorithms harmonize beautifully with `std::vector` due to its random-access nature. Algorithms requiring frequent reordering, however, might be better paired with other containers.

Exceptions

Pushing beyond capacity or accessing out-of-bounds indices can throw exceptions. Notably, operations are exception-safe, preserving vector states even if operations (like insertions) throw exceptions.

Customization

With custom allocators, tweak memory allocation strategies. However, `std::vector` does not naturally support custom comparators or hash functions.

Example

In this example, we will show the following best-practices and use of `std::vector`:

- Preallocating memory with reserve
- Using `emplace_back` for efficient insertion

- Using iterators for traversal and modification

- Employing std::vector with custom objects

- Using algorithms such as std::remove with std::vector

Here is the code example:

```cpp
#include <algorithm>
#include <iostream>
#include <vector>

class Employee {
public:
  Employee(int _id, const std::string &_name)
      : id(_id), name(_name) {}

  int getId() const { return id; }
  const std::string &getName() const { return name; }

  void setName(const std::string &newName) {
    name = newName;
  }

private:
  int id{0};
  std::string name;
};

int main() {
  std::vector<Employee> employees;

  employees.reserve(5);
  employees.emplace_back(1, "Lisa");
  employees.emplace_back(2, "Corbin");
  employees.emplace_back(3, "Aaron");
  employees.emplace_back(4, "Amanda");
  employees.emplace_back(5, "Regan");

  for (const auto &emp : employees) {
    std::cout << "ID: " << emp.getId()
              << ", Name: " << emp.getName() << "\n";
  }

  auto it = std::find_if(
```

```
        employees.begin(), employees.end(),
        [](const Employee &e) { return e.getId() == 3; });

    if (it != employees.end()) { it->setName("Chuck"); }

    std::cout << "\nAfter Modification:\n";
    for (const auto &emp : employees) {
      std::cout << "ID: " << emp.getId()
                << ", Name: " << emp.getName() << "\n";
    }

    employees.erase(std::remove_if(employees.begin(),
                                   employees.end(),
                                   [](const Employee &e) {
                                     return e.getId() == 2;
                                   }),
                    employees.end());

    std::cout << "\nAfter Removal:\n";

    for (const auto &emp : employees) {
      std::cout << "ID: " << emp.getId()
                << ", Name: " << emp.getName() << "\n";
    }

    return 0;
  }
```

The preceding example demonstrates the efficiency and flexibility of std::vector combined with C++ STL algorithms. It showcases managing and manipulating a list of Employee objects in various ways.

Now, let us look at a std::vector<bool> example.

std::vector<bool> is a somewhat controversial specialization in the C++ Standard Library. It was designed to use only one bit per boolean value, thereby saving space. However, this space optimization has led to several unexpected behaviors and quirks, especially compared to std::vector for other types.

For those reasons, many experts advise caution when using std::vector<bool>. Nevertheless, if one still wishes to utilize it, here's a canonical example illustrating its use and some of its quirks:

```
#include <iostream>
#include <vector>
```

```cpp
int main() {
  std::vector<bool> boolVec = {true, false, true, true,
                               false};

  boolVec[1] = true;
  std::cout << "Second element: " << boolVec[1] << '\n';

  auto ref = boolVec[1];
  ref = false;

  std::cout << "Second element after modifying copy: "
            << boolVec[1] << '\n';

  // Iterating over the vector
  for (bool val : boolVec) { std::cout << val << ' '; }
  std::cout << '\n';

  // Pushing values
  boolVec.push_back(false);

  // Resizing
  boolVec.resize(10, true);

  // Capacity and size
  std::cout << "Size: " << boolVec.size()
            << ", Capacity: " << boolVec.capacity()
            << '\n';

  // Clearing the vector
  boolVec.clear();

  return 0;
}
```

The key takeaways from the preceding code are as follows:

- `std::vector<bool>` offers memory savings by storing booleans as individual bits.

- When accessing an element from `std::vector<bool>`, you don't get a normal reference as you do with other vector types. Instead, you get a proxy object. This is why modifying `ref` in the example doesn't change the actual value in the vector.

- Other operations, such as iteration, resizing, and capacity checks, work similarly to other `std::vector` types.

For many applications, the peculiarities of `std::vector<bool>` might outweigh its memory-saving benefits. If the memory optimization isn't crucial and the behavior quirks can be problematic, consider using alternative containers such as `std::deque<bool>`, `std::bitset`, or a third-party bitset/vector library.

Best practices

Let us explore the best practices of using `std::vector`:

- **Space-efficient specialization**: It's essential to recognize that `std::vector<bool>` isn't just a simple vector of boolean values. It's specialized to save space, and this space efficiency comes at a cost: elements aren't real bools but bitfield proxies. This specialization can lead to unique behavior in certain operations, making it vital to understand its intricacies fully.

- **Dynamic resizing**: A key feature of `std::vector` is its ability to resize dynamically. While this is powerful, predicting and guiding this resizing with the `reserve` function can be beneficial. Preallocating memory helps in minimizing reallocations and ensures efficient performance.

- **The power of emplace_back**: Although `push_back` is a frequently used method to add elements, `emplace_back` provides a more efficient way to construct objects directly in the vector. Constructing objects in place can often enhance performance, especially with complex objects.

- **Random access**: `std::vector` provides excellent random access performance. However, operations in the middle, such as insertions or deletions, can be more time-consuming due to the need to move subsequent elements. For tasks that require frequent middle operations, it is worthwhile to consider alternative STL containers.

- **Bounds checking**: Always ensure that vector element access is within bounds. While direct index access is fast, it doesn't offer safety against out-of-bounds errors. The `.at()` member function, on the other hand, provides bounds-checked access and will throw a `std::out_of_range` exception if an invalid index is used.

- **Synchronization in multithreading**: Synchronization is crucial if you're working with multiple threads that access a `std::vector`. While `std::vector` isn't inherently thread-safe, you can achieve thread safety with appropriate synchronization tools such as mutexes.

- **(Maybe) Avoid list-like use**: `std::vector` isn't optimized for frequent middle insertions or deletions. That said, its cache-friendliness and ability to quickly search may still mean it is the best data type to use. Using it as a linked list can be suboptimal, but only for specific use cases (perhaps very large data types or very large datasets.) For such patterns, containers like `std::list` may be better suited. Never assume, however, that a `std::list` will perform better just because you require frequent insertions and deletions.

- **Don't assume automatic updates**: In the context of other containers, such as `std::map`, where vectors might be values, don't fall into the trap of assuming automatic updates. It's essential to manage and update these nested containers explicitly.

std::deque

`std::deque` is a double-ended queue. On the surface, it looks like `std::vector` with better insertions and deletions at both the beginning and the end. While that's true, remember that this flexibility comes at the cost of a slightly more complex internal structure. If your application requires rapid insertions and deletions at both ends but does not need the tight memory layout of `std::vector`, `std::deque` is your container of choice.

Purpose and suitability

`std::deque` is a container that provides rapid insertions and deletions at both its beginning and end. Its primary strengths are as follows:

- Efficient *O(1)* insertions and deletions at both ends

- Dynamic size with no need for manual memory management

- Fairly good cache performance for front and back operations

`std::deque` shines in the following contexts:

- You require random-access capabilities but expect frequent modifications at both ends.

- You need a dynamically sized container but do not want the memory overhead of a `std::list`.

If only end modifications are necessary, `std::vector` could be a better choice.

Ideal use cases

The following are some of the ideal use cases of `std::deque`:

- **Fast insertion at both ends**: The name deque is short for *double-ended queue*. Unlike `std::vector`, which primarily allows for fast insertion at the back, `std::deque` supports quick insertion and deletion at both the front and the back, making it ideal for scenarios requiring operations on both ends.

- **General purpose queue and stack**: Due to its double-ended nature, `std::deque` can serve as a queue (FIFO data structure) and a stack (LIFO data structure). It's versatile in this regard, unlike other containers specializing in one or the other.

- **Random access**: Just like arrays and `std::vector`, `std::deque` offers constant-time random access to elements, making it suitable for applications that need to access elements by index.

- **Dynamic growth**: While `std::vector` grows in one direction, `std::deque` can grow in both directions. This makes it especially useful for situations where the dataset might expand unpredictably on both ends.

- **Buffered data streams**: When building applications such as media players that buffer data, std::deque can be helpful. As data is consumed from the front (played), new data can be buffered at the back without reshuffling the entire dataset.

- **Sliding window algorithms**: In algorithms that require a *sliding window* approach, where elements are continuously added and removed from both ends of a data structure, std::deque offers an efficient solution.

- **Adaptable to other data structures**: With its flexibility, std::deque can easily be adapted into other custom data structures. For example, a balanced tree or a specific kind of priority queue might leverage the capabilities of std::deque.

- **Undo/redo mechanisms with a limit**: For software applications that provide undo and redo functionality but want to limit the number of stored actions, a std::deque can efficiently handle adding new actions and automatically removing the oldest ones.

When considering std::deque, it is essential to weigh the benefits of its double-ended and random-access nature against its slightly higher per-element overhead compared to std::vector. Other data structures might be more space-efficient in scenarios with only one-sided growth.

Performance

The algorithmic performance of std::deque is characterized as follows:

- **Insertion:** *O(1)* for both front and back; *O(n)* in the middle
- **Deletion:** *O(1)* for both front and back; *O(n)* for the middle
- **Access:** Consistent *O(1)* for random access
- **Memory overhead:** Slightly higher than std::vector due to segmented memory

Memory management

std::deque uses segmented allocation, which means it allocates chunks of memory as needed. Unlike std::vector, it doesn't double its size; thus, there is no excessive memory overhead. Custom allocators can affect memory allocation strategies.

Thread safety

Concurrent reads are safe. But like most STL containers, simultaneous writes or a mix of reads and writes require external synchronization mechanisms, such as mutexes.

Extensions and variants

`std::deque` stands between `std::vector` and `std::list` in terms of performance and memory characteristics. However, it uniquely offers fast operations at both ends.

Sorting and searching complexity

The sorting and search complexity is characterized as follows:

- **Sorting**: As with most random-access containers, *O(n log n)* with `std::sort()`
- **Searching**: *O(n)* for unsorted; *O(log n)* for sorted data with `std::binary_search()`

Interface and member functions

Apart from the familiar (`push_back`, `push_front`, `pop_back`, `pop_front`, `begin`, and `end`), get familiar with the following:

- `emplace_front` and `emplace_back`: In-place construction at respective ends
- `resize`: Adjust the container size, extending or truncating it as needed

Comparisons

Compared to `std::vector`, `std::deque` provides better front operations. Against `std::list`, it gives better random access but may suffer in terms of middle insertions/deletions. The non-contiguous storage of `std::deque` can be a disadvantage when it comes to iterating over elements compared to `std::vector` due to poorer cache performance.

Interactions with algorithms

`std::deque` can leverage most STL algorithms effectively due to its random-access nature. Algorithms requiring swift end modifications are particularly suited for `std::deque`.

Exceptions

Going beyond size or accessing out-of-range indices can lead to exceptions. If operations such as insertions throw exceptions, the container remains intact, ensuring exception safety.

Customization

`std::deque` can be used with custom allocators to tailor memory allocation behavior, but it does not support custom comparators or hash functions.

Example

In this example, we will show the following best practices and use of `std::deque`:

- Using `std::deque` to maintain a list of elements, taking advantage of its dynamic size
- Inserting elements at both the front and back
- Efficient removal of elements from both the front and back
- Using `std::deque` as a sliding window to process elements in chunks
- Applying STL algorithms such as `std::transform`

Here is the code example:

```cpp
#include <algorithm>
#include <deque>
#include <iostream>

// A function to demonstrate using a deque as a sliding
// window over data.
void processInSlidingWindow(const std::deque<int> &data,
                            size_t windowSize) {
  for (size_t i = 0; i <= data.size() - windowSize; ++i) {
    int sum = 0;

    for (size_t j = i; j < i + windowSize; ++j) {
      sum += data[j];
    }

    std::cout << "Average of window starting at index "
              << i << ": "
              << static_cast<double>(sum) / windowSize
              << "\n";
  }
}

int main() {
  std::deque<int> numbers;

  for (int i = 1; i <= 5; ++i) {
    numbers.push_back(i * 10);    // 10, 20, ..., 50
    numbers.push_front(-i * 10);  // -10, -20, ..., -50
  }
```

```cpp
    std::cout << "Numbers in deque: ";
    for (const auto &num : numbers) {
      std::cout << num << " ";
    }
    std::cout << "\n";

    numbers.pop_front();
    numbers.pop_back();

    std::cout << "After removing front and back: ";

    for (const auto &num : numbers) {
      std::cout << num << " ";
    }
    std::cout << "\n";

    processInSlidingWindow(numbers, 3);

    std::transform(numbers.begin(), numbers.end(),
                   numbers.begin(),
                   [](int n) { return n * 2; });

    std::cout << "After doubling each element: ";

    for (const auto &num : numbers) {
      std::cout << num << " ";
    }
    std::cout << "\n";

    return 0;
}
```

In the preceding example, we do the following:

- We demonstrate the dynamic nature of std::deque by adding elements to both the beginning and end of the container.

- We showcase the efficient operations of pop_front() and pop_back().

- A sliding window function processes the elements in chunks, taking advantage of the random access nature of std::deque.

- Finally, we use the std::transform algorithm to manipulate the data.

Best practices

Let us explore the best practices of using `std::deque`:

- **Segmented memory**: One of the characteristics of `std::deque` is its segmented memory. This can sometimes lead to performance nuances that are less predictable compared to the contiguous memory layout of `std::vector`.

- **Not a vector**: It's essential not to equate `std::deque` with `std::vector` when it comes to memory behavior. The two have different architectures, leading to varied performances in specific scenarios.

- **Middle operations**: `std::deque` provides quick insertions and deletions at both ends but not in the middle. If middle operations are measured to be a bottleneck, consider other containers such as `std::vector` and `std::list`.

- **Both ends advantage**: Utilize `std::deque` for its core strength: constant-time operations at both ends. Should you predominantly use only one end, `std::vector` could offer better performance. Even with this advantage, do not assume that `std::deque` will perform better than `std::vector`. You may find that `std::vector`'s contiguous storage and cache-friendliness allow it to outperform `std::deque` even with front insertions.

- **Non-contiguous nature**: Since `std::deque` doesn't guarantee contiguous memory, it can pose challenges when dealing with APIs or libraries that demand raw arrays. Always be aware of this distinction.

- **In-place creation**: Harness the power of `emplace_front` and `emplace_back` when adding elements. These functions construct elements directly within the deque, optimizing memory usage and performance.

- **Consistent front and back operations**: Consider `std::deque` when the front and back operations are frequent and the measured performance loss is acceptable. Its architecture is optimized for these operations, providing consistent performance.

- **Size assurance**: Before attempting random access on `std::deque`, always ensure you're within its size boundaries to prevent undefined behavior.

- **Synchronization**: If multiple threads are accessing or modifying `std::deque`, make sure to use appropriate synchronization mechanisms, such as mutexes or locks, to ensure data integrity and prevent race conditions.

std::list

`std::list` is a doubly linked list. Unlike the previous containers, it does not store its elements contiguously. This means you lose out on the cache-friendliness but gain immense flexibility. Insertions and deletions, regardless of position, are a constant-time operation as long as you have an iterator to the position. However, access time is linear, making it less suited for tasks where random access is frequent. `std::list` is best suited for scenarios where the dataset experiences frequent insertions and deletions from both the middle and the ends, and direct access isn't a priority.

Purpose and suitability

`std::list` is a doubly-linked list provided by the STL. Its strengths include the following:

- Facilitating constant-time insertions and deletions at any position (while sacrificing cache friendliness and fast searching)

- Preserving iterator validity during modifications (except when the element referred to by the iterator is removed)

It's best chosen in the following situations:

- Frequent insertions and deletions from both the container's front and middle are expected.

- Random access isn't a primary requirement.

- Iterator validity preservation is vital.

- You have inherently cache-unfriendly (large) data stored in each node.

When considering between different containers, lean towards `std::list` for its linked-list benefits. If random access is vital, `std::vector` or `std::deque` may be better choices.

Ideal use cases

The following are some of the ideal use cases of `std::list`:

- **Bidirectional traversal**: Unlike `std::forward_list`, `std::list` provides bidirectional traversal capabilities, allowing you to iterate through the elements both forward and backward, which is beneficial for certain algorithms.

- **Fast insertions and deletions**: `std::list` offers constant time insertions and deletions at any position, provided you have an iterator to the position. This makes it suitable for applications where such operations are frequent. Note, however, that the cost of searching for the position to perform the insertion may outweigh the benefits of the insertion operation itself. Often, `std::vector` will outperform `std::list` even for frequent insertions and deletions.

- **Maintaining order without continuous resizing**: When you want to maintain the order of elements without the overhead of continuous resizing or the need for random access, `std::list` can be a good choice.

- **Complex data movement**: When applications require operations such as moving chunks of data within the list or transferring elements between lists without data copying, `std::list` proves efficient due to its splicing capabilities.

- **Queue implementations**: While `std::queue` is the standard choice, `std::list` can be employed to implement double-ended queues (deque) because of its bidirectional nature.

- **Undo/Redo functionality in applications**: The ability to traverse both forwards and backward makes `std::list` apt for maintaining an undo and redo history in software applications.

- **Cache implementations**: When a **Least Recently Used** (LRU) cache is to be implemented, `std::list` is often a good choice due to its efficiency in moving elements around.

- **Circular lists**: Given its doubly-linked nature, `std::list` can be adapted to create circular lists where the last element links back to the first.

- **Graph representations**: For representing graphs using adjacency lists where bidirectional traversal of edges may be required, `std::list` can be used.

While `std::list` is versatile, one should be cautious of its limitations. It doesn't support direct access or indexing, unlike arrays or `std::vector`. Therefore, it is crucial to choose `std::list` when its specific strengths align well with the application's requirements. It is also cache-unfriendly and expensive to perform a linear search on.

Performance

The algorithmic performance of `std::list` is characterized as follows:

- **Insertion**: *O(1)* anywhere in the list.

- **Deletion**: *O(1)* for a known position.

- **Access**: *O(n)* due to its linked nature.

- **Memory overhead**: Generally higher than vector due to storage of next and previous pointers.

- **Trade-offs**: This structure allows for swift insertions and deletions but at the cost of slower access times, cache misses, and increased memory overhead. Generally, `std::vector` will outperform `std::list` for most use cases.

Memory management

Unlike `std::vector`, `std::list` does not reallocate en masse. Each element's allocation is independent. Allocators can still influence individual node allocation, granting more specific memory management.

Thread safety

Concurrent reads are safe. However, modifications, or simultaneous reads and writes, require external synchronization. Mutexes or similar constructs can be employed.

Extensions and variants

`std::forward_list` is a singly-linked variant, optimizing for space but losing the ability to traverse backward.

Sorting and searching complexity

The sorting and search complexity is characterized as follows:

- **Sorting**: Utilize `std::list::sort()`, typically *O(n log n)*
- **Searching**: Linear *O(n)* with `std::find()` due to lack of random access

Interface and member functions

Noteworthy functions are as follows:

- `emplace_front/emplace_back`: Direct in-place construction
- `splice`: Transfers elements from one list to another
- `merge`: Combines two sorted lists
- `unique`: Removes duplicate elements

Comparisons

When juxtaposed with `std::vector` or `std::deque`, `std::list` seems like it would be superior for frequent insertions and deletions in the middle. However, it does not offer the speedy random access the former containers do. This means that the cost of finding where to perform an insertion or deletion outweighs the benefits of the insertion or deletion itself.

Interactions with algorithms

While `std::list` can work with many STL algorithms, those requiring random access (e.g., `std::random_shuffle`) aren't ideal.

Exceptions

Out-of-bounds or illegal operations might throw exceptions. However, many of `std::list`'s operations offer strong exception safety, ensuring the list remains consistent.

Customization

Custom allocators can be employed to influence the node memory allocation. Unlike containers such as `std::set` or `std::map`, custom comparators aren't typical with `std::list`.

Example

In this example, we will show the following best practices and use of `std::list`:

- Exploiting the bidirectional nature of `std::list` to traverse and modify elements in both forward and reverse directions

- Efficiently inserting and removing elements from anywhere in the list

- Using `std::list`'s member functions such as `sort()`, `merge()`, `splice()`, and `remove_if()`

- Applying external STL algorithms like `std::find`

Here is the code example:

```
#include <algorithm>
#include <iostream>
#include <list>

void display(const std::list<int> &lst) {
  for (const auto &val : lst) { std::cout << val << " "; }
  std::cout << "\n";
}

int main() {
  std::list<int> numbers = {5, 1, 8, 3, 7};

  std::cout << "Numbers in reverse: ";
  for (auto it = numbers.rbegin(); it != numbers.rend();
       ++it) {
    std::cout << *it << " ";
  }
  std::cout << "\n";

  auto pos = std::find(numbers.begin(), numbers.end(), 8);
  numbers.insert(pos, 2112);
  std::cout << "After insertion: ";
  display(numbers);

  numbers.sort();
  std::list<int> more_numbers = {2, 6, 4};
  more_numbers.sort();
  numbers.merge(more_numbers);
  std::cout << "After sorting and merging: ";
  display(numbers);
```

```
std::list<int> additional_numbers = {99, 100, 101};
numbers.splice(numbers.end(), additional_numbers);
std::cout << "After splicing: ";
display(numbers);

numbers.remove_if([](int n) { return n % 2 == 0; });
std::cout << "After removing all even numbers: ";
display(numbers);

return 0;
}
```

In this example, we do the following:

- We traverse the `std::list` in reverse using reverse iterators.

- We showcase the ability to efficiently insert elements at a desired position.

- We demonstrate the use of `std::list`-specific operations such as `sort()`, `merge()`, and `splice()`.

- Finally, we use a lambda with `remove_if()` to conditionally remove elements from the list.

This example illustrates various capabilities of `std::list`, including operations that are especially efficient with this container and ones that use its bidirectional nature.

Best practices

Let us explore some best practices for using `std::list`:

- **Prefer std::vector**: Generally, do not use `std::list` unless you have profiled your code against a data type such as `std::vector` and found a measurable performance improvement.

- **Sorting with std::list**: Using the `sort()` member function provided by `std::list` itself is essential rather than resorting to `std::sort`. This is due to c requiring random access iterators, which `std::list` doesn't support.

- **Limitations in random access**: `std::list` doesn't offer *O(1)* random access due to its doubly-linked structure. For frequent random access, containers such as `std::vector` or `std::deque` may be more suitable.

- **Bidirectional overhead**: The bidirectional nature of `std::list` means it maintains two pointers per element. This enables backward and forward traversal but does come at a memory cost. If memory usage is critical and bidirectional traversal isn't required, `std::forward_list` offers a cleaner alternative.

- **Optimizing insertions and deletions**: An iterator pointing to a specific location in the `std::list` can transform operations from *O(n)* to *O(1)*. Harness the power of iterators for more efficient insertions and deletions.

- **The power of splicing**: `std::list` offers the unique ability to transfer elements between lists in constant time using the `splice` function. This operation is both efficient and can simplify list manipulations.

- **Direct construction**: Using `emplace_front` and `emplace_back`, you can construct elements in place, eliminating the need for temporary objects and potentially speeding up your code.

- **Reiterating memory overhead**: While it has been mentioned, it is vital to always factor in the memory implications of the two pointers per element in `std::list`. Especially in memory-sensitive scenarios, being aware of this overhead can be critical in making informed container choices.

std::forward_list

`std::forward_list` is a singly linked list. It's similar to `std::list`, but each element points only to the next element and not the previous. This reduces memory overhead compared to `std::list` but at the cost of bidirectional iteration. Choose `std::forward_list` when you require a list structure but don't need to traverse backward and wish to save on memory overhead.

Purpose and suitability

The `std::forward_list` is a singly linked list container in the STL. Its primary appeal lies in the following:

- Efficient insertions and deletions at any location in the list

- Consuming less memory than `std::list` since it doesn't store previous pointers

It's especially fitting in the following contexts:

- You require constant-time insertions or deletions irrespective of the position.

- Memory overhead is a concern.

- Bidirectional iteration is not needed.

While `std::vector` excels in random access, turn to `std::forward_list` if you value insertion and deletion efficiency above all.

Ideal use cases

The following are some of the ideal use cases of `std::forward_list`:

- **Memory efficiency**: `std::forward_list` uses a singly-linked list, which has less overhead than doubly-linked lists since it only has to maintain a link in one direction. This makes it suitable for scenarios where space conservation is a priority.

- **Fast insertions at the front**: When the primary operation inserts elements at the list's beginning, `std::forward_list` offers optimal efficiency.

- **Sequence with unpredictable growth**: In applications where the growth of the sequence is not known in advance, and dynamic resizing is essential, `std::forward_list` can be a fitting choice.

- **Avoiding reverse iteration**: In scenarios where reverse traversal of the list is unnecessary or should be avoided, `using std::forward_list` ensures one-directional movement.

- **Stack implementations**: As a data structure that supports efficient front insertion and removal, `std::forward_list` can be employed to design stack-like behavior.

- **Graph representations**: When representing graphs where the nodes have several outgoing connections but don't need backtracking, `std::forward_list` can store these edges.

- **Event queues**: For applications that process events in a first-in-first-out manner without the need for backward traversal, `std::forward_list` provides the necessary structure.

- **Garbage collection algorithms**: In some custom garbage collection scenarios, a list of items to be examined in a forward-only fashion might use `std::forward_list`.

It's essential to understand that while `std::forward_list` offers advantages in specific use cases, it lacks some functionalities other containers offer, such as the bidirectional traversal seen in `std::list`. Choosing `std::forward_list` is appropriate when its benefits align with the application's needs.

Performance

The algorithmic performance of `std::forward_list` is characterized as follows:

- **Insertion**: *O(1)* irrespective of the position.

- **Deletion**: *O(1)* for any spot.

- **Access**: *O(n)* since sequential access is the only option.

- **Memory overhead**: Minimal, as only the next pointers are stored.

- **Trade-offs**: The sacrifice of quick access times is balanced by efficient insertions and deletions. This efficiency, as in `std::list`, is usually outweighed by its cache unfriendliness and slow search performance compared to `std::vector`. Generally, `std::vector` will outperform `std::forward_list` for most use cases.

Memory management

Memory is allocated as and when an element is inserted. Each node stores the element and a pointer to the next node. Custom allocators can adjust this allocation strategy.

Thread safety

Concurrent reads are safe. However, writes or a combination of reads and writes require external synchronization.

Extensions and variants

For those desiring bidirectional iteration capabilities, `std::list` (a doubly-linked list) is a viable alternative.

Sorting and searching complexity

The sorting and search complexity is characterized as follows:

- **Sorting**: Typically *O(n log n)* with `std::sort()`
- **Searching**: *O(n)* since there's no random access

Special interface and member functions

Noteworthy member functions are as follows:

- `emplace_front`: For direct element construction
- `remove`: To get rid of elements by value
- `splice_after`: For transferring elements from another `std::forward_list`

Remember, there's no `size()` or `push_back()` function in `std::forward_list`.

Comparisons

Against `std::list`, `std::forward_list` uses less memory but doesn't support bidirectional iteration. Compared to `std::vector`, it doesn't allow random access but ensures consistent insertion and deletion times.

Interactions with algorithms

Given its forward-only nature, `std::forward_list` might not gel with algorithms needing bidirectional or random access iterators.

Exceptions

Exceptions can arise during memory allocation failures. Most operations on `std::forward_list` offer strong exception safety guarantees.

Customization

You can adjust the memory allocation strategy using custom allocators. `std::forward_list` doesn't inherently support custom comparators or hash functions.

Example

`std::forward_list` is a singly-linked list, which is particularly efficient at insertions/deletions from the front. It consumes less memory than `std::list` because it doesn't store backward pointers for each element.

One common use case for a `std::forward_list` is implementing a hash table with chaining to resolve collisions. Here's a basic version of a chained hash table using `std::forward_list`:

```cpp
#include <forward_list>
#include <iostream>
#include <vector>

template <typename KeyType, typename ValueType>
class ChainedHashTable {
public:
  ChainedHashTable(size_t capacity) : capacity(capacity) {
    table.resize(capacity);
  }

  bool get(const KeyType &key, ValueType &value) const {
    const auto &list = table[hash(key)];
    for (const auto &bucket : list) {
      if (bucket.key == key) {
        value = bucket.value;
        return true;
      }
    }
    return false;
```

```cpp
    }

    void put(const KeyType &key, const ValueType &value) {
      auto &list = table[hash(key)];
      for (auto &bucket : list) {
        if (bucket.key == key) {
          bucket.value = value;
          return;
        }
      }
      list.emplace_front(key, value);
    }

    bool remove(const KeyType &key) {
      auto &list = table[hash(key)];
      return list.remove_if([&](const Bucket &bucket) {
        return bucket.key == key;
      });
    }

private:
  struct Bucket {
    KeyType key;
    ValueType value;
    Bucket(KeyType k, ValueType v) : key(k), value(v) {}
  };

  std::vector<std::forward_list<Bucket>> table;
  size_t capacity;
  size_t hash(const KeyType &key) const {
    return std::hash<KeyType>{}(key) % capacity;
  }
};

int main() {
  ChainedHashTable<std::string, int> hashTable(10);

  hashTable.put("apple", 10);
  hashTable.put("banana", 20);
  hashTable.put("cherry", 30);

  int value;
  if (hashTable.get("apple", value)) {
```

```
      std::cout << "apple: " << value << "\n";
    }

    if (hashTable.get("banana", value)) {
      std::cout << "banana: " << value << "\n";
    }

    hashTable.remove("banana");

    if (!hashTable.get("banana", value)) {
      std::cout << "banana not found!\n";
    }

    return 0;
}
```

In this example, we do the following:

- The hash table consists of a `std::vector` of `std::forward_list` called table. Each slot in the vector corresponds to a hash value and potentially holds multiple keys (in a `forward_list`) that collide with that hash value.

- The `emplace_front` function of `forward_list` is particularly useful in this context because we can add new key-value pairs to the front of the list in constant time.

- We use `forward_list::remove_if` for removing a key-value pair, which scans through the list and removes the first matching key.

Best practices

Let us explore the best practices of using `std::forward_list`:

- **Prefer std::vector**: Generally, do not use `std::forward_list` unless you have profiled your code against a data type such as `std::vector` and found a measurable performance improvement.

- **Utilizing std::forward_list effectively**: The `std::forward_list` is a specialized container optimized for certain scenarios in the world of singly linked lists. Understanding its strengths and limitations is crucial to use it effectively.

- **Space and operational considerations**: If memory conservation is crucial and the primary operations are insertions or deletions without needing bidirectional traversal, `std::forward_list` is a solid choice. However, it lacks fast direct access to elements, requiring an $O(n)$ operation.

- **Forward iteration only**: The `std::forward_list` supports only forward iteration. If bidirectional traversal is necessary, consider other containers such as `std::list`.

- **No random access**: This container is unsuitable for scenarios where quick random access to elements is required.

- **Size calculation**: The absence of a `size()` member function means that determining the list's size requires an *O(n)* operation. For a quick check on whether the list is empty, utilize the `empty()` function, which is efficient.

- **Efficient additions**: `std::forward_list` offers efficient insertions and deletions. Specifically, `emplace_front` is useful for in-place element construction, reducing overhead.

- **Sorting and removing duplicates**: Utilize the `sort()` function to maintain element order. To remove consecutive duplicate elements, apply the `unique()` function.

- **Cautions with iterators**: It's imperative to recheck iterator validity after modifications, especially post insertions or deletions, as they may become invalidated.

- **Concurrency considerations**: Ensure synchronized access to `std::forward_list` in multi-threaded applications to prevent data races or inconsistencies.

- **Memory considerations**: Compared to `std::list`, the `std::forward_list` often uses less memory because it maintains only one pointer per element (forward pointer), making it a more memory-efficient choice when bidirectional iteration is not required.

std::string

Within the STL, `std::string` is a class designed to manage sequences of characters. `std::string` simplifies text handling by providing a range of string manipulation and analysis features. `std::string` is not classified under the *sequence containers* category in the formal C++ Standard Library documentation, though it behaves very much like one. Instead, it is categorized under a separate *Strings* category, recognizing its general container-like behavior and its specialized nature for text handling.

Purpose and suitability

`std::string` represents a dynamic sequence of characters and is essentially a specialization of `std::vector<char>`. It is designed for the following:

- Manipulating textual data

- Interacting with functions that expect string input or produce string output

It's particularly suitable in the following contexts:

- Dynamic text modification is frequent.

- Efficient access to individual characters is desired.

Choose `std::string` for most string manipulation tasks. If you require string views without ownership, consider `std::string_view`.

Ideal use cases

The following are some of the ideal use cases of `std::string`:

- **Text processing**: Parsing files, processing logs, or any other task requiring dynamic text manipulation
- **User input/output**: Accepting user inputs; producing human-readable output
- **Data serialization**: Encoding data as a string for transport/storage

Performance

The algorithmic performance of `std::string` is characterized as follows:

- **Insertion**: *O(1)* average for the end, *O(n)* for elsewhere
- **Deletion**: *O(n)* since elements might need shifting
- **Access**: A rapid *O(1)* for any position
- **Memory overhead**: Generally low but can grow if reserved capacity isn't used

Memory management

`std::string` dynamically allocates memory. When the buffer is filled, it reallocates, often doubling its size. Custom allocators can modify this behavior.

Thread safety

Concurrent reading is safe, but simultaneous modifications require synchronization, typically using mutexes.

Extensions and variants

`std::wstring` is a wide-character version useful for certain localization tasks. `std::string_view` offers a non-owning view into a string, enhancing performance in specific scenarios. Also consider `std::u8string`, `std::u16string`, and `std::u32string`.

Sorting and searching complexity

The algorithmic performance of `std::string` is characterized as follows:

- **Searching**: *O(n)* for linear search
- **Sorting**: *O(log n)* using `std::binary_search()` is possible for sorted sequences

Special interface and member functions

Apart from the well-known ones (`substr`, `find`, and `append`), get familiar with the following:

- `c_str()`: Returns a C-style string (provides functionalities for interacting with null-terminated C-strings)
- `data()`: Direct access to underlying character data
- `resize()`: Adjusts string length
- `shrink_to_fit()`: Reduces memory usage

Comparisons

While `std::string` manages text, `std::vector<char>` might seem similar but lacks string semantics, such as automatic null termination.

Interactions with algorithms

STL algorithms work seamlessly with `std::string`, though some, such as sorting, might seldom apply to textual content.

Exceptions

Bad accesses (e.g., `at()`) can throw. Operations are generally exception-safe, meaning a string remains valid even if an operation throws.

Customization

`std::string` supports custom allocators, but custom comparators or hash functions aren't applicable.

Example

The `std::string` in C++ is a versatile container that provides a series of member functions for different purposes, from text manipulation to searching and comparison. Here's an advanced example illustrating best practices when using `std::string`:

```
#include <algorithm>
#include <iostream>
#include <string>

int main() {
  std::string s = "Hello, C++ World!";
```

```cpp
    std::cout << "Size: " << s.size() << "\n";
    std::cout << "First char: " << s[0] << "\n";

    std::string greet = "Hello";
    std::string target = "World";
    std::string combined = greet + ", " + target + "!";
    std::cout << "Combined: " << combined << "\n";

    if (s.find("C++") != std::string::npos) {
      std::cout << "String contains 'C++'\n";
    }

    std::transform(
        s.begin(), s.end(), s.begin(),
        [](unsigned char c) { return std::toupper(c); });
    std::cout << "Uppercase: " << s << "\n";

    std::transform(
        s.begin(), s.end(), s.begin(),
        [](unsigned char c) { return std::tolower(c); });
    std::cout << "Lowercase: " << s << "\n";

    s.erase(std::remove(s.begin(), s.end(), ' '), s.end());
    std::cout << "Without spaces: " << s << "\n";

    std::string first = "apple";
    std::string second = "banana";

    if (first < second) {
      std::cout << first << " comes before " << second
                << "\n";
    }

    int number = 2112;
    std::string numStr = std::to_string(number);
    std::cout << "Number as string: " << numStr << "\n";

    int convertedBack = std::stoi(numStr);
    std::cout << "String back to number: " << convertedBack
                << "\n";

    return 0;
}
```

In the preceding example, we did the following:

- We demonstrated basic string operations, including construction, accessing characters, and concatenation.

- We used the `find` function to check for substrings.

- We used `std::transform` with `std::toupper` and `std::tolower` to convert the entire string to uppercase and lowercase, respectively.

- We removed characters from the string using `erase` combined with `std::remove`.

- We compared two strings using the natural ordering provided by the overloaded comparison operators of `std::string`.

- We converted numbers to strings and vice versa using the `std::to_string` and `std::stoi` functions.

These operations showcase various `std::string` best practices and its seamless integration with other STL components.

Best practices

Let us explore the best practices of using `std::string`:

- **Efficiency in concatenation**: Looping with the `+ operator` for string concatenation might hit performance, given the probable reallocations and copies. Switch to `+=` within loops to boost efficiency.

- **Preallocate memory wisely**: When you foresee multiple string appends, utilize `reserve()` to preallocate adequate memory, curtailing reallocations and bolstering performance.

- **Iterative modulation prudence**: Altering a string during iteration can serve you surprises. Exercise caution and avoid concurrent modifications while iterating.

- **Harness built-in string operations**: Instead of handcrafting loops, lean on `std::string` member functions such as `find()`, `replace()`, and `substr()`. They simplify the code, enhance readability, and may boost performance.

- **Guarded element access**: Before diving into string elements, verify your indices. Out-of-bounds access is a one-way ticket to undefined behavior.

- **Embracing string views**: Tap into `std::string_view` for a lightweight reference to part or whole of a string. When modifications aren't on your agenda, it is an efficient alternative to traditional string slicing.

- **Go beyond std::string**: The landscape doesn't end with `std::string`. It's a derivative of the `std::basic_string` template, which can cater to custom character types and specialized character behaviors.

- **Encodings**: Tread with Awareness. Lean on `std::string` for ASCII and UTF-8 needs. Are you venturing into UTF-16 or UTF-32 territories? Look towards `std::wstring` and its wide character comrades. Always stay vigilant with encodings to avert potential data mishaps.

- **Capitalizing on internal optimizations**: The **Small String Optimization** (**SSO**) is an ace up many standard libraries' sleeves. It allows the storage of small strings directly within the string object, evading dynamic allocation. It's a boon for performance with diminutive strings.

> **Just how small is a small string?**
>
> The exact length of a *small string* varies by implementation. However, a typical size of the small string buffer is usually between 15 and 23 characters.

- **Comparison caveats**: When comparing strings, remember that the `compare()` function of `std::string` offers more granularity than the `==` operator. It can give insights into lexical ordering, which might be vital for sorting operations.

- **Stream operations and strings**: While `std::stringstream` provides a flexible way to concatenate and convert strings, it might come with overheads. When performance is pivotal, prefer direct string operations.

- **String-to-number conversions**: For converting strings to numbers and vice-versa, the STL provides utilities such as `std::stoi` and `std::to_string`, among others. These are safer and often more efficient than manual parsing.

7

Advanced Ordered Associative Container Usage

Associative containers in C++ allow developers to manage data in ways that align more naturally with real-world scenarios, such as using keys to retrieve values. This chapter gets into both ordered and unordered associative containers, their unique attributes, and ideal application environments. For the intermediate C++ developer, understanding when to use a map over an unordered map or the nuances between a set and a multiset can be pivotal in optimizing performance, memory usage, and data retrieval speed. Furthermore, mastering best practices will empower developers to write efficient, maintainable, and bug-free code, ensuring containers serve their purpose effectively in diverse application contexts.

In essence, ordered associative containers, with their strict order and unique (or, sometimes, not so unique) elements, provide powerful tools in the C++ developer's arsenal. They are tailor-made for scenarios that involve relationships, ordering, and uniqueness. Understanding their characteristics and use cases is the first step in leveraging their full potential.

This chapter provides a reference for the following containers:

- `std::set`
- `std::map`
- `std::multiset`
- `std::multimap`

Technical requirements

The code in this chapter can be found on GitHub:

`https://github.com/PacktPublishing/Data-Structures-and-Algorithms-with-the-CPP-STL`

std::set

At its heart, a `std::set` container is a collection of unique elements where each element follows a strict order. You can think of it as a club where each member is distinct and all have a particular rank. The container ensures that no two elements are the same, making it exceptionally useful in situations where duplicates are not desired.

Purpose and suitability

`std::set` is an associative container designed to store a sorted set of unique objects of type `Key`. Its strengths are as follows:

- Ensuring all elements are unique

- Automatically sorting elements as they are inserted

It is particularly suitable in the following scenarios:

- When duplicate elements are not desired

- When the ordering of elements matters

- When frequent lookups and insertions are anticipated

Ideal use cases

The following are some ideal use cases of `std::set`:

- **Unique collection**: If you need to maintain a collection of items where duplicates are not allowed, `std::set` naturally enforces this. For instance, it will be useful when collecting a list of unique student IDs or product codes.

- **Ordered data**: `std::set` keeps its elements in a sorted order as per the comparison criteria. It's beneficial when you require data to be inherently sorted, such as when maintaining a leaderboard where scores are continuously inserted but should always be in order.

- **Membership checks**: Due to its tree-based nature, `std::set` offers logarithmic time complexity for lookups. This makes it apt for scenarios where frequent membership checks are necessary – for instance, checking if a particular user is part of a VIP list.

- **Set operations**: When working with mathematical set operations such as union, intersection, or difference, `std::set` can be invaluable. It's particularly useful in situations where you might want to find common elements between two collections or determine which elements are exclusive to one set.

- **Event scheduling**: For applications that deal with events scheduled at different times, a `std::set` container can be used to keep track of these times. Given its ordered nature, you can swiftly determine the next event or if a particular time slot is already booked.

It's worth noting that while `std::set` is adept at these tasks, it is crucial to evaluate the specific requirements of the problem at hand. If ordering is not essential and you primarily need quick insertions, deletions, and lookups without regard for order, `std::unordered_set` might be a more suitable choice.

Performance

The algorithmic performance of `std::set` is characterized as follows:

- **Insertion**: Typically *O(log n)* due to the balanced binary search tree structure
- **Deletion**: *O(log n)* for individual elements
- **Access (finding elements)**: *O(log n)*
- **Memory overhead**: Generally higher than `std::vector` due to the tree structure

Memory management

Internally, `std::set` uses a tree structure, typically a balanced binary search tree. Memory allocation can be influenced using custom allocators.

Thread safety

Similar to `std::vector`, concurrent reads are safe, but modifications or a combination of reads and modifications necessitate external synchronization.

Extensions and variants

The C++ **Standard Template Library** (**STL**) also offers `std::multiset` (which allows repeated elements) and `std::unordered_set` (a hash table, providing average *O(1)* insert/find at the cost of no ordering).

Sorting and searching complexity

The sorting and search complexity is characterized as follows:

- **Sorting**: Elements are automatically sorted upon insertion
- **Searching**: *O(log n)* with the `find` member function

Special interface and member functions

Some handy member functions to note are as follows:

- `emplace`: Insert elements in place
- `count`: Return the number of elements (always 0 or 1 in a set)
- `lower_bound` and `upper_bound`: Provide bounds for a specific key

Comparisons

In contrast to `std::vector`, `std::set` excels in ensuring uniqueness and maintaining order but may not be optimal for frequent random access or if order isn't a concern.

Interactions with algorithms

Given its bidirectional iterators, many STL algorithms are compatible with `std::set`. However, algorithms requiring random access might not be ideal.

Exceptions

No exceptions are thrown due to capacity issues since `std::set` does not have a fixed capacity. Exceptions can arise from allocators during memory allocation.

Customization

`std::set` allows custom allocators for memory management. You can also provide a custom comparator to define how a set's elements are ordered.

Example

`std::set` is a sorted associative container that contains unique elements. It is typically used to represent a collection where the existence of an element is more important than the number of times it appears. The following code is an example illustrating best practices when using `std::set`:

```
#include <algorithm>
#include <iostream>
#include <set>
#include <vector>

int main() {
  std::set<int> numbers = {5, 3, 8, 1, 4};

  auto [position, wasInserted] = numbers.insert(6);
```

```
if (wasInserted) {
  std::cout << "6 was inserted into the set.\n";
}

auto result = numbers.insert(5);
if (!result.second) {
  std::cout << "5 is already in the set.\n";
}

if (numbers.find(3) != numbers.end()) {
  std::cout << "3 is in the set.\n";
}

numbers.erase(1);

std::cout << "Elements in the set:";
for (int num : numbers) { std::cout << ' ' << num; }
std::cout << '\n';

std::set<int> moreNumbers = {9, 7, 2};
numbers.merge(moreNumbers);

std::cout << "After merging:";
for (int num : numbers) { std::cout << ' ' << num; }
std::cout << '\n';

if (numbers.count(2)) {
  std::cout << "2 exists in the set.\n";
}

std::set<std::string, bool (*)(const std::string &,
                              const std::string &)>
    caseInsensitiveSet{[](const std::string &lhs,
                          const std::string &rhs) {
      return std::lexicographical_compare(
          lhs.begin(), lhs.end(), rhs.begin(), rhs.end(),
          [](char a, char b) {
            return std::tolower(a) < std::tolower(b);
          });
    }};

caseInsensitiveSet.insert("Hello");
if (!caseInsensitiveSet.insert("hello").second) {
```

```
        std::cout << "Duplicate insertion (case-insensitive) "
                    "detected.\n";
    }

    return 0;
}
```

Here is the example output:

```
6 was inserted into the set.
5 is already in the set.
3 is in the set.
Elements in the set: 3 4 5 6 8
After merging: 2 3 4 5 6 7 8 9
2 exists in the set.
Duplicate insertion (case-insensitive) detected.
```

In this example, we did the following:

- We demonstrated basic `std::set` operations such as insertion, finding an element, and erasing.

- We showcased how a set inherently sorts its elements and how to iterate over them.

- The use of the `merge` function was illustrated to merge another set into our primary set.

- The `count` method was used to check for the existence of an element in a set, which can only be 0 or 1 due to the uniqueness constraint.

- Lastly, we used a custom comparator to create a case-insensitive set of strings.

Best practices

Let us explore the best practices of using `std::set`:

- **Understand access patterns**: In `std::set`, access time is not constant as in `std::vector` or `std::array`. Due to its tree-based structure, element retrieval typically takes logarithmic time. When designing algorithms, factor this in.

- **Understand its immutable nature**: Once an element enters a `std::set` container, it is immutable. Altering it directly via an iterator could breach the set's internal ordering. If modification is imperative, erase the old element and insert its updated version.

- **Set selection criteria**: If order significance doesn't resonate with your use case, especially with voluminous data, lean toward `std::unordered_set`. Thanks to its hash-based design, it frequently trumps `std::set` in performance metrics, barring worst-case scenarios.

- **Leverage in-place construction**: Minimize overheads by using `emplace` to create elements right within a set. This technique forestalls unnecessary object copying or movement.

- **Navigate element alterations**: Direct tinkering of set elements is a no-go. The best approach when you need a modification is a two-step process: remove the original and introduce its altered counterpart.

- **Check presence efficiently**: The `find` method is your go-to for determining if an element resides in a set. It's more succinct and expressive than `count` in the context of `std::set`, given a set's unique element nature.

- **Beware of comparator pitfalls**: When supplying custom comparators, ensure they impose a strict weak ordering. A faulty comparator can disrupt a set's internal balance, leading to erratic behavior. Always validate custom comparators against the standard library's requirements using tools such as `std::is_sorted`.

- **Address multithreading concerns:** `std::set` is not intrinsically thread-safe. If concurrent access by multiple threads is anticipated, guard the set with synchronization primitives such as `std::mutex` or consider using concurrent containers provided by certain C++ libraries.

- **Iteration insights**: When iterating over a `std::set` container, remember that the elements are sorted. This can often obviate the need for additional sorting operations that you might apply on other containers.

- **Size and capacity**: Unlike `std::vector`, `std::set` doesn't support `reserve` or `capacity` operations. The tree grows as elements are added. For efficiency, when removing elements, consider occasional `shrink_to_fit` operations available in some implementations.

std::map

A sibling to the `std::set` container, `std::map` is about relationships. It connects unique keys to specific values, forming a pair. In layman's terms, imagine a dictionary where each word (key) has a unique definition (value).

Purpose and suitability

`std::map` is an ordered associative container that stores key-value pairs, ensuring unique keys. Its underlying data structure is typically a balanced binary tree (such as a **red-black tree** (**RBT**)). The main advantages include the following:

- Logarithmic access, insertion, and deletion times
- Maintaining key-value pairs in sorted order by keys

Use `std::map` in the following scenarios:

- When you need to associate values with unique keys
- When maintaining the order of keys is important
- When frequent access, insertion, or deletion operations are required, and they need to be efficient

Ideal use cases

The following are some ideal use cases of `std::map`:

- **Dictionary or phonebook**: As with traditional dictionaries or phonebooks, `std::map` shines when associating unique keys with specific values. For example, it is useful when mapping a person's name (unique key) to their contact details or a word to its definition.

- **Configuration settings**: When building software with configurable options, a `std::map` container can associate different configuration keys with their respective values, ensuring easy retrieval and modification of settings.

- **Student record system**: Educational institutions might maintain a record system where student IDs (ensured to be unique) act as keys, mapping to comprehensive student profiles comprising names, courses, grades, and other details.

- **Frequency counter**: When analyzing data, particularly in fields such as text processing or data analytics, it is common to determine the frequency of unique items. In such scenarios, `std::map` can associate distinct items with their occurrence counts, ensuring efficient updates and retrievals.

- **Inverted index**: An inverted index maps terms or keywords to a list of documents or locations in which they appear. It is commonly used in search engines and databases. Using a `std::map` container for this purpose ensures that terms are sorted and can be efficiently accessed or updated.

- **Caching mechanisms**: In systems where expensive computations are done repeatedly, caching the results for specific inputs can save time. `std::map` can serve as a cache, mapping input values to their computed results.

- **Order-based operations**: Since `std::map` inherently maintains its elements in sorted order based on its keys, it is apt for scenarios where operations dependent on this order are frequent – for example, fetching the *top 10* or *lowest 5* based on some criteria.

Always consider the specific needs of your problem. While `std::map` offers ordering and unique key-value association, if ordering isn't required, `std::unordered_map` might be a more performance-efficient alternative due to its average constant-time complexity for most operations.

Performance

The algorithmic performance of `std::map` is characterized as follows:

- **Insertion**: *O(log n)*
- **Deletion**: *O(log n)*
- **Access**: *O(log n)* to locate a key
- **Memory overhead**: Generally higher than hash-based counterparts due to tree-based structure

The primary trade-off is balancing memory overhead with the efficiency of ordered operations and the flexibility of key-value pair manipulation.

Memory management

`std::map` efficiently manages its memory internally, ensuring balanced trees. However, specific behavior can be influenced by custom allocators, allowing for more control.

Thread safety

Concurrent reads are safe. However, concurrent writes or mixed read-writes require external synchronization, such as utilizing mutexes.

Extensions and variants

`std::multimap` allows multiple values per key, whereas `std::unordered_map` offers a hash-table-based alternative without ordering but with potential *O(1)* average access times.

Sorting and searching complexity

The sorting and search complexity is characterized as follows:

- **Sorting**: Being ordered, `std::map` inherently maintains sorting
- **Searching**: *O(log n)*

Special interface and member functions

Some handy member functions to note are as follows:

- `emplace`: Directly constructs a key-value pair in place
- `at`: Throws an exception if the key doesn't exist
- `operator[]`: Accesses or creates a value for a given key
- `lower_bound` and `upper_bound`: Provide iterators pointing to positions relative to a key

Comparisons

Compared to `std::unordered_map`, `std::map` excels in scenarios where key order matters or when the dataset might grow and shrink frequently. For situations demanding raw performance and where the order is insignificant, `std::unordered_map` might be preferable.

Interactions with algorithms

While many STL algorithms can work with `std::map`, its bidirectional iterators limit its compatibility with algorithms requiring random access.

Exceptions

Operations such as `at()` can throw out-of-range exceptions. Most operations on `std::map` provide strong exception safety, ensuring the map remains unchanged if an exception is thrown.

Customization

You can provide custom comparators to dictate the order of keys or use custom allocators to influence memory management.

Example

In `std::map`, keys are sorted and unique, making it easy to find specific entries. The following code is an example illustrating best practices when using `std::map`:

```cpp
#include <algorithm>
#include <iostream>
#include <map>
#include <string>

int main() {
  std::map<std::string, int> ageMap = {
      {"Lisa", 25}, {"Corbin", 30}, {"Aaron", 22}};

  ageMap["Kristan"] = 28;
  ageMap.insert_or_assign("Lisa", 26);

  if (ageMap.find("Corbin") != ageMap.end()) {
    std::cout << "Corbin exists in the map.\n";
  }

  ageMap["Aaron"] += 1;

  std::cout << "Age records:\n";
  for (const auto &[name, age] : ageMap) {
    std::cout << name << ": " << age << '\n';
  }

  ageMap.erase("Corbin");
```

```
  if (ageMap.count("Regan") == 0) {
    std::cout << "Regan does not exist in the map.\n";
  }

  std::map<std::string, int,
           bool (*)(const std::string &,
                    const std::string &)>
       customOrderMap{[](const std::string &lhs,
                         const std::string &rhs) {
         return lhs > rhs; // reverse lexicographic order
       }};

  customOrderMap["Lisa"] = 25;
  customOrderMap["Corbin"] = 30;
  customOrderMap["Aaron"] = 22;

  std::cout << "Custom ordered map:\n";
  for (const auto &[name, age] : customOrderMap) {
    std::cout << name << ": " << age << '\n';
  }

  return 0;
}
```

Here is the example output:

```
Corbin exists in the map.
Age records:
Aaron: 23
Corbin: 30
Kristan: 28
Lisa: 26
Regan does not exist in the map.
Custom ordered map:
Lisa: 25
Corbin: 30
Aaron: 22
```

In this example, we did the following:

- We demonstrated the basic operations of std::map, such as insertion, modification, checking for the existence of a key, and iterating over its elements.

- We used structured bindings (C++17) to restructure the key-value pairs when iterating.

- We illustrated the use of `count` to check if a key exists in the map.

- We created a custom-ordered map by providing a custom comparator that sorts the keys in reverse lexicographical order.

Best practices

Let us explore the best practices of using `std::map`:

- **Immutable key principle**: Once a key-value pair is inserted into `std::map`, the key remains constant for the lifetime of that element. Modifying it directly is not allowed. Should you need to update the key, the correct approach is to remove the old key-value pair and insert a new one with the desired key.

- **Select appropriate containers**: If maintaining the order of the key-value pairs is not a requirement, consider leveraging `std::unordered_map`. Its hash table-based implementation may offer faster average-time complexities for many operations compared to the RBT of `std::map`, reducing potential overhead.

- **Efficient insertions with emplace**: Utilize the `emplace` method, which constructs the element in place within the map, avoiding temporary object creation and unnecessary copies. When paired with tools such as `std::make_pair` or `std::piecewise_construct`, it optimizes performance for insertions.

- **Safe key access**: The `operator[]` method, though convenient, can be a double-edged sword. If the specified key does not exist, it inserts the key with a default-initialized value into the map. When you wish to only query, without potential insertions, use the `find` method instead. The `find` method returns an iterator to the element if found and to the `end()` method if not.

- **Custom sorting with comparators**: The default sorting of `std::map` might not always fit the use case. You can customize the order by providing a comparator when defining the map. Ensure this comparator enforces a strict weak ordering to maintain the integrity of the map's internal structures.

- **Concurrency and synchronization**: In environments where multiple threads access a `std::map` container, synchronization becomes imperative. Consider using `std::mutex` or other STL synchronization primitives to lock access during write operations, preserving data consistency.

- **Efficient membership checks**: When validating whether a key exists, use the `count` method for a direct count result. For a map, this will always return `0` or `1`, making it a fast way to check membership.

- **Iterators and erasure**: When erasing elements using iterators, remember that the `erase` operation invalidates the iterator. Use the returned iterator from `erase` to continue operations safely.

- **Range operations**: For bulk operations, `std::map` offers range methods such as `equal_range`, which can return the bounds of a subrange of elements with keys equivalent to a given key. Utilize them for efficient subrange manipulations.

- **Memory management with allocators**: If specific memory management behaviors are required, remember that `std::map` supports custom allocators. This allows for better control over allocation and deallocation processes.

std::multiset

While a `std::set` container prides itself on its exclusivity, `std::multiset` is a bit more accommodating. It still maintains order, but it allows multiple elements to have the same value. This container is like a club where members have ranks, but there's room for more than one member at each rank.

Purpose and suitability

`std::multiset` is an associative container that stores sorted elements and allows multiple occurrences of an element. Its key strengths are as follows:

- Maintaining a sorted order of elements

- Allowing duplicates

- Offering logarithmic time complexity for insertion, deletion, and search

It's particularly suitable in the following scenarios:

- When duplicate values need to be retained

- When you require elements to always remain sorted

- When random access is not a necessity

Ideal use cases

The following are some ideal use cases for `std::multiset`:

- **Ranking systems**: In scenarios such as gaming leaderboards or student grade systems where multiple entities might have identical scores or grades, a `std::multiset` container is beneficial. It allows for the storage of duplicate values while maintaining them in a sorted order.

- **Statistics calculations**: When working with a set of numerical data and needing to compute the median, mode, or other statistics, a `std::multiset` container is invaluable due to its inherent sorted nature and its ability to accommodate repeated numbers.

- **Event management**: In events where attendees can select multiple time slots or sessions they're interested in, a `std::multiset` container can help in efficiently managing and tracking these selections, especially when a popular session is chosen multiple times.

- **Inventory management**: In businesses, certain items can be more popular and purchased more frequently. A `std::multiset` container can represent such items, allowing easy tracking and replenishment based on demand.

- **Document term frequency**: In text processing or search engine scenarios, while an inverted index (such as with `std::map`) maps terms to documents, a `std::multiset` container can be used to keep track of how frequently terms appear across multiple documents, even if some terms are common and appear repeatedly.

- **Spatial data structures**: In computational geometry or graphics, structures such as sweep line algorithms use `std::multiset` to manage events or points efficiently, especially when multiple events share the same position.

- **Handling collisions**: In scenarios where collisions (identical values from different sources) are expected and need to be retained for further processing, `std::multiset` shines.

Remember, while `std::multiset` is designed to handle multiple instances of the same value in a sorted manner, if the sorted property isn't essential and you want to keep track of multiple items, structures such as `std::unordered_multiset` can be more performance-efficient in some cases due to hash-based implementations.

Performance

The algorithmic performance of `std::multiset` is characterized as follows:

- **Insertion**: *O(log n)*
- **Deletion**: *O(log n)*
- **Access**: Elements are accessed in *O(log n)* time
- **Memory overhead**: Overhead is present due to internal balancing (typically implemented as a balanced binary search tree)

Memory management

`std::multiset` does not dynamically resize like `std::vector`. Instead, it uses dynamic memory allocation for nodes as elements are inserted. Allocators can influence node memory management.

Thread safety

Concurrent reads are safe. However, modifications (insertions or deletions) require external synchronization. Utilizing mutexes or other synchronization primitives is recommended for concurrent writes.

Extensions and variants

`std::set` is a direct variant that disallows duplicates. There's also `std::unordered_multiset`, which offers average constant-time complexity for operations but does not maintain order.

Sorting and searching complexity

The sorting and search complexity is characterized as follows:

- **Sorting**: Elements are always sorted; thus, no sort operation is required
- **Searching**: $O(log\ n)$ due to its tree-based nature

Special interface and member functions

While it provides regular functions (`insert`, `erase`, `find`), some handy ones include the following:

- `count`: Returns the total number of elements matching a specified key
- `equal_range`: Provides range (iterators) of all instances of an element

Comparisons

Against `std::set`, `std::multiset` allows duplicates but at the cost of slightly increased memory. Against sequence containers such as `std::vector`, it maintains sorted order but doesn't offer constant-time access.

Interactions with algorithms

Algorithms that benefit from sorted data (such as binary searches or set operations) work well with `std::multiset`. Those requiring random access or frequent reordering might not be suitable.

Exceptions

Memory allocation failures can throw exceptions. Most `std::multiset` operations provide strong exception-safety guarantees.

Customization

In `std::multiset`, customization entails the following:

- Custom allocators can be used to control memory allocation.

- Custom comparators can be provided to dictate the order of element storage.

Example

`std::multiset` is a container that can store multiple keys, including duplicate keys. The keys are always sorted from the lowest key to the highest. `std::multiset` is typically used in situations where you need to maintain a sorted set of elements, and duplicates are allowed.

The following code is an example of using `std::multiset`, demonstrating some of its unique features and best practices:

```
#include <iostream>
#include <iterator>
#include <set>
#include <string>

int main() {
  std::multiset<int> numbers = {5, 3, 8, 5, 3, 9, 4};

  numbers.insert(6);
  numbers.insert(5); // Inserting another duplicate

  for (int num : numbers) { std::cout << num << ' '; }
  std::cout << '\n';

  std::cout << "Number of 5s: " << numbers.count(5)
            << '\n';

  auto [begin, end] = numbers.equal_range(5);

  for (auto it = begin; it != end; ++it) {
    std::cout << *it << ' ';
  }
  std::cout << '\n';

  numbers.erase(5);

  std::multiset<std::string, std::greater<>> words = {
      "apple", "banana", "cherry", "apple"};
```

```
  for (const auto &word : words) {
    std::cout << word << ' ';
  }
  std::cout << '\n';

  std::multiset<int> dataset = {1, 2, 3, 4, 5,
                                6, 7, 8, 9, 10};

  const auto start = dataset.lower_bound(4);
  const auto stop = dataset.upper_bound(7);

  std::copy(start, stop,
            std::ostream_iterator<int>(std::cout, " "));
  std::cout << '\n';

  return 0;
}
```

Here is the example output:

```
3 3 4 5 5 5 6 8 9
Number of 5s: 3
5 5 5
cherry banana apple apple
4 5 6 7
```

Key takeaways from the preceding example are as follows:

- `std::multiset` automatically sorts keys.
- It can store duplicate keys, and this property can be utilized for certain algorithms or storage patterns where duplicates are meaningful.
- Using `equal_range` is a best practice to find all instances of a key. This method returns both the beginning and the end iterators, covering all instances of the key.
- Custom comparators, such as `std::greater<>`, can be used to reverse the default ordering.
- `lower_bound` and `upper_bound` can be used for efficient range queries.

Remember, if you don't need to store duplicates, then `std::set` is a more appropriate choice.

Best practices

Let us explore the best practices of using `std::multiset`:

- **Select the appropriate set type**: If the dataset doesn't necessitate duplicate values, avoid using `std::multiset` to prevent undue overhead. Instead, favor `std::set`, which inherently manages unique elements and can be more efficient.

- **Understand access characteristics**: Remember that `std::multiset` doesn't offer the same constant-time access that `std::vector` provides. Accessing elements is logarithmic in complexity due to the underlying tree-based data structure.

- **Account for memory consumption**: The ability of `std::multiset` to hold duplicate elements can lead to elevated memory usage, especially when those duplicates are numerous. It's crucial to analyze memory requirements and ensure the container's suitability for the application.

- **Custom comparator considerations**: When employing a custom comparator for sorting elements within `std::multiset`, ensure that it imposes a strict weak ordering. Any inconsistency in ordering can lead to undefined behavior. Test the comparator rigorously to confirm its reliability.

- **Leverage member functions for element queries**: Instead of manually iterating over the multiset to check for an element's existence, take advantage of the `find` and `count` member functions. They offer a more efficient and direct way to perform such checks.

- **Be decisive about duplicates**: Before opting for `std::multiset`, clearly outline the reasons for needing duplicate entries. If the rationale isn't strong, or duplicates don't benefit your application logic significantly, consider using `std::set`.

std::multimap

Extending the principles of `std::map`, the `std::multimap` container allows for one key to be associated with multiple values. It's like a dictionary where a word might have several related definitions.

Purpose and suitability

`std::multimap` is an associative container within the STL. Its distinguishing features are as follows:

- Storing key-value pairs
- Allowing multiple values with the same key
- Storing elements in a sorted manner, as determined by the key

It's particularly suitable in the following scenarios:

- When you need to maintain a collection with non-unique keys

- When you want sorted access based on keys

- When key-value mapping is paramount

Choose `std::multimap` when you expect multiple values under the same key. If unique keys are necessary, you might want to look into `std::map`.

Ideal use cases

The following are some ideal use cases of `std::multimap`:

- **Multiple entries per key**: Consider a business directory where a single business name (key) might have multiple branches or phone numbers (values). Using `std::multimap`, you can associate one key with several values.

- **Multi-language dictionary**: In a language translation application, a single word in one language might have multiple translations in another. A `std::multimap` container can effectively map these multiple meanings.

- **Airport flight schedules**: Airports can have multiple flights departing to the same destination at different times. A `std::multimap` container can associate a destination (key) with various flight details or times (values).

- **Event scheduling**: For event managers, a particular date (key) might have several events or tasks. Using `std::multimap`, one can easily keep track of all events for a specific date.

- **Graph representations**: In computational structures, a node in a graph might be connected to multiple other nodes. Representing such relationships using `std::multimap` can be handy, especially when weights or other data associated with the edges are required.

- **Course enrollment systems**: In educational institutions, a single course (key) can have multiple enrolled students or multiple instructors (values). This system can be easily managed using a `std::multimap` container.

- **Patient record systems**: In healthcare, a specific doctor (key) might see multiple patients or have several appointments (values) on a particular day. A `std::multimap` container is apt for such use cases.

- **Media tagging systems**: In media libraries, a particular tag or category (key) can be associated with multiple songs, videos, or photos (values). Using `std::multimap` helps in organizing and retrieving media based on tags efficiently.

Remember that `std::multimap` is a go-to when one-to-many relationships are prevalent. However, if order and sorting aren't crucial and efficient retrieval is more important, considering structures such as `std::unordered_multimap` can be beneficial due to their hash-based nature.

Performance

The algorithmic performance of std::multimap is characterized as follows:

- **Insertion**: Logarithmic $O(log\ n)$ in most cases
- **Deletion**: Logarithmic $O(log\ n)$ generally
- **Access**: $O(log\ n)$ for specific keys
- **Memory overhead**: It is a bit higher due to maintaining the tree-based structure and potential balancing

Memory management

`std::multimap` internally employs a tree structure, typically an RBT. Thus, memory allocation and balancing operations can occur. Allocators can influence its memory handling.

Thread safety

Multiple reads are safe. However, writes or combinations of reads and writes require external synchronization. Using tools such as mutexes is advisable.

Extensions and variants

For hash-table-based key-value mapping, consider `std::unordered_multimap`. For unique key-value mapping, `std::map` is more appropriate.

Sorting and searching complexity

The sorting and search complexity is characterized as follows:

- **Sorting**: Sorting is inherent, as elements are maintained in key order
- **Searching**: $O(log\ n)$ to locate a specific key

Special interface and member functions

Standard functions such as `insert`, `erase`, and `find` are available. The following are also available:

- `count`: Returns the number of elements with a particular key
- `equal_range`: Retrieves the range of elements with a specific key

Comparisons

Against `std::unordered_multimap`, `std::multimap` offers ordered access but might have a slightly higher overhead due to its tree-based nature.

Interactions with algorithms

Since `std::multimap` maintains ordered access, algorithms that benefit from sorted data (such as `std::set_intersection`) can be useful. However, remember that data is key-ordered.

Exceptions

Trying to access non-existent keys or out-of-bound scenarios can throw exceptions. Most operations are strongly exception-safe, ensuring the container remains valid even if an exception is thrown.

Customization

Custom allocators can refine memory management. `std::multimap` also allows custom comparators to dictate the ordering of keys.

Example

`std::multimap` is a container that maintains a collection of key-value pairs, where multiple pairs can have the same key. The keys in `std::multimap` are always sorted.

The following code is an example of using `std::multimap`, demonstrating some of its unique features and best practices:

```cpp
#include <iostream>
#include <map>
#include <string>

int main() {
  std::multimap<std::string, int> grades;

  grades.insert({"John", 85});
  grades.insert({"Corbin", 78});
  grades.insert({"Regan", 92});
  grades.insert({"John", 90}); // John has another grade

  for (const auto &[name, score] : grades) {
    std::cout << name << " scored " << score << '\n';
  }
  std::cout << '\n';
```

```
    std::cout << "John's grade count:"
              << grades.count("John") << '\n';

    auto [begin, end] = grades.equal_range("John");
    for (auto it = begin; it != end; ++it) {
      std::cout << it->first << " scored " << it->second
                << '\n';
    }
    std::cout << '\n';

    grades.erase("John");

    std::multimap<std::string, int, std::greater<>>
        reverseGrades = {{"Mandy", 82},
                         {"Mandy", 87},
                         {"Aaron", 90},
                         {"Dan", 76}};

    for (const auto &[name, score] : reverseGrades) {
      std::cout << name << " scored " << score << '\n';
    }

    return 0;
}
```

Here is the example output:

```
Corbin scored 78
John scored 85
John scored 90
Regan scored 92

John's grade count:2
John scored 85
John scored 90

Mandy scored 82
Mandy scored 87
Dan scored 76
Aaron scored 90
```

Key takeaways from the preceding code are as follows:

- `std::multimap` automatically sorts keys.

- It can store multiple key-value pairs with the same key.

- Using `equal_range` is a best practice to find all instances of a key. This method returns both the beginning and the end iterators, covering all instances of the key.

- `grades.count("John")` efficiently counts the number of key-value pairs with the specified key.

- Custom comparators, such as `std::greater<>`, can change the ordering from the default ascending order to descending.

A `std::multimap` container is useful when you need a dictionary-like data structure that supports duplicate keys. If duplicates aren't needed, `std::map` would be a more appropriate choice.

Best practices

Let us explore the best practices of using `std::multimap`:

- **Understand access time**: Do not expect constant-time access from `std::multimap`. The access complexity is logarithmic, attributed to its tree-based underpinning.

- **Recognize it is distinctly different from std::map**: It's essential not to mistakenly assume that keys in `std::multimap` are unique, as in `std::map`. A `std::multimap` container permits multiple entries for a single key. If your application demands unique keys, then `std::map` is the appropriate choice.

- **Harness its sorted property**: One of the strengths of `std::multimap` is the inherent sorted nature of its elements based on the keys. Exploit this characteristic to your advantage, especially when performing operations that benefit from ordered data, such as range searches or ordered merges.

- **Contemplate on order significance**: If maintaining the order of elements is not a paramount requirement, and you prioritize average-case performance, `std::unordered_multimap` might be a more fitting alternative due to its hashing mechanism. However, it is worth noting that worst-case performance and memory overheads can differ.

- **Verify key existence prior to access**: Before retrieving values associated with a key, ensure the key's presence in the multimap. This can be accomplished using member functions such as `find` or `count`. It helps prevent potential pitfalls and ensure robust code.

- **Use custom comparators for tailored sorting**: Should you have a specific ordering requirement that deviates from the default, use custom comparators. Ensure that your comparator enforces a strict weak ordering to guarantee consistent and defined behavior of the multimap.

- **Efficiently handle multiple values for a key**: When dealing with a key with multiple associated values, use the `equal_range` member function. It provides a range (beginning and end iterators) of all elements with a particular key, enabling efficient iteration over those specific elements.

- **Beware of large datasets**: As with any tree-based structure, `std::multimap` can become inefficient with large datasets, especially if frequent insertions and deletions are commonplace. In such scenarios, evaluate the structure's performance and consider alternatives or optimization strategies.

8

Advanced Unordered Associative Container Usage

While our journey with ordered associative containers has provided us with the prowess of relationship mapping and the power of ordering, it is time to venture into a domain that prioritizes speed over sorted behavior: unordered associative containers. As their name suggests, these containers do not guarantee any specific order of their elements, but they make up for it with potentially faster access times.

In the world of computing, there are always trade-offs. Unordered associative containers might relinquish the beauty of order, but in many scenarios, they make up for it with speed, especially when hashing operates at its best. Whether you're developing a high-frequency trading system, a caching mechanism, or a real-time multiplayer game backend, understanding when to harness the power of unordered associated containers can make a difference.

This chapter provides references for the following containers:

- `std::unordered_set`
- `std::unordered_map`
- `std::unordered_multiset`
- `std::unordered_multimap`

Technical requirements

The code in this chapter can be found on GitHub:

`https://github.com/PacktPublishing/Data-Structures-and-Algorithms-with-the-CPP-STL`

std::unordered_set

This container is akin to `std::set` but with a twist: it does not maintain the elements in any particular order. Instead, it employs a hashing mechanism to access its elements quickly. This hash-based approach can offer constant time average complexity for most operations, given a good hash function.

Purpose and suitability

`std::unordered_set` is a hash-based container in the C++ **Standard Template Library** (**STL**) that stores unique elements in no particular order. Its core strengths include the following:

- Providing average constant-time operations for insertions, deletions, and searches
- Handling non-trivial data types effectively

You should choose `std::unordered_set` in the following scenarios:

- When you need rapid checks for the existence of elements
- When the order of elements is not a concern
- When frequent insertions and deletions are expected

However, if the ordering of elements is crucial, `std::set` might be a better alternative.

Ideal use cases

The following are some of the ideal use cases for `std::unordered_set`:

- **Fast membership checks**: If the primary goal is determining whether a particular item exists in a collection, `std::unordered_set` is your candidate.
- **Eliminating duplicates**: You can use `std::unordered_set` to create a collection of unique items from an existing dataset.
- **High-volume data storage**: You can use `std::unordered_set` where quick insertions and deletions are more critical than maintaining order.
- **When the order doesn't matter**: Prefer `std::unordered_set` over `std::set` when the order of elements doesn't matter since `std::unordered_set` provides faster lookup, insertion, and removal operations. However, `std::unordered_set` may use more memory than `std::set`.

Performance

The algorithmic performance of `std::unordered_set` is characterized as follows:

- **Insertion**: Average-case *O(1)*, worst-case *O(n)* due to potential hash collisions
- **Deletion**: Average-case *O(1)*, worst-case *O(n)* due to potential hash collisions
- **Access**: *O(1)*
- **Memory overhead**: Generally higher than ordered containers due to hashing mechanisms

The key trade-off here revolves around average versus worst-case scenarios, especially concerning hash collisions.

Memory management

`std::unordered_set` manages its memory using a series of buckets to store elements. The number of buckets can grow, usually when the load factor exceeds a certain threshold. Using custom allocators can help tailor this behavior.

Thread safety

Concurrent reading is safe. However, operations that modify the set (such as insertions or deletions) require external synchronization mechanisms, such as mutexes.

Extensions and variants

`std::unordered_multiset` is a close relative, allowing multiple instances of an element to be used. If ordered storage is vital, `std::set` and `std::multiset` come into play.

Sorting and searching complexity

Its sorting and search complexity is characterized as follows:

- **Sorting**: This is not inherently supported as `std::unordered_set` is not ordered.
- **Searching**: It has an average *O(1)* time due to hashing, but its worst-case scenario can be *O(n)* with poor hashing.

Special interface and member functions

Some handy member functions to note are as follows:

- `emplace`: This allows elements to be constructed directly.

- bucket: This can retrieve the bucket number for a given element.
- load_factor and max_load_factor: These are required for managing performance characteristics.

Comparisons

Compared to std::set, std::unordered_set generally offers faster operations but loses the inherent order and might have a higher memory overhead.

Interactions with algorithms

Due to its unordered nature, std::unordered_set might not be the best candidate for STL algorithms that require ordered data. However, algorithms revolving around unique elements can fit well.

Exceptions

Operations can throw exceptions if allocations fail or if hash functions throw. Ensure your hash functions are exception-free to guarantee the container's exception safety.

Customization

Custom hash functions and equality predicates can be applied to fine-tune the container's behavior for specific data types. Moreover, custom allocators can also be beneficial in some scenarios.

Example

std::unordered_set stores unique elements in no particular order. The primary operations it supports are insertion, deletion, and member checking. Unlike std::set, which uses a balanced binary tree internally, std::unordered_set uses a hash table, making the average insertion, deletion, and search complexities *O(1)*, albeit with higher constants and worse worst-case performance.

The following code shows an example demonstrating best practices when using std::unordered_set:

```cpp
#include <iostream>
#include <unordered_set>
#include <vector>

void displaySet(const std::unordered_set<int> &set) {
  for (const int &num : set) { std::cout << num << " "; }
  std::cout << '\n';
}

int main() {
```

```cpp
  std::unordered_set<int> numbers;

  for (int i = 0; i < 10; ++i) { numbers.insert(i); }

  displaySet(numbers);

  int searchValue = 5;
  if (numbers.find(searchValue) != numbers.end()) {
    std::cout << searchValue << " found in the set."
              << '\n';
  } else {
    std::cout << searchValue << " not found in the set."
              << '\n';
  }

  numbers.erase(5);
  displaySet(numbers);

  std::cout << "Size: " << numbers.size() << '\n';
  std::cout << "Load factor: " << numbers.load_factor()
            << '\n';

  numbers.rehash(50);
  std::cout << "Number of buckets after rehash: "
            << numbers.bucket_count() << '\n';

  std::vector<int> moreNumbers = {100, 101, 102, 103};
  numbers.insert(moreNumbers.begin(), moreNumbers.end());
  displaySet(numbers);

  return 0;
}
```

Here's the example output:

```
9 8 7 6 5 4 3 2 1 0
5 found in the set.
9 8 7 6 4 3 2 1 0
Size: 9
Load factor: 0.818182
Number of buckets after rehash: 53
103 102 101 100 9 8 7 6 4 3 2 1 0
```

Here are some key takeaways from the preceding code:

- `std::unordered_set` allows rapid insertions, deletions, and lookups.

- `find` can be used to check for the existence of an element.

- The `rehash` method can change the number of buckets in the underlying hash table, which might help when you know the number of elements in advance and wish to reduce the overhead of rehashing.

- Always be cautious about the load factor (covered in the following Best practices section) and consider rehashing when necessary to maintain efficient performance.

- Remember that the order of elements in `std::unordered_set` is not guaranteed. The order can change over time as elements are inserted or deleted.

Using `std::unordered_set` is appropriate when you need rapid lookups and are not worried about the order of elements. If ordering is essential, you might want to consider using `std::set` instead.

Best practices

Let's explore the best practices of using `std::unordered_set`:

- **Order assumptions**: `std::unordered_set` is designed without the need to maintain any specific order of its elements. Never rely on any sequential consistency within this container.

- **Hash collision awareness**: Hash collisions can detrimentally affect performance, transforming average-case constant-time operations into worst-case linear-time operations. Always be aware of this, especially when designing hash functions or handling large datasets.

- **Bucket count and load factor management**: The performance of `std::unordered_set` can be intimately tied to its bucket count and load factor. Consider the load factor and rehashing policies of `std::unordered_set` for performance tuning. The **load factor** is the ratio of the number of elements in the container to the size of the bucket array. If the load factor is too high, too many elements are in each bucket, which can slow down lookup and insertion operations. On the other hand, if the load factor is too low, the bucket array is too large, which can waste memory. Ensure you understand and monitor the following:

  - `bucket_count()`: The current number of buckets

  - `load_factor()`: The current number of elements divided by the bucket count

  - `max_load_factor()`: The load factor threshold, which, when surpassed, triggers a rehash

- **Hash function customization**: The default hash function might not always provide optimal performance, especially for user-defined types. Consider implementing custom hash functions using the C++11 `std::hash` standard template specialization. This allows hashing behavior to be fine-tuned.

- **Rehashing**: Monitor the load factor and proactively invoke `rehash()` or `reserve()` when necessary. This can help prevent unexpected performance drops, especially when inserting new elements.

- **Uniform hash distribution**: A good hash function will distribute values uniformly across buckets, minimizing the chance of collisions. Ensure your hash function achieves this by testing its distribution with sample data before deploying it in performance-critical applications. Use a well-designed hash function that distributes elements evenly across the buckets to avoid performance degradation.

- **Ordered container alternatives**: If element ordering becomes necessary for your application, `std::unordered_set` is not the ideal choice. Consider migrating to `std::set` or leveraging other ordered containers within the STL.

- **Concurrency concerns**: When using `std::unordered_set` in multi-threaded applications, ensure proper synchronization mechanisms are in place. Concurrent reads are safe, but writes or simultaneous reads and writes demand external synchronization.

- **Size and capacity management**: Although `std::unordered_set` dynamically manages its size, it is beneficial to use functions such as `reserve()` if you have an estimate of the number of elements to be stored. This can help in reducing the number of rehashes and improve performance.

- **Erase elements efficiently**: Utilize the `erase` member function judiciously. Remember that erasing by the iterator is faster ($O(1)$) than erasing by the key value ($O(n)$) in the worst case.

- **Memory footprint**: Be aware that `std::unordered_set`, due to its hashing mechanism, might have a higher memory overhead than other containers. Consider this aspect, especially in memory-sensitive applications.

std::unordered_map

Think of this container as an unsorted version of `std::map`. It associates keys with values but without imposing any order. Instead, it banks on hashing for swift operations.

Purpose and suitability

`std::unordered_map` is a hash table-based key-value container in the STL. Its core strengths are as follows:

- Fast average-case key-based access, insertion, and removal
- Ability to maintain a key-value association

This container is the go-to in the following circumstances:

- When insertions, deletions, and lookups must be swift on average

- When the order of elements isn't a concern

Ideal use cases

The following are some of the ideal use cases for `std::unordered_map`:

- **Fast associative lookups**: When you need quick access to values based on unique keys, `std::unordered_map` provides average constant-time complexity for `search`, `insert`, and `delete` operations

- **Cache systems**: When implementing cache mechanisms where the priority is rapid key-based access over the order of items, `std::unordered_map` is ideal

- **Frequency analysis**: For tasks such as counting the occurrence of words in a document or the number of visits to a website from unique IP addresses, `std::unordered_map` allows you to map items to their occurrence counts efficiently

- **Grouping or bucketing**: In scenarios such as classifying objects or grouping records based on certain attributes, `std::unordered_map` can map the attribute to a list or set of objects

- **Dynamic configuration**: In applications that require dynamic settings that can be modified at runtime, `std::unordered_map` can associate setting keys with their current values for quick lookups and modifications

- **Database indexing**: While traditional databases have indexing mechanisms, for simpler or in-memory databases, `std::unordered_map` can serve as an efficient index for quick record access based on unique identifiers

- **Real-time analytics**: In real-time systems that analyze and categorize streaming data, `std::unordered_map` offers an efficient way to update and access data categories or counters based on unique keys

- **Networking applications**: For tasks such as tracking the number of packets sent from different network nodes or routing tables in networking applications, `std::unordered_map` provides an efficient structure to handle key-value pairs

- **Game scoreboards**: In gaming, where scores or the attributes of players need to be constantly updated and retrieved based on player IDs or names, `std::unordered_map` proves invaluable

- **Resource management**: In systems or applications that need to manage resources, such as thread pools or connection pools, `std::unordered_map` can associate resource keys with their status or attributes

To summarize, `std::unordered_map` is optimal for scenarios that demand quick associative lookups, insertions, and deletions without needing the keys to maintain any specific order. If a key's sequence or sorted nature is a priority, structures such as `std::map` would be more suitable.

Performance

The algorithmic performance of `std::unordered_map` is characterized as follows:

- **Insertion**: *O(1)* average-case, *O(n)* worst-case

- **Deletion**: *O(1)* average-case, *O(n)* worst-case

- **Access**: *O(1)* average-case, *O(n)* worst-case due to potential hash collisions

- **Memory overhead**: Generally higher than ordered map counterparts due to the hashing infrastructure

Memory management

`std::unordered_map` manages its memory automatically, resizing when load factors exceed certain thresholds. Allocators can offer finer control over this process.

Thread safety

Concurrent reading is safe. However, modifications or mixed read-writes necessitate external synchronization, such as using mutexes.

Extensions and variants

`std::map` is the ordered counterpart, providing log(n) guarantees at the cost of maintaining order. Based on your requirements, decide whether you need order or average-case speed.

Sorting and searching complexity

Its sorting and search complexity is characterized as follows:

- **Sorting**: Not applicable as `std::unordered_map` is inherently unordered
- **Searching**: Fast *O(1)* average-case key-based lookups

Special interface and member functions

Apart from the standard functions (`insert`, `erase`, `find`), become familiar with the following:

- `emplace`: Constructs key-value pairs in place

- `bucket_count`: Returns the number of buckets
- `load_factor`: Provides the current load factor

Comparisons

Compared to `std::map`, `std::unordered_map` trades order for faster average-case operations. The unordered variant often outperforms in scenarios where constant order isn't vital.

Interactions with algorithms

Most STL algorithms that work with sequences aren't directly applicable to key-value map structures. Still, the container provides methods that are optimized for its use case.

Exceptions

Failures in memory allocation or the hash function can throw exceptions. Some operations, such as `at()`, can throw `std::out_of_range`. It's crucial to ensure exception safety, especially during insertions or emplacements.

Customization

You can supply custom hash functions and key equality functions to optimize further or adapt behavior. Additionally, custom allocators are available for memory management tweaks.

Example

`std::unordered_map` is a container that associates keys with values. It is similar to `std::map`, but while `std::map` maintains its elements in a sorted manner (based on keys), `std::unordered_map` does not maintain any order. Internally, it uses a hash table, which gives it an *O(1)* complexity for insertions, deletions, and lookups.

The following code shows an example demonstrating best practices when using `std::unordered_map`:

```cpp
#include <iostream>
#include <unordered_map>

void displayMap(
    const std::unordered_map<std::string, int> &map) {
  for (const auto &[key, value] : map) {
    std::cout << key << ": " << value << '\n';
  }
}
```

```cpp
int main() {
  std::unordered_map<std::string, int> ageMap;

  ageMap[„Lisa"] = 28;
  ageMap[„Corbin"] = 25;
  ageMap[„Aaron"] = 30;

  std::cout << "Corbin's age: " << ageMap["Corbin"]
            << '\n';

  if (ageMap.find("Daisy") == ageMap.end()) {
    std::cout << "Daisy not found in the map." << '\n';
  } else {
    std::cout << "Daisy's age: " << ageMap["Daisy"]
              << '\n';
  }

  ageMap["Lisa"] = 29;
  std::cout << "Lisa's updated age: " << ageMap["Lisa"]
            << '\n';

  displayMap(ageMap);

  std::cout << "Load factor: " << ageMap.load_factor()
            << '\n';
  std::cout << "Bucket count: " << ageMap.bucket_count()
            << '\n';

  ageMap.rehash(50);
  std::cout << "Bucket count after rehash:"
            << ageMap.bucket_count() << '\n';

  // Remove an entry
  ageMap.erase("Aaron");
  displayMap(ageMap);

  return 0;
}
```

Here's the example output:

```
Corbin's age: 25
Daisy not found in the map.
Lisa's updated age: 29
```

```
Aaron: 30
Corbin: 25
Lisa: 29
Load factor: 0.6
Bucket count: 5
Bucket count after rehash:53
Corbin: 25
Lisa: 29
```

Here are some key takeaways from the preceding code:

- Use the `operator[]` or the `insert` method to add elements to the map. Note that using an index operator on a non-existent key will create it with a default value.

- The `find` method checks for the existence of a key. It's more efficient than using the `index` operator when you want to check a key's existence without potential insertion.

- Always be aware of the map's load factor and consider rehashing if necessary to maintain efficient performance.

- As with `std::unordered_set`, the order of elements in `std::unordered_map` is not guaranteed. It can change as elements are inserted or removed.

`std::unordered_map` is suitable when you need quick key-based access and don't care about the order of elements. If ordering is essential, then `std::map` would be a more appropriate choice.

Best practices

Let's explore the best practices of using `std::unordered_map`:

- **Element order is not guaranteed**: Do not assume the map maintains element order.

- **Beware of hash collisions**: Ensure you account for potential worst-case performance in hash-collision scenarios.

- **Monitor bucket count and load factors**: Be mindful of the bucket count and load factors in `std::unordered_map` to maintain optimal performance. Regularly check the load factor and consider rehashing if necessary.

- **Use custom hash functions**: Employ suitable hash functions for your key type. The performance of `std::unordered_map` is highly dependent on the effectiveness of the hash function used. A poorly designed hash function can lead to poor performance due to cache misses and collision resolution overhead.

- **Use custom allocators**: Use custom allocators for `std::unordered_map` to improve memory efficiency, particularly in scenarios with high insertions and deletions.

- **Check for an existing key**: Always check for an existing key before insertion to avoid overwriting.

- **Use emplace**: Use `emplace` to construct entries in place, reducing overhead.
- **Avoid default initialization**: Using the default initialization in `std::unordered_map` is expensive when using `operator[]` for accessing elements, which can be a performance pitfall.

std::unordered_multiset

This container is a flexible counterpart to `std::unordered_set`, allowing multiple occurrences of an element. It amalgamates the speed of hashing with the liberty of non-unique elements.

Purpose and suitability

`std::unordered_multiset` is a hash table-based container that allows you to store multiple equivalent items in an unordered manner. Its primary attractions are as follows:

- Quick average-case insertion and lookup times
- The ability to store multiple items with the same value

It's particularly suitable in the following scenarios:

- When the order of elements doesn't matter
- When you anticipate having multiple elements with the same value
- When you want average-case constant time complexity for insertions and lookups

When searching for a container where duplicates are permissible and order isn't crucial, `std::unordered_multiset` is a compelling choice.

Ideal use cases

The following are some of the ideal use cases for `std::unordered_multiset`:

- **Non-unique element storage**: When storing elements where duplicates are allowed and the order is not important, `std::unordered_multiset` is suitable. It permits the storage of multiple identical elements.
- **Frequency distribution analysis**: For tasks such as identifying the distribution of values, `std::unordered_multiset` can be an efficient structure where each unique value is stored alongside its duplicates.
- **Collisions in hashing mechanisms**: In applications that utilize hashing, `std::unordered_multiset` can be useful for managing hash collisions by storing collided items together.
- **Networking**: When analyzing packets with duplicate signatures or patterns, `std::unordered_multiset` can store these repeating patterns for further analysis.

- **Real-time data duplication analysis**: In scenarios where you want to analyze and identify repeated data in real-time, `std::unordered_multiset` is efficient as it allows constant time average complexity for inserts.

- **Tag systems**: For applications that allow users to tag items, where a tag can be associated with multiple items and vice versa, `std::unordered_multiset` can efficiently manage these tag occurrences.

- **Multi-criteria grouping**: In applications that need to group items based on more than one attribute, and duplicates for each attribute are allowed, `std::unordered_multiset` provides a way to manage these grouped items.

- **Database record redundancy**: In some database tasks, where the redundancy of certain records or attributes is necessary, `std::unordered_multiset` can be an efficient in-memory tool to manage these redundant data points.

`std::unordered_multiset` is best suited for scenarios where quick insertions and lookups are needed, duplicates are allowed, and the order of elements is not significant. When unique keys or ordered data structures are a requirement, other containers, such as `std::unordered_set` or `std::map`, may be more appropriate.

Performance

The algorithmic performance of `std::unordered_multiset` is characterized as follows:

- **Insertion**: *O(1)* average-case though worst-case can be *O(n)*

- **Deletion:** *O(1)* average-case

- **Access**: No direct access like an array, but finding an element is *O(1)* average-case

- **Memory overhead**: Typically, this is higher than ordered containers due to hashing mechanisms

One trade-off is that while `std::unordered_multiset` offers average-case *O(1)* insertion, lookup, and deletion, worst-case performance can degrade to *O(n)*.

Memory management

`std::unordered_multiset` dynamically manages its bucket list. The container can be resized, which might happen automatically when elements are inserted and the size exceeds `max_load_factor`. Allocators can be used to influence memory allocation.

Thread safety

Reading from the container is thread-safe, but modifications (for example, insertions or deletions) require external synchronization. Multiple threads writing to `std::unordered_multiset` simultaneously can lead to race conditions.

Extensions and variants

`std::unordered_set` functions similarly but doesn't allow duplicate elements. It contrasts with `std::multiset`, which keeps its elements ordered but permits duplicates.

Sorting and searching complexity

Its sorting and search complexity is characterized as follows:

- **Sorting**: Not inherently sorted, but you can copy elements to a vector and sort them
- **Searching**: *O(1)* average-case complexity for lookups due to hashing

Special interface and member functions

While it offers standard functions (`insert`, `erase`, `find`), you can also explore the following:

- `count`: Returns the number of elements that match a specific value
- `bucket`: Returns the bucket number for a given value
- `max_load_factor`: Manages when the container decides to resize

Comparisons

Compared to `std::multiset`, this container offers faster average-case performance but at the expense of order and potentially higher memory usage.

Interactions with algorithms

Hash-based containers such as `std::unordered_multiset` don't always benefit as much from STL algorithms that have been optimized for ordered containers. Algorithms that don't rely on element order are preferable (that is, `std::for_each`, `std::count`, `std::all_of`, `std::transform`, and others).

Exceptions

Standard exceptions can be thrown for bad allocations. It's critical to know that operations on `std::unordered_multiset` offer strong exception safety.

Customization

The container supports custom allocators and hash functions, allowing for refined control over memory allocation and hashing behavior.

Example

std::unordered_multiset is similar to std::unordered_set but allows multiple occurrences of the same element. Like other unordered containers, it uses a hash table internally, so it doesn't maintain any order of elements. The key characteristic of unordered_multiset is its ability to store duplicates, which can be useful in certain applications, such as counting or categorizing items based on some criterion.

The following example demonstrates some best practices when using std::unordered_multiset:

```cpp
#include <algorithm>
#include <iostream>
#include <string>
#include <unordered_set>

int main() {
  std::unordered_multiset<std::string> fruits;

  fruits.insert("apple");
  fruits.insert("banana");
  fruits.insert("apple");
  fruits.insert("orange");
  fruits.insert("apple");
  fruits.insert("mango");
  fruits.insert("banana");

  const auto appleCount = fruits.count("apple");
  std::cout << "Number of apples: " << appleCount << '\n';

  auto found = fruits.find("orange");
  if (found != fruits.end()) {
    std::cout << "Found: " << *found << '\n';
  } else {
    std::cout << "Orange not found!" << '\n';
  }

  auto range = fruits.equal_range("banana");
  for (auto itr = range.first; itr != range.second;
       ++itr) {
    std::cout << *itr << " ";
  }
  std::cout << '\n';

  fruits.erase("apple");
```

```
    std::cout << "Number of apples after erase:"
              << fruits.count("apple") << '\n';
    std::cout << "Load factor: " << fruits.load_factor()
              << '\n';
    std::cout << "Bucket count: " << fruits.bucket_count()
              << '\n';

    fruits.rehash(50);
    std::cout << "Bucket count after rehashing: "
              << fruits.bucket_count() << '\n';

    for (const auto &fruit : fruits) {
      std::cout << fruit << " ";
    }
    std::cout << '\n';

    return 0;
}
```

Here's the example output:

```
Number of apples: 3
Found: orange
banana banana
Number of apples after erase:0
Load factor: 0.363636
Bucket count: 11
Bucket count after rehashing: 53
mango banana banana orange
```

Here are some key takeaways from the preceding code:

- `std::unordered_multiset` can store duplicate values. Use the `count` method to check how many occurrences of a given element exist in the container.

- The `equal_range` function provides a range of iterators pointing to all instances of a specific element.

- As with other unordered containers, be conscious of the load factor and consider rehashing when necessary.

- Remember that the elements in `unordered_multiset` are unordered. If you need ordered data with duplicate values, you should use `std::multiset`.

- You'd need to iterate through the set and use the iterator-based `erase()` method to erase specific occurrences of a duplicate value. In the preceding example, we removed all occurrences of `apple` for simplicity.

Use `std::unordered_multiset` to keep track of elements where the order doesn't matter, and duplicates are allowed. It offers efficient constant-time average complexity for insertions, deletions, and lookups.

Best practices

Let's explore the best practices of using `std::unordered_multiset`:

- **Distinguish from std::unordered_set**: It's crucial to recognize the key differences between `std::unordered_multiset` and `std::unordered_set`. Unlike `std::unordered_set`, `std::unordered_multiset` allows duplicates. Choose `std::unordered_multiset` if your application must store multiple equivalent keys.

- **Handle duplicates**: One of the primary features of `std::unordered_multiset` is its ability to handle duplicate elements. This is particularly useful in scenarios where you need to track multiple instances of an element. However, this also means that operations such as `find()` will return an iterator to the first instance of the element, and iterating through all duplicates might be necessary for certain operations.

- **Load factor and performance**: Similar to `std::unordered_set`, the performance of `std::unordered_multiset` is affected by the load factor. A higher load factor can cause more hash collisions, impacting performance. Conversely, a lower load factor, while reducing collisions, can lead to memory inefficiency. Use `load_factor()` to monitor and `rehash()` or `max_load_factor()` to manage the load factor effectively.

- **Custom hash function**: Customizing the hash function is especially important in `std::unordered_multiset` for efficient element distribution, especially when dealing with custom or complex data types. Implement a specialized hash function using `std::hash` template specialization to ensure uniform distribution and minimize collision.

- **Unordered nature and alternatives**: If your application logic requires ordered data, `std::unordered_multiset` may not be the right choice due to its unordered nature. In such cases, consider using `std::multiset`, which maintains order but still allows duplicates.

- **Efficient element erasure**: Use the `erase()` function to remove elements. Removing an element by an iterator is an $O(1)$ operation, whereas removing by value can take up to $O(n)$ in the worst case. Be mindful of this when designing your erasure strategy, especially in performance-critical applications.

- **Memory usage considerations**: Like `std::unordered_set`, `std::unordered_multiset` can have higher memory overhead due to its hashing mechanism. This should be a consideration in environments where memory is a constraint.

- **Concurrency and synchronization**: Similar to other unordered containers, `std::unordered_multiset` supports concurrent reads but requires external synchronization mechanisms for writes or concurrent reads and writes. This is crucial in multi-threaded environments to avoid data races and maintain data integrity.

- **Interactions with STL algorithms**: While most STL algorithms are compatible with `std::unordered_multiset`, be aware of algorithms that expect a sorted range since they are not suitable for an unordered container. Always ensure that the chosen algorithm aligns with the characteristics of `std::unordered_multiset`.

std::unordered_multimap

By blending the principles of `std::unordered_map` and the flexibility of multiplicity, this container allows a single key to be associated with multiple values without the need to maintain a specific order.

Purpose and suitability

`std::unordered_multimap` is a hash-based container that permits multiple values to be associated with a single key. Unlike `std::unordered_map`, it doesn't enforce unique keys. It's especially apt in the following scenarios:

- When quick average-case lookup times are desired

- When you anticipate multiple values for the same key

- When key order doesn't matter, as elements aren't stored in any particular order

Choose `std::unordered_multimap` for situations that require non-unique keys and swift lookups. If order or unique keys matter, consider other options.

Ideal use cases

The following are some of the ideal use cases for `std::unordered_multimap`:

- **One-to-many relationships**: When one key can be associated with multiple values, `std::unordered_multimap` is a suitable container. For example, one author (key) can have numerous books in a database of authors and their books (values).

- **Reverse lookup tables**: If you need a fast way to associate several items with one key, such as in applications that find all items linked to a particular attribute, `std::unordered_multimap` is beneficial.

- **Collisions in hashing systems**: In scenarios that use hashing mechanisms, `std::unordered_multimap` can manage hash collisions by linking collided keys to their respective values.

- **Tagging systems**: In systems where multiple tags can be associated with a single item or a single tag can be associated with multiple items, `std::unordered_multimap` can organize these tag-to-item or item-to-tag relationships.

- **Database joins**: When simulating inner joins in databases where multiple records from one table match with multiple records from another table, `std::unordered_multimap` can be an efficient in-memory tool.

- **Grouping by attributes**: If you need to group items based on an attribute that isn't unique, `std::unordered_multimap` can serve as a storage system. As an example, this can be useful if you're grouping people by their birth year, where one year (key) can correspond to many people (values).

- **Lookup systems with variations**: For lookup systems where one key might correspond to multiple slight variations in values, `std::unordered_multimap` is useful. An example would be color-naming systems, where one color can have several associated names.

- **Spatial indexing**: In applications such as game development, you might need to find objects in a particular location quickly. Using spatial keys (such as grid coordinates), `std::unordered_multimap` can associate one coordinate with multiple objects in that space.

`std::unordered_multimap` is a highly versatile tool that's apt for applications where fast insertions and lookups are crucial, and one key should be linked to multiple values. When unique keys or ordered data structures are required, other containers, such as `std::unordered_map` or `std::set`, might be more fitting.

Performance

The algorithmic performance of `std::unordered_multimap` is characterized as follows:

- **Insertion**: Average-case $O(1)$, worst-case $O(n)$
- **Deletion**: Average-case $O(1)$, worst-case $O(n)$
- **Access**: Average-case $O(1)$, worst-case $O(n)$
- **Memory overhead**: Moderate due to hashing infrastructure, potentially increasing with hash collisions

Its trade-offs include speedy average-case operations but potential slowdowns if hash collisions become prevalent.

Memory management

`std::unordered_multimap` resizes when the load factor exceeds its maximum value. Allocators can be used to customize memory behavior, including allocation and deallocation strategies.

Thread safety

Reading from different instances is thread-safe. However, concurrent reading and writing to the same instance necessitates external synchronization.

Extensions and variants

`std::unordered_map` is a variant that holds unique keys. If you need ordered key behavior, `std::multimap` and `std::map` are tree-based alternatives.

Sorting and searching complexity

Its sorting and search complexity is characterized as follows:

- **Sorting**: Not inherently sortable as it is unordered; must be copied to a sortable container
- **Searching**: Average-case $O(1)$ due to hashing, but can degrade in the presence of many hash collisions

Special interface and member functions

Beyond common functions (`insert`, `find`, `erase`), dive into the following:

- `emplace`: Directly constructs the element in the container
- `bucket`: Fetches the bucket number for a given key
- `load_factor`: Provides the ratio of elements to buckets

Comparisons

Compared to `std::unordered_map`, this container allows non-unique keys. If key order matters, `std::multimap` is a tree-based alternative.

Interactions with algorithms

Being unordered, many STL algorithms designed for ordered sequences might not be directly applicable or would necessitate a different approach.

Exceptions

Failures in memory allocation or hash function complications can throw exceptions. Container operations offer basic exception safety, ensuring the container remains valid.

Customization

You can use custom allocators for memory adjustments. Custom hash functions or key equality predicates can also optimize behavior for specific use cases.

Example

std::unordered_multimap is similar to std::unordered_map but allows for multiple key-value pairs with equivalent keys. It is an associative container, meaning its value type is formed by combining its key and mapped types.

The following code example demonstrates some best practices when using std::unordered_multimap:

```cpp
#include <iostream>
#include <string>
#include <unordered_map>

int main() {
  std::unordered_multimap<std::string, int> grades;

  grades.insert({"Lisa", 85});
  grades.insert({"Corbin", 92});
  grades.insert({"Lisa", 89});
  grades.insert({"Aaron", 76});
  grades.insert({"Corbin", 88});
  grades.insert({"Regan", 91});

  size_t lisaCount = grades.count("Lisa");
  std::cout << "Number of grade entries for Lisa: "
            << lisaCount << '\n';

  auto range = grades.equal_range("Lisa");
  for (auto it = range.first; it != range.second; ++it) {
    std::cout << it->first << " has grade: " << it->second
              << '\n';
  }

  auto lisaGrade = grades.find("Lisa");
  if (lisaGrade != grades.end()) {
    lisaGrade->second = 90; // Updating the grade
  }

  grades.erase("Corbin"); // This will erase all grade
```

```
                    // entries for Corbin
std::cout
    << "Number of grade entries for Corbin after erase: "
    << grades.count("Corbin") << '\n';

std::cout << "Load factor: " << grades.load_factor()
          << '\n';
std::cout << "Bucket count: " << grades.bucket_count()
          << '\n';

grades.rehash(50);
std::cout << "Bucket count after rehashing: "
          << grades.bucket_count() << '\n';

for (const auto &entry : grades) {
  std::cout << entry.first
            << " received grade: " << entry.second
            << '\n';
}

return 0;
}
```

Here's the example output:

```
Number of grade entries for Lisa: 2
Lisa has grade: 85
Lisa has grade: 89
Number of grade entries for Corbin after erase: 0
Load factor: 0.363636
Bucket count: 11
Bucket count after rehashing: 53
Regan received grade: 91
Aaron received grade: 76
Lisa received grade: 90
Lisa received grade: 89
```

Here are some key takeaways from the preceding code:

- With `std::unordered_multimap`, it is possible to insert multiple key-value pairs with the same key.

- You can use `equal_range` to get a range of iterators to all the key-value pairs with a specific key.

- The `count` method helps you determine the number of key-value pairs with a specific key.

- Like other unordered containers, you should be aware of the load factor and might want to rehash it if necessary to achieve optimal performance.

- Using the `erase()` method with a key will remove all the key-value pairs associated with that key.

- Since it is an unordered container, the order of the elements is not guaranteed.

- Use `std::unordered_multimap` when you need to keep track of multiple values associated with the same key and don't need the key-value pairs to be sorted. It provides average constant-time complexity for most operations.

Best practices

Let's explore the best practices of using `std::unordered_multimap`:

- **Avoid assuming order**: The *unordered* part of `std::unordered_multimap` signifies that the container maintains no specific order for its key-value pairs. Iterating through the container does not guarantee any particular sequence.

- **Handle non-unique keys**: One of the distinguishing features of `std::unordered_multimap` is its ability to store multiple entries for a single key. Remember this when inserting, erasing, or searching to avoid unintended logic errors.

- **Load factor management**: The load factor (calculated as the ratio of the number of elements to the number of buckets) impacts performance. A higher load factor increases the likelihood of hash collisions, potentially degrading access/insertion performance. Use the `load_factor()` function to monitor the current load factor. If it gets too high, consider rehashing the container using the `rehash()` function. It's also possible to set a desired upper limit on the load factor with the `max_load_factor()` function.

- **Efficient hash function design**: The default hash function might not be ideal for all data types. Inefficient hash functions can degrade performance significantly. Crafting a specialized hash function ensures a more uniform distribution across buckets, thus reducing the chances of collisions. Utilize the `std::hash` template specialization for custom data types to ensure efficient and consistent hashing.

- **Handle hash collisions**: Even with an efficient hash function, collisions might occur. The container handles these internally, but awareness of them helps with making better design decisions. Collisions can lead to a performance drop in insertion and search operations, so balancing the load factor and the number of buckets is essential.

- **Mindful iteration**: When iterating, one key might appear multiple times with different associated values due to the possibility of multiple values for a single key. Use `equal_range()` when iterating through all values associated with a specific key.

- **Iterator invalidation**: Iterator invalidation can be a concern, especially after operations such as rehashing. Always ensure that iterators, pointers, or references to the elements are not used after they might have been invalidated.

- **In-place construction**: To efficiently insert elements without the overhead of temporary object creation, use the `emplace` or `emplace_hint` methods. These allow the key-value pair to be constructed directly within the container.

- **Concurrency considerations**: Concurrent reads are thread-safe, but you'll need external synchronization for any modifications or concurrent reads and writes. Use synchronization primitives such as mutexes in multi-threaded scenarios.

- **Interactions with STL algorithms**: Many STL algorithms can be employed with `std::unordered_multimap`. However, ensure the selected algorithm doesn't expect ordering or unique keys, since those assumptions would contradict the container's properties.

9

Advanced Container Adaptor Usage

Container adaptors, as their name suggests, adapt underlying containers to provide specific interfaces and functionalities. Think of them as a way to enhance or modify an existing container so that it serves a different purpose without having to reinvent the wheel. They wrap around base containers and provide a distinct set of member functions, imbuing them with behavior that can be useful in various programming scenarios.

This chapter provides references for the following containers:

- `std::stack`
- `std::queue`
- `std::priority_queue`
- `std::flat_set`
- `std::flat_map`
- `std::flat_multiset`
- `std::flat_multimap`

Technical requirements

The code in this chapter can be found on GitHub:

`https://github.com/PacktPublishing/Data-Structures-and-Algorithms-with-the-CPP-STL`

std::stack

`std::stack` is a data structure that represents a stack, a **last-in, first-out** (**LIFO**) data structure. It is implemented as an adapter class, which means it is built on top of other containers, such as std::deque, std::vector, and std::list, providing a simple and easy-to-use interface for working with stacks. You can push elements onto the top of the stack, pop elements from the top, and access the top element without accessing elements at other positions. std::stack is commonly used for tasks that require a stack-like behavior, such as tracking function call sequences, parsing expressions, and managing temporary data. It provides a convenient way to manage data to ensure the most recently added element is the first to be removed.

Purpose and suitability

std::stack is a container adapter that's designed to provide a LIFO data structure. It operates on top of another container, such as std::vector, std::deque, or std::list.

It's particularly suitable in the following scenarios:

- When a LIFO behavior is needed
- When you only need to access the most recently added element
- When insertions and deletions happen solely at one end

Choose std::stack when you require a simple interface to manage data in a LIFO manner. For more flexible operations, consider its underlying container.

Ideal use cases

The following are some of the ideal use cases for std::stack:

- **Expression evaluations and parsing**: An example of this is evaluating postfix expressions
- **Backtracking algorithms**: An example of this is performing depth-first search in graphs
- **Undo operations in software**: Maintaining a history of user actions to revert them

Performance

Since std::stack is a container adaptor, its algorithmic performance is dependent on the underlying container implementation:

- **Insertion (push)**: *O(1)*
- **Deletion (pop)**: *O(1)*
- **Access (top)**: *O(1)*
- **Memory overhead**: Directly tied to the underlying container

Memory management

std::stack behaves like its underlying container does. For instance, if std::vector is the base, resizing might involve reallocation, doubling its memory.

Thread safety

Like most STL containers, std::stack isn't thread-safe for write operations. External synchronization is necessary for concurrent writes or a combination of reads and writes.

Extensions and variants

std::queue and std::priority_queue are other adapters in the STL, serving **first-in, first-out (FIFO)** behaviors and priority-driven access, respectively.

Sorting and searching complexity

Sorting and searching are not inherently suited for std::stack. You might have to transfer elements to a different container to sort or search.

Special interface and member functions

std::stack is designed to offer three special member functions:

- push: Pushes an element onto the top of the stack
- pop: Removes (pops) an element from the top of the stack
- top: Gets the value of the top element in the stack without removing it

Comparisons

Compared to the raw underlying containers, std::stack offers a restricted interface tailored for LIFO operations.

Interactions with algorithms

Direct interactions with STL algorithms are limited due to the lack of iterator support. For algorithmic operations, consider the underlying container directly.

Exceptions

Attempting operations on an empty stack, such as pop or top, doesn't throw but leads to undefined behavior. Ensure the stack isn't empty before such operations.

Customization

While the behavior of `std::stack` can't be altered much, using custom allocators or selecting a specific underlying container can influence performance and storage characteristics.

Example

The following code shows an example demonstrating the use of `std::stack`. This example implements a function to evaluate **Reverse Polish Notation** (**RPN**) expressions, a postfix mathematical notation. Using a stack is a natural fit for this type of problem:

```cpp
#include <iostream>
#include <sstream>
#include <stack>
#include <string>

double evaluateRPN(const std::string &expression) {
  std::stack<double> s;
  std::istringstream iss(expression);
  std::string token;

  while (iss >> token) {
    if (token == "+" || token == "-" || token == "*" ||
        token == "/") {
      if (s.size() < 2) {
        throw std::runtime_error("Invalid RPN expression");
      }

      double b = s.top();
      s.pop();
      double a = s.top();
      s.pop();

      if (token == "+") {
        s.push(a + b);
      } else if (token == "-") {
        s.push(a - b);
      } else if (token == "*") {
        s.push(a * b);
      } else if (token == "/") {
        if (b == 0.0) {
          throw std::runtime_error("Division by zero");
        }
        s.push(a / b);
```

```
      }
    } else {
      s.push(std::stod(token));
    }
  }

  if (s.size() != 1) {
    throw std::runtime_error("Invalid RPN expression");
  }

  return s.top();
}

int main() {
  try {
    // Evaluate RPN expressions
    std::cout << "46 2 + = " << evaluateRPN("46 2 +")
              << "\n"; // 48
    std::cout << "5 1 2 + 4 * + 3 - = "
              << evaluateRPN("5 1 2 + 4 * + 3 -")
              << "\n"; // 14
    std::cout << "3 4 5 * - = " << evaluateRPN("3 4 5 * -")
              << "\n"; // -17
  } catch (const std::exception &e) {
    std::cerr << "Error: " << e.what() << "\n";
  }

  return 0;
}
```

Here's the example output:

```
46 2 + = 48
5 1 2 + 4 * + 3 - = 14
3 4 5 * - = -17
```

In the preceding example, the following occurs:

- We use `std::stack` to manage operands and evaluate the RPN expression.

- Operands are pushed onto the stack. When an operator is encountered, the necessary number of operands (usually two) are popped from the stack. Next, the operation is performed. Finally, the result is pushed back onto the stack.

- If the expression is valid at the end of the evaluation, there should be precisely one number on the stack: the result.

- The function handles possible errors, such as an invalid RPN expression or division by zero.

This is a typical use of `std::stack` as it showcases the LIFO nature of the data structure and its principle operations (`push`, `pop`, and `top`).

Best practices

Let's explore the best practices of using `std::stack`:

- **Maintain a LIFO discipline**: A stack is designed for LIFO operations. Avoid manipulating the underlying container directly to access anything other than the top element. Bypassing the LIFO logic compromises the purpose and integrity of using a stack.

- **Perform safety checks with empty()**: Before invoking `top()` or `pop()`, always validate if the stack is empty using the `empty()` function. Accessing or popping from an empty stack leads to undefined behavior and potential runtime errors.

- **Choose an underlying container**: By default, `std::stack` uses `std::deque` as its container, which typically provides efficient push and pop operations. While you can customize this with containers such as `std::vector` or `std::list`, be aware of their respective performance and memory characteristics. For instance, while `std::vector` might have occasional resizing overheads, `std::list` has per-element overheads.

- **Concurrency requires external synchronization**: `std::stack` itself does not guarantee thread safety. If you're accessing or modifying a stack from multiple threads, employ proper synchronization mechanisms, such as `std::mutex`, to prevent data races and maintain consistency.

- **Be wary of direct container access**: While the `std::stack` interface restricts you to the top element, the underlying container might not. Directly using the underlying container can provide broader access and introduce errors if you're not cautious.

- **Efficient element construction with emplace**: Instead of pushing an already constructed element, use `emplace` to construct the element directly within the stack. This can reduce the need for temporary objects and potential copy/move operations, leading to more efficient and concise code.

- **Exception safety**: Certain operations might provide basic or strong exception safety, depending on the underlying container. Awareness of these guarantees is essential, especially if your application requires a certain level of exception safety.

- **Mind the stack's capacity**: While `std::stack` doesn't expose capacity or reservation mechanisms directly, the underlying container, especially if it's `std::vector`, might have such behaviors. If you're confident about the stack's growth patterns, consider using an appropriate underlying container and managing its capacity for optimization.

- **Beware of aliases and auto**: When employing type aliases or automatic type deduction using `auto`, be explicitly aware of your stack's type. This includes the type of elements it holds and the underlying container. This clarity ensures you remain informed about the stack's performance characteristics and limitations.

- **Avoid std::stack<bool> pitfalls**: Just as with `std::vector<bool>`, using `std::stack<bool>` with certain underlying containers can have unexpected behaviors or inefficiencies due to container specializations. If you need a stack of Boolean values, consider alternatives or be well-informed about the specific container's behavior with Boolean types.

std::queue

`std::queue` represents a FIFO data structure. It is implemented as an adapter class and is typically based on other underlying containers, such as `std::deque` or `std::list`. `std::queue` provides a straightforward interface for working with queues, allowing you to enqueue (push) elements at the back and dequeue (pop) elements from the front. It is commonly used in C++ for situations where data needs to be processed in the order it was added, such as task scheduling, breadth-first traversal of graphs or trees, and managing work items in multi-threaded programs. `std::queue` ensures that the element in the queue that is the longest is the first to be dequeued, making it a useful tool for managing ordered data processing.

Purpose and suitability

`std::queue` is a container adapter that's built on top of another container such as `std::deque`, `std::list`, or `std::vector`. Its primary purpose is to provide FIFO data access.

It's especially suitable in the following scenarios:

- When sequential access is needed
- When elements are to be processed in their insertion order

If searching, sorting, or random access is a primary concern, `std::queue` might not be the optimal choice.

Ideal use cases

The following are some of the ideal use cases for `std::queue`:

- **Task scheduling**: Manage tasks in the order they arrive
- **Data serialization**: Ensure data is processed in the order it's received
- **Tree Traversal:** Breadth-first traversal of graphs or trees

Performance

Since `std::queue` is a container adaptor, its algorithmic performance depends on the underlying container implementation:

- **Insertion (push)**: *O(1)*
- **Deletion (pop)**: *O(1)*
- **Access (front and back)**: *O(1)*
- **Memory overhead**: Depends on the underlying container

The performance characteristics derive mainly from the base container, which is typically `std::deque`.

Memory management

Its memory behavior depends on the underlying container. For instance, if you're using `std::deque`, it manages blocks of memory and can grow both ends.

Thread safety

Reads and writes aren't inherently thread-safe. External synchronization, such as mutexes, is necessary if concurrent access is required.

Extensions and variants

`std::priority_queue` is another adapter that provides access to the top-most element based on a priority, not insertion order.

Sorting and searching complexity

Sorting and searching does not apply to `std::queue`. `std::queue` is designed for FIFO access. Sorting or random searching would require manual iteration through the underlying container, which is suboptimal and defies the purpose of a queue.

Special interface and member functions

Its primary operations include `push()`, `pop()`, `front()`, and `back()`. `size()` and `empty()` are used for size checks and emptiness.

Comparisons

Compared to `std::stack`, which offers LIFO access, `std::queue` ensures FIFO behavior. If random access is required, then `std::vector` might be more appropriate.

Interactions with algorithms

Direct interaction with most STL algorithms is limited due to the lack of iterators. If algorithmic operations are needed, you'd typically work on the underlying container directly.

Exceptions

The exceptions that are thrown depend on the operations of the underlying container. However, accessing elements from an empty queue (using `front()` or `back()`) can lead to undefined behavior.

Customization

Memory management can be customized by choosing an appropriate underlying container and possibly using custom allocators.

Example

One everyday use case for `std::queue` is implementing a **breadth-first search** (**BFS**) algorithm on a graph. Let's create an example that showcases a BFS traversal using `std::queue`. Here is a basic BFS implementation on an undirected graph that uses an adjacency list representation:

```cpp
#include <iostream>
#include <queue>
#include <vector>

class Graph {
public:
  Graph(int vertices) : numVertices(vertices) {
    adjList.resize(vertices);
  }

  void addEdge(int v, int w) {
    adjList[v].push_back(w);
    adjList[w].push_back(v);
  }

  void BFS(int startVertex) {
    std::vector<bool> visited(numVertices, false);
    std::queue<int> q;

    visited[startVertex] = true;
    q.push(startVertex);

    while (!q.empty()) {
```

```cpp
        int currentVertex = q.front();
        std::cout << currentVertex << " ";
        q.pop();

        for (int neighbor : adjList[currentVertex]) {
          if (!visited[neighbor]) {
            visited[neighbor] = true;
            q.push(neighbor);
          }
        }
      }
    }
  }

private:
  int numVertices{0};
  std::vector<std::vector<int>> adjList;
};

int main() {
  Graph g(6);

  g.addEdge(0, 1);
  g.addEdge(0, 2);
  g.addEdge(1, 3);
  g.addEdge(1, 4);
  g.addEdge(2, 4);
  g.addEdge(3, 4);
  g.addEdge(3, 5);

  std::cout << "BFS starting from vertex 0: ";
  g.BFS(0); // Output: 0 1 2 3 4 5

  return 0;
}
```

Here's the example output:

BFS starting from vertex 0: 0 1 2 3 4 5

The following points explain the code:

- The Graph class uses an adjacency list (adjList) to represent the graph.

- The BFS traversal starts from a given vertex, marks it as visited, and then explores its neighbors. Neighbors are added to the queue and processed in the order they are encountered (FIFO order), ensuring a breadth-first traversal.

- As vertices are visited, they are marked in the visited vector to ensure they're not processed multiple times.

- The BFS function uses the primary operations of `std::queue:` `push` to add vertices to the queue, `front` to inspect the next vertex to be processed, and `pop` to remove it.

Best practices

Let's explore the best practices of using `std::queue`:

- **Maintain a FIFO discipline**: A queue is inherently designed for FIFO operations. Attempting to use it for other purposes, such as random access or stack operations with LIFO order, can lead to suboptimal designs and complexities.

- **Avoid direct iterator usage**: `std::queue` does not expose direct iterators. If you need to iterate over the elements, consider if a queue is the proper data structure for your needs or if the underlying container should be accessed directly.

- **Ensure safety with empty()**: Before accessing elements with `front()` or `back()`, always check if the queue is empty using the `empty()` function. This prevents undefined behavior that could arise from trying to access elements in an empty queue.

- **Be mindful of the underlying container**: The default container for `std::queue` is `std::deque`, but you can use others, such as `std::list`. Each container has its characteristics, trade-offs, and memory overhead. For example, while `std::list` offers efficient insertions and deletions, its memory overhead per element is higher than `std::deque`.

- **External synchronization is necessary for concurrency**: If multiple threads access the queue, ensure you provide proper synchronization mechanisms, such as `std::mutex`, to avoid data races and inconsistencies. The operations on `std::queue` itself are not inherently thread-safe.

- **Push and pop considerations**: When pushing or popping elements, be aware that the operations might involve memory allocations or deallocations, especially if the underlying container is a `std::vector` container (though this is rare for a queue). This can be a performance concern in real-time or performance-critical applications.

- **Use emplace for in-place construction**: Instead of pushing an already constructed element, consider using `emplace` to construct the element directly within the queue. This can lead to more efficient code as it avoids temporary object creation.

- **Avoid capacity-related assumptions**: Unlike `std::vector`, `std::queue` doesn't have capacity-related member functions. Without explicit knowledge or control, do not make assumptions about the underlying container's size or capacity.

- **Choose containers with appropriate exception guarantees**: If exception safety is a concern, ensure the underlying container provides the necessary exception guarantees. For example, `std::deque` provides strong exception safety for its operations, ensuring data isn't corrupted during exceptions.

- **Be cautious with type aliases**: If you're using type aliases or auto-typing, be sure you know the exact type of your queue, especially if you're working with queues of different underlying containers in the same code base. This ensures you don't mistakenly assume a different container type's characteristics or performance trade-offs.

std::priority_queue

Purpose and suitability

`std::priority_queue` is an adapter container built on top of a random-access container type, primarily `std::vector`. Its core strength revolves around the following:

- Always having the highest priority element at the top
- Ensuring efficient insertion and retrieval of the top element

It shines in the following scenarios:

- When priority-based access is required
- When insertions are random but access always targets the element of the highest importance

In scenarios where order is not a concern or insertion order matters more than access priority, `std::priority_queue` might not be the ideal choice.

Ideal use cases

The following are some of the ideal use cases for `std::priority_queue`:

- **Job scheduling**: Assigning jobs based on their urgency or priority
- **Pathfinding algorithms**: An example of such an algorithm is Dijkstra's algorithm, where nodes with the shortest tentative distance are processed first
- **Simulation systems**: For events that should be processed based on priority rather than sequence

Performance

Since `std::priority_queue` is a container adaptor, its algorithmic performance depends on the underlying container implementation:

- **Insertion**: *O(log n)*, as the element is placed in its suitable position based on its priority
- **Deletion**: *O(log n)* for the top element as the queue restructures itself

- **Access**: *O(1)* to the top element

- **Memory overhead**: Moderate, contingent on the underlying container

Note that when using `std::vector` as the underlying container, additional memory overheads might appear when it resizes.

Memory management

This is inherently dependent on the underlying container. With `std::vector`, memory reallocation might happen upon reaching capacity. Allocators can be utilized for customization.

Thread safety

Concurrent access requires caution. Multiple reads are safe, but simultaneous reads or writes demand external synchronization mechanisms, such as mutexes.

Extensions and variants

If you want a container that ensures sequence preservation, you might consider `std::queue`. If an associative container with key-value pairs and inherent ordering is needed, `std::map` or `std::set` might be more apt.

Sorting and searching complexity

Sorting does not apply to `std::priority_queue`. Direct access to the top priority element for searching is *O(1)*. However, searching for other elements is not straightforward and isn't the primary intent of this container.

Special interface and member functions

Beyond the basics (`push`, `pop`, `top`), explore the following:

- `emplace`: Directly constructs an element within the priority queue

- `size`: Retrieves the number of elements

- `swap`: Exchanges the contents of two priority queues

Comparisons

In contrast to `std::queue`, which respects FIFO ordering, `std::priority_queue` always ensures the highest priority element is accessible. Compared with `std::set`, the latter allows ordered access to all elements, while the former focuses on priority.

Interactions with algorithms

Given the lack of iterators, most STL algorithms can't interact directly with `std::priority_queue`. However, it naturally aligns with user-defined algorithms that focus on the highest-priority elements, such as those that use `push()` and `pop()`.

Exceptions

Throwing can occur during underlying container operations, such as memory allocation. Exception safety often aligns with that of the underlying container.

Customization

Here are some customization options:

- **Allocators**: Customize memory allocation using custom allocators
- **Comparators**: Modify the priority logic using custom comparator functions, allowing for a custom definition of *priority*

Example

`std::priority_queue` is often used in scenarios where elements need to be processed based on their priorities. One of the most common examples of using `std::priority_queue` is implementing Dijkstra's shortest path algorithm for weighted graphs.

The following code shows an example of implementing Dijkstra's algorithm with `std::priority_queue`:

```cpp
#include <climits>
#include <iostream>
#include <list>
#include <queue>
#include <vector>

class WeightedGraph {
public:
  WeightedGraph(int vertices) : numVertices(vertices) {
    adjList.resize(vertices);
  }

  void addEdge(int u, int v, int weight) {
    adjList[u].push_back({v, weight});
    adjList[v].push_back({u, weight});
  }
```

```cpp
  void dijkstra(int startVertex) {
    std::priority_queue<std::pair<int, int>,
                        std::vector<std::pair<int, int>>,
                        std::greater<std::pair<int, int>>>
        pq;
    std::vector<int> distances(numVertices, INT_MAX);

    pq.push({0, startVertex});
    distances[startVertex] = 0;

    while (!pq.empty()) {
      int currentVertex = pq.top().second;
      pq.pop();

      for (auto &neighbor : adjList[currentVertex]) {
        int vertex = neighbor.first;
        int weight = neighbor.second;

        if (distances[vertex] >
            distances[currentVertex] + weight) {
          distances[vertex] =
              distances[currentVertex] + weight;
          pq.push({distances[vertex], vertex});
        }
      }
    }

    std::cout << "Distances from vertex " << startVertex
              << ":\n";
    for (int i = 0; i < numVertices; ++i) {
      std::cout << i << " -> " << distances[i] << '\n';
    }
  }

private:
  int numVertices{0};
  std::vector<std::list<std::pair<int, int>>> adjList;
};

int main() {
  WeightedGraph g(5);
```

```
    g.addEdge(0, 1, 9);
    g.addEdge(0, 2, 6);
    g.addEdge(0, 3, 5);
    g.addEdge(1, 3, 2);
    g.addEdge(2, 4, 1);
    g.addEdge(3, 4, 2);

    g.dijkstra(0);

    return 0;
}
```

Here's the example output:

```
Distances from vertex 0:
0 -> 0
1 -> 7
2 -> 6
3 -> 5
4 -> 7
```

The following happens in this implementation:

- The `WeightedGraph` class uses an adjacency list to represent the graph, where each list element is a pair representing the neighboring vertex and the weight of the edge.

- The `dijkstra` function calculates the shortest distance from a given vertex to all other vertices in the graph.

- `std::priority_queue` is used to select the next vertex with the shortest known distance to process.

- Distances to vertices are updated based on the currently processed vertex and its neighbors.

- As the algorithm progresses, `priority_queue` ensures that vertices are processed in increasing order of their known shortest distances.

Using `std::priority_queue` provides an efficient way to always process the vertex with the smallest known distance in Dijkstra's algorithm.

Best practices

Let's explore the best practices of using `std::priority_queue`:

- **Top-element access:** The primary purpose of `std::priority_queue` is to efficiently access the highest-priority element, not to provide ordered access to all its elements. Do not assume you can access the elements in a fully sorted order.

- **Custom priority rules**: If the default comparison logic doesn't meet your needs, always provide a custom comparator. This ensures that the queue maintains elements according to your specific priority rules.

- **Underlying container choices**: By default, `std::priority_queue` uses `std::vector` as its underlying container. While this is often suitable, switching to containers such as `std::deque` or `std::list` can influence performance. Choose the container that aligns with your specific requirements.

- **Check for emptiness**: Before trying to access the top element or perform a pop operation, always verify that the queue isn't empty. This prevents undefined behavior.

- **Avoid underlying container manipulation**: Directly manipulating the underlying container can disrupt the integrity of the priority queue. Avoid this to ensure that the priority order remains consistent.

- **Efficient element construction**: To construct elements directly within the priority queue, prefer the `emplace` method over `push`. This provides more efficient in-place construction and can save on unnecessary copies or moves.

- **Thread safety**: Like other STL containers, `std::priority_queue` is not inherently thread-safe. If you need to access or modify it across multiple threads, ensure you use appropriate synchronization mechanisms.

- **Awareness of internal sorting**: While it's tempting to think of the priority queue as always holding a sorted list of elements, remember that it only ensures that the top-most element is the highest priority. The internal order of other elements is not guaranteed to be sorted.

- **No iterators**: Unlike many other STL containers, `std::priority_queue` does not provide iterators to its elements. This design intentionally keeps users from inadvertently breaking the queue's priority invariants.

- **Size considerations**: Be mindful of the size and capacity of the underlying container, especially if you're dealing with large datasets. Periodically checking and managing capacity can help in optimizing memory usage.

By following these best practices, you can ensure that you use `std::priority_queue` in a manner that is efficient and consistent with its design intentions.

std::flat_set

`std::flat_set` is a sorted associative container that's designed to store a collection of unique elements in a sorted order. What sets `std::flat_set` apart from other associative containers, such as `std::set`, is that it is implemented as a flat container, often based on a sorted `std::vector` container. This means that elements are stored contiguously in memory, leading to optimal memory usage and faster iteration times compared to traditional tree-based associative containers.

`std::flat_set` maintains its elements in a sorted order, allowing for efficient searching, insertion, and deletion operations, while also providing similar functionality and interface to other set-like containers in the C++ STL. It is especially useful when you need the advantages of both sorted storage and efficient memory management.

Purpose and suitability

`std::flat_set` is a container that represents an associative set stored in a sorted flat array. It merges the benefits of a `std::vector` container (such as cache-friendliness) with those of a `std::set` container (such as ordered storage).

Use `std::flat_set` in the following scenarios:

- When you need ordered data with set properties

- When memory allocation overhead is a concern

- When you want to leverage cache locality advantages similar to those of `std::vector`

If you need to perform many insertions and deletions, other set types, such as `std::set`, may be more suitable due to their tree-based implementation.

Ideal use cases

The following are some of the ideal use cases for `std::flat_set`:

- **Large data initialization**: Given its contiguous memory storage, bulk loading data into a `std::flat_set` container and sorting it can be efficient

- **Fast lookups**: Benefiting from cache locality, searches within a `std::flat_set` container can be notably faster than tree-based sets for smaller sizes

- **Intersecting/Synthesizing sets**: If you're performing operations to combine or intersect sets, the linear nature of `std::flat_set` can be advantageous

Performance

Since `std::flat_set` is a container adaptor, its algorithmic performance depends on the underlying container implementation:

- **Insertion**: $O(n)$ since shifting may be required

- **Deletion**: $O(n)$ for the same reasons

- **Access**: $O(\log n)$ for lookup using binary search

- **Memory overhead**: Less than tree-based structures due to fewer memory allocations

The trade-off is the speed of lookups versus the cost of insertion and deletion, especially as the set grows.

Memory management

`std::flat_set` uses a contiguous block of memory (similar to `std::vector`). Reallocations occur when this block is exhausted. You can influence the allocation strategy using custom allocators.

Thread safety

As with most STL containers, concurrent reads are safe, but writes or mixed operations necessitate external synchronization.

Extensions and variants

`std::flat_map` is a cousin of `std::flat_set` that stores key-value pairs in a flat structure. It offers similar performance characteristics and uses.

Sorting and searching complexity

Its sorting and search complexity is characterized as follows:

- **Sorting**: Inherent to the container and usually *O(n log n)*
- **Searching**: *O(log n)* due to binary search on sorted data

Special interface and member functions

Apart from the typical set functions (`insert`, `erase`, `find`), consider the following:

- `reserve`: Allocates memory in anticipation of insertions
- `capacity`: Returns the current allocation size

Comparisons

In contrast to `std::set`, `std::flat_set` offers better cache locality but can become inefficient with frequent insertions/deletions in large datasets.

Interactions with algorithms

STL algorithms that require random-access iterators, such as `std::sort()`, can be applied directly. However, remember that `std::flat_set` maintains its sorted order, so sorting manually is redundant.

Exceptions

Misusing iterators or exceeding capacity can cause exceptions. Many operations provide strong exception safety, ensuring container consistency.

Customization

`std::flat_set` permits custom allocators, allowing for refined memory control. You can also supply custom comparators for specialized sorting.

Best practices

Let's explore the best practices of using `std::flat_set`:

- **Optimal usage scenarios**: `std::flat_set` is best suited for use cases where the set is built once and queried multiple times. If your application demands frequent insertions and deletions, a traditional tree-based `std::set` container might be more appropriate.

- **Cache locality**: One of the primary advantages of `std::flat_set` over other set implementations is its continuous memory layout, making it cache-friendly. This can lead to significant performance improvements for smaller datasets or when the data can fit into the cache.

- **Efficient merging**: If you have multiple `std::flat_set` containers and need to merge them, consider inserting all elements into a single container first, then sort and make the entire collection unique. This approach is often more efficient than merging sorted sets element by element.

- **Memory management**: Using the `reserve` method is advisable if you have a reasonable estimate of the number of elements you'll be inserting. This can minimize memory reallocations and enhance performance.

- **Alternative set implementations**: For datasets that are constantly changing in size or require frequent element modifications, consider switching to a `std::set` container, which is tree-based and can handle such modifications more gracefully.

- **Maintaining element order**: Since `std::flat_set` maintains its elements in a sorted order, it's crucial to avoid manually sorting the container. Adding elements to a `std::flat_set` container will keep them in order based on the provided comparator.

- **Element access and search**: While `std::flat_set` offers member functions such as `find` for efficient searching, they are optimized for its internal structure. Using these member functions is generally more efficient than applying generic algorithms. If you ever need to use algorithms, ensure they are designed for sorted sequences, such as `std::lower_bound` or `std::upper_bound`.

- **Custom comparators**: The default comparator for `std::flat_set` is `std::less`. However, if your data requires custom sorting logic, ensure you provide a custom comparator during the set's construction. Remember, this comparator should give a strict weak ordering to maintain the set's properties.

- **Avoid frequent reallocations**: Continuously adding elements without reserving memory or deleting elements can lead to frequent memory reallocations. This can negate some of the performance benefits `std::flat_set` provides. If your use case has such patterns, evaluate if other containers might be more suitable.

- **Iterators and modifications**: Unlike `std::set`, modifying elements (for example, through iterators) in a `std::flat_set` container without ensuring the order can lead to undefined behavior. Always confirm that the sorted order is maintained post modifications.

- **Interactions with algorithms**: Due to its contiguous memory layout, `std::flat_set` works well with algorithms that have been optimized for random-access iterators. However, be cautious with algorithms that modify the order or content as they can violate the set's properties.

std::flat_map

`std::flat_map` is a sorted associative container that combines the features of a map and a flat container. Similar to `std::map`, it allows you to store key-value pairs, and the keys are unique and ordered. However, unlike `std::map`, which is typically implemented as a balanced binary search tree, `std::flat_map` is implemented as a flat container, often based on a sorted `std::vector` container. This means that `std::flat_map` offers efficient memory usage and faster iteration times than traditional tree-based associative containers such as `std::map`. Elements in a `std::flat_map` container are stored contiguously in memory, which can lead to better cache locality and improved performance for certain use cases.

`std::flat_map` provides functionality and interface similar to `std::map`, allowing you to perform operations such as insertion, deletion, and searching while maintaining the elements in a sorted order. It's beneficial when you need both the advantages of sorted storage and the benefits of a flat container.

Purpose and suitability

`std::flat_map` is a container that pairs together keys and values, functioning as an associative array. The following reasons set it apart from other map containers:

- It uses a vector-like structure, granting advantages in cache locality.

- This contiguous memory layout fosters improved lookup times in some scenarios.

Its niche lies in the following scenarios:

- When the map is mainly built once and then often queried

- When iteration speed and cache locality take precedence over insertion/deletion speed

- When a sorted map representation is essential

If you foresee frequent modifications post-initialization, consider using `std::map`.

Ideal use cases

The following are some of the ideal use cases for `std::flat_map`:

- **Configuration data**: Storing configuration key-value pairs loaded once at startup but queried frequently during application runtime

- **Spatial indexing**: In graphics or game development, quick iteration and retrieval are more critical than frequent modifications

- **Data serialization**: For datasets that require sorting and occasional lookups but aren't modified regularly

Performance

- **Insertion**: $O(n)$ due to the underlying vector structure

- **Deletion**: $O(n)$ because elements may need to be shifted

- **Access**: $O(\log n)$ due to binary search on the sorted array

- **Memory overhead**: Generally, this is low, but it can escalate if the reserved capacity isn't utilized efficiently

Memory management

`std::flat_map`, like `std::vector`, may reallocate when its capacity is surpassed. It's wise to employ `reserve` if you can predict the eventual size. Allocators can provide control over memory management behaviors.

Thread safety

While concurrent reads are safe, writes or a mixture of both necessitate external synchronization – for example, using mutexes.

Extensions and variants

For unordered associative containers, the STL offers `std::unordered_map`. If a balanced tree structure with ordered keys is preferred, then `std::map` is your go-to.

Sorting and searching complexity

Its sorting and search complexity is characterized as follows:

- **Sorting**: Inherent to its structure, it always maintains order
- **Searching**: *O(log n)* due to binary search

Interface and member functions

Common members such as `insert`, `find`, and `erase` are present. However, you should also explore the following gems:

- `emplace`: Directly constructs elements in place
- `lower_bound` and `upper_bound`: These provide efficient range searches
- `at`: Provides direct access to values by key with bounds-checking

Comparisons

`std::flat_map` excels in iteration and lookup performance, especially for smaller datasets. However, if frequent modifications dominate your use case, you might lean toward `std::map`.

Interactions with algorithms

Due to its random-access nature, `std::flat_map` pairs well with STL algorithms that thrive on such iterators. However, any algorithm that disrupts the key order should be approached cautiously.

Exceptions

Exceeding capacity or accessing out-of-bounds keys might trigger exceptions. Many operations offer strong exception safety, preserving map states if exceptions arise.

Customization

`std::flat_map` allows for custom allocators, and you can specify a custom comparator during construction to dictate the key order.

Best practices

Let's explore the best practices of using `std::flat_map`:

- **Insertion and deletion**: Avoid using `std::flat_map` for frequent insertions and deletions due to the high cost. For such cases, consider alternatives, such as `std::map`.

- **Key modifications**: Do not alter keys directly using iterators. This disrupts the sorted order of the map. If keys need to be modified, consider erasing the old key-value pair and inserting a new one to ensure order maintenance.

- **Memory management**: If you can predict the map's eventual size, employ `reserve()` to reduce the frequency of memory reallocations, enhancing performance.

- **Element construction**: Utilize `emplace` to construct key-value pairs in place efficiently, maximizing performance and avoiding unnecessary temporary object creation.

- **Container choice**: Consider alternatives for use cases dominated by constant modifications, especially insertions and deletions. Containers such as `std::map` may offer better performance profiles in such scenarios.

- **Concurrency**: Ensure thread safety during multi-threaded access. Concurrent reads are generally safe, but writing or mixed read-write operations require external synchronization, such as mutexes.

- **Lookup and iteration**: Capitalize on the strengths of `std::flat_map`. It offers superior cache locality and efficient lookups, especially when the map is mainly queried post-initialization.

- **Order maintenance**: Given the sorted nature of `std::flat_map`, be cautious of operations that may disrupt this order. Always validate the order after any modifications to ensure the container's integrity.

- **Interface usage**: Familiarize yourself with and employ member functions such as `lower_bound` and `upper_bound` for efficient range-based queries, leveraging the container's sorted characteristics.

- **Custom comparators**: While the default comparator (`std::less`) works for many scenarios, `std::flat_map` allows you to specify custom comparators during instantiation, tailoring the key order to specific needs.

std::flat_multiset

`std::flat_multiset` is a container that was introduced in the C++ STL that's designed to store elements in a sorted order. Unlike `std::multiset`, which is typically implemented as a red-black tree, `std::flat_multiset` stores its elements in a contiguous memory block, similar to a `std::vector` container. This design choice offers improved cache performance due to data locality, making it efficient for scenarios where the container is not frequently modified after being filled.

Purpose and suitability

`Std::flat_multiset` is a container that stores elements in a sorted array, similar to `std::flat_set`, but allows for multiple occurrences of equivalent elements.

This container offers the following:

- Efficient lookup times thanks to its sorted nature
- Improved cache locality and predictability in memory usage

It's especially suitable in the following scenarios:

- When duplicates are permissible and you need sorted access
- When cache locality is prioritized
- When the dataset's size is relatively stable post-initialization

However, other containers might be more appropriate when frequent insertions or deletions become the norm.

Ideal use cases

The following are some of the ideal use cases for `std::flat_multiset`:

- **Historical records**: Storing repeated events in chronological order, such as transaction logs
- **Frequency counter**: Counting occurrences of elements when order and access speed are vital
- **Sorted buffers**: Temporary storage during processing, where the order is crucial, and duplicates are expected

Performance

Since `std::flat_multiset` is a container adaptor, its algorithmic performance depends on the underlying container implementation:

- **Insertion**: $O(n)$ since maintaining order may necessitate element shifting
- **Deletion**: $O(n)$ due to the possibility of shifting to fill gaps
- **Access**: $O(log\ n)$ for lookups owing to binary search
- **Memory overhead**: It uses continuous memory, such as `std::vector`, but the lack of tree structures minimizes memory overhead

Memory management

`std::flat_multiset` manages memory in chunks. Pre-allocating memory using `reserve()` can prevent frequent reallocations. Custom allocators can further modify allocation behavior.

Thread safety

Simultaneous reads are safe. However, concurrent modifications or simultaneous reads and writes need external synchronization mechanisms.

Extensions and variants

While `std::flat_multiset` stores multiple instances of an element, `std::flat_set` is its unique element counterpart. For hash-based approaches, you might want to look at `std::unordered_multiset`.

Sorting and searching complexity

Its sorting and search complexity is characterized as follows:

- **Sorting**: This is inherent since `std::flat_multiset` maintains order
- **Searching**: Efficient $O(log\ n)$ due to binary searching

Special interface and member functions

`std::flat_multiset` offers much the same interface as its underlying type. Here are some especially useful functions:

- `equal_range`: Returns range of equivalent elements
- `count`: Efficiently counts the occurrences of an element
- `emplace`: Constructs elements directly in place

Comparisons

Compared to `std::multiset`, `std::flat_multiset` offers a better cache locality but may suffer from frequent modifications. It excels in read-heavy scenarios post-initialization.

Interactions with algorithms

Being sorted, `std::flat_multiset` resonates well with binary search-based algorithms. However, those that shuffle or reorder might not be ideal.

Exceptions

Attempting to access out-of-bounds or mismanaging memory can lead to exceptions. Generally, operations are exception-safe, ensuring the container remains consistent.

Customization

`std::flat_multiset` supports custom allocators, allowing for memory allocation fine-tuning. Moreover, custom comparators can adjust the sorting behavior.

Best practices

Let's explore the best practices of using `std::flat_multiset`:

- **Insertion and deletion efficiency**: Opt for `std::flat_multiset` primarily in scenarios where the set size stabilizes post-initialization. Frequent insertions or deletions will lead to inefficiencies due to the need to maintain a sorted order, often leading to element shifting.

- **Iterator validity**: Unlike some tree-based counterparts, such as `std::multiset`, the iterators for `std::flat_multiset` can become invalidated post-modification, especially those that change the container's size. Always reassess iterator validity after altering the container.

- **Memory management with reserve()**: If you have a rough estimate of the eventual size of your `std::flat_multiset` container, employ `reserve()` to allocate sufficient memory upfront. This prevents recurrent and costly reallocations. While reserving space for anticipated growth is important, over-reservation can lead to unnecessary memory consumption. Aim for a balance between the two.

- **Choosing between std::flat_multiset and std::flat_set**: In scenarios where duplicate elements are expected, and sorting is essential, `std::flat_multiset` is more suitable than `std::flat_set`. It retains all instances of an element, whereas the latter only keeps unique entries.

- **Container alternatives for dynamic data**: If your use case requires regular insertions and deletions, reconsider your container choice. Containers such as `std::list` or `std::multiset` might offer more efficiency for such operations.

- **Efficient element construction**: Instead of inserting pre-constructed elements, utilize `emplace()` to construct elements directly within the set. This can eliminate unnecessary temporary constructions and copies, particularly for complex data types.

- **Concurrency concerns**: Concurrent reading from `std::flat_multiset` is safe. Writing operations, whether they're insertions, deletions, or modifications, require synchronization in a multi-threaded environment to ensure data integrity and prevent data races.

- **Interaction with STL algorithms**: Due to its sorted nature, `std::flat_multiset` pairs well with STL algorithms that benefit from sorted datasets, such as `std::lower_bound` or `std::upper_bound`. However, remember that algorithms that alter the order or introduce elements might invalidate this inherent sorting.

- **Customization**: While the default comparators work for basic types, for custom data types or specific sorting needs, provide a custom comparator to `std::flat_multiset` to control its ordering behavior.

- **Exception safety**: Be aware of operations that can throw exceptions, such as memory allocation failures. Ensuring exception-safe code will prevent data inconsistencies and potential memory leaks.

std::flat_multimap

`std::flat_multimap` is a container adapter that combines the characteristics of associative and sequence containers. It stores key-value pairs, similar to `std::multimap`, but with a significant distinction: the elements are stored in a flat, contiguous memory space, akin to a `std::vector` container. This storage approach enhances cache performance due to improved data locality, which is especially beneficial for read-intensive operations.

Purpose and suitability

`Std::flat_multimap` is a container within the STL that's optimized for fast associative lookups. Its distinguishing features include the following:

- Storage in a sorted contiguous block of memory, akin to `std::vector`
- Allows multiple key-value pairs with identical keys

It is most suitable in the following scenarios:

- When cache locality and associative lookups are both desired
- When the dataset stabilizes post-initialization since it's not optimized for frequent insertions or deletions

Pick `std::flat_multimap` over other containers when the advantages of flat storage and allowance for key duplicity align with your use case.

Ideal use cases

The following are some of the ideal use cases for `std::flat_multimap`:

- **Web browser history**: Storing URLs with timestamps. Multiple entries (timestamps) can exist for the same URL (key).

- **Word frequency counter**: When words in a piece of text can have multiple meanings and you want to store each meaning alongside its count.

- **Event scheduler**: To maintain events (values) that occur at specific times (keys), where multiple events might happen at the same timestamp.

Performance

Since `std::flat_multimap` is a container adaptor, its algorithmic performance depends on the underlying container implementation:

- **Insertion**: *O(n)* due to potential element shifting
- **Deletion**: *O(n)* due to maintaining order
- **Access**: *O(log n)* due to binary search on a sorted array
- **Memory overhead**: Relatively low with advantages in cache locality

The trade-off lies in enjoying faster lookups at the cost of slower insertions and deletions.

Memory management

`std::flat_multimap` manages memory akin to `std::vector`. The `reserve()` function can anticipate and allocate memory for growth. Custom allocators can further tailor memory behaviors.

Thread safety

Concurrent reads are safe. However, writes or mixed read-writes require synchronization mechanisms such as mutexes.

Extensions and variants

For a container without duplicate key allowance, there's `std::flat_map`. For unsorted and bucketed storage, you might want to consider `std::unordered_multimap`.

Sorting and searching complexity

Its sorting and search complexity is characterized as follows:

- **Sorting**: Inherent to the container and managed internally
- **Searching**: *O(log n)* due to binary search

Interface and member functions

Apart from the standard functions (`insert`, `erase`, `find`), explore the following:

- `equal_range`: Returns bounds of all entries matching a key
- `emplace`: Directly constructs key-value pairs inside the map

Comparisons

Compared to `std::multimap`, `std::flat_multimap` offers better cache locality but slower modifications. When juxtaposed with `std::unordered_multimap`, it trades faster lookups for inherent sorting.

Interactions with algorithms

`std::flat_multimap` is beneficial with algorithms such as `std::lower_bound` and `std::upper_bound` due to its sorted nature. However, be cautious with algorithms that modify order or introduce elements.

Exceptions

Key insertions or lookups won't throw, but be wary of memory allocation failures, especially during insertions, which can cause exceptions. Exception safety is prioritized, with many operations offering strong guarantees.

Customization

While custom allocators are permitted, `std::flat_multimap` relies on its internal sorting mechanism. Thus, custom comparators are essential to define key order.

Best practices

Let's explore the best practices of using `std::flat_multimap`:

- **Insertion and deletion frequency**: Refrain from using `std::flat_multimap` when the use case involves continuous or frequent insertions and deletions. Due to the container's linear nature, such operations can be costly.

- **Iterator expectations**: Be aware that `std::flat_multimap` only supports input, output, forward, and bidirectional iterators. It does not provide random-access iterators.

- **Key data type considerations**: Prefer concise and lightweight data types for keys. Using large custom data types can exacerbate the costs of element shifting during insertions and deletions.

- **Memory allocation management**: If you have an estimate of the eventual size of `std::flat_multimap`, leverage the `reserve()` function. Pre-allocating memory can mitigate expensive reallocations and copying.

- **Entry construction**: Utilize the `emplace` method for in-situ construction of key-value pairs. This can be more efficient than creating and inserting an entry separately.

- **Container suitability**: Should the dataset be dynamic with frequent changes, consider the merits of alternative associative containers such as `std::multimap` or `std::unordered_multimap`. These containers might offer better performance for such scenarios.

- **Concurrency**: In multi-threaded environments, ensure that proper synchronization mechanisms, such as mutexes, are in place for write operations to `std::flat_multimap`. Concurrent reads are typically safe but write operations can lead to race conditions without proper synchronization.

- **Key ordering**: Implement and utilize custom comparators when the default key comparison doesn't suffice. This ensures that `std::flat_multimap` retains its internal ordering based on your specific requirements.

- **Search efficiency**: Due to the sorted nature of `std::flat_multimap`, binary search algorithms, such as `std::lower_bound` and `std::upper_bound`, can be used efficiently for operations such as range queries or finding specific keys.

- **Exception safety**: Avoid potential memory allocation failures, especially during insertions. Many operations on `std::flat_multimap` offer strong exception guarantees, ensuring that the container remains consistent, even if an operation throws an exception.

- **Value handling**: Given the allowance for key duplicity in `std::flat_multimap`, use member functions such as `equal_range` to handle and process all entries associated with a specific key.

- **Capacity management**: Regularly monitor the capacity and size of `std::flat_multimap` using member functions such as `capacity()` and `size()`. If excess reserved space isn't being utilized, consider using `shrink_to_fit()` to release this memory.

10

Advanced Container View Usage

At their core, views are non-owning ranges, meaning they provide a view (hence the name) of other data structures without taking ownership of the underlying data. This makes them incredibly lightweight and versatile. With views, you can perform various operations on data without copying it, ensuring efficient code that maximizes performance and minimizes overhead.

This chapter focuses on the following containers:

- `std::span`
- `std::mdspan`

Technical requirements

The code in this chapter can be found on GitHub:

`https://github.com/PacktPublishing/Data-Structures-and-Algorithms-with-the-CPP-STL`

std::span

`std::span` is a template class introduced in C++20 that provides a view of a contiguous sequence of elements, similar to a lightweight, non-owning reference. It represents a range over some contiguous storage, such as an array or a portion of a vector, without owning the underlying data.

The primary purpose of `std::span` is to safely and efficiently pass arrays of data to functions without needing to pass the size explicitly, as the size information is encapsulated within the `std::span` object. It can be considered a safer, more flexible alternative to raw pointer-and-size or pointer-and-length parameter passing.

Purpose and suitability

`std::span` is a non-owning view of a contiguous sequence, often an array or a segment of another container. It is a lightweight, flexible, and safe way to refer to such sequences, ensuring no extraneous copies.

`std::span` is best suited in the following scenarios:

- When a temporary view of data is needed
- When the underlying data's ownership is managed elsewhere
- When you want to avoid unnecessary data copying but still need random access

Consider using `std::span` to provide functions with access to parts of data without granting ownership.

Ideal use cases

The following are some of the ideal use cases of `std::span`:

- **Processing data segments**: Parsing a subsegment of a large data block, such as processing headers in a networking buffer
- **Function interfaces**: Granting functions a view of data without transferring ownership or risking resource leaks
- **Data views**: Quickly and safely offering multiple views on a data source without duplicating the source

Performance

The algorithmic performance of `std::span` is characterized as follows:

- **Insertion**: Not applicable, as `std::span` doesn't own its data
- **Deletion**: Not applicable
- **Access**: *O(1)*, just like direct array access
- **Memory overhead**: Minimal, as it essentially holds a pointer and a size

Remember, the performance of `std::span` mainly derives from its non-owning characteristic.

Memory management

No allocations are done by `std::span`. It simply references memory owned elsewhere. Thus, concerns about memory behavior primarily relate to the underlying data, not the span itself.

Thread safety

Multiple concurrent reads through a span are safe. However, as with any data structure, concurrent writes or write-read combinations require synchronization.

Extensions and variants

`std::span` is unique in the **Standard Template Library** (**STL**) and designed for its purpose. While containers such as `std::string_view` offer a similar view concept, they cater to specific data types.

Sorting and searching complexity

Sorting isn't directly applicable to `std::span`, since it doesn't own its data. Searching, however, is $O(n)$ for an unsorted sequence and $O(log\ n)$ for sorted data using appropriate STL algorithms.

Interface and member functions

Key functions in this category include the following:

- `size()`: Returns the number of elements
- `data()`: Provides access to the underlying data
- `subspan()`: Generates another span from the current one

Comparisons

Compared to `std::vector` or `std::array`, `std::span` doesn't manage or own data. It offers a way to safely view sections of these containers (or others) without copying.

Interactions with algorithms

STL algorithms requiring access (and not structure modification) can interact with `std::span` seamlessly. Those requiring insertions or deletions should be avoided.

Exceptions

Operating beyond the bounds of the span can trigger exceptions. Always ensure the underlying data's validity during the span's entire lifetime.

Customization

`std::span` isn't typically customized with allocators, comparators, or hash functions due to its non-owning nature.

Example

Let's look at an example demonstrating the use of std::span to process the headers of a **User Datagram Protocol (UDP)** packet.

UDP headers typically consist of the following:

- **Source port**: 2 bytes

- **Destination port**: 2 bytes

- **Length**: 2 bytes

- **Checksum**: 2 bytes

We'll create a simple structure representing the header, and then we'll use std::span to handle a buffer containing the header and data of a UDP packet. Let's explore the following code:

```
#include <cstdint>
#include <iostream>
#include <span>

struct UDPHeader {
  uint16_t srcPort{0};
  uint16_t destPort{0};
  uint16_t length{0};
  uint16_t checksum{0};

  void display() const {
    std::cout << "Source Port: " << srcPort << "\n"
              << "Destination Port: " << destPort << "\n"
              << "Length: " << length << "\n"
              << "Checksum: " << checksum << "\n";
  }
};

void processUDPPacket(std::span<const uint8_t> packet) {
  if (packet.size() < sizeof(UDPHeader)) {
    std::cerr << "Invalid packet size!\n";
    return;
  }

  auto headerSpan = packet.subspan(0, sizeof(UDPHeader));

  const UDPHeader &header =
      *reinterpret_cast<const UDPHeader *>(
```

```
                headerSpan.data());
    header.display();

    auto dataSpan = packet.subspan(sizeof(UDPHeader));
    std::cout << "Data size: " << dataSpan.size()
              << " bytes\n";
}

int main() {
    uint8_t udpPacket[] = {0x08, 0x15, // Source port
                           0x09, 0x16, // Destination port
                           0x00, 0x10, // Length
                           0x12, 0x34, // Checksum
                           // Some data
                           0x01, 0x02, 0x03, 0x04, 0x05,
                           0x06};

    processUDPPacket(udpPacket);

    return 0;
}
```

Here is the example output:

```
Source Port: 5384
Destination Port: 5641
Length: 4096
Checksum: 13330
Data size: 6 bytes
```

The key points from the preceding code are as follows:

- We define a UDPHeader structure to represent the header fields.
- In the processUDPPacket function, we use std::span to handle the buffer.
- We then create a subspan for the header and reinterpret it as the UDPHeader structure.
- The remaining part of the buffer is the data, which we handle using another subspan.

std::span offers a view of a contiguous sequence of objects, making it suitable for safely accessing memory regions, such as networking buffers, without owning the underlying data.

Best practices

Let us explore the best practices of using `std::span`:

- **Dangling references**: Ensure that the underlying data of `std::span` outlives the span itself. This is critical to avoid dangling references.

- **Non-owning nature**: Understand that `std::span` is not a data-owning container. It only provides a view of the data, unlike containers such as `std::vector` that manage their data.

- **Mutual reflection**: Be aware that any modifications to the underlying data will immediately reflect in the `std::span` view. This joint reflection means data integrity must be maintained throughout the span's life cycle.

- **Data lifetime**: Use `std::span` judiciously. Always ensure the span's duration is shorter than or equal to the lifetime of the underlying data.

- **Copy management**: Favor `std::span` in function interfaces to prevent unnecessary data copying. This can optimize performance, especially when working with large data blocks.

- **Bounds checking**: As with any data access, always validate bounds before accessing elements through `std::span`. Utilize functions such as `size()` for bounds verification.

- **Safety over raw pointers**: Opt for `std::span` over raw pointer and length pairs. It offers a type-safe, more readable alternative, reducing the risk of common pointer errors.

- **Data abstraction**: Leverage `std::span` for abstracting data segments. It's especially beneficial when different components or functions of a program need access to varying data sections without full ownership.

- **Interactions with STL algorithms**: Since `std::span` offers random access iterators, it's compatible with most STL algorithms. However, be cautious when using algorithms that might expect data ownership or mutation capabilities beyond the scope of `std::span`.

- **Data synchronization**: In multithreaded scenarios, ensure proper synchronization when accessing or modifying the underlying data through `std::span`, given its direct reflection properties.

std::mdspan

`std::mdspan`, introduced in the C++23 standard, is a multidimensional span template class that extends the concept of `std::span` to multiple dimensions. It provides a view of a multidimensional contiguous sequence of elements without owning the underlying data. This class is handy for numerical computations and algorithms that operate on multidimensional data structures, such as matrices and tensors.

Purpose and suitability

`std::mdspan` is a multidimensional span in the C++ STL. It is a non-owning view of a multidimensional array, offering efficient access and manipulation.

Its strengths are as follows:

- Representing and accessing multidimensional data without owning it
- Facilitating interoperability with other languages and libraries that work with multidimensional arrays

`std::mdspan` is particularly suitable in the following scenarios:

- When you must work with multidimensional data from other libraries or APIs without copying
- When you require flexibility in indexing and slicing through multidimensional datasets.

Ideal use cases

The following are some of the ideal use cases of `std::mdspan`:

- **Image processing**: Accessing pixels in a 2D image or frames in a 3D video stream
- **Scientific computing**: Manipulating data in matrix formats for mathematical computations
- **Data wrangling**: Efficiently re-indexing, slicing, or reshaping multidimensional datasets
- **Interoperability**: Interfacing with other languages or libraries that manage multidimensional data structures

Performance

The algorithmic performance of `std::mdspan` is characterized as follows:

- **Access**: Typically *O(1)* for any position.
- **Memory overhead**: Minimal, as `std::mdspan` only provides a view of existing data.
- **Trade-offs**: The primary trade-off is the lack of ownership. Ensure underlying data outlives the `std::mdspan` itself.

Memory management

Since `std::mdspan` doesn't own its data, it does not control memory allocation or deallocation. Ensure the underlying data remains valid during the `mdspan` lifespan.

Thread safety

Like `std::span`, multiple concurrent reads are safe, but writes or mixed reads and writes necessitate external synchronization.

Extensions and variants

`std::span` can be seen as a 1D variant. While `std::span` provides a view of linear data, `std::mdspan` extends this concept to multidimensional data.

Sorting and searching complexity

Sorting and searching are not inherently properties of `std::mdspan`, given its nature. External algorithms would need to be adapted to their multidimensional characteristics.

Special interface and member functions

`std::mdspan` offers the following special interface and member functions:

- `extent`: Returns the size in a given dimension
- `strides`: Provides the number of elements between successive items in each dimension
- `rank`: Gives the number of dimensions

Comparisons

Against raw multidimensional arrays or pointers, `std::mdspan` offers a safer and more flexible interface, albeit without data ownership.

Interactions with algorithms

While many STL algorithms are designed for linear data structures, specific algorithms, especially custom ones for multidimensional data, can be adapted to work with `std::mdspan`.

Exceptions

Given its non-owning nature, accessing data through an invalidated `std::mdspan` (if the underlying data is destroyed) is an undefined behavior and won't throw standard exceptions. Always ensure data validity.

Customization

`std::mdspan` can be customized using layout policies to define data storage patterns.

Best practices

Let us explore the best practices of using `std::mdspan`:

- **Ownership awareness**: `std::mdspan` is a non-owning view. Ensure that you never mistakenly treat it as a data-owning container. This oversight can introduce dangling references and undefined behavior.

- **Efficient data access**: Pay attention to the layout and stride when using `std::mdspan`. Understanding and adjusting these aspects can optimize your data access patterns, making them more cache-friendly.

- **Inter-language interoperability**: If you're interfacing with libraries from other programming languages, be particularly vigilant about data layouts. Languages have their conventions, such as row-major or column-major storage. Aligning `std::mdspan`'s layout with the expected convention can prevent subtle bugs and inefficiencies.

- **Lifetime management**: It's paramount that the data to which `std::mdspan` points remain valid for the span's entire lifetime. Avoid situations where the underlying data could be destroyed or go out of scope while an active `std::mdspan` references it.

- **Explicit layout specification**: When working alongside different libraries, especially those external to the C++ STL, be overt about the expected data layouts. Such clarity prevents ambiguities and ensures consistent data interpretation.

- **API design**: When designing APIs that manipulate multidimensional data, prefer using `std::mdspan` as a parameter. This choice offers safety from dangling references (compared to raw pointers) and greater expressiveness regarding multidimensional data operations.

- **Bound checks**: Test the dimensions and bounds before accessing data through `std::mdspan`. While `std::mdspan` offers some level of type safety, out-of-bounds access still leads to undefined behavior. Consider using functions such as `extents` to ascertain dimensions.

- **Custom layouts**: You can customize how `std::mdspan` interprets the underlying data using layout policies for advanced use cases. This flexibility can be particularly valuable when needing non-standard data arrangements or optimizing for specific hardware architectures.

- **Thread safety**: Like its sibling `std::span`, `std::mdspan` itself doesn't guarantee thread safety for the underlying data. If multithreaded access is anticipated, ensure the underlying data structure or its operations are thread-safe.

- **Leverage STL algorithms**: While `std::mdspan` doesn't naturally fit all STL algorithms due to its multidimensional nature, you can still use many algorithms on a flattened view or individual slices of the data. Being familiar with STL algorithms can help you avoid reinventing the wheel.

Part 3:
Mastering STL Algorithms

In this Part, you will acquire a robust understanding of the algorithmic backbone of the C++ STL. We establish a foundation with fundamental algorithms, emphasizing sorting, searching, and element comparison, essential to efficient data manipulation. We then dive into the transformative power of STL through copying, moving, filling, and generating operations, revealing techniques for optimal data manipulation while underpinning the importance of modern idioms like **Return Value Optimization (RVO)**.

Continuing, we explore numeric operations, from simple summations to complex inner products, and extend our focus to range-based operations, underscoring their significance in modern C++. The subsequent chapter transitions to the structured manipulation of data sets through partitioning, heap operations, and permutations, illustrating their pivotal roles in data organization and analysis.

Finally, we conclude by introducing the concept of ranges, an evolution in STL that brings a more expressive and efficient approach to algorithmic operations. We dissect the advantages and best practices of range-based algorithms for sorting and searching, advocating for their adoption in contemporary C++ development. Best practices are highlighted throughout, providing you with a clear pathway to writing clean, efficient, and maintainable code with STL algorithms.

This part has the following chapters:

- *Chapter 11: Fundamental Algorithms and Searching*
- *Chapter 12: Manipulation and Transformation*
- *Chapter 13: Numeric and Range-Based Operations*
- *Chapter 14: Permutations, Partitions, and Heaps*
- *Chapter 15: Modern STL with Ranges*

11

Fundamental Algorithms and Searching

This chapter covers some of the most crucial and commonly used C++ **Standard Template Library** (**STL**) algorithms. The chapter equips readers with the knowledge and skills to manipulate and analyze data effectively by focusing on sorting, conditional checks, finding, and searching techniques. Understanding these fundamental algorithms is paramount for developers keen on ensuring efficient and robust applications. The chapter also emphasizes best practices, ensuring code is correct and optimized.

This chapter covers the following main topics:

- Sorting
- Checking conditions
- Counting and finding
- Searching and comparison
- Best practices

Technical requirements

The code in this chapter can be found on GitHub:

```
https://github.com/PacktPublishing/Data-Structures-and-Algorithms-
with-the-CPP-STL
```

Sorting

Sorting is a fundamental concept every programmer encounters, yet it is not just about ordering elements. It's about optimization, understanding the nature of your data, and selecting the right approach to arrange that data meaningfully. The vast toolkit of the C++ STL has a rich array of sorting algorithms tailored to various scenarios and datasets. But how do you choose? How do you effectively wield these tools for optimal results? Let's embark on this enlightening journey together.

To begin with, why do we sort? Sorting makes data aesthetically appealing and paves the way for efficient searching, data analysis, and optimized data structures. Whether it is sorting names in an address book or products by price in an online store, the act of sorting is deeply woven into the fabric of computing.

The STL provides a primary sorting function: `std::sort`. This function is versatile and can sort almost any sequence of elements, from arrays to vectors. Under the hood, `std::sort` is typically implemented using an introsort, a hybrid sorting algorithm that combines quicksort, heapsort, and insertion sort, ensuring speed and adaptability. Here's a simple example of `std::sort`:

```
std::vector<int> numbers = {5, 3, 8, 1, 4};
std::sort(numbers.begin(), numbers.end());
```

But sorting isn't always about ascending order or numbers. With `std::sort`, custom comparators allow you to define the order. Imagine you have a list of products and want to sort them by their names in descending order. You can do it in the following manner:

```
std::sort(products.begin(), products.end(), [](const Product& a, const
Product& b) {
    return a.name > b.name;
});
```

It's not just about regular sorting. When you have almost sorted data, `std::partial_sort` comes to the rescue. This function sorts a range so that a particular subrange is sorted. Say you want to find the top three students by their score; `std::partial_sort` can make this task efficient.

However, knowing the algorithm is only half the battle; understanding when to use which function is critical. If you aim to sort a list of a million numbers, `std::sort` is your best friend. But if you're dealing with a smaller dataset where you must maintain the original order of equal elements, `std::stable_sort` is a more suitable option.

There are also niche sorting functions tailored for specific scenarios. For instance, when dealing with large datasets where you're interested in a subset of sorted data, `std::nth_element` is a fantastic tool. It rearranges elements such that the element at the nth position is the one that would be in that position in a sorted sequence.

Selecting the suitable algorithm also involves understanding the nature of your data. If you have a smaller dataset or a nearly sorted list, insertion sort might be your best bet. On the other hand, for larger datasets, more advanced algorithms such as mergesort or quicksort are more fitting. Knowing the underlying mechanics of these algorithms and their performance metrics helps make informed decisions.

Sorting in the STL is not just about arranging data but choosing the optimal way. It's a dance of understanding your data, the nature of your application, and the tools at your disposal. Next, we will learn how to check various conditions on our sorted data.

Checking conditions

The elegance of the C++ STL doesn't just lie in its vast assortment of containers and algorithms. It also resides in its fine-tuned ability to let developers efficiently check and validate data using condition-based operations. With the might of predicate functions, these operations empower programmers to answer questions such as *Does this dataset hold a particular property?* and *Are all elements in this range positive?*

One of the most intuitive and fundamental operations is `std::all_of`. With this algorithm, you can check if all elements in a range satisfy a given predicate. If you had a list of students' grades, you could use `std::all_of` to see if all grades were positive (and they should be!).

By contrast, its counterpart `std::none_of` checks if none of the elements in a range satisfy a given predicate. Let's say you're working with a list of student grades and want to ensure that no one has scored below passing marks. In this case, `std::none_of` becomes an invaluable asset.

Rounding up the trio is `std::any_of`, which checks if at least one element in a sequence meets a specific condition. This becomes particularly handy in scenarios where you're looking for the existence of a condition, such as finding if any grades are As (>= 90).

Let's look at a code example illustrating the usage of `std::all_of`, `std::none_of`, and `std::any_of`:

```cpp
#include <algorithm>
#include <iostream>
#include <vector>

int main() {
  std::vector<int> grades = {85, 90, 78, 92,
                             88, 76, 95, 89};

  if (std::all_of(grades.begin(), grades.end(),
                  [](int grade) { return grade > 0; })) {
    std::cout << "All students have positive grades.\n";
  } else {
    std::cout << "Not all grades are positive.\n";
  }

  if (std::none_of(grades.begin(), grades.end(),
                   [](int grade) { return grade < 80; })) {
    std::cout
        << "No student has scored below passing marks.\n";
  } else {
    std::cout << "There are students who scored below "
                 "passing marks.\n";
```

```
    }

    if (std::any_of(grades.begin(), grades.end(),
                    [](int grade) { return grade >= 95; })) {
      std::cout << "There's at least one student with an "
                   "'exceptional' grade.\n";
    } else {
      std::cout
          << "No student has an 'exceptional' grade.\n";
    }

    return 0;
}
```

Here's the example output:

```
All students have positive grades.
There are students who scored below passing marks.
There's at least one student with an 'exceptional' grade.
```

In this example, we've used a set of student grades as our dataset. We use the described algorithms to check if all grades are positive, if no student scored below passing marks (considered 80 in this case), and if there's at least one student who achieved an *exceptional* grade (90 or above).

Moving beyond these fundamental checks, there are more specialized algorithms such as std::is_ sorted, which, as the name suggests, verifies if a range is sorted. For instance, with a dataset of product prices, this function quickly checks if the sequence is in ascending order, ensuring integrity before performing other operations.

Another intriguing algorithm is std::is_partitioned. Imagine you have a mixed data collection, and you've used some criteria to partition it, such as dividing numbers into even and odd. This algorithm checks if such a partitioning exists in a sequence based on a predicate.

While these functions offer direct ways to validate data, sometimes the need is more nuanced. Consider the situation where you want to compare two sequences to check if they're permutations of each other. The STL offers std::is_permutation for this very purpose. Whether it is strings, numbers, or custom objects, this function can ascertain if one sequence is a reordering of another.

Let's use a dataset of product prices to demonstrate the use of std::is_permutation:

```
#include <algorithm>
#include <iostream>
#include <vector>

int main() {
```

```cpp
std::vector<double> prices = {5.99, 10.49, 20.89, 25.55,
                              30.10};

if (std::is_sorted(prices.begin(), prices.end())) {
  std::cout << "The product prices are sorted in"
               "ascending order.\n";
} else {
  std::cout << "The product prices are not sorted.\n";
}

auto partitionPoint = std::partition(
    prices.begin(), prices.end(),
    [](double price) { return price < 20.0; });

if (std::is_partitioned(
        prices.begin(), prices.end(),
        [](double price) { return price < 20.0; })) {
  std::cout << "Prices are partitioned with prices less "
               "than $20 first.\n";
} else {
  std::cout << "Prices are not partitioned based on the "
               "given criteria.\n";
}

std::vector<double> shuffledPrices = {25.55, 5.99, 30.10,
                                      10.49, 20.89};

// Using std::is_permutation to ascertain if
// shuffledPrices is a reordering of prices
if (std::is_permutation(prices.begin(), prices.end(),
                        shuffledPrices.begin())) {
  std::cout
      << "Sequences are permutations of each other.\n";
} else {
  std::cout << "Sequences are not permutations of each "
               "other.\n";
}

return 0;
}
```

Here's the example output:

```
The product prices are sorted in ascending order.
Prices are partitioned with prices less than $20 first.
Sequences are permutations of each other.
```

In this example, we've used the described algorithms on a dataset of product prices. The prices are first checked to see if they're sorted. Then, they're partitioned based on a price criterion. Finally, we verify if two sequences of prices are permutations of each other.

Utilizing these condition-checking functions isn't just about invoking them on datasets. True power comes from crafting meaningful predicates. By harnessing the capabilities of lambdas or functor objects, you can design intricate conditions that precisely capture your requirements. Whether checking the validity of user inputs, validating data before processing, or ensuring the sanctity of results post-processing, predicate-based functions are your trusty tools.

But like any powerful toolkit, these functions must be used judiciously. Over-relying on checks can lead to performance overhead, especially on large datasets. Striking a balance between validation and performance is crucial. Often, understanding the nature of your data and the broader context of the application can guide you in efficiently using these algorithms.

In wrapping up this exploration of condition-checking algorithms, it is evident that they form an essential part of the STL's algorithmic suite. They provide a robust foundation upon which more advanced operations can be built. As we journey ahead, you'll see how these foundational checks intertwine with other algorithms, such as counting and finding, painting a holistic picture of data processing in the captivating world of C++.

Counting and finding

In the data we deal with daily, managing or validating the data and actively searching, locating, and quantifying specific elements or patterns within it often becomes essential. The STL equips developers with a treasure trove of precise algorithms for counting and finding.

Let's start with the simple yet powerful `std::count` and its twin `std::count_if`. While `std::count` can swiftly tell you how many times a specific value appears in a range, `std::count_if` takes it up a notch, letting you count occurrences based on a predicate. Imagine you have a collection of student marks and wish to find out how many scored above 90. With `std::count_if`, it's a cakewalk, as shown here:

```cpp
#include <algorithm>
#include <iostream>
#include <vector>

int main() {
  std::vector<int> grades = {85, 90, 78, 92,
```

```
                              88, 76, 95, 89};

  const auto exact_count =
      std::count(grades.begin(), grades.end(), 90);

  std::cout << "Number of students who scored exactly 90:"
            << exact_count << "\n";

  const auto above_count =
      std::count_if(grades.begin(), grades.end(),
                    [](int grade) { return grade > 90; });

  std::cout << "Number of students who scored above 90:"
            << above_count << "\n";

  return 0;
}
```

Here's the example output:

```
Number of students who scored exactly 90: 1
Number of students who scored above 90: 2
```

Here, we have utilized `std::count` to check the number of students who scored precisely 90 and then employed `std::count_if` to count the students scoring above 90.

Beyond just counting, sometimes the goal is to locate a specific element. This is where `std::find` and `std::find_if` come into play. In comparison, `std::find` looks for an exact match, and `std::find_if` searches based on a predicate. For those times when you're eager to know the position of the first element that meets a condition, these functions are your go-to.

Yet, life isn't always about the first match. Occasionally, it is the last match that matters. In such scenarios, `std::find_end` proves invaluable. Especially useful in situations such as locating the last occurrence of a subsequence within a larger sequence, this function ensures you don't miss out on the nuances in your data.

Let's look at a code example using `std::list` containing a structure of student names and grades. We'll then use `std::find_if` and `std::find_end` to locate students based on their grades, as demonstrated here:

```
#include <algorithm>
#include <iostream>
#include <list>

struct Student {
```

```
    std::string name;
    int grade{0};

    Student(std::string n, int g) : name(n), grade(g) {}
};

int main() {
  std::list<Student> students = {
      {"Lisa", 85},   {"Corbin", 92}, {"Aaron", 87},
      {"Daniel", 92}, {"Mandy", 78},  {"Regan", 92},
  };

  auto first_92 = std::find_if(
      students.begin(), students.end(),
      [](const Student &s) { return s.grade == 92; });

  if (first_92 != students.end()) {
    std::cout << first_92->name
              << "was the first to score 92.\n";
  }

  std::list<Student> searchFor = {{"", 92}};
  auto last_92 = std::find_end(
      students.begin(), students.end(), searchFor.begin(),
      searchFor.end(),
      [](const Student &s, const Student &value) {
        return s.grade == value.grade;
      });

  if (last_92 != students.end()) {
    std::cout << last_92->name
              << "was the last to score 92.\n";
  }

  return 0;
}
```

Here's the example output:

```
Corbin was the first to score 92.
Regan was the last to score 92.
```

In this example, we use `std::find_if` to find the first student who scored 92. Then, we use `std::find_end` to find the last student who scored 92. The `std::find_end` function is a bit tricky in this case because it is meant for finding subsequences, but by providing it with a single-element list (which acts as our *subsequence*), we can still use it to find the last occurrence of a particular grade.

For those who work with sorted data, STL doesn't disappoint. With `std::lower_bound` and `std::upper_bound`, you can efficiently find the beginning and end of a range of values equal to a given value in a sorted sequence. Furthermore, `std::binary_search` lets you quickly ascertain if an element exists in the sorted range. Remember, these functions capitalize on the sorted nature of the data, making them considerably faster than their generic counterparts.

Let's define a `Student` structure and use a `std::set` of `Student` objects. We'll modify the comparison operators to sort based on grades as follows:

```cpp
#include <algorithm>
#include <iostream>
#include <set>
#include <string>

struct Student {
  std::string name;
  int grade{0};

  bool operator<(const Student &other) const {
    return grade < other.grade; // Sorting based on grade
  }
};

int main() {
  std::set<Student> students = {
      {"Amanda", 68},  {"Claire", 72}, {"Aaron", 85},
      {"William", 85}, {"April", 92},  {"Bryan", 96},
      {"Chelsea", 98}};

  Student searchStudent{"", 85};

  const auto lb = std::lower_bound(
      students.begin(), students.end(), searchStudent);

  if (lb != students.end() && lb->grade == 85) {
    std::cout
        << lb->name
        << " is the first student with a grade of 85.\n";
  }

  const auto ub = std::upper_bound(
```

```
                students.begin(), students.end(), searchStudent);

     if (ub != students.end()) {
       std::cout << ub->name
                 << " is the next student after the last one "
                    "with a grade of 85, with a grade of "
                 << ub->grade << ".\n";
     }

     if (std::binary_search(students.begin(), students.end(),
                            searchStudent)) {
       std::cout << "There's at least one student with a "
                    "grade of 85.\n";
     } else {
       std::cout << "No student has scored an 85.\n";
     }

     return 0;
   }
```

Here's the example output:

```
Aaron is the first student with a grade of 85.
April is the next student after the last one with a grade of 85, with
a grade of 92.
There's at least one student with a grade of 85.
```

In this example, `Student` structures are sorted in `std::set` based on their grades. The names are then used in the output.

Speaking of speed, the adjacency algorithms – `std::adjacent_find` being a prime example – allow for the rapid location of consecutive duplicates in a sequence. Imagine a sensor sending data, and you wish to identify if there are back-to-back duplicate readings quickly. This function is your go-to solution.

Let's look at an example of a `std::list` of structures where each entry has a sensor reading (a temperature) and the time it was taken:

```
#include <algorithm>
#include <chrono>
#include <iomanip>
#include <iostream>
#include <list>

struct SensorData {
```

```cpp
  int temperature{0};
  std::chrono::system_clock::time_point timestamp;
};

int main() {
  const auto now = std::chrono::system_clock::now();
  std::list<SensorData> sensorReadings = {
      {72, now - std::chrono::hours(10)},
      {73, now - std::chrono::hours(9)},
      {75, now - std::chrono::hours(8)},
      {75, now - std::chrono::hours(7)},
      {76, now - std::chrono::hours(6)},
      {78, now - std::chrono::hours(5)},
      {78, now - std::chrono::hours(4)},
      {79, now - std::chrono::hours(3)},
      {80, now - std::chrono::hours(2)},
      {81, now - std::chrono::hours(1)}};

  auto it = sensorReadings.begin();

  while (it != sensorReadings.end()) {
    it = std::adjacent_find(
        it, sensorReadings.end(),
        [](const SensorData &a, const SensorData &b) {
          return a.temperature == b.temperature;
        });

    if (it != sensorReadings.end()) {
      int duplicateValue = it->temperature;

      std::cout << "Found consecutive duplicate readings "
                   "of value: "
                << duplicateValue
                << " taken at the following times:\n";

      while (it != sensorReadings.end() &&
             it->temperature == duplicateValue) {
        const auto time =
            std::chrono::system_clock::to_time_t(
                it->timestamp);

        std::cout << "\t"
                  << std::put_time(std::localtime(&time),
```

```
                                        "%Y-%m-%d %H:%M:%S\n");
        ++it;
      }
    }
  }

  return 0;
}
```

In this example, each `SensorData` structure contains a temperature and its recorded timestamp. We're using `std::adjacent_find` with a custom comparator to check for back-to-back duplicate temperature readings. When we find such a reading, we display the time the reading was taken and the temperature value.

Here's the example output:

```
Found consecutive duplicate readings of value: 75 taken at the
following times:
    2099-10-01 03:14:51
    2099-10-01 04:14:51
Found consecutive duplicate readings of value: 78 taken at the
following times:
    2099-10-01 06:14:51
    2099-10-01 07:14:51
```

As with all tools, understanding when and how to use these algorithms is pivotal. While it might be tempting to employ binary searches frequently due to their speed, they're only applicable to sorted data. Otherwise, using them might lead to incorrect results. Similarly, while counting occurrences might seem straightforward, using the correct counting function, depending on whether you have a specific value or a condition, can significantly affect your program's clarity and efficiency.

Given all of the options for data handling in C++, counting and finding are foundational and complex. They pave the way for more advanced operations, and a mastery over them ensures you're well on your way to becoming adept at handling even the most complex data scenarios. Given our sorted data, we can expand our toolset further by examining efficient searching and comparison with the STL.

Searching and comparison

Searching through data is a common yet crucial operation that most software requires. Whether you're trying to retrieve specific user details from a database or find a book's position in a sorted list, a robust search technique is paramount. With its plethora of algorithms, the STL offers several methods to search through sequences efficiently. Moreover, the library provides intuitive ways to compare sequences and retrieve extreme values, making data analysis more streamlined.

When working with sorted data, `std::binary_search` is a power player. It's a testament to the importance of keeping data sorted wherever feasible. By repeatedly dividing the dataset in half, it locates the desired element, making it an exceptionally speedy tool. However, this is merely a boolean operation; it informs if the element exists, but not where it exists. For that, we lean on `std::lower_bound` and `std::upper_bound`. These functions retrieve iterators pointing to the first occurrence and just past the last occurrence of an element. Combining these two can give a range representing all instances of a value in a sorted sequence.

Yet, not all data is sorted, and not all searches are for exact matches. The STL doesn't leave you in the lurch. Functions such as `std::find` and `std::find_if` shine in these situations, providing flexibility to search based on actual values or predicates.

After searching, a natural progression is comparing elements. Often, we need to determine if one sequence is lexicographically less than, greater than, or equal to another. This is where `std::lexicographical_compare` steps in, allowing you to compare two sequences like dictionary ordering. It's a must-have when working with strings or custom data types, ensuring you can quickly sort and rank data as required.

Here's an example to demonstrate the use of `std::lexicographical_compare`:

```cpp
#include <algorithm>
#include <iostream>
#include <string>
#include <vector>

int main() {
  std::vector<char> seq1 = {'a', 'b', 'c'};
  std::vector<char> seq2 = {'a', 'b', 'd'};
  std::vector<char> seq3 = {'a', 'b', 'c', 'd'};

  if (std::lexicographical_compare(
          seq1.begin(), seq1.end(), seq2.begin(),
          seq2.end())) {
    std::cout << "Sequence 1 is lexicographically less"
                 "than Sequence 2"
              << "\n";
  } else {
    std::cout
        << "Sequence 1 is not lexicographically less"
           "than Sequence 2"
        << "\n";
  }

  if (std::lexicographical_compare(
          seq1.begin(), seq1.end(), seq3.begin(),
```

```
                seq3.end()))  {
    std::cout << "Sequence 1 is lexicographically less"
                   "than Sequence 3"
                << "\n";
  } else {
    std::cout
        << "Sequence 1 is not lexicographically less"
           "than Sequence 3"
        << "\n";
  }

  // For strings
  std::string str1 = "apple";
  std::string str2 = "banana";

  if (std::lexicographical_compare(
          str1.begin(), str1.end(), str2.begin(),
          str2.end()))  {
    std::cout << "String 1 (apple) is lexicographically "
                   "less than String 2 (banana)"
                << "\n";
  } else {
    std::cout << "String 1 (apple) is not "
                   "lexicographically less "
                   "than String 2 (banana)"
                << "\n";
  }

  return 0;
}
```

Here is the example output:

```
Sequence 1 is lexicographically less than Sequence 2
Sequence 1 is lexicographically less than Sequence 3
String 1 (apple) is lexicographically less than String 2 (banana)
```

This demonstrates how `std::lexicographical_compare` can be used to determine the relative ordering of two sequences.

But what if you're only interested in the extremes? Perhaps you want to find the highest score in an exam or the lowest price in a list of products. Here, `std::max_element` and `std::min_element` are your stalwarts. They return iterators pointing to the maximum and minimum elements, respectively.

If you're looking for both, `std::minmax_element` does the trick, giving you a pair of iterators in one go:

```cpp
#include <algorithm>
#include <iostream>
#include <vector>

int main() {
  std::vector<int> scores = {85, 93, 78, 90, 96, 82};

  const auto max_it =
      std::max_element(scores.begin(), scores.end());

  if (max_it != scores.end()) {
    std::cout << "The highest score is: "<< *max_it
              << "\n";
  }

  const auto min_it =
      std::min_element(scores.begin(), scores.end());

  if (min_it != scores.end()) {
    std::cout << "The lowest score is: "<< *min_it
              << "\n";
  }

  const auto minmax =
      std::minmax_element(scores.begin(), scores.end());

  if (minmax.first != scores.end() &&
      minmax.second != scores.end()) {
    std::cout << "The lowest and highest scores are: "
              << *minmax.first << " and " << *minmax.second
              << ", respectively.\n";
  }

  std::vector<double> productPrices = {99.99, 79.99, 49.99,
                                       59.99, 89.99};

  // Find the minimum and maximum prices
  auto minmaxPrices = std::minmax_element(
      productPrices.begin(), productPrices.end());

  if (minmaxPrices.first != productPrices.end() &&
```

```
                minmaxPrices.second != productPrices.end()) {
            std::cout
                << "The cheapest and priciest products cost: $"
                << *minmaxPrices.first << " and $"
                << *minmaxPrices.second << ", respectively.\n";
        }

        return 0;
    }
```

Here is the example output:

```
The highest score is: 96
The lowest score is: 78
The lowest and highest scores are: 78 and 96, respectively.
The cheapest and priciest products cost: $49.99 and $99.99,
respectively.
```

This demonstrates using `std::max_element`, `std::min_element`, and `std::minmax_element` to find the extreme values in sequences.

To wrap up, the power of searching and comparison in STL isn't just in the breadth of its functions but in its adaptability. With iterators and predicates, these algorithms are remarkably versatile, ensuring you can adapt them to various scenarios. As developers, these tools become extensions of our thinking, guiding us toward efficient and elegant solutions. As we progress further, remember these operations form the foundation for more advanced techniques and best practices, fortifying our capabilities in data handling and algorithmic problem-solving in C++.

Best practices

The elegance of the C++ STL lies in its vast array of utilities and its potential for optimization. However, merely knowing the algorithms isn't the endgame. How you use them, combine them, and make subtle decisions can spell the difference between an efficient program and a sluggish one. So, let's delve into the best practices, ensuring that your forays into STL are correct and performed at peak efficiency:

- **Know your data**: Before choosing any algorithm, you need to assess the nature of your data. Is it mostly sorted or completely random? Is it sparse or densely populated? The answers to these questions can dictate the choice of algorithm. For instance, using `std::binary_search` on a mostly sorted array may be counterproductive when `std::find` can serve the purpose with less overhead.

- **Leverage the sorted nature of your data structures**: On the topic of sorted data, always leverage the sorted nature of your data structures wherever possible. Sorted data structures, such as `std::set` and `std::map`, have inherent advantages in searching and inserting elements.

However, they can also lead to pitfalls. Continuously adding elements to such containers may not be efficient, and sometimes, batch insertions followed by a sort operation can be more optimal.

- **Avoid needless reallocations**: Memory reallocation is one of the most expensive operations regarding time performance. When working with containers such as `std::vector`, using the `reserve` method, it is crucial to have a fair estimate of the size and reserve the memory upfront. This way, as you call `push_back` to add elements, the vector does not have to reallocate memory frequently, offering a significant performance boost.

- **Prefer algorithms with predicate versions**: Algorithms such as `std::count_if` and `std::find_if` allow custom conditions to be set, making them flexible and adaptable to a broader range of scenarios than their non-predicate counterparts. Moreover, lambdas in C++11 and beyond have made using these algorithms even more concise and expressive.

- **Be wary of algorithmic complexity**: While the STL provides tools, it does not change the fundamental nature of algorithms. A linear search will always be linear, and a binary search will be logarithmic. Recognize the complexity of your algorithm and question whether that's the best for your application's requirements.

- **Opt for stack over heap allocation**: Opt for stack over heap allocation when feasible in terms of memory performance. Containers such as `std::array`, which are stack-allocated, can be faster to access than their heap-allocated counterparts due to cache locality. However, this comes with the trade-off of fixed sizes. Hence, understanding the memory requirements beforehand can help strike the right balance.

- **Iterators are your friends**: Iterators are your friends, but they can also be your downfall if not used carefully. Always ensure that the iterators you use are valid. Operations such as insertion and deletion, especially in containers such as `std::vector`, can invalidate iterators, leading to undefined behavior.

- **Benchmark and profile**: Assumptions and best practices are starting points, but real performance metrics come from profiling your application. Tools such as gprof, Valgrind, and Celero can be invaluable in highlighting bottlenecks and guiding you toward the right optimizations. These best practices outline how to optimize C++ STL usage, emphasizing the importance of understanding the nature of data, leveraging sorted data structures, avoiding unnecessary memory reallocations, preferring algorithms with predicate versions, being aware of algorithmic complexity, choosing stack over heap allocation when appropriate, using iterators judiciously, and the significance of benchmarking and profiling to identify performance bottlenecks. They underscore that while STL offers powerful utilities, efficient programming depends on how these tools are employed and combined.

Summary

In this chapter, we have thoroughly examined the core algorithms that operate on STL containers and their role in efficient C++ programming. We began by exploring the essentials of sorting algorithms and understanding how they organize data for better accessibility and performance. We then delved into various methods for checking container conditions and techniques for counting and finding elements, which are vital for data analysis and manipulation.

This chapter has armed you with strategies for effectively searching and comparing elements. We also focused on best practices that ensure these operations are performed with optimal efficiency and minimal error.

This knowledge has provided a foundation for implementing complex algorithms and performing data manipulations and everyday tasks in intermediate to advanced C++ development.

In the next chapter, we will extend our understanding of algorithms further. We will learn about copying and moving semantics within STL containers, **Return Value Optimization** (**RVO**), and techniques for filling, generating, removing, and replacing elements. Additionally, we will explore the nuances of swapping and reversing elements and conclude with deduplication and sampling strategies. These topics will contribute to a holistic understanding of data manipulation and transformation.

12

Manipulation and Transformation

This chapter discusses data manipulation techniques provided by the C++ **Standard Template Library** (**STL**). These techniques of manipulating data structures, whether copying, generating new data, removing outdated entries, or performing advanced operations such as swapping or reversing, form a significant part of most applications. This chapter will expose you to many methods and nuances, allowing you to choose the right tool for your tasks. Accompanied by best practices, this chapter ensures you understand and apply these techniques efficiently.

This chapter will cover the following main topics:

- Copying and moving in STL containers
- Exploring return value optimization
- Filling and generating in STL containers
- Removing and replacing in STL containers
- Swapping and reversing in STL containers
- Best practices

Technical requirements

The code in this chapter can be found on GitHub:

```
https://github.com/PacktPublishing/Data-Structures-and-Algorithms-
with-the-CPP-STL
```

Copying and moving in STL containers

The STL in C++ is known for its robust data structures and algorithms. Among its most fundamental aspects are the operations of copying and moving containers. These operations are not only crucial for data manipulation but also play a significant role in the efficiency and performance of C++ applications. This section explores the nuances of copying and moving within the STL, exploring their semantics, implications on performance, and the strategic decision-making involved in choosing one over the other.

Copying semantics in the STL

Copying, in the most rudimentary sense, refers to creating a replica of an object. In the STL, when you copy a container, you duplicate its contents into a new one. One way to visualize this is to imagine photocopying a document. The original remains unchanged, and you have a new document with the same content.

For instance, consider the following:

```
std::vector<int> original{1, 2, 3};
std::vector<int> duplicate(original); // Copy constructor
```

The `duplicate` vector is now a replica of the original vector. Both containers are entirely independent; modifying one won't affect the other. While this sounds straightforward, the devil is often in the detail. Copying can be an expensive operation, especially for large containers. Each element of the original container is duplicated, which might lead to performance pitfalls in applications where time efficiency is paramount.

Moving semantics in the STL

Introduced in C++11, **move semantics** ushered a paradigm shift in managing resources. Instead of duplicating the content, moving transfers the ownership of resources from one object (the *source*) to another (the *destination*).

Imagine you have a box of toys (`std::vector`). Instead of creating a new box and transferring toys one by one (copying), you simply hand over the box to someone else (moving). The original box is empty, and the other person owns all the toys.

Here's how it looks in the code:

```
std::vector<int> original{1, 2, 3};
std::vector<int> destination(std::move(original)); // Move constructor
```

Post this operation, `destination` owns the data, while `original` is in a valid but unspecified state (often empty). This mechanism offers significant performance benefits, especially with large datasets, as it eliminates the overhead of duplicating data.

Copying versus moving – a deliberate choice

Now, equipped with an understanding of both mechanics, the onus is on the developer to make an informed choice. Copying ensures data integrity as the original remains untouched. This is useful when the original data still plays a role in subsequent operations. However, if the original container's data is disposable or you're sure it won't be needed afterward, opting for a move operation can dramatically enhance performance.

Yet, caution is advised. The careless use of move semantics might lead to surprises, especially if one assumes data still resides in the source container. Always be conscious of the state of your objects after any operation.

Here's an example demonstrating the potential pitfalls of the careless use of move semantics:

```
#include <iostream>
#include <vector>

void printVector(const std::vector<int> &vec,
                 const std::string &name) {
  std::cout << name << ": ";
  for (int val : vec) { std::cout << val << " "; }
  std::cout << "\n";
}

int main() {
  std::vector<int> source = {10, 20, 30, 40, 50};

  std::vector<int> destination = std::move(source);

  std::cout
      << "Trying to access the 'source' vector after "
         "moving its data:\n";

  printVector(source, "Source");
  printVector(destination, "Destination");

  source.push_back(60);
  std::cout << "After trying to add data to 'source' "
               "post-move:\n";
  printVector(source, "Source");

  return 0;
}
```

The following is the output of the preceding code:

```
Trying to access the 'source' vector after moving its data:
Source:
Destination: 10 20 30 40 50
After trying to add data to 'source' post-move:
Source: 60
```

As shown, the `source` vector is in a valid but unspecified state after moving data from `source` to `destination`. It's empty, but operations such as `push_back` can still be performed. The key takeaway is that one should be aware of such states and not assume that the `source` container's data is intact after a move.

In essence, the power of the STL is magnified when the developer understands the nuances of its operations. Copying and moving are foundational pillars, determining how data is managed and how efficiently an application runs. As we venture deeper into manipulation and transformation techniques in subsequent sections, always keep these mechanics in mind. They often form the bedrock upon which advanced techniques are built.

Exploring return value optimization

Return value optimization (**RVO**) deserves special mention. Modern compilers optimize returning objects from functions, effectively transforming what looks like a copy into a move, making the operation highly efficient. This is a testament to the evolving nature of C++ and its inclination towards performance optimization.

Here's a code example to demonstrate the concept of RVO:

```cpp
#include <iostream>
#include <vector>

class Sample {
public:
  Sample() { std::cout << "Constructor called!\n"; }

  Sample(const Sample &) {
    std::cout << "Copy Constructor called!\n";
  }

  Sample(Sample &&) noexcept {
    std::cout << "Move Constructor called!\n";
  }

  ~Sample() { std::cout << "Destructor called!\n"; }
};

Sample createSample() { return Sample(); }

int main() {
  std::cout << "Creating object via function return:\n";
  Sample obj = createSample();
  return 0;
}
```

In this code, when the function `createSample` is called, it returns a `Sample` object. Without RVO, we might expect a sequence of calls: `Constructor -> Copy Constructor` (or `Move Constructor`) `-> Destructor`. However, because of RVO, many modern compilers will optimize the creation so that only the constructor is called. The output typically would be as follows:

```
Creating object via function return:
Constructor called!
Destructor called!
```

The absence of a call to the Copy Constructor (`Sample(const Sample&)`) or Move Constructor (`Sample(Sample&&) noexcept`) indicates that RVO took place. The object was constructed directly in the memory location of `obj` without the need for additional copying or moving.

Next, let's explore efficient ways of automatically populating STL containers using the concepts of filling and generating elements.

Filling and generating in STL containers

Populating containers and generating data within them is akin to molding clay into a sculpture. The data structure is your foundation, and the techniques to fill and generate data give life to your programs. As we continue to unearth the vast capabilities of the STL, this segment is dedicated to the pivotal techniques of *filling and generating* in STL containers. Let's roll up our sleeves and dive into the art and science of crafting data structures with precision!

Populating with static assignment

Imagine a scenario where you need a container filled with a specific value, be it zeroes, a particular character, or any other repeating pattern. The STL simplifies this with methods tailored for static assignments.

For instance, the `std::vector` offers an overload of its constructor that allows you to specify a size and a default value:

```
std::vector<int> v(5, 2112);
```

Such a method ensures uniformity of data, which is essential for operations that rely on homogeneous collections. This isn't exclusive to vectors. Many STL containers provide similar functionalities, ensuring developers have the necessary tools for various contexts.

Dynamic generation with the STL

While static assignment has its charm, more often, there's a need for dynamic data generation. Whether it is for creating test cases, simulating scenarios, or any situation demanding a specific pattern, the STL doesn't disappoint.

The STL provides the `std::generate` and `std::generate_n` algorithms for these needs. These functions assign values to a container based on a generator function.

Consider the following example:

```
std::vector<int> v(5);
std::generate(v.begin(), v.end(), [n = 0]() mutable { return n++; });
```

Here, we've leveraged a lambda function to generate consecutive integers dynamically. This method offers unparalleled flexibility, allowing developers to generate data as simple as incrementing numbers or as complex as values based on intricate formulas or computations.

Ensuring relevance and efficiency

Now, having the tools is only half the battle. Employing them effectively is where mastery shines. When filling and generating data, do the following:

- **Choose appropriately**: Consider the data's lifecycle. If the dataset remains static post-creation, static assignments are straightforward and efficient. However, for ever-evolving data, dynamic generation methods provide flexibility and adaptability.

- **Mind the size**: Overpopulating can lead to memory inefficiencies, while underpopulating might result in incomplete operations or unexpected behaviors. Always be keenly aware of the size requirements.

- **Harness the power of lambdas**: With C++11 and onward, lambdas concisely define quick functions. They are invaluable in dynamic generation, allowing for tailored functions without the verbosity of traditional function definitions.

- **Consider real-world contexts**: Always relate to the problem at hand. If you're populating a container to simulate real-world data, ensure that your filling and generating techniques mirror realistic scenarios. It's not just about filling containers but filling them with purpose.

To summarize, the ability to effectively fill and generate data in STL containers is a testament to the library's robustness. Whether you're aiming for uniformity with static assignments or seeking the dynamic flair of generated patterns, the STL is well-equipped to handle your needs. As we progress toward more intricate manipulations in the coming sections, always remember that data is the heart of your application. How you shape and nurture it often determines the rhythm and pulse of your programs.

Removing and replacing in STL containers

In data manipulation using the C++ STL, we often find ourselves adding or viewing elements and engaging in curating them. As we peel the layers of this chapter, the art of *removing and replacing* emerges as an essential skill, striking the perfect balance between retaining the valuable and discarding the redundant. By mastering these operations, you can elevate your proficiency in handling STL containers, enhancing data relevance and overall efficiency.

The essence of removal

When we dive into the rich waters of data storage in the STL, there's an undeniable need for refining. Whether it is the removal of outdated records, anomalies, or any redundancies, the STL has powerful tools to assist you. One can pinpoint specific values or conditions for purging using functions such as erase and remove. For instance, with `std::remove`, it's possible to relocate particular elements to the end of a sequence container, while `erase` can permanently eliminate them. It's this tandem of operations that ensures a seamless cleanup.

Yet, while removal operations are efficient, caution is essential. Mindlessly erasing elements can disturb container continuity and even impact performance. The key is to employ these operations judiciously and be constantly aware of iterator validity and potential reallocations, especially in dynamic containers such as `std::vector`.

Replacement

Imagine having a collection of dated values or placeholder elements, and the need arises to update them. The STL doesn't leave you stranded. Functions such as `std::replace` and `std::replace_if` are your allies in this endeavor. With `std::replace`, you can seamlessly swap old values with new ones throughout your collection. For more complex scenarios, where the replacement criteria aren't just a simple value match, `std::replace_if` steps into the spotlight. `std::replace_if` allows conditions often expressed through lambdas or function objects to dictate the replacement.

For a hands-on example, consider a collection where negative values are deemed errors and need updating. With `std::replace_if`, you can hunt down every negative value and replace it with a default or corrected value, all in a single, elegant line of code.

Let's look at an example of using `std::replace` and `std::replace_if`:

```cpp
#include <algorithm>
#include <iostream>
#include <vector>

int main() {
  std::vector<int> values = {10, -1, 20, -2, 30};

  // Using std::replace to update a specific value
  std::replace(values.begin(), values.end(), -1,
               0); // Replace -1 with 0

  // Using std::replace_if to update based on a condition
```

```
std::replace_if(
    values.begin(), values.end(),
    [](int value) {
      return value < 0;
    },  // Lambda function for condition
    0); // Replace negative values with 0

// Printing the updated collection
for (int value : values) { std::cout << value << " "; }
std::cout << std::endl;

return 0;
}
```

Here is the example output:

```
10 0 20 0 30
```

In this example, we use `std::replace` to find and replace a specific value (-1) with 0. We then use `std::replace_if` with a lambda function to identify negative values and replace them with 0. This example demonstrates the use of `std::replace` for simple, direct replacements and `std::replace_if` for more complex scenarios where a condition (such as identifying negative values) dictates the replacement.

A balancing act

Balancing removal and replacement requires a sense of rhythm and balance. While it is tempting to curate aggressively, sometimes retaining specific data, even if outdated or redundant, can serve as a historical record or a point of reference. Therefore, always approach removal and replacement with a clear objective, ensuring data integrity, relevance, and efficiency aren't compromised.

In this section, we've honed the skill of curating and modifying collections, focusing on removing and replacing them. This process is pivotal, as it balances the retention of valuable data with the elimination of redundancy, enhancing both data relevance and container efficiency. We've explored the strategic use of functions such as `erase` and `remove` for precision in data refinement and the importance of cautious removal to maintain container integrity and performance. We learned about the replacement techniques using `std::replace` and `std::replace_if`, which are instrumental in updating collections, especially when dealing with complex conditions. These tools not only ensure the freshness and accuracy of data but also highlight the flexibility and power of the STL in data manipulation.

Next, we approach swapping and reversing, demonstrating how to efficiently alter the order and positioning of elements within containers, a vital aspect of managing and manipulating data structures in C++.

Swapping and reversing in STL containers

While we have traversed through adding, initializing, and refining our STL containers, there lies an equally intriguing domain where we maneuver and shuffle elements to align with our requirements. This section promises to take you on an expedition, showcasing the capabilities of the STL in repositioning and reshuffling elements while also touching upon intricate manipulations including deduplication and sampling.

Swapping – the art of interchanging

In many real-world scenarios, the need arises to interchange content between containers. Whether for load balancing, data synchronization, or other computational tasks, the STL offers the swap function, an efficient and streamlined mechanism.

For instance, the `std::swap` can be used with almost all STL containers. If you've two `std::vectors` and wish to exchange their contents, `std::swap` does the magic in constant time without any overhead of copying or moving individual elements. This efficiency is derived from the fact that underlying data pointers are swapped, not the actual content.

Reversing – a glimpse from the end

Sometimes, looking at things from a different perspective brings clarity, and the same holds true for data. The STL provides the `std::reverse` algorithm, which inverts the order of elements within a container, offering a fresh view or aiding specific computational needs. Whether analyzing data trends or catering to a reverse chronological requirement, `std::reverse` ensures your containers can flip their sequence in linear time.

Deduplication – singling out the unique

As our data grows, so does the likelihood of redundancies. However, the STL is well prepared to tackle such situations. The `std::unique` algorithm helps remove consecutive duplicates in a sorted sequence. While it does not delete the duplicates directly, it repositions them to the end of the container, making it convenient to erase them if needed. When paired with `std::sort`, `std::unique` becomes a potent tool in ensuring that your container retains only singular instances of every element.

Sampling – a slice of the whole

On occasions, there's a need to sample a subset from a more extensive collection. While the STL does not provide a direct *sample* function, one can derive a sample with a combination of other tools, like random shuffle algorithms. By randomly shuffling and then selecting the first n elements, you get a representative sample that can be used for testing, analysis, or any other purpose.

Swapping, reversing, deduplication, and sampling are just glimpses into the expansive capabilities of the STL. They represent the dynamic nature of data and the myriad ways we might need to interact with it. As you continue your journey, remember that the STL is more than just tools and functions; it's a suite designed to move, mold, and manage your data efficiently.

Best practices

Let's review optimal ways of implementing STL algorithms to ensure efficiency, maintain data integrity, and recognize the most apt methods suitable for diverse use cases.

- **Choose the right algorithm**: One size does not fit all. A quintessential practice is to ascertain the selection of the correct algorithm for the right task. Study the properties, strengths, and weaknesses of each algorithm before deciding. For instance, `std::sort` is versatile but may not be optimal for partially sorted sequences, where `std::partial_sort` or `std::stable_sort` may prevail.

- **Prefer algorithms over hand-written loops**: When confronted with tasks like searching or sorting, favor STL algorithms over hand-written loops as they are optimized and tested extensively, rendering them more reliable and often faster.

- **Use const correctness**: Ensure you use `const` wherever possible. It maintains data integrity and provides better interface insights, avoiding accidental modifications.

- **Leverage safe algorithms**: Many STL algorithms have safer counterparts that prevent unexpected behaviors. For example, `std::copy_n` ensures no out-of-bound accesses compared to `std::copy`.

- **Discern between algorithm types**: The STL provides diverse algorithms catering to different needs—mutating, non-mutating, and removing. Recognize the type needed for your task. For instance, if the intention is not to modify the container, opt for non-mutating algorithms such as `std::count`.

- **Identify specific needs**: Evaluate your requirements meticulously. If you need to traverse a list and make modifications based on some conditions, algorithms such as `std::transform` would be more suited than `std::for_each`.

- **Utilize reserve for vectors**: When using vectors, and the size is known beforehand, use `std::vector::reserve` to preallocate memory. This practice avoids unnecessary reallocations, enhancing performance.

- **Use appropriate data structures**: Each data structure has its pros and cons. Selecting the right one, such as `std::set` for frequent lookups, can significantly optimize performance.

- **Embrace move semantics**: In situations involving heavy objects, opt for move semantics to avoid deep copies and enhance performance. Algorithms such as `std::move` help in achieving this.

Summary

This chapter covered the essential techniques for altering and shaping data within STL containers. We began by understanding the nuances of copying and moving semantics in the STL, learning to make deliberate choices between copying versus moving elements depending on the context to optimize performance and resource management. We then explored RVO, a technique for optimizing compilers that removes redundant object copying.

We then examined the methods for filling and generating container contents, which are vital to efficiently initializing and modifying large datasets. We covered the mechanisms for removing and replacing elements within containers, balancing the need for data integrity with performance. The chapter also introduced the operations of swapping and reversing elements, deduplication to eliminate duplicates, and sampling to create representative subsets of data. Throughout, we focused on best practices to ensure that these operations are executed with precision and efficiency.

As we build more complex programs, we frequently encounter the need to manipulate large data sets. Proficiency in these operations enables the creation of more sophisticated and performant applications, making the information valuable and vital for modern C++ programming.

In the next chapter, we will focus on basic and advanced numeric operations such as generating sequences, summing elements, and working with adjacent differences and inner products. We will also look at operations on sorted ranges, consolidating our understanding of how to apply STL algorithms to numerical data, thereby enhancing our toolkit for algorithmic problem-solving in C++. This next chapter will continue to build on the foundation laid by previous chapters, ensuring a cohesive and comprehensive understanding of the STL's capabilities.

13

Numeric and Range -Based Operations

In this chapter, you will uncover the potential of the powerful numeric and sorting operations of the C++ **Standard Template Library** (**STL**). These functions breathe life into sequences, making tasks such as accumulation, transformation, and querying using sorted ranges a breeze. Readers will gain insights into elementary and advanced numeric operations and discover the utility of working with sorted collections. When paired with best practices, this chapter ensures developers have a robust toolset to optimize, parallelize, and handle numeric data with finesse.

This chapter will cover the following main topics:

- Basic numeric operations
- Advanced numeric operations
- Operations on sorted ranges
- Best practices

Technical requirements

The code in this chapter can be found on GitHub:

https://github.com/PacktPublishing/Data-Structures-and-Algorithms-with-the-CPP-STL

Basic numeric operations

Unearthing the power of the C++ STL's numeric functions is a refreshing experience. In this section, we'll dive deep into the foundational numeric operations. By mastering these, you'll unlock the capability to generate sequences, compute comprehensive summaries, and efficiently execute sophisticated operations on contiguous elements. So, buckle up, and let's get started!

Generating sequences with std::iota

The first treasure we're going to unearth is `std::iota`. It's a simple yet powerful tool in the numeric operations chest. `std::iota` fills a range with a sequence of consecutive values. Starting from an initial value, it assigns increasing values to subsequent elements in the range. Here, you can see that `std::itoa` fills a vector with five consecutive integers, starting with 1:

```
std::vector<int> vec(5);
std::iota(vec.begin(), vec.end(), 1);
// vec now holds: {1, 2, 3, 4, 5}
```

This function is a boon when you want a container to hold many contiguous sequences of numbers without manually inputting each one. Consider a scenario where you want a `std::vector` to hold timesteps for a constructive simulation:

```
#include <iostream>
#include <numeric>
#include <vector>

int main() {

  const int numTimeSteps = 100;

  std::vector<double> timeSteps(numTimeSteps);

  // Generate a sequence of time steps using std::iota
  double timeStep = 0.01; // Time step size
  std::iota(timeSteps.begin(), timeSteps.end(), 0);

  // Scale the time steps to represent actual time
  for (double &t : timeSteps) { t *= timeStep; }

  // Now, timeSteps contains a sequence of time points for
  // simulation

  // Simulate a simple system over time (e.g., particle
  // movement)
  for (const double t : timeSteps) {
    // Simulate the system's behavior at time t
    // ...
    std::cout << "Time: " << t << std::endl;
  }

  return 0;
}
```

Here is the example output:

```
Time:0
Time: 0.01
Time: 0.02
Time: 0.03
Time: 0.04
Time: 0.05
...
```

In this example, std::iota is used to generate a sequence of time steps, which can be used to model the behavior of a system over time. While this is a simplified example, in real-world applications, you can use std::iota as a foundation for more complex simulations and modeling scenarios, such as physics simulations, financial modeling, or scientific research.

std::iota helps create a time series or discrete event timeline, which can be a fundamental component in various computational simulations and modeling tasks. Its value becomes more apparent when integrated into larger, more complex systems where time sequencing or indexing is crucial.

Summing elements with std::accumulate

Say you have a sequence of numbers and wish to find their sum (or maybe a product). Enter std::accumulate. This algorithm is primarily used to compute the sum over a range of elements. Let's look at the following simple example in action:

```cpp
std::vector<int> vec = {1, 2, 3, 4, 5};
int sum = std::accumulate(vec.begin(), vec.end(), 0);
// sum will be 15
```

It is primarily used to compute the sum of a range of elements, but its power doesn't stop there. With its flexible design, std::accumulate can also be employed for other operations, such as finding products or concatenating strings. By providing a custom binary operation, its applications are broadened significantly. Here is a simple example of how std::accumulate can be used with strings:

```cpp
#include <iostream>
#include <numeric>
#include <string>
#include <vector>

int main() {

  std::vector<std::string> words = {"Hello", ", ", "world",
                                    "!"};

  std::string concatenated = std::accumulate(
```

```
        words.begin(), words.end(), std::string(""),
        [](const std::string &x, const std::string &y) {
          return x + y;
        });

    std::cout << "Concatenated string: " << concatenated
              << std::endl;

    return 0;
}
```

Here is the example output:

Concatenated string: Hello, world!

With some creativity, `std::accumulate` can become a versatile tool in your algorithmic toolbox.

Adjacent elements and their interactions with std::adjacent_ difference

Sometimes, we're interested in individual elements and pairs of adjacent elements. The STL has got your back here with `std::adjacent_difference`.

`std::adjacent_difference` calculates the difference between an element and its predecessor and stores it in another sequence. This operation is beneficial in tasks such as computing discrete derivatives.

The following code demonstrates the usage of `std::adjacent_difference`:

```
std::vector<int> vec = {2, 4, 6, 8, 10};
std::vector<int> result(5);
std::adjacent_difference(vec.begin(), vec.end(), result.begin());
// result holds: {2, 2, 2, 2, 2}
```

Not just for differences, you can pass custom binary operations to `std::adjacent_difference` to achieve varied results, such as ratios. Let's look at the following example:

```
#include <iostream>
#include <numeric>
#include <vector>

int main() {
  std::vector<double> values = {8.0, 16.0, 64.0, 256.0,
                                4096.0};

  // Create a vector to store the calculated ratios
```

```cpp
std::vector<double> ratios(values.size());

// Write a lambda to use in adjacent_difference
auto lambda = [](double x, double y) {
  if (x == 0.0) {
    // Handle division by zero for the first element
    return 0.0;
  } else {
    // Calculate the ratio between y and x
    return y / x;
  }
};

// Calculate the ratios between consecutive elements
std::adjacent_difference(values.begin(), values.end(),
                         ratios.begin(), lambda);

// The first element in the ratios vector is 0.0 because
//there's no previous element

// Print the calculated ratios for the remaining elements
std::cout << "Ratios between consecutive elements:\n";

for (size_t i = 1; i < ratios.size(); ++i) {
  std::cout << "Ratio " << i << ": " << ratios[i]
            << "\n";
}

return 0;
}
```

Here is the example output:

```
Ratios between consecutive elements:
Ratio 1: 0.5
Ratio 2: 0.25
Ratio 3: 0.25
Ratio 4: 0.0625
```

Inner products with std::inner_product

This function is a marvel for those who've dabbled in linear algebra. `std::inner_product` calculates the dot product of two ranges. As you might recall, the dot product is the sum of the products of corresponding pairs from two sequences. Let's look at how to compute the dot product of two vectors:

```
std::vector<int> vec1 = {1, 2, 3};
std::vector<int> vec2 = {4, 5, 6};
int product = std::inner_product(vec1.begin(), vec1.end(),
                                 vec2.begin(), 0);
// product will be 32 (because 1*4 + 2*5 + 3*6 = 32)
```

`std::inner_product` isn't just limited to integers or plain multiplication. Custom binary operations can be tailored to work on different types and operations.

Here are some real-world examples to demonstrate that `std::inner_product` can work with custom binary operations tailored to different types and operations beyond just integers and plain multiplication:

- **Calculating weighted average**: You can use `std::inner_product` to calculate the weighted average of elements in two containers, where one container holds values, and the other container holds the corresponding weights. The custom binary operation would perform the element-wise multiplication of the values and weights and then sum them up to find the weighted average.

- **Financial portfolio valuation**: Suppose you have a financial portfolio with different assets, each having a price and quantity. You can use `std::inner_product` with a custom binary operation to calculate the portfolio's total value by multiplying the asset prices by their respective quantities and summing them up.

- **Vector dot product**: In a 3D graphics application, you might need to calculate the dot product of two 3D vectors, which involves multiplying their corresponding components and summing the results. `std::inner_product` can be used with a custom binary operation for this purpose.

- **Matrix multiplication**: In linear algebra, matrix multiplication involves multiplying the rows and columns of two matrices and summing the results to obtain a new matrix. `std::inner_product` can be adapted with a custom binary operation to perform matrix multiplication efficiently.

- **Complex number operations**: You can use `std::inner_product` to perform complex number operations, such as calculating the inner product of two complex vectors or finding the sum of the squares of complex numbers. The custom binary operation would be tailored to complex number arithmetic.

- **String concatenation**: If you have a vector of strings and want to concatenate them into a single string, you can use `std::inner_product` with a custom binary operation that concatenates strings. This allows you to join a collection of strings efficiently.

- **Color blending in image processing**: In image processing, color blending operations involve combining pixel values from two images using a specific blending formula. `std::inner_product` can be adapted with a custom binary operation to perform color blending based on the desired algorithm.

These examples illustrate that `std::inner_product` is a versatile algorithm that can be customized for various types and operations. This makes it useful in many real-world applications beyond simple integer multiplication.

In this section, we have seen that the basic numeric operations provided by the C++ STL pave the way for the efficient computation, generation, and manipulation of sequences. They transform how developers approach problems, allowing for swift and effective solutions. As we've seen, these algorithms are versatile and, with a pinch of creativity, can be adapted to a myriad of tasks.

With these tools in your utility belt, you're now equipped to generate sequences, compute quick summaries, and perform intricate operations on consecutive elements.

Advanced numeric operations

In order to take our journey with the numeric operations of the C++ STL a step further, let's look at the advanced numerical procedures that elevate data handling and make parallelism and concurrency allies in the pursuit of performance.

Remember our discussion about generating sequences and computing summaries? Well, imagine supercharging these operations to process enormous volumes of data efficiently by harnessing the power of multiple processors. This is precisely where advanced numeric operations shine. Parallel algorithms, introduced in C++17, provide the means to achieve this, ensuring our computations are both swift and efficient, even in concurrent environments.

When dealing with vast datasets, sequential processing often doesn't cut it. Take the example of summing up a large vector of numbers. Doing it in a straight line gets the job done but might not be the quickest. However, the operation can be sped up significantly by splitting the data and working on chunks concurrently. This is the essence of parallel algorithms, and functions such as `std::reduce` exemplify this. Instead of sequentially accumulating values, `std::reduce` can accumulate subtotals in parallel and then combine them, offering a significant boost in performance for large datasets.

To see this in action, let's calculate the sum of all numbers in a large vector in parallel:

```
#include <execution>
#include <iostream>
#include <numeric>
#include <vector>

int main() {
  // Create a large vector of numbers
```

```
   const int dataSize = 1000000;
   std::vector<int> numbers(dataSize);

   // Initialize the vector with some values (e.g., 1 to
   // dataSize)
   std::iota(numbers.begin(), numbers.end(), 1);

   // Calculate the sum of the numbers in parallel
   int parallelSum = std::reduce(
       std::execution::par, numbers.begin(), numbers.end());

   std::cout << "Parallel Sum: " << parallelSum
             << std::endl;
   return 0;
}
```

Here is the example output:

```
Parallel Sum: 1784293664
```

Diving into parallel operations requires a nuanced approach. While the promise of speed is tempting, one must be cautious. Parallelism introduces challenges such as ensuring thread safety and managing data races. Thankfully, the STL offers a remedy through execution policies. By specifying an execution policy, such as `std::execution::par`, when invoking an algorithm, we can direct it to run in parallel. Additionally, there's `std::execution::par_unseq` for parallel and vectorized execution, ensuring even greater throughput.

Speaking of transformation, let's look into `std::transform_reduce`. This is a fusion of `std::transform` and `std::reduce`. It applies a transformation function to each range element and reduces the results into a single value, which can be parallelized. For instance, if we had a vector of numbers and wanted to square each element and then sum up the squared values, `std::transform_reduce` would be our go-to, especially when dealing with a substantial amount of data.

Let's see how we can use `std::transform_reduce` to square each element of a vector and then sum up the squared values:

```
#include <algorithm>
#include <execution>
#include <iostream>
#include <numeric>
#include <vector>

int main() {
  const long int dataSize = 1000;
  std::vector<long int> numbers(dataSize);
```

```
    std::iota(numbers.begin(), numbers.end(), 1);

    // Use std::transform_reduce to square each element and
    // sum them up in parallel
    long int parallelSumOfSquares = std::transform_reduce(
        std::execution::par, numbers.begin(), numbers.end(),
        0, // Initial value for the accumulation
        std::plus<long int>(),
        [](long int x) { return x * x; });

    std::cout << "Parallel Sum of Squares:"
              << parallelSumOfSquares << "\n";
    return 0;
}
```

Here is the example output:

Parallel Sum of Squares: 333833500

Another feather in the cap of advanced operations is the `std::inclusive_scan` and `std::exclusive_scan` duo. These are powerful tools for generating prefix sums. `std::inclusive_scan` includes the ith input element in the ith sum, whereas `std::exclusive_scan` doesn't. Like their fellow advanced numeric operations, they, too, can be supercharged with parallel execution for heightened performance.

Important note

A **prefix sum**, also known as a **scan** operation, is a computational operation that generates an output array or sequence from an input array or sequence by calculating the cumulative sum of elements up to a specific position. In other words, for each element at index i in the input sequence, the corresponding element in the output sequence contains the sum of all elements from index 0 to i in the input sequence.

Parallel operations can be resource-intensive. It's essential to ensure that the hardware can handle the parallelism and that the amount of data is large enough to justify the overhead of concurrent execution. Additionally, always be vigilant about potential pitfalls such as data races or deadlocks. The key is constantly weighing the pros and cons, analyzing the specific requirements, and choosing the most suitable approach.

Operations on sorted ranges

The allure of sorting isn't just about placing elements for the sake of neatness. Instead, it is about the power it grants us in subsequent operations—streamlined navigation, efficient querying, and enhanced manipulation capabilities. For C++ developers, understanding operations on sorted ranges is like acquiring a new set of superpowers. Armed with the C++ STL's tools for these sorted sequences, the world of efficient algorithmic operations becomes an open field, ready for exploration.

So, what's the big deal about having sorted ranges? Consider the difference between looking for a book in a disordered pile versus finding it on a neatly organized shelf. When the data are sorted, algorithms can take shortcuts, such as dividing and conquering, leading to logarithmic rather than linear-time complexities.

A primary technique leveraged for sorted ranges is **binary search**. In C++, `std::lower_bound` and `std::upper_bound` are your go-to functions for this purpose. The former finds the first position where a value should be inserted to maintain the order, while the latter identifies the last suitable spot. Together, they can determine the range of entries equivalent to a given value. If you've ever marveled at the rapidity with which some applications return search results, binary search techniques such as these are often to thank.

Continuing on the topic of queries, `std::equal_range` steps in as a combination of the aforementioned functions, returning both the lower and upper bounds of a value in a sorted range; if you just need a straightforward check, `std::binary_search` tells you if an element exists in the sorted range. These tools simplify querying, making it both swift and precise.

However, operations on sorted ranges aren't confined to searches. Set operations, reminiscent of our elementary math lessons, come alive with sorted data. If you've two sorted sequences and wish to determine their common elements, `std::set_intersection` is the tool for the job. For those elements that belong to one sequence but not to the other, turn to `std::set_difference`. If you're in the mood to combine the elements of two sequences while maintaining the sort order, `std::set_union` stands ready. Last but not least, for finding elements unique to each sequence, `std::set_symmetric_difference` serves the purpose.

Imagine the power that these operations grant. Comparing two large datasets to find commonalities or differences is a frequent requirement in many applications, from databases to data analytics. By working on sorted ranges, these operations become feasible and efficient.

Sorted operations presume, quite reasonably, that the data is sorted. If this invariant isn't maintained, the results can be unpredictable. So, ensuring the sort order is paramount before diving into these operations. Thankfully, with functions such as `std::is_sorted`, one can verify the sorted nature of a range before venturing further.

Let's pull all of these concepts together into a quick example of how they can be used:

```cpp
#include <algorithm>
#include <iostream>
#include <vector>

int main() {
  std::vector<int> d = {10, 20, 30, 40, 50,
```

```
                         60, 70, 80, 90};
int tgt = 40;
auto lb = std::lower_bound(d.begin(), d.end(), tgt);
auto ub = std::upper_bound(d.begin(), d.end(), tgt);

bool exists =
    std::binary_search(d.begin(), d.end(), tgt);

std::vector<int> set1 = {10, 20, 30, 40, 50};
std::vector<int> set2 = {30, 40, 50, 60, 70};
std::vector<int> intersection(
    std::min(set1.size(), set2.size()));

auto it = std::set_intersection(set1.begin(), set1.end(),
                                set2.begin(), set2.end(),
                                intersection.begin());

std::vector<int> difference(
    std::max(set1.size(), set2.size()));

auto diffEnd = std::set_difference(
    set1.begin(), set1.end(), set2.begin(), set2.end(),
    difference.begin());
bool isSorted = std::is_sorted(d.begin(), d.end());

std::cout << "Lower Bound:"
          << std::distance(d.begin(), lb) << "\n";
std::cout << "Upper Bound:"
          << std::distance(d.begin(), ub) << "\n";
std::cout << "Exists: " << exists << "\n";

std::cout << "Intersection: ";
for (auto i = intersection.begin(); i != it; ++i)
  std::cout << *i << " ";
std::cout << "\n";

std::cout << "Difference: ";
for (auto i = difference.begin(); i != diffEnd; ++i)
  std::cout << *i << " ";
std::cout << "\n";

std::cout << "Is Sorted: " << isSorted << "\n";
return 0;
}
```

Here is the example output:

```
Lower Bound: 3
Upper Bound: 4
Exists: 1
Intersection: 30 40 50
Difference: 10 20
Is Sorted: 1
```

It is evident from these examples that operations on sorted ranges unlock a realm of possibilities. They exemplify the blend of mathematical theory and practical coding, creating a robust framework for developers to navigate, query, and manipulate data with unparalleled efficiency. As we move forward, we'll explore the best practices associated with numeric and range-based operations, ensuring that as we harness their power, we do so with precision, efficiency, and finesse. The journey of discovery and mastery continues!

Best practices

The following best practices are associated with numeric and range-based operations:

- **Selecting the most suitable algorithm based on data attributes**: Effectively using the numeric and range-based operations from the C++ STL requires more than just knowing their functionalities; it's crucial to discern when and where to employ them to ensure optimal performance and data preservation. Different datasets exhibit varying properties such as size, distribution, and repetition frequency. These properties can influence the performance of certain operations. For example, `std::stable_sort` may prove more efficient than other sorting methods for a nearly sorted dataset. Thus, understanding your dataset's characteristics is pivotal when deciding appropriate operations.

- **Maintaining data integrity in sorted operations**: Preserving data integrity is paramount, especially in processes that rely on sorted datasets. Many range-based operations, such as binary searches and set operations, presuppose the data range is already sorted. Implementing these operations without this assurance might lead to unreliable outcomes or errors. It's a misconception to assume that once data is sorted, it remains sorted indefinitely. Simple modifications can alter the dataset's order. Hence, verifying the order with `std::is_sorted` before proceeding with sorted operations is recommended.

- **Using parallel algorithms judiciously**: With the growing emphasis on concurrency, parallel algorithms present an attractive option to boost performance. The C++ STL provides parallel versions of many standard algorithms. While these algorithms capitalize on multiple CPU cores to deliver faster results, they can also introduce challenges, especially regarding thread safety. A primary concern in concurrent programming is a shared mutable state. Issues arise when multiple threads attempt to simultaneously modify the same data. To use parallel algorithms safely, it's critical that threads either work on distinct data sections or employ synchronization tools, such as mutexes, to manage simultaneous data modifications.

Furthermore, parallelism isn't always the answer. The overhead from managing multiple threads can sometimes negate the benefits of parallel execution, especially for small datasets or straightforward tasks. To determine the effectiveness of parallelism in a given scenario, it's beneficial to profile your code in both sequential and parallel configurations. This assessment aids in choosing the most efficient method.

In this section, we've explored how to choose the right algorithms in the C++ STL based on data properties, emphasizing the importance of dataset characteristics such as size and distribution. Selecting an appropriate algorithm, such as `std::stable_sort`, for nearly sorted data is crucial for optimal performance. We also highlighted the necessity of maintaining data order for sorted operations, using tools such as `std::is_sorted` to ensure data integrity. Parallel algorithms were discussed, focusing on their benefits and complexities, such as thread safety. The key takeaway is that parallelism, while powerful, requires careful consideration, especially regarding dataset size and task complexity.

Summary

In this chapter, we have immersed ourselves in the versatile world of algorithms provided by the C++ STL that handle numeric sequences and operate on sorted ranges. We started with basic numeric operations, such as generating sequences with `std::iota`, summing elements with accumulate, and exploring the interactions of adjacent elements with `std::adjacent_difference`. The chapter explored more complex tasks, such as computing inner products with `std::inner_product`.

These operations are essential in data handling and analysis within STL containers, facilitating tasks from simple accumulations to complex transformations. The information presented is crucial for developers, as it enhances efficiency and efficacy when performing numerical computations and prepares them for high-performance scenarios, especially when dealing with large datasets.

The chapter also covered advanced numeric operations, which are particularly beneficial in parallel computing environments. We learned how to employ parallel algorithms for data transformation and summarization, ensuring high performance in concurrent environments. Operations on sorted ranges were explored, illustrating the efficiency of binary search techniques and the functionality of set operations, which are significantly optimized by the data's sorted nature.

In the next chapter, we will venture into ranges, representing a more contemporary approach to sequences in C++. We will explore why there has been a shift toward range-based operations, understand the essence and power of these modern STL components, and explore their composability for sorting and searching algorithms. This upcoming chapter will empower readers with the knowledge to embrace the full potential of the modern STL, making informed decisions on when and how to apply these new tools in their C++ programming endeavors.

14

Permutations, Partitions, and Heaps

This chapter explores some of the most essential yet often overlooked aspects of the algorithmic library of the C++ **Standard Template Library** (**STL**). The chapter sheds light on sequence organization through partitioning, sequence variation via permutations, and the fascinating world of heap-based operations. These operations are the backbone of many advanced algorithms and data structures. By understanding and mastering them, developers can enhance the efficiency of their applications, optimize data handling, and ensure the integrity of their datasets.

In this chapter, we will cover the following topics related to STL:

- Partitioning
- Permutations
- Heap operations
- Best practices

Technical requirements

The code in this chapter can be found on GitHub:

```
https://github.com/PacktPublishing/Data-Structures-and-Algorithms-
with-the-CPP-STL
```

Partitioning

Partitioning, in its simplest form, is about organizing sequences based on specific criteria, ensuring that all elements for which the requirements hold true precede those for which it does not. It is about segregating data efficiently, optimizing its organization for rapid access, and enhancing computational efficiency.

The C++ STL offers a rich set of algorithms for partitioning tasks. While one might be tempted to use simple loops and conditionals to achieve such tasks, these STL functions are optimized, tested, and designed to offer the best performance. These algorithms are implemented by experts who have a deep understanding of the underlying system, handle the edge cases, and typically take advantage of compiler optimizations and even (potentially) parallelization.

std::partition and its power

One of the most foundational functions in this category is `std::partition`. This function reorganizes elements in a range based on a predicate. It ensures that all elements satisfying the predicate come before those that don't. But here's a vital thing to remember: the order of the elements is not guaranteed to be preserved. If order matters to you, then `std::stable_partition` is your friend. While it may have a slightly higher overhead, it retains the relative order of the elements.

Let's look at an example. Consider a sequence of integers, and suppose you'd like to separate even numbers from odd ones. A call to `std::partition` with an appropriate lambda can swiftly complete the job, as shown in the following code:

```
std::vector<int> numbers = {7, 1471414, 3, 18, 9, 518955};
auto it = std::partition(numbers.begin(), numbers.end(), [](int n) {
return n % 2 == 0; });
```

After this operation, the iterator will iterate over the range of odd numbers.

Checking partitions with std::is_partitioned

Once a range is partitioned, it might be beneficial to ensure that the partitioning holds true, especially in larger systems or when integrating multiple algorithms. Enter `std::is_partitioned`, a handy function that checks whether a range is partitioned based on a given predicate. This can be particularly useful when building upon multiple operations, ensuring that assumptions about data layout hold firm.

The utility of std::partition_point

After partitioning, one might ask, *Where's the dividing line?* That's where `std::partition_point` comes into play. This function returns an iterator pointing to the first element in the newly partitioned range, which does not satisfy the predicate. It assumes the range is partitioned and leverages binary search, ensuring a swift response.

Partitioning beyond basic sequences

While the preceding examples primarily use vectors, partitioning isn't limited to them. One can employ these techniques on arrays, lists, and even more advanced containers. However, it is crucial to remember that the underlying container characteristics, such as random access capability, can influence the efficiency of these operations.

Combining these partitioning functions, one can build efficient, flexible, and highly organized systems that cater to diverse computational needs. Consider the following real-world applications:

- **Sorting algorithms**: `std::is_partitioned` and `std::partition` can be used in various sorting algorithms such as Quicksort and Hoare partitioning. They help in efficiently partitioning elements based on a condition.

- **Searching algorithms**: `std::partition_point` can be used in binary search algorithms. It helps find the first element in a partitioned range that doesn't satisfy a given condition. This can be useful for searching in sorted datasets.

- **Filtering data**: In real-world applications, you often need to filter data based on specific criteria. `std::partition` can efficiently separate elements that meet a condition from those that do not; for example, filtering even and odd numbers from a list.

- **Grouping data**: When working with datasets, you might want to group elements based on specific criteria. `std::partition` can help separate elements into different partitions based on these criteria.

- **Parallel processing**: In parallel programming, you may need to split a dataset into two partitions for parallel processing. `std::partition` can be used to efficiently divide the data based on certain conditions, improving parallelization.

- **Data analysis**: When analyzing data, you may need to separate outliers or anomalies from the primary dataset. `std::partition` can be used to partition the data and then analyze the outliers separately.

- **Game development**: In game development, you might use partitioning to separate visible objects from hidden ones for rendering optimization.

- **Database queries**: When querying a database, you can use partitioning to separate the data that matches specific filter conditions from the rest of the dataset.

- **Resource management**: In resource management scenarios, such as memory allocation, you can use partitioning to efficiently segregate used and unused memory blocks efficiently. As developers, we constantly grapple with diverse data and its efficient handling. Partitioning offers a structured way to handle this, enabling optimized organization and rapid data access. While seemingly simple, it forms the backbone of many advanced algorithms.

By mastering partitioning with the STL, one not only enhances individual operations but elevates the overall efficiency and structure of applications. As we progress to permutations and heap operations in subsequent sections, remember the foundational importance of efficient data organization.

Permutations

A journey into permutations is a journey into how the elements of a sequence can be arranged. With the vastness of the sequences and datasets handled by developers today, the ability to organize, shuffle, rotate, and switch elements around becomes a fascinating exercise and a critical requirement for many applications. The C++ STL, with its power-packed permutation algorithms, offers a path to unlock this potential effortlessly. In this section, we will learn how to generate, manipulate, and rotate permutations, along with practical examples.

Generating permutations with std::next_permutation

Imagine listing all possible permutations of a dataset, analyzing them, and perhaps using them for a brute-force solution to a problem. The STL provides `std::next_permutation` for this exact purpose. Given a range, this function rearranges its elements to the next lexicographically greater permutation. When all permutations have been exhausted, the function returns `false`, offering a clear signal to the developer.

Consider a simple sequence: {1, 2, 3}. With successive calls to `std::next_permutation`, one can generate {1, 3, 2}, {2, 1, 3}, and so forth until the sequence loops back, as illustrated by the following code:

```cpp
std::vector<int> data = {1, 2, 3};
do {
  for (int num : data) { std::cout << num << " "; }
  std::cout << "\n";
} while (std::next_permutation(data.begin(), data.end()));
```

Predecessor permutations with std::prev_permutation

Sometimes, looking backward is essential, exploring permutations that precede the current arrangement. The twin to our previously discussed function, `std::prev_permutation`, does just that. It transforms the sequence into its immediate lexicographically smaller permutation.

Shuffling elements randomly with std::shuffle

While structured permutations have their place, there are times when randomness is the order of the day.

Enter `std::shuffle`, an algorithm that rearranges elements in a completely random order. Paired with a robust random number generator, it ensures true randomness, which is crucial for many applications.

Real-world uses for `std::shuffle` include the following:

- **Card games and board games**: In card games such as poker or board games such as chess, you often need to shuffle a deck of cards or randomize the starting positions of pieces. `std::shuffle` can be used to achieve this randomness.

- **Quiz or test questions**: When presenting multiple-choice questions in a quiz or test, it's essential to randomize the order of answer choices to avoid bias. `std::shuffle` can be used to shuffle the answer choices.

- **Random sampling**: When selecting, if you need to select a random subset of elements from a larger dataset, you can shuffle the dataset using `std::shuffle`, and then pick the first N elements.

- **Game development**: In video game development, you might want to randomize the spawning locations of enemies or the order of power-ups. `std::shuffle` can help introduce randomness into the game.

- **Music playlists**: When creating a playlist of songs or videos, you can use `std::shuffle` to randomize the order of tracks, providing variety to the listeners.

- **Testing and debugging**: In testing and debugging scenarios, you might want to introduce randomness to simulate different conditions. `std::shuffle` can be used to shuffle inputs or events to test different code paths.

- **Machine learning and data science**: When training machine learning models or conducting experiments in data science, you may need to shuffle the dataset to ensure that the model doesn't learn any order-related biases.

- **Randomized algorithms**: In computer science, some algorithms are randomized for various purposes, such as Quicksort's pivot selection. `std::shuffle` can be used to generate the randomization needed for such algorithms.

- **Lottery and gambling simulations**: In simulations or applications related to lotteries or gambling, you can use `std::shuffle` to simulate random outcomes or the shuffling of cards or dice.

- **Cryptographic applications**: While `std::shuffle` is unsuitable for cryptographic purposes, the concept of shuffling is crucial in cryptographic algorithms for purposes such as card-shuffling functionality for secure card games.

Rotating sequences with std::rotate

Not all permutations involve intricate rearrangements. Sometimes, it is about simple rotations. `std::rotate` moves elements so that the chosen element becomes the new first element. It's like turning a dial where the numbers rotate around a central point.

The following is a simple example demonstrating the use of `std::rotate`:

```
std::vector<int> nums = {1, 2, 3, 4, 5};
std::rotate(nums.begin(), nums.begin() + 2, nums.end());
// nums now holds {3, 4, 5, 1, 2}
```

Let us now look at the wide range of real-world applications of `std::rotate`:

- **Text editors and word processors**: When users perform text editing operations such as moving a block of text or shifting paragraphs, `std::rotate` can be used to reposition the text efficiently.

- **Game development**: In game development, you might need to cycle through textures or images used for animation. `std::rotate` can be used to swap or cycle image resources.

- **Scheduling and time management**: In scheduling applications, you might want to shift a schedule by rotating the appointments or tasks for a day or a week to accommodate changes.

- **Circular buffers**: Circular buffers, often used in embedded systems and data streaming applications, employ `std::rotate` to efficiently manage the movement of data in and out of the buffer.

- **Data encryption**: In some encryption algorithms, data bits are shifted or rotated as part of the encryption process. `std::rotate` can be used for such bit manipulation.

- **Sorting algorithms**: Some sorting algorithms, such as Timsort, use `std::rotate` as part of the sorting process to handle partially ordered data efficiently.

- **Image processing**: In image processing, you might need to rotate pixel values to perform image transformations or manipulations.

- **Numerical analysis**: In numerical analysis and scientific computing, `std::rotate` can be used to shift elements in vectors or arrays when solving equations or performing iterative calculations.

- **Memory management**: In memory management scenarios, you might need to shift memory blocks to optimize memory allocation and defragmentation.

- **Algorithm optimization**: In algorithm design, rotating elements can help improve the efficiency of certain operations by reducing the number of swaps or data movements.

- **Game puzzles**: In puzzle games such as the Rubik's Cube, `std::rotate` can be used to simulate the rotation of puzzle pieces.

- **Data visualization**: In data visualization tools, `std::rotate` can be employed to create animated effects by rotating or shifting data points.

Permutations with the STL bring forth an exciting blend of mathematical theory and practical computing. They embody the spirit of reorganization, viewing data from different perspectives and ensuring no stone (or sequence!) is left unturned. As we delve deeper into heaps and their operations in the following sections, remember this power of permutation, which can transform and re-envision sequences in countless ways.

Heap operations

The journey into algorithmic wonders would be incomplete without exploring heaps. **Heaps** are unique structures prioritizing data in a specific order, ascending or descending. At the heart of a heap lies its promise: the element with the highest (or lowest) priority will always be at the top. With the C++ STL, managing heaps becomes intuitive, lending efficiency and power to applications requiring priority-based operations.

Constructing heaps with std::make_heap

Creating a heap from a random data collection is the first step in the process. With `std::make_heap`, one can swiftly transform any sequence into a max heap, where the largest element is at the beginning. The following code demonstrates the use of `std::make_heap`:

```
std::vector<int> v = {3, 7, 2, 5, 1, 7, 4, 9};
std::make_heap(v.begin(), v.end());
```

With the simple call above, our `v` vector now holds a valid max heap. Based on the given comparator or default comparison, the most significant element will always be at the front.

Adding and removing elements – std::push_heap and std::pop_heap

With heaps, the operations aren't just about looking at the top element. Adding and removing data from the heap is fundamental. When a new element is added to the underlying sequence, `std::push_heap` ensures it is placed appropriately in the heap, as shown in the following code:

```
v.push_back(8);  // Add element to vector
std::push_heap(v.begin(), v.end());  // Re-adjust the heap
```

Conversely, to remove the top element, `std::pop_heap` is used. This function doesn't erase the element but moves it to the end of the sequence, making it convenient for removal, as illustrated in the following code:

```
std::pop_heap(v.begin(), v.end());
v.pop_back();  // Remove the former top element
```

Adding and removing elements from a heap is the core of heap-based operations. Now, let's move on to something a bit more advanced: heap-based sorting.

Heap-based sorting – the power of std::sort_heap

Heaps are more than just priority management. Their structure allows for an efficient sorting mechanism. `std::sort_heap` turns the heap into a sorted range in ascending order, as shown in the following code:

```
std::sort_heap(v.begin(), v.end());
```

It's worth noting that heap-based sorting can be especially effective when dealing with datasets where insertion and extraction operations are frequent, making it a valuable tool in a developer's toolkit.

Checking heap validity with std::is_heap

Ensuring that a sequence maintains its heap properties is crucial. `std::is_heap` offers a quick validity check, returning `true` if the given range forms a heap and `false` otherwise, as shown in the following code:

```
bool isHeap = std::is_heap(v.begin(), v.end());
```

This function is especially valuable when working with complex sequences, ensuring data operations haven't disrupted the heap structure.

The significance of heaps in today's computing

Heaps are integral in modern-day computing, from task scheduling to network packet management. Their structure facilitates efficient priority management, making them indispensable in scenarios including simulations, event-driven programming, and more.

These heap-based operations can be used in many real-world scenarios:

- **Priority queues**: Heaps are frequently employed to create priority queues, where elements of higher priority are processed ahead of those with lower priority. In C++ STL, the `std::priority_queue` container employs a heap internally to effectively manage the highest-priority element at the fore.

- **Job scheduling**: In job scheduling algorithms, tasks or jobs often have associated priorities or deadlines. A min-heap can be used to prioritize and schedule tasks efficiently.

- **Dijkstra's shortest path algorithm**: Dijkstra's algorithm for finding the shortest path in a weighted graph uses a priority queue implemented with a min-heap to select the next vertex to explore.

- **Huffman coding**: A popular data compression technique, Huffman coding builds a binary tree with characters' frequencies as weights. A min-heap can be used to efficiently merge nodes during tree construction.

- **Heap sort**: Heap sort is a comparison-based sorting algorithm that uses a binary heap data structure to repeatedly extract the maximum (for a max-heap) or minimum (for a min-heap) element from an unsorted array, resulting in a sorted array. It is an in-place sorting algorithm with a time complexity of $O(n \log n)$.

- **Event scheduling**: In discrete event simulation or real-time systems, events often have associated timestamps. A min-heap can be used to schedule and process events in chronological order.

- **Memory management**: Dynamic memory allocation and deallocation in some memory management systems use heaps to efficiently allocate and free memory blocks.

- **Load balancing:** Tasks or processes are distributed among available resources in load balancing algorithms. A min-heap can help manage resource availability and task assignment.

- **Online median calculation**: When processing a continuous stream of data, you can maintain two heaps (a max-heap and a min-heap) to calculate the median of the data efficiently.

- **Merge sorted files**: When merging multiple sorted files or streams, a min-heap can be used to select the smallest element among all available elements, facilitating the merge process.

- **Disk space management**: In file systems, managing free disk space efficiently often involves maintaining a heap of available disk blocks.

- **Job prioritization in print queues**: Print job queues can prioritize print jobs based on various factors such as user priority or document size, which can be efficiently managed using a priority queue implemented with a heap.

The heap operations provided by the C++ STL equip developers with the means to handle priority-driven tasks efficiently. They merge the theoretical elegance of data structures with practical utility. As we transition to best practices in the next section, it is essential to internalize the role heaps play in shaping efficient, responsive, and reliable applications.

Best practices

Navigating permutations, partitions, and heaps offers valuable insights into the capabilities of the C++ STL. These foundational elements can significantly boost application performance and reliability when used effectively. Following best practices is critical to maximizing these benefits and ensuring consistent, optimized data operations. These best practices include the following:

- **Simplify permutation tasks**: Though permutations provide a broad range of sequence variations, it's important not to overcomplicate the process. Choose permutation operations that directly serve the task at hand. For intricate operations, breaking them down can help maintain clarity and focus.

- **Utilize STL permutation functions**: The STL offers convenient functions such as `std::next_permutation` and `std::prev_permutation` to traverse permutations. Utilizing these functions eliminates the need to generate permutations manually and promotes efficient and error-free operations.

- **Optimal partitioning**: A precise and unambiguous predicate is essential when dividing data. Unclear criteria can yield unpredictable partitions and potentially decrease application efficiency. Being familiar with your data's characteristics can aid in effective partitioning. If the data has inherent order or structure, it's advantageous to factor that into the partitioning algorithms to enhance performance and reduce resource use.

- **Maintain comparator consistency**: For heap operations, using comparators consistently is crucial. Any inconsistency in their use can disturb the heap structure and lead to unexpected results. For example, suppose you use one comparator to build a max-heap and switch to a different comparator for extracting elements. In that case, the heap's structure might be disturbed, and you might not get the expected maximum element.

- **Prioritize heap access**: Heaps are optimized for priority-based access. Directly accessing or altering elements can destabilize the heap's structure. Instead, utilize STL functions such as `std::push_heap` and `std::pop_heap` to preserve heap integrity.

- **Choose sorting methods wisely**: Heap-based sorting benefits datasets undergoing regular changes. However, conventional sorting methods such as `std::sort` may be more efficient for more static datasets.

These partitioning, permutation, and heap concepts can significantly improve application performance and reliability. Simplifying permutation tasks to avoid complexity, utilizing STL permutation functions for efficiency, ensuring clear criteria for data partitioning, maintaining comparator consistency for heap operations, prioritizing heap access with appropriate functions, and choosing sorting methods based on the dataset's characteristics and update frequency are all helpful. Following best practices in these areas is essential for maximizing the benefits of the C++ STL and ensuring consistent and optimized data operations in programming.

Summary

Throughout this chapter, we have covered the manipulation of sequences. We explored partitioning techniques, which organize data based on specific predicates, and examined various permutation algorithms that enable reordering elements within a range. We also investigated the heap operations provided by STL, which facilitate priority queue implementations and efficient sorting.

Understanding these operations is essential for developers because they underpin many higher-level algorithms and are foundational to efficient data processing. Mastery of partitioning allows for quick segregation of data, permutations enable the exploration of all possible orderings of a dataset, and heaps provide a means to maintain a collection always sorted by priority. These tools are fundamental for tasks requiring optimized data retrieval, manipulation, and organization.

In the next chapter, we will explore the range concept, which offers a more expressive approach to handling sequences of elements. The chapter will discuss the advantages of range-based operations for sorting and searching algorithms, highlighting their enhanced composability and readability. As we progress into this chapter, we will gain insights into the practical application of these modern techniques, ensuring our continued growth as adept and contemporary C++ developers.

15

STL with Ranges

This chapter discusses the transformative adoption of ranges in C++, marking a paradigm shift from traditional iterators. As an integral facet of modern C++, ranges champion expressive and ergonomic code. Through this chapter, you will grasp the mechanics of utilizing ranges with standard algorithms, achieving cleaner code that's simultaneously intuitive and powerful. By mastering ranges, C++ developers can harness a more compositional and streamlined approach to algorithm application, setting the stage for more maintainable and efficient code bases.

This chapter will cover the following topics:

- Introduction to ranges
- Ranges for sorting algorithms
- Ranges for searching algorithms
- Best practices

Technical requirements

The code in this chapter can be found on GitHub:

https://github.com/PacktPublishing/Data-Structures-and-Algorithms-with-the-CPP-STL

Introduction to ranges

Programming paradigms evolve, and C++ is no exception. As the journey through the vast landscape of the C++ **Standard Template Library** (**STL**) unfolds, it is evident that adaptability and growth have been at their core. One such evolutionary step, which stands out for its expressiveness and efficiency, is the advent of ranges in modern C++. But what exactly are ranges?

Understanding the essence of ranges

Ranges, in the simplest of terms, are an abstraction over sequences of values. Unlike traditional iterators, which typically require pairs of `begin` and `end` to define a sequence, ranges encapsulate this information within a unified entity. This seemingly subtle shift has profound implications, reshaping how we approach algorithms and data manipulations.

At a glance, the following shows the verbose legacy way to sort a vector:

```
std::sort(v.begin(), v.end());
```

However, with ranges, we could express it as follows:

```
std::ranges::sort(v);
```

The beauty lies in the clarity and conciseness. No longer must we juggle multiple iterators; the range elegantly conveys the intent.

Why the shift to ranges?

The evolution from iterators to ranges wasn't just a whimsical design choice; it addressed pressing needs in the C++ community, such as the following:

- **Expressiveness**: The preceding example shows that the code becomes more readable. Expressing algorithms over entire sequences without explicitly mentioning boundary iterators facilitates a more natural, declarative style of coding.

- **Composability**: Ranges enable a more functional approach to programming in C++. This means algorithms can be seamlessly composed, leading to modular and easily understandable code.

- **Error minimization**: By reducing the need to manage individual iterators, there's a lower chance of errors related to mismatched or incorrectly used iterators. This leads to safer and more maintainable code.

A glimpse into range operations

Ranges aren't just about cleaner syntax; they offer a plethora of operations that can transform sequences in expressive ways. Some operations include the following:

- **Filtering**: Easily refine sequences based on certain conditions

- **Transformations**: Modify sequences by applying functions to their elements

- **Concatenation**: Seamlessly join multiple sequences

With ranges, these operations can be chained, leading to code that's both intuitive and powerful. For instance, transforming and filtering a sequence becomes a straightforward task with ranges.

Looking ahead – the power of modern STL

The introduction of ranges in the STL represents a significant stride toward a more expressive and ergonomic C++. As developers embark on this new chapter, they'll find that the familiar operations they have come to rely on have been enhanced and primed for the modern challenges of the software industry.

Ranges in C++ significantly enhance code quality and developer productivity. Ranges offer a more declarative approach to data manipulation, promoting cleaner and more readable code. They enable operations on collections of data without the explicit need to handle iterators or create temporary containers. This abstraction not only reduces boilerplate but also minimizes the likelihood of errors associated with manual iterator management. Furthermore, ranges facilitate lazy evaluation, where computations are deferred until values are actually needed. This can lead to performance improvements, especially in scenarios involving large datasets or complex filtering criteria. Looking ahead, ranges have the potential to revolutionize C++ coding practices by simplifying algorithm applications, enhancing composability, and potentially introducing more opportunities for compiler optimizations. As the C++ language evolves, ranges will likely become integral in writing more efficient, maintainable, and intuitive code.

In this section, we explored the concept of ranges in modern C++, a significant advancement in the C++ STL. Ranges represent an abstraction over sequences, offering a unified way to handle data sequences as opposed to the traditional pair of iterators. This shift to ranges improves code expressiveness, readability, and maintainability. Ranges reduce the need for verbose iterator management, minimizing errors and enhancing code clarity. They support a variety of operations such as filtering, transformations, and concatenation, which can be seamlessly chained for more intuitive and powerful coding. The advent of ranges in C++ marks a step toward more declarative data manipulation, promising improvements in developer productivity and code quality. As C++ continues to evolve, ranges are poised to play a crucial role in shaping more efficient and ergonomic coding practices.

In the following sections, we'll delve deeper into the nuances of ranges, exploring their applications with classic STL algorithms, and uncovering best practices to ensure that they're leveraged to their utmost potential.

Ranges for sorting algorithms

Sorting is a fundamental operation, a bedrock in the vast universe of algorithms. Over the years, the STL has empowered us with robust sorting capabilities. With the introduction of ranges, this power has been augmented by simplifying the syntax and infusing a heightened sense of expressiveness into the mix.

In this section, we will explore how ranges simplify the implementation of sorting algorithms in C++. We will examine how range-based sorting reduces the syntactical overhead and potential errors associated with traditional iterator-based methods. Furthermore, we will discuss how ranges enhance the readability and maintainability of sorting code, making it easier to understand and modify.

Traditional STL sorting – a recap

Before diving into the enhancements brought by ranges, let's quickly recall the conventional STL sorting approach. Traditionally, the `std::sort` function is employed, requiring two iterators marking the beginning and the end of the sequence:

```
std::vector<int> nums = {4, 1, 3, 2};
std::sort(nums.begin(), nums.end());
```

While effective, this approach leaves room for enhancement in readability and user-friendliness. To address this, enter the STL's range-based sorting.

Range-based sorting – the basics

Redefining elegance, the range-based `std::ranges::sort` function allows us to pass the sequence to be sorted directly. No fussing with iterators. Given our earlier example, with ranges, the sorting becomes the following:

```
std::vector<int> nums = {4, 1, 3, 2};
std::ranges::sort(nums);
```

The concise nature of range-based sorting makes it a joy to use, reducing potential error avenues and enhancing readability.

Embracing composability in sorting

One of the crown jewels of ranges is their ability to facilitate composability, which shines exceptionally bright in sorting scenarios. Consider the need to sort only a subset of a sequence or the necessity to chain multiple operations before sorting. Ranges cater to such needs seamlessly.

For example, imagine the requirement to sort only the even numbers from a sequence in reverse order. With ranges, this can be expressed in a few lines, harnessing the power of filtering combined with sorting:

```
#include <algorithm>
#include <iostream>
#include <ranges>
#include <vector>

int main() {
  std::vector<int> data = {5, 2, 9, 1, 5, 6, 8, 7, 3, 4};

  // Create a view of the data that filters even numbers
  // and then sorts them
  auto even_sorted =
```

```
        data | std::views::filter([](int x) {
          return x % 2 == 0;
        }) |
        std::views::transform([](int x) { return -x; }) |
        std::ranges::to<std::vector<int>>();

    std::sort(even_sorted.begin(), even_sorted.end());

    // Display the sorted even numbers
    std::cout << "Sorted even numbers: ";

    for (int num : even_sorted) { std::cout << num << " "; }

    std::cout << "\n";
    return 0;
}
```

Here is the example output[1]:

```
Sorted even numbers: -8 -6 -4 -2
```

In this example, vector data contains a sequence of integers. We use a range pipeline to create a view that first filters out the even numbers using `std::views::filter`. Then, we use `std::views::transform` to negate the numbers, allowing them to be sorted in reverse order. Finally, `std::ranges::to` is used to convert the view into a vector. The sorted even numbers are then displayed. This showcases the composability of ranges, allowing for concise and expressive manipulation of data sequences.

The ability to chain operations, leading from filtering to sorting fluidly, exemplifies the compositional strength of ranges.

Advantages beyond syntax – why ranges shine in sorting

Beyond the evident syntactical elegance, using ranges with STL sorting algorithms offers a buffet of benefits, such as the following:

- **Safety**: The encapsulation of `begin` and `end` in a single entity diminishes the risk of mismatched iterators, elevating code safety.

- **Flexibility**: Ranges, coupled with views, provide a dynamic toolkit. Whether sorting with custom comparators or adapting to different data structures, the range-based approach remains consistent and straightforward.

---

1 This example has been tested to work with Visual Studio v17.8.6 but does not yet compile with GCC v13.2 or Clang v17.0.1.

- **Expressive power**: Ranges foster a declarative coding style, wherein the intent of the code stands out. This expressiveness proves invaluable when sorting complex data types or applying multifaceted logic.

The revolution of ranges in sorting

Sorting, an operation as old as programming itself, witnesses a rejuvenation with the introduction of ranges. Combining traditional STL sorting prowess with the modern elegance of ranges can revolutionize our implementations with more intuitive, maintainable, and efficient code.

Ranges have transformed sorting algorithms in modern C++. We have seen the traditional iterator-based approach of STL sorting with the more streamlined and readable range-based approach. The traditional method, using `std::sort` with iterators, is effective but can be improved in terms of readability and user-friendliness. Range-based sorting, using `std::ranges::sort`, simplifies this by allowing direct passing of the sequence, reducing syntactical complexity and potential errors. A key highlight is the composability of ranges, particularly beneficial in sorting scenarios.

The advantages of using ranges in sorting extend beyond syntax. They provide safety by encapsulating the beginning and end of sequences into a single entity, reducing the risk of mismatched iterators. They offer flexibility with dynamic tools for sorting using custom comparators or different data structures. Moreover, ranges enable a declarative coding style, making the code's intent more apparent, especially beneficial for sorting complex data types or applying intricate logic.

The introduction of ranges in C++ has married the traditional strength of STL sorting algorithms with the modern finesse of ranges. This revolution leads to more intuitive, maintainable, and efficient code implementations. The exploration continues in subsequent sections, delving deeper into the interaction of ranges with other STL algorithms for searching and uncovering best practices for their effective utilization.

Ranges for searching algorithms

When delving into the domain of algorithmic searching within the STL, it's evident that the advent of ranges heralds an era of simplified and expressive code. To appreciate this evolution, looking back at the traditional search methods in the STL is essential.

The classic way of searching within a container involved using functions such as `std::find` or `std::find_if`, wherein you'd provide iterators marking the search range:

```
std::vector<int> nums = {1, 2, 3, 4, 5};
auto it = std::find(nums.begin(), nums.end(), 3);
```

Effective? Yes. Optimal in terms of expressiveness and adaptability? Perhaps not.

Finding elegance – range-based searching

The transition to more readable and concise code is evident using the range-based approach. With ranges, searching operations become inherently more declarative, as shown in the following code:

```
std::vector<int> nums = {1, 2, 3, 4, 5};
auto it = std::ranges::find(nums, 3);
```

Beyond mere simplicity, the real power of range-based searching emerges when combined with other range adaptors, opening a gateway to more adaptive and modular code.

Chaining and filtering – the beauty of composability

The elegance of code often lies in its ability to express complex operations in a simple, readable manner. Ranges, with their composability, play a pivotal role in achieving such elegance. Let's consider a nuanced example to understand this better: finding the first three numbers in a sequence that are both prime and greater than a specified value. This task, when approached with traditional STL methods, might involve cumbersome loops and condition checks. However, ranges transform it into an efficient and easily understandable series of operations.

Let's look at an interesting example to illustrate this concept:

```
#include <iostream>
#include <ranges>
#include <vector>

bool is_prime(int number) {
  if (number <= 1) return false;

  for (int i = 2; i * i <= number; i++) {
    if (number % i == 0) return false;
  }

  return true;
}

int main() {
  std::vector<int> nums = {4,  6,  8,  9,  10, 11,
                           13, 15, 17, 19, 23, 25};

  auto prime_greater_than_10 =
      nums |
      std::views::filter([](int n) { return n > 10; }) |
      std::views::filter(is_prime) | std::views::take(3);
```

```
std::cout
    << "First three prime numbers greater than 10: ";

for (int num : prime_greater_than_10) {
  std::cout << num << " ";
}

std::cout << "\n";
return 0;
}
```

Here is the example output:

First three prime numbers greater than 10: 11 13 17

In this example, we start with a nums vector containing a sequence of integers. Using ranges, we chain together three operations:

1. Filtering for numbers greater than 10: `std::views::filter([](int n) { return n > 10; })` selects numbers greater than.

2. Filtering for prime numbers: `std::views::filter(is_prime)` uses the `is_prime` function to keep only prime numbers

Taking the first three elements: `std::views::take(3)` limits the results to the first three elements that meet the previous criteria.

The result is a seamless integration of conditions in a single, readable line of code. This example not only demonstrates the power of chaining and filtering but also highlights how ranges can significantly enhance the expressiveness and adaptability of C++ code. The combination of simplicity and expressiveness is what makes ranges an invaluable feature in modern C++ development.

Understanding views in searches

Views are pivotal in the range-based landscape, especially in searching scenarios. Unlike containers, views don't own their elements. They present a transformed *view* of their source data, which can be another range (such as a container). When incorporated into searches, views don't modify the original data but provide a new perspective, which can be particularly useful in modular and reusable code.

The extended toolkit – more than just find

While `std::ranges::find` is a cornerstone, the modern range-based approach offers a broad spectrum of searching algorithms. Functions such as `std::ranges::search`, which locates a subsequence, or `std::ranges::find_end`, which finds the last occurrence of a sequence, encapsulate the richness of range-based searching. Their true power is unlocked with other range adaptors, offering a palette of possibilities for efficient and expressive searching tasks.

Transitioning from traditional methods, range-based searching in the STL stands as a testament to the evolution of C++ toward more readable, modular, and expressive code. As we advance further into the world of ranges, harnessing these tools and techniques will be paramount for those eager to craft efficient and maintainable code.

Best practices

The transition to range-based STL is undoubtedly exhilarating. With this newfound expressiveness and clarity, we have powerful tools at our fingertips. However, understanding a set of best practices is essential to maximize the potential of ranges and ensure the maintainability of your code base. Let us look at some of the best practices that we can implement.

Embracing the power of chaining

One of the standout features of ranges is their natural ability to chain operations. Chaining not only enhances readability but also improves efficiency by avoiding intermediary storage:

```
std::vector<int> nums = {5, 8, 10, 14, 18};
auto result = nums | std::views::filter([](int n) { return n % 2 == 0;
})
                   | std::views::transform([](int n) { return n * 2;
});
```

This elegant one-liner filters out odd numbers and then doubles the even ones. By promoting such chaining, you can foster cleaner, more concise code.

Guarding against range pitfalls – lifetime awareness

Going all out with ranges is tempting, especially with their composability. Yet, caution is advised. One of the most common pitfalls is the unintentional dangling of views, as shown in the following code:

```
auto doubledEvens() {
    std::vector<int> nums = {1, 2, 3, 4, 5};
    return nums | std::views::filter([](int n) { return n % 2 == 0; })
               | std::views::transform([](int n) { return n * 2; });
}
```

The preceding code returns a view on a local variable. As this function exits, the local variable will be destroyed. Since a view of this destroyed variable is being returned, it will lead to undefined behavior. Always be aware of the lifetime of the underlying data when working with views.

Performance considerations – laziness and evaluation

Ranges, especially views, operate lazily. This means that they evaluate their elements only when accessed. While this can be a boon for efficiency, it might also lead to pitfalls, especially when combined with stateful operations or side effects, as illustrated in the following example:

```
int x = 0;
auto range = std::views::iota(1) | std::views::transform([&x](int n) {
return x += n; });
```

If `range` is evaluated multiple times, the side effect in the lambda accumulates, leading to unexpected results. It is advisable to force an eager evaluation for such scenarios, perhaps by converting the range to a container.

Readability over brevity – striking the balance

While ranges enable concise code, remember the cardinal rule: code is read more often than written. Overly compacted chains of range operations can be challenging to understand, especially for those new to the code base. Strike a balance between brevity and clarity.

Adhering to range idioms – keep it standard

As with other parts of the C++ language, certain idioms and patterns have emerged for using ranges. When possible, prefer the standard idioms. (For example, use `std::ranges::sort` for sorting and `std::ranges::find` for finding. Both of these are better than writing your own loops to do essentially the same thing.) This makes your code more understandable to other C++ developers and ensures that you benefit from community-tested patterns.

This section highlights key best practices for effectively using range-based STL in C++. It emphasizes the importance of embracing the power of chaining, which enhances code readability and efficiency by avoiding intermediary storage. However, it also cautions against common pitfalls, such as dangling views, and advises awareness of the lifetime of underlying data. The section notes the lazy evaluation nature of ranges, recommending eager evaluation in scenarios involving stateful operations or side effects to avoid unexpected results. Additionally, it advises maintaining a balance between code conciseness and readability, ensuring that code remains accessible and understandable. Finally, it suggests adhering to established range idioms, leveraging standard patterns for better clarity and community alignment. These practices aim to maximize the potential of ranges while ensuring maintainable and robust code.

Summary

In this chapter, we explored the concept of ranges in the C++ STL and how they enhance how we work with sequences of elements. We began with an introduction to ranges, understanding their essence and the motivations behind the shift to this new paradigm. We saw how range operations facilitate more expressive and readable code, and we delved into the composability that ranges introduce to sorting algorithms.

The chapter then focused on range-based sorting, discussing the basic concepts and the advantages ranges bring to the table, such as cleaner syntax and improved composability. We also examined the application of ranges in searching algorithms, appreciating the elegant and powerful ways ranges enable us to chain operations and apply filters.

Ranges help us write cleaner code in a way that better expresses our intent. The shift to ranges represents a significant evolution in the STL, offering enhanced clarity and efficiency in code. It allows us to compose complex operations in a more readable and maintainable way, which is beneficial for both the development process and the longevity of the code base.

Now that we have a strong understanding of STL data types, algorithms, and other core concepts, we will use this knowledge in the next chapter to create our own container types that integrate seamlessly with the existing STL algorithms and iterators. We will cover the essential requirements for STL compatibility, such as iterator implementation and value semantics. We will guide you through the effective use of operator overloading and the creation of custom hash functions. By learning to create STL-compatible containers, we can extend the STL to suit their specific needs, ensuring that their custom types can benefit from the power and flexibility of the STL algorithms and practices.

Part 4:
Creating STL-Compatible Types and Algorithms

This part of our book is dedicated to the creation and integration of custom types and algorithms within the C++ Standard Template Library ecosystem. We start by exploring the construction of STL-compatible containers, detailing the essential requirements for seamless interoperability with STL algorithms. We discuss the importance of crafting robust iterators and the nuances of operator overloading to provide intuitive and consistent behavior for custom types. Special attention is given to creating custom hash functions to facilitate the use of user-defined types with unordered associative containers.

Next, we get into the intricacies of developing STL-compatible algorithms. This includes mastering template functions, understanding the subtleties of overloading, and leveraging inline functions for performance. We will emphasize the use of predicates and functors for enhanced flexibility.

Finally, we are introduced to type traits and policies, powerful tools that allow developers to craft more adaptable and modular code. We gain insights into implementing these concepts effectively, ensuring that your custom types and algorithms not only integrate well with the STL but also adhere to best practices in modern C++ programming.

By the end of this part, you will have gained the knowledge to extend the STL to fit your unique requirements, fostering a deeper understanding of template metaprogramming and the powerful abstractions provided by C++.

This part has the following chapters:

- *Chapter 16: Creating STL-Types Containers*
- *Chapter 17: Creating STL-Compatible Algorithms*
- *Chapter 18: Type Traits and Policies*

16

Creating STL-Types Containers

Developers can harness unparalleled interoperability, consistency, and efficiency by integrating custom types with the C++ **Standard Template Library** (**STL**). This chapter focuses on the essential aspects of creating custom types that effortlessly interoperate with STL algorithms, emphasize proper operator overloading, and implement robust iterators. By the end of this chapter, you will be proficient in designing and implementing custom types, ensuring they fully utilize the strengths of the STL and elevate the overall effectiveness of your applications.

In this section, we will cover the following topics:

- The advantages of STL-compatible types
- Interacting with STL algorithms
- Essential requirements for compatibility
- Crafting iterators for custom types
- Effective operator overloading
- Creating custom hash functions

Technical requirements

The code in this chapter can be found on GitHub:

```
https://github.com/PacktPublishing/Data-Structures-and-Algorithms-
with-the-CPP-STL
```

The advantages of STL-compatible types

Building STL-compatible types in C++ offers many advantages for developers seeking to elevate their programming prowess. One of the foremost reasons is the ability to tailor containers to specific needs and performance requirements. While the STL provides a rich set of generic containers, custom containers allow us to finely tune data structures when standard ones fall short in catering to intricate application demands or optimization goals. Moreover, crafting our own containers grants us enhanced control over critical aspects, such as memory layout, allocation strategies, and container behaviors. This granular control empowers us to optimize memory usage and boost application efficiency. Beyond the tangible benefits, embarking on the journey of building custom containers is an invaluable opportunity to deepen our understanding of C++ internals and intricacies. It's a path that leads to a higher level of expertise in a language known for its depth and precision.

One language, one approach

First and foremost, making custom types STL-friendly offers an undeniable benefit – uniformity. Consider the vast plethora of algorithms and containers within the STL. From sorting routines to complex data structures, the STL is the bedrock of C++ development. By aligning your types with the STL, you ensure they can seamlessly interoperate with this expansive library.

Picture this – a developer new to your code base, already familiar with STL, finds themselves at home when they see that your custom types follow the same patterns. This consistent approach significantly reduces the learning curve, offering a familiar and intuitive experience. Imagine the convenience of using the `std::for_each` algorithm on your custom type, just as one would with `std::vector` or `std::list`. This unity in design boosts productivity and fosters code readability.

Reusability – the gift that keeps giving

Building upon the notion of uniformity, there's another equally compelling argument for STL compatibility – reusability. Adhering to STL conventions makes your custom types reusable across diverse scenarios. Think of the vast collection of algorithms provided by the STL. Once your type is STL-compatible, it can immediately benefit from all these algorithms without reinventing the wheel.

Moreover, reusability isn't just limited to algorithms. The chances are that if your type is STL-compatible, other developers can adopt it in their projects with ease. Over time, this encourages collaborative development and fosters an ecosystem where code is written, shared, reviewed, and improved upon by a broader community.

Efficiency in the familiar

At the heart of the STL lies a commitment to performance. The library is meticulously optimized to ensure efficiency. By making your types STL-compatible, you position them to leverage these optimizations. Whether it is a sorting routine or a complex associative container, you can be confident that your type will benefit from all of the performance optimizations within the STL.

Furthermore, an STL-friendly design often guides developers away from common pitfalls. Given that the STL has been tried and tested over the years, aligning with its conventions inherently encourages best practices in type design.

Paving the way forward

With an evident appreciation of the merits of STL-compatible types, the journey ahead becomes even more interesting. The stage is set as we recognize the value of uniformity, reusability, and efficiency that comes with STL compatibility. The subsequent sections will uncover the intricacies of ensuring your custom types align with STL and shine in their uniqueness. From interacting with STL algorithms to the nuances of crafting custom iterators, the roadmap is clear – creating types that stand tall in their compatibility and versatility.

In this section, we explored the advantages of making custom types STL-compatible. This journey has equipped you with the understanding of why STL-friendly design is not merely a choice but also a significant stride in C++ development. We looked at the virtues of uniformity, reusability, and efficiency, highlighting how these qualities elevate your custom types within the C++ landscape.

As we move on to the next section, *Interacting with STL algorithms*, we'll transition from the *why* to the *how* of STL compatibility. This upcoming section will guide you through the crucial role of iterators in interfacing with STL algorithms, adapting your custom types to meet algorithmic expectations, and handling errors effectively.

Interacting with STL algorithms

This section will focus on equipping you with the skills necessary to seamlessly integrate custom types with STL algorithms, a critical aspect of advanced C++ programming. This integration is not just about conforming to standards but also about creating a symbiotic relationship, where custom types and STL algorithms enhance each other's capabilities. You will learn how to design and implement robust iterators for your custom types, which is crucial for enabling smooth interaction with STL algorithms. Understanding the specific requirements of different STL algorithms and tailoring your custom types to meet these needs is also a key focus. This includes supporting various operations, such as copying, comparison, and arithmetic, which are essential for algorithms to function correctly.

We will also cover the nuances of error handling and feedback mechanisms, teaching you how to make your custom types not only facilitate the operations of STL algorithms but also respond appropriately to unexpected scenarios. Emphasizing algorithmic efficiency, we will guide you through best practices to ensure that your custom types do not become performance bottlenecks. By the end of this section, you will have gained invaluable insights into creating custom types that are not only compatible with STL algorithms but also optimized for performance, making your C++ programming more effective and your applications more efficient and maintainable.

The centrality of iterators

Iterators serve as the bridge between custom types and STL algorithms. At their core, STL algorithms predominantly rely on iterators to navigate and manipulate data within containers. Hence, any custom type aiming for flawless integration must prioritize a robust iterator design. While we'll touch upon crafting iterators in a dedicated section, it is essential to understand their pivotal role. Providing a suite of iterators – ranging from forward iterators to bidirectional and even random-access ones – enhances the spectrum of STL algorithms that your custom type can interact with.

Adapting to algorithmic expectations

Each STL algorithm has a set of requirements or expectations from the containers it interacts with. For instance, the `std::sort` algorithm operates optimally with random-access iterators. As such, to ensure that a custom type meshes well with this sorting routine, it should ideally support random-access iterators.

But the relationship goes deeper. Some algorithms expect the ability to copy elements, some require comparison operations, while others might need arithmetic operations. Therefore, understanding the prerequisites of the algorithms you aim to support is crucial. The more you fine-tune your custom type based on these expectations, the better the synergy.

Error handling and feedback mechanisms

A robust custom type does not merely facilitate an algorithm's operations but also offers feedback mechanisms. Suppose an STL algorithm encounters an unexpected scenario while operating on your custom type. In such a case, how does your type respond? Implementing mechanisms to handle potential issues and provide meaningful feedback is integral. This could be in the form of exceptions or other error-handling paradigms that C++ supports.

Let's look at the following example:

```cpp
#include <algorithm>
#include <iostream>
#include <stdexcept>
#include <vector>

class CustomType {
public:
  CustomType(int value = 0) : value_(value) {}

  // Comparison operation
  bool operator<(const CustomType &other) const {
    return value_ < other.value_;
  }

  // Arithmetic operation
  CustomType operator+(const CustomType &other) const {
    return CustomType(value_ + other.value_);
  }
```

```cpp
  // Copy operation
  CustomType(const CustomType &other)
      : value_(other.value_) {}

private:
  int value_{0};
};

class CustomContainer {
public:
  using iterator = std::vector<CustomType>::iterator;
  using const_iterator =
      std::vector<CustomType>::const_iterator;

  iterator begin() { return data_.begin(); }
  const_iterator begin() const { return data_.begin(); }
  iterator end() { return data_.end(); }
  const_iterator end() const { return data_.end(); }

  void push_back(const CustomType &value) {
    data_.push_back(value);
  }

private:
  std::vector<CustomType> data_;
};

int main() {
  CustomContainer container;
  container.push_back(CustomType(3));
  container.push_back(CustomType(1));
  container.push_back(CustomType(2));

  try {
    std::sort(container.begin(), container.end());
  } catch (const std::exception &e) {
    // Handle potential issues and provide meaningful
    // feedback
    std::cerr << "An error occurred: " << e.what() << "\n";
    return 1;
  }
```

```
    return 0;
}
```

The preceding example has a `CustomType` that supports comparison, arithmetic, and copy operations. We also have a `CustomContainer` that provides random-access iterators (through the underlying `std::vector`). The `std::sort` algorithm is used to sort the elements in the container. If an error occurs during the sorting process, it is caught and handled in the `catch` block.

Algorithmic efficiency and your type

STL algorithms are known for their performance, often crafted with intricate optimizations. However, the custom type can bottleneck the algorithm's efficiency if it is not designed with performance in mind. Consider scenarios where the algorithm might need to access elements or frequently iterate over the custom container. Any latency in these fundamental operations can amplify during the algorithm's execution.

As a best practice, continually benchmark your custom type's performance when subjected to STL algorithms. Profiling tools can offer insights into potential bottlenecks and guiding optimizations.

Laying a solid foundation

In essence, the journey to making custom types STL algorithm-friendly is multifaceted. Starting from the foundational element of iterators, venturing into understanding algorithmic expectations, emphasizing error handling, and prioritizing efficiency form the crux of this endeavor.

In this section, we have immersed ourselves in the process of integrating custom types with STL algorithms. This helps our code form a symbiotic relationship with the STL, where custom types and STL algorithms mutually enhance each other's functionality. We explored the critical role of iterators as the vital link between custom types and STL algorithms, understanding their necessity for smooth data navigation and manipulation. Additionally, we learned about adapting custom types to meet the specific requirements of various STL algorithms, ensuring optimal performance and effective integration.

As we move forward to the next section, *Essential requirements for compatibility*, our focus will shift from the broad interactions with STL algorithms to the specific requirements and standards for achieving true STL compatibility.

Essential requirements for compatibility

In this section, we focus on the foundational aspects that make a custom type truly compatible with the STL. Understanding and implementing the key elements we will outline is crucial for leveraging the full potential of STL's robust and versatile toolkit. We will cover the essentials, such as the design of iterators, adherence to value semantics, operational guarantees, and the provision of size and capacity information, each playing a vital role in ensuring seamless integration with STL algorithms.

The goal here is to equip your custom types with the capability to not only interact with but also enhance the efficiency and functionality of STL algorithms. This requires an understanding of the STL's expectations in terms of performance, behavior under operations, and exception safety. By meeting these requirements, you will be able to create custom types that are not just functional but also optimized for performance and reliability within the STL framework.

The cornerstones of compatibility

Venturing into the world of STL compatibility is akin to joining an exclusive club. The key to entry is understanding and adhering to foundational requirements. Once you've got these down pat, the immense benefits of the STL are yours for the taking. Let's embark on this transformative journey and unravel the essential components for seamless integration.

The vitality of iterators

An STL-compatible type is synonymous with iterators. They're the veins that channel data to and from the STL's algorithms. However, it is not enough to merely provide an iterator. The nature and capabilities of your iterators define which algorithms can interact with your custom type. A forward iterator might grant basic functionalities, but you'd need bidirectional or even random-access iterators if you wish to leverage more advanced algorithms. Ensuring your custom type exposes the appropriate iterator opens the doors to a broader range of algorithmic interactions.

Embracing value semantics

C++ and its STL thrive on value semantics. This means that objects clearly understand copy, assignment, and destruction. When constructing an STL-compatible type, it is imperative to define clear and efficient copy constructors, copy assignment operators, move operations, and destructors. A well-defined semantic behavior ensures that algorithms can seamlessly create, modify, or destroy instances of your custom type without unforeseen consequences.

Operational guarantees

Algorithms rely on certain operations being performed in predictable time frames. For instance, `std::vector` guarantees constant-time access to its elements. If your custom type promises similar access, it should consistently deliver on that promise. Providing accurate operational guarantees ensures that the algorithm performs optimally and as expected.

Size and capacity queries

STL algorithms often require information about the size of a container or, in some cases, its capacity. Your custom type needs to furnish these details promptly. Functions such as `size()`, `empty()`, and potentially, `capacity()` should be integral components of your design.

Element access and manipulation

Beyond understanding the structure, STL algorithms need to access and manipulate the elements within. This calls for member functions or operators to facilitate direct access, insertion, and removal. The more versatile these operations, the broader the range of algorithms your custom type can befriend.

Consistency in exception safety

Exception safety is the assurance that your code won't leak resources or end up undefined when exceptions occur. The STL adopts a nuanced approach to exception safety, often categorized into levels such as "basic" and "strong." Aligning your custom type's exception safety guarantees with those of the STL ensures smoother interactions and fortifies your type's reliability.

Let's look at an example:

```
#include <algorithm>
#include <iostream>
#include <vector>

// Custom type that is STL-compatible
class CustomType {
public:
  using iterator = std::vector<int>::iterator;
  using const_iterator = std::vector<int>::const_iterator;

  // Constructors
  CustomType() = default;
  CustomType(const CustomType &other) : data(other.data) {}
  CustomType(CustomType &&other) noexcept
      : data(std::move(other.data)) {}

  // Assignment operators
  CustomType &operator=(const CustomType &other) {
    if (this != &other) { data = other.data; }
    return *this;
  }

  CustomType &operator=(CustomType &&other) noexcept {
    if (this != &other) { data = std::move(other.data); }
    return *this;
  }

  ~CustomType() = default;
```

```
  // Size and capacity queries
  size_t size() const { return data.size(); }
  bool empty() const { return data.empty(); }

  // Element access and manipulation
  int &operator[](size_t index) { return data[index]; }

  const int &operator[](size_t index) const {
    return data[index];
  }

  void push_back(int value) { data.push_back(value); }
  void pop_back() { data.pop_back(); }

  // Iterators
  iterator begin() { return data.begin(); }
  const_iterator begin() const { return data.begin(); }
  iterator end() { return data.end(); }
  const_iterator end() const { return data.end(); }

private:
  std::vector<int> data;
};

int main() {
  CustomType custom;

  // Fill with some data
  for (int i = 0; i < 10; ++i) { custom.push_back(i); }

  // Use STL algorithm with our custom type
  std::for_each(
      custom.begin(), custom.end(),
      [](int &value) { std::cout << value << ' '; });

  return 0;
}
```

Here is the example output:

```
0 1 2 3 4 5 6 7 8 9
```

This code defines a `CustomType` class that is compatible with the STL. It provides iterators and defines copy and move constructors, assignment operators, and a destructor. It also provides functions to query size and capacity and to access and manipulate elements. The `main` function demonstrates how to use an STL algorithm (`std::for_each`) with an instance of `CustomType`.

Looking forward to enhanced integration

With a grasp of these foundational requirements, you're well on your way to crafting types that resonate harmoniously with the STL. Remember, it is a partnership. While the STL offers algorithms and utilities of unparalleled power, your custom types bring unique functionalities and nuances. When these worlds collide in compatibility, the result is coding magic.

As we progress to the subsequent sections, we'll deepen our understanding, touching upon the intricate art of crafting iterators and the subtleties of operator overloading. Each step you take solidifies your position in the elite club of STL integration, unlocking greater programming prowess.

Crafting iterators for custom types

Iterators are, without a doubt, the heartbeat of data access in the world of the STL. They act as bridges, connecting custom data structures with the vast array of STL algorithms. A well-crafted iterator ensures seamless data access and modification, making your custom types feel like they've been part of the STL family all along.

Creating STL iterators for custom types is pivotal in C++ programming, as they act as essential bridges, enabling seamless integration and interaction between custom types and the myriad of STL algorithms. They facilitate the traversal and manipulation of data within custom containers, ensuring that these types can fully leverage the power and efficiency of STL's algorithms. Without properly designed iterators, custom types would be isolated, unable to tap into the extensive and optimized functionalities that the STL offers.

Choosing the right iterator type

There is a myriad of iterator types to pick from, each bringing its own capabilities to the table. A forward iterator enables one-way movement through a sequence, while a bidirectional iterator offers you the ability to traverse in reverse. Stepping it up, random-access iterators allow swift jumps to any position in a data structure. When crafting iterators for your custom types, it is crucial to identify which type aligns with the nature of your data and the operations you wish to support. The chosen type sets the stage for the algorithms that can be utilized and the efficiency of those operations.

The selection of an iterator type should be guided by the inherent characteristics of your data structure and the efficiency requirements of the operations you intend to perform. Forward iterators are the simplest, supporting only one-directional traversal. They are suitable for data structures requiring only sequential access, such as singly linked lists. This simplicity can lead to more optimized performance for such tasks.

Bidirectional iterators, which allow traversal in both directions, are apt for structures such as doubly linked lists, where reverse iteration is as fundamental as forward iteration. The added flexibility of moving backward comes with a slight increase in complexity, but if your data structure and algorithms benefit from bidirectional traversal, this is a justified choice.

Random access iterators offer the most flexibility, enabling direct access to any element in constant time, akin to array indexing. They are indispensable for data structures such as vectors and arrays, where such capabilities are essential. However, this level of functionality is not necessary for all data types and can add unnecessary overhead if the data structure does not inherently support fast random access.

In essence, while you can design a data structure to use a more advanced iterator type such as random access, doing so without a need for its capabilities can lead to inefficiencies. The iterator choice should align with the natural behavior and requirements of your data structure to ensure optimal performance and resource utilization. It is about finding the right balance between the functionality provided by the iterator and the nature of the data structure it is intended for.

Crafting the basic components

At its core, an iterator must support a set of basic operations that define its behavior. This includes dereferencing to access the underlying data, incrementing and potentially decrementing to navigate through the data, and comparison to determine the relative positions of two iterators. Implementing these operations effectively ensures that your custom type's iterators play nicely with STL algorithms.

Addressing iterator categories with type traits

STL algorithms, being the discerning entities they are, often look for clues about the nature of an iterator. They use these hints to optimize their behavior. This is where type traits come into play. By specializing `std::iterator_traits` for your custom iterator, you're effectively whispering in the algorithm's ear, telling it what to expect. This knowledge equips algorithms to make the best choices in their operations, ensuring peak performance.

End iterators – signifying the finish line

Every journey needs a clear destination, and iterators are no exception. Beyond the iterators that allow access to data, it is paramount to provide an *end* iterator. This special iterator doesn't point to valid data but signifies the boundary – the point past the last valid element. STL algorithms rely on this sentinel to know when to stop their operations, making it an essential part of any iterator suite.

Considerations for const iterators

Just as a library provides regular books and reference-only texts, data structures often need to cater to modification and mere viewing. **Const iterators** cater to the latter scenario, allowing data to be accessed without the risk of modification. Crafting const iterators ensures that your custom type can be safely used in scenarios where data integrity is paramount.

Let's look at an illustrative C++ code example that demonstrates the creation of a custom iterator for a custom data structure:

```cpp
#include <iostream>
#include <iterator>
#include <vector>

// Define a custom data structure for custom iterators.
class MyContainer {
public:
  MyContainer(std::initializer_list<int> values)
      : data(values) {}

  // Custom iterator for MyContainer.
  class iterator {

  private:
    std::vector<int>::iterator it;

  public:
    iterator(std::vector<int>::iterator iter) : it(iter) {}

    // Dereferencing operator to access the underlying
    // data.
    int &operator*() { return *it; }

    // Increment operator to navigate through the data.
    iterator &operator++() {
      ++it;
      return *this;
    }

    // Comparison operator to determine the relative
    // positions of two iterators.
    bool operator==(const iterator &other) const {
      return it == other.it;
    }

    bool operator!=(const iterator &other) const {
      return it != other.it;
    }
```

```
  };

  // Begin and end functions to provide iterators.
  iterator begin() { return iterator(data.begin()); }
  iterator end() { return iterator(data.end()); }

  // Additional member functions for MyContainer as needed.
 private:
  std::vector<int> data;
  };

int main() {
  MyContainer container = {1, 2, 3, 4, 5};

  // Using custom iterators to iterate through the data.
  for (MyContainer::iterator it = container.begin();
       it != container.end(); ++it) {
    std::cout << *it << " ";
  }

  std::cout << "\n";
  return 0;
}
```

Here is the example output:

```
1 2 3 4 5
```

Performance optimizations and advanced techniques

Crafting an iterator isn't just about functionality but also finesse. Consider memory caching techniques, prefetching, and other optimizations to enhance performance. Remember, an iterator is a frequently used component, and any efficiency improvements can have a significant ripple effect on overall application performance.

Embracing the iterative spirit

With a deep dive into the world of iterators behind us, it is clear that they are more than just tools – they are a testament to the versatility and power of the STL. By meticulously crafting iterators for your custom types, you enhance interoperability with STL algorithms and elevate the user experience, making data access intuitive and efficient. Throughout this section, we learned why it is important to choose the right iterator types, how to write basic iterators, and the things to consider when building const iterators. In the next section, we'll explore the nuances of operator overloading, ensuring that our custom types genuinely feel at home in the world of C++ and STL.

Effective operator overloading

Next, let's work to understand the strategic implementation of operator overloading in C++, a feature that significantly enhances the functionality and integration of custom types. Operator overloading allows custom types to emulate the behavior of built-in types, providing a seamless interface for STL algorithms to work with these types as efficiently as they do with native C++ types. This feature is instrumental in ensuring that custom types are not just compatible with STL algorithms but also optimized for their efficient execution.

The focus here is on designing operator overloads that facilitate the integration of custom types into the STL framework. For example, overloading arithmetic operators such as +, -, and * allows custom types to directly participate in STL algorithms that perform mathematical operations, such as `std::transform` or `std::accumulate`. Similarly, overloading relational operators such as ==, <, and > enables custom types to be effectively used with STL algorithms that require element comparisons, such as `std::sort` or `std::binary_search`. The key is to ensure that these overloaded operators mimic the behavior of their counterparts for built-in types, maintaining the intuitive nature of operations and enhancing the predictability of algorithm outcomes. By carefully implementing operator overloading, we can ensure that custom types not only interact flawlessly with STL algorithms but also contribute to the overall efficiency and readability of C++ programs.

Operator overloading in C++

Operator overloading allows custom types in C++ to have specialized behaviors for standard operators. By leveraging this feature, developers can implement operations on custom types as straightforwardly as with built-in types, enhancing code readability and consistency.

Considerations in overloading

Although operator overloading can make expressions more expressive, it's crucial to use it judiciously. The primary objective should be to enhance clarity, not introduce confusion. A fundamental guideline is that an overloaded operator should behave similarly to its counterpart for built-in types. Deviating from this standard can produce code that is difficult to understand and maintain.

Implementing arithmetic operators for custom types

For a custom mathematical vector type, it's reasonable to implement operations such as addition (+), subtraction (-), and multiplication (*). Overloading these operators ensures that developers can operate on your custom type just as with primitive data types.

Overloading relational operators for clear comparisons

Relational operators (==, ! =, <, <=, >, >=) are not limited to primitive types. By overloading these operators for custom types, you provide a direct method to compare instances. This capability simplifies tasks such as sorting a list of custom objects.

Consider a custom `Product` class with an overload of the +, <, =, and += operators. The implementation is straightforward and provides a very intuitive way to interact with the class:

```cpp
#include <iostream>
#include <string>

class Product {
public:
  std::string name;
  double price;

  Product(const std::string &n, double p)
      : name(n), price(p) {}

  // Overloading the addition operator (+) to combine
  // prices
  Product operator+(const Product &other) const {
    return Product(name + " and " + other.name,
                   price + other.price);
  }

  // Overloading the less than operator (<) to compare
  // prices
  bool operator<(const Product &other) const {
    return price < other.price;
  }

  // Overloading the assignment operator (=) to copy
  // products
  Product &operator=(const Product &other) {
    if (this == &other) { return *this; }

    name = other.name;
    price = other.price;
    return *this;
  }

  // Overloading the compound assignment operator (+=) to
```

```
  // add prices
  Product &operator+=(const Product &other) {
    price += other.price;
    return *this;
  }
};

int main() {
  Product widget("Widget", 25.99);
  Product gadget("Gadget", 19.95);

  // Using the overloaded operators
  Product combinedProduct = widget + gadget;

  // Using the compound assignment operator
  widget += gadget;

  bool widgetIsCheaper = widget < gadget;
  bool gadgetIsCheaper = gadget < widget;

  std::cout << "Combined Product: " << combinedProduct.name
            << " ($" << combinedProduct.price << ")"
            << "\n";

  std::cout << "Is Widget cheaper than Gadget? "
            << (widgetIsCheaper ? "Yes": "No") << "\n";

  std::cout << "Is Gadget cheaper than Widget? "
            << (gadgetIsCheaper ? "Yes": "No") << "\n";

  std::cout << "Updated widget: " << widget.name << " ($"
            << widget.price << ")"
            << "\n";

  return 0;
}
```

Here is the example output:

```
Combined Product: Widget and Gadget ($45.94)
Is Widget cheaper than Gadget? No
Is Gadget cheaper than Widget? Yes
Updated widget: Widget ($45.94)
```

This example demonstrates how to leverage operator overloads on custom types. These overloads (especially comparisons) are required for types to be compatible with various STL algorithms.

Simplifying tasks with assignment and compound assignment

Overloading assignment (=) and compound assignment operators (+=, -=, |=, >>=, and many more) offer a straightforward method to modify instances of your custom type, eliminating the need for lengthier function calls.

Stream operators for efficient I/O

I/O operations are central to most applications. Overloading the stream insertion (<<) and extraction (>>) operators enables custom types to work effortlessly with C++ streams, ensuring a uniform I/O interface.

Operator precedence and associativity in overloading

When defining operator overloads, keeping the established precedence and associativity rules in C++ in mind is essential. This ensures that expressions involving your custom type are processed as expected.

The role of operator overloading in C++

Operator overloading enhances the integration of custom types in C++. It facilitates concise and intuitive operations, enabling custom types to work well with STL algorithms and containers. By using this feature thoughtfully, developers can create custom types that offer functionality and ease of use.

In subsequent sections, we'll look at the tools and practices that can optimize your C++ development experience, aiming to make application development effective and straightforward.

Creating custom hash functions

As we have seen, the STL offers a vast array of container classes such as `std::unordered_map`, `std::unordered_set`, and `std::unordered_multiset`, which rely heavily on hash functions for their efficient operation. When working with custom types, creating custom hash functions tailored to your data structures is imperative. In this section, we will learn about the significance of implementing custom hash functions, explore the characteristics of a good hash function, and provide an illustrative example of how to integrate a custom type with an STL container, using a custom hash function.

Interoperability with STL containers

STL containers such as `std::unordered_map` or `std::unordered_set` use hash tables to store and retrieve elements efficiently. To make your custom types compatible with these containers, you need to provide a way for them to compute a hash value, which is used to determine the storage location of an element within the container. Without a custom hash function, the STL containers would not know how to hash your custom objects correctly.

By implementing custom hash functions, you ensure that your custom types can seamlessly interoperate with STL containers, providing the following benefits:

- **Efficiency**: Custom hash functions can be optimized for your specific data structure, leading to faster access and retrieval times within STL containers. This optimization can significantly boost the overall performance of your application.

- **Consistency**: Custom hash functions enable hashing consistency for your custom types. Without them, different instances of the same custom type may yield different hash values, causing problems retrieving elements from containers.

- **Correctness**: A well-designed custom hash function ensures that your custom types are correctly hashed, preventing collisions and maintaining the integrity of your data within the container.

Custom type semantics

Custom types often have unique semantics and internal structures that require special handling when hashing. STL containers, by default, use the `std::hash` function provided by the standard library. This function may not adequately handle the intricacies of your custom type.

By crafting your custom hash function, you can tailor the hashing process to the specific requirements of your data structure. For instance, you might want to consider the internal state of your custom type, selectively hash some members while excluding others, or even apply additional transformations to ensure an optimal distribution of elements in the container.

The characteristics of a good hash function

Adhering to specific characteristics that define a good hash function is essential when creating a custom hash function. A good hash function should possess the following properties:

- **Deterministic**: A hash function should always produce the same value for the input. This property ensures that the elements are consistently placed in the same location within the container.

- **Uniform distribution**: Ideally, a hash function should distribute values uniformly across the entire range of possible hash values. Uneven distribution can lead to performance issues, as some buckets may become overloaded while others remain underutilized.

- **Minimal collisions**: Collisions occur when two different elements produce the same hash value. A good hash function minimizes collisions by ensuring that distinct inputs generate distinct hash values. This reduces the likelihood of performance degradation in STL containers.

- **High efficiency**: Efficiency is crucial for hash functions, especially when dealing with large datasets. A good hash function should be computationally efficient, ensuring minimal overhead when computing hash values.

- **Mixes well**: A hash function should produce hash values that are well-mixed, meaning small changes in the input should result in significantly different hash values. This property helps maintain a balanced distribution of elements within the container.

Example for the creation of a custom hash function

Let's illustrate the creation of a custom hash function with an example. Suppose we have a custom `Person` class with a name and age. We want to use `std::unordered_map` to store `Person` objects, and we need a custom hash function to achieve this. The following code is an implementation of such a hash function:

```cpp
#include <iostream>
#include <string>
#include <unordered_map>

class Person {
public:
  Person(const std::string &n, int a) : name(n), age(a) {}

  std::string getName() const { return name; }
  int getAge() const { return age; }

  bool operator==(const Person &other) const {
    return name == other.name && age == other.age;
  }

private:
  std::string name;
  int age{0};
};

struct PersonHash {
  std::size_t operator()(const Person &person) const {
    // Combine the hash values of name and age using XOR
    std::size_t nameHash =
        std::hash<std::string>()(person.getName());

    std::size_t ageHash =
        std::hash<int>()(person.getAge());
```

```
        return nameHash ^ ageHash;
    }
};

int main() {
    std::unordered_map<Person, std::string, PersonHash>
        personMap;

    // Insert Person objects into the map
    Person person1("Alice", 30);
    Person person2("Bob", 25);

    personMap[person1] = "Engineer";
    personMap[person2] = "Designer";

    // Access values using custom Person objects
    std::cout << "Alice's profession: " << personMap[person1]
            << "\n";

    return 0;
}
```

In this example, we define the `Person` class with custom equality operators and a custom hash function, `PersonHash`. The `PersonHash` hash function combines the hash values of the `name` and `age` members, using XOR to ensure a well-mixed hash result. This custom hash function allows us to use `Person` objects as keys in `std::unordered_map`.

By implementing a custom hash function tailored to the specific needs of our custom type, we enable smooth integration with STL containers and ensure efficient, consistent, and correct operations.

In conclusion, custom hash functions are essential when working with custom types in STL containers. They facilitate efficient, consistent, and correct storage and retrieval of elements within these containers. Adhering to the characteristics of a good hash function and crafting one that suits your custom type's semantics is crucial. The example we provided demonstrates how to create a custom hash function for a custom type and use it effectively with an STL container. This knowledge enables you to make the most of the C++ STL when dealing with your custom data structures.

Summary

In this chapter, we explored the fundamental aspects of creating STL-type containers in C++. We started by exploring the advantages of using STL-compatible types, emphasizing the benefits of consistency, reusability, and efficiency. These advantages lay the groundwork for a smoother and more efficient development process.

Then, we discussed how to interact with STL algorithms, emphasizing the centrality of iterators in navigating and manipulating container elements. We highlighted the importance of adapting your custom types to algorithmic expectations, handling errors gracefully, and optimizing for algorithmic efficiency.

We also covered the essential requirements for compatibility, including the importance of iterators, value semantics, operational guarantees, size and capacity queries, and element access and manipulation. Understanding these concepts ensures your custom types seamlessly integrate with the STL.

Furthermore, we explored the process of crafting iterators for custom types and operator overloading. Finally, we touched upon creating custom hash functions, which is essential when your custom types are used in associative containers such as `std::unordered_map`.

The information presented in this chapter equips you with the foundational knowledge needed to create STL-compatible custom containers effectively. It allows you to harness the full power of the C++ STL in your projects, resulting in more efficient and maintainable code.

In the following chapter, we will explore the world of template functions, overloading, inline functions, and creating generic algorithms. You will better understand how to develop algorithmic solutions that seamlessly work with various custom container types. We will venture into the intricacies of function templates, SFINAE, overloading algorithms, and customization using predicates and functors. By the end of the chapter, you will be well-equipped to build your own STL-compatible algorithms and further enhance your C++ programming skills.

17

Creating STL
-Compatible Algorithms

This chapter discusses creating versatile and efficient algorithms in C++. Developers will learn type-generic programming, understand the function overloading, and learn to tailor existing algorithms to specific needs. The chapter will include theory, best practices, and hands-on techniques. By the end, we will be equipped to develop powerful and adaptable algorithms for various scenarios.

In this chapter, we will cover the following main topics:

- Template functions
- Overloading
- Creating generic algorithms
- Customizing existing algorithms

Technical requirements

The code in this chapter can be found on GitHub:

```
https://github.com/PacktPublishing/Data-Structures-and-Algorithms-
with-the-CPP-STL
```

Template functions

One of the hallmarks of the C++ **Standard Template Library** (**STL**) is its commitment to type-generic programming. This allows algorithms to be written to operate on multiple data types, effectively sidestepping the restrictions of traditional type-specific functions. C++ achieves this remarkable feat using template functions. Let us explore these template functions.

A primer on function templates

At the heart of type-generic programming lies the function template, an incredible tool that allows developers to write functions without specifying the exact data types they will operate on. Instead of committing to a single type, templates let you define a blueprint, making the function adaptable to various types. Here's a simple example: imagine writing a function that swaps the values of two variables. With function templates, this `swap` function can cater to integers, floats, strings, and even custom types!

Variadic templates – multiplicity in templates

Variadic templates elevate the power of function templates by allowing you to write functions that accept a variable number of template arguments. This is especially handy when crafting algorithms that need to operate on different numbers of inputs. They become indispensable when you think of functions that combine, transform, or process multiple containers or elements simultaneously. As you explore the STL, you'll see many instances where this flexibility becomes crucial.

SFINAE – fine-tuning template substitution

Substitution failure is not an error (**SFINAE**) sounds like a cryptic concept, but it is a cornerstone for creating resilient template functions in C++. It's a mechanism that allows the compiler to discard specific template overloads based on whether the type substitution leads to a valid result. In essence, it is like giving the compiler a set of rules on which template to pick based on the specifics of the provided types.

Imagine you're writing a function template that operates on STL containers. With SFINAE, you can direct the compiler to pick a particular overload when the container is a sequence container and another when it is an associative container. The magic here lies in ensuring that the template substitution remains valid.

Harnessing SFINAE with std::enable_if

The `std::enable_if` utility is a boon when working with SFINAE. It's a type trait that can conditionally remove or add a particular function overload from the set of overloads considered during template substitution. Coupling `std::enable_if` with type traits allows you to fine-tune your algorithms to cater to specific STL container characteristics.

Let's look at an example that demonstrates the concepts of function templates, variadic templates, and SFINAE:

```
#include <iostream>
#include <map>
#include <type_traits>
#include <vector>
```

```cpp
// Function Template
template <typename T> void swap(T &a, T &b) {
  T temp = a;
  a = b;
  b = temp;
}

// Variadic Template
template <typename... Args> void print(Args... args) {

  (std::cout << ... << args) << '\n';
}

// SFINAE with std::enable_if
template <typename T, typename std::enable_if<
                          std::is_integral<T>::value>::type
                          * = nullptr>
void process(T t) {
  std::cout << "Processing integral: " << t << '\n';
}

template <typename T,
          typename std::enable_if<std::is_floating_point<
              T>::value>::type * = nullptr>
void process(T t) {
  std::cout << "Processing floating point: " << t << '\n';
}

// SFINAE for STL containers
template <
    typename T,
    typename std::enable_if<std::is_same<
        T, std::vector<int>>::value>::type * = nullptr>
void processContainer(T &t) {
  std::cout << "Processing vector: ";
  for (const auto &i : t) { std::cout << i << ' '; }

  std::cout << '\n';
}

template <
    typename T,
```

```
      typename std::enable_if<std::is_same<
          T, std::map<int, int>>::value>::type * = nullptr>
  void processContainer(T &t) {
    std::cout << "Processing map: ";
    for (const auto &[key, value] : t) {
      std::cout << "{" << key << ": " << value << "} ";
    }

    std::cout << '\n';
  }

  int main() {
    // Function Template
    int a = 5, b = 10;
    swap(a, b);
    std::cout << "Swapped values: " << a << ", " << b
              << '\n';

    // Variadic Template
    print("Hello", " ", "World", "!");

    // SFINAE with std::enable_if
    process(10);
    process(3.14);

    // SFINAE for STL containers
    std::vector<int> vec = {1, 2, 3, 4, 5};
    processContainer(vec);

    std::map<int, int> map = {{1, 2}, {3, 4}, {5, 6}};
    processContainer(map);

    return 0;
  }
```

Here is the example output:

```
Swapped values: 10, 5
Hello World!
Processing integral: 10
Processing floating point: 3.14
Processing vector: 1 2 3 4 5
Processing map: {1: 2} {3: 4} {5: 6}
```

This code demonstrates the concepts of function templates, variadic templates, and SFINAE. The `swap` function is a simple function template that swaps two variables of any type. The `print` function is a variadic template that prints any number of arguments. The `process` functions demonstrate SFINAE with `std::enable_if`, where different overloads are chosen based on the type of argument. Finally, the `processContainer` functions show how SFINAE can be used to differentiate between different STL containers.

Understanding and mastering function templates will be pivotal as you venture deeper into creating STL-compatible algorithms. They ensure that your algorithms are versatile, adapting to various types and scenarios. But more than just flexibility, templates bolster efficiency. By working closely with the type system, your algorithms can be optimized for specific types, yielding performance benefits.

Function templates, variadic templates, and SFINAE are more than just tools; they are the bedrock upon which the STL's type-generic paradigm stands. By leveraging these, you are aligning with the STL's philosophy and elevating your algorithms' adaptability and power.

As we progress further into the chapter, we'll review overloading techniques, understand the nuances of creating truly generic algorithms, and learn the art of customizing existing ones for specific needs. Each step brings us closer to mastering the art of crafting exceptional STL-compatible algorithms.

Overloading

Function overloading is a cornerstone of C++ programming, enabling developers to define multiple versions of a function with the same name but different parameters. This ability is especially crucial when crafting algorithms that interact with the diverse palette of STL containers, each with its unique characteristics and requirements. With overloading, you can tailor your algorithms to specific containers or situations, ensuring optimal performance and flexibility.

Crafting multiple algorithm versions for STL containers

A need to treat specific containers differently based on their inherent properties might arise when designing algorithms compatible with STL containers. For instance, an algorithm interacting with `std::vector` might have different requirements than when dealing with `std::map`. By utilizing function overloading, you can design separate versions of the algorithm optimized for each container type, ensuring that each interaction is as efficient as possible.

Function resolution – navigating the intricacies

Function overloading comes with challenges, and understanding function resolution is pivotal. When multiple overloaded functions are potential candidates for a call, the compiler follows a strict set of rules to determine the best match. It considers the number of arguments, their types, and their potential type conversions. As you overload functions for STL-compatible algorithms, being aware of these rules is paramount. It ensures that the correct version of your function gets invoked and prevents any unexpected behaviors or ambiguities.

Overloading with care – clarity and consistency

The power to overload functions can be both a boon and a pitfall. While it allows for greater flexibility, it also introduces the risk of cluttering your code base with too many function variations, potentially leading to confusion. A golden rule when overloading is to maintain clarity and consistency.

Ask yourself whether the overloaded version offers a different or optimized approach for a particular STL container or scenario. If it doesn't, perhaps relying on a generic version that can cater to multiple scenarios is more prudent. A well-designed function signature, combined with meaningful parameter names, can often convey the function's purpose, reducing the need for excessive overloading.

Furthermore, ensure that your documentation is precise. Mention the purpose of each overloaded version, the scenarios in which it should be used, and how it differs from other versions. This not only aids other developers who might use or maintain your algorithms but also serves as a valuable reference for your future self.

With a firm grasp on overloading, you are now poised to dive further into the world of STL-compatible algorithms. The techniques you've acquired here lay the foundation for creating generic algorithms and customizing existing ones to cater to specific needs. The journey ahead is exciting, filled with opportunities to design robust, versatile algorithms that seamlessly integrate with the vast expanse of STL containers, genuinely exemplifying the essence of C++ programming.

Creating generic algorithms

In this section, we will learn about constructing algorithms that transcend type-specific boundaries, a fundamental aspect of advanced C++ programming. This approach is crucial for developing robust and versatile software, as it allows algorithms to operate seamlessly across a diverse array of data types and structures. This section will guide you through the principles and techniques necessary to design algorithms that are not just efficient but also adaptable and type-agnostic, aligning perfectly with the philosophy of the STL.

The ability to write generic algorithms is invaluable. It ensures that your code is not only reusable across various applications but also capable of handling unforeseen future requirements. This versatility is especially important in C++ programming, where the complexity and diversity of data types can pose significant challenges. By focusing on a type-independent approach and embracing tools such as iterators, predicates, and functors, you will learn to create algorithms that are not constrained by type-specific limitations. This knowledge will empower you to write code that is more maintainable, scalable, and aligned with best practices in C++ programming. As we work through these concepts, you'll gain the skills to make your algorithms a perfect fit for the STL, enhancing both their utility and performance.

Toward a type-independent approach

As you create generic algorithms, one guiding principle is the type-independent approach. The strength of C++ and the STL is their ability to craft algorithms that, at their core, do not care about the type they operate on. They focus on logic, and the underlying machinery handles the type-specific details, primarily templates and iterators.

Embracing iterators – the bridge to generics

In many ways, iterators are the secret sauce behind the generic nature of STL algorithms. Think of iterators as bridging the gap between type-specific containers and type-agnostic algorithms. When crafting a generic algorithm, you typically wouldn't accept a container as a parameter. Instead, you'd accept iterators, and these iterators abstract away the underlying container and its type.

For example, instead of designing an algorithm specifically for `std::vector<int>`, accept iterators as parameters. This makes your algorithm applicable to `std::vector<int>` and potentially to any container that provides the required iterator type.

```cpp
// This function only takes a specific kind of vector
void printElements(const std::vector<int> &vec) {
  std::for_each(vec.begin(), vec.end(),
                [](int x) { std::cout << x << " "; });
  std::cout << "\n";
}

// Template function that operates on iterators, making it
// applicable to any container type
template <typename Iterator>
void printElements(Iterator begin, Iterator end) {
  while (begin != end) {
    std::cout << *begin << " ";
    ++begin;
  }
  std::cout << "\n";
}
```

These examples show how a function that takes iterators as parameters can be more versatile than one that takes a reference to a container.

Predicates – customizing algorithm behavior

But what if you wish to introduce a hint of customization? What if you want your generic algorithm to have a configurable behavior? Enter predicates.

Predicates are Boolean-valued unary or binary functions (or function objects). When passed to an algorithm, they can influence its behavior. For instance, when sorting a collection, you can provide a predicate to determine the ordering of elements. By harnessing predicates, your algorithms can remain generic but still be tailored to specific scenarios without hardcoding any behavior.

The magic of functors – enhancing flexibility

While predicates allow customization, functors (or function objects) take this to another level. A **functor** is an object that can be called as if it were a function. The essential advantage here is statefulness. Unlike simple function pointers or lambdas, functors can maintain state, providing a more significant degree of flexibility.

Imagine designing a generic algorithm that applies a transformation to each element in an STL container. By accepting a functor as a parameter, users of your algorithm can not only specify the transformation logic but also carry some state with it, making for robust and adaptable solutions.

With iterators, predicates, and functors in your toolkit, you're well-equipped to craft generic algorithms that are versatile yet type-agnostic. Always focus on the logic, keep the type specifics abstracted away, and provide avenues (such as predicates and functors) for users to inject custom behavior.

As you move ahead, remember that the essence of generic programming is adaptability. Algorithms should be built to cater to a wide range of scenarios and types. The upcoming section will guide you through adapting and extending the already robust set of STL algorithms, amplifying the power of your C++ code base.

Customizing existing algorithms

The STL provides for adapting and enhancing its already robust set of algorithms. This skill is crucial for any proficient C++ programmer, as it allows for the fine-tuning of algorithms to meet specific needs without starting from scratch. In this section, you will learn how to use design patterns, such as the **decorator pattern**, and lambda functions to modify existing algorithms, making them more suitable for your unique requirements.

In practical programming scenarios, you often encounter situations where an existing STL algorithm *almost* meets your needs but requires some adjustments. Knowing how to customize these algorithms, as opposed to creating entirely new ones, can save significant time and effort. This section will teach you to leverage existing solutions and adapt them creatively, ensuring efficiency and maintainability. You will discover how to integrate design patterns to add new behaviors or modify existing ones and how to use lambda functions for concise and effective customizations.

Looking at the decorator pattern in action

When confronted with an STL algorithm that almost fits the bill but not entirely, resisting the urge to reinvent the wheel is crucial. Instead, adapting these algorithms using tried and true design patterns can often lead to a more elegant, efficient, and maintainable solution.

One of the most potent design patterns in this context is the decorator pattern. It allows you to take an existing algorithm and add or modify behaviors without altering its structure. Consider a scenario where you have a sorting algorithm and want to add logging capabilities. Instead of rewriting or overloading the function, use the decorator pattern to create a new algorithm that calls the original sorting function and adds logging on top. The beauty here is in the separation of concerns and the ability to chain decorators for multiple additional behaviors.

Let's look at the decorator pattern in action. We will use it to add logging to an STL comparison function:

```cpp
#include <algorithm>
#include <functional>
#include <iostream>
#include <vector>

// Decorator for adding logging to the compare function
template <typename Compare> class LoggingCompareDecorator {
public:
  LoggingCompareDecorator(Compare comp) : comp(comp) {}

  template <typename T>
  bool operator()(const T &lhs, const T &rhs) {
    bool result = comp(lhs, rhs);
    std::cout << "Comparing " << lhs << " and " << rhs
              << ": "
              << (result ? "lhs < rhs" : "lhs >= rhs")
              << "\n";
    return result;
  }

private:
  Compare comp;
};

int main() {
  std::vector<int> numbers = {4, 2, 5, 1, 3};

  // Original comparison function
  auto comp = std::less<int>();
```

```
// Decorating the comparison function with logging
LoggingCompareDecorator<decltype(comp)> decoratedComp(
    comp);

// Using the decorated comparison in sort algorithm
std::sort(numbers.begin(), numbers.end(), decoratedComp);

// Output the sorted numbers
std::cout << "Sorted numbers: ";
for (int num : numbers) { std::cout << num << " "; }
std::cout << "\n";

return 0;
}
```

Here is the example output:

```
Comparing 2 and 4: lhs < rhs
Comparing 4 and 2: lhs >= rhs
Comparing 5 and 2: lhs >= rhs
Comparing 5 and 4: lhs >= rhs
Comparing 1 and 2: lhs < rhs
Comparing 2 and 1: lhs >= rhs
Comparing 3 and 1: lhs >= rhs
Comparing 3 and 5: lhs < rhs
Comparing 5 and 3: lhs >= rhs
Comparing 3 and 4: lhs < rhs
Comparing 4 and 3: lhs >= rhs
Comparing 3 and 2: lhs >= rhs
Sorted numbers: 1 2 3 4 5
```

In this example, LoggingCompareDecorator is a template class that takes a comparison function object (comp) and adds logging around it. operator() is overridden to add logging before calling the original comparison function. The original sorting algorithm (std::sort) is used with the decorated comparison function, thereby adding logging to each comparison operation without altering the sorting algorithm itself. This demonstrates the decorator pattern by allowing additional behavior (logging) to be added to an existing function (std::less) in a manner that is clean and maintainable and adheres to the separation of concerns principle.

Harnessing the power of lambda functions

Lambda functions are magnificent tools in the C++ arsenal. They enable developers to define anonymous functions in place, making code concise and, in many cases, more readable. When customizing existing STL algorithms, lambdas can be a game-changer.

Imagine you're using the `std::transform` algorithm, which applies a function to every element in a container. The beauty of `std::transform` is its flexibility in accepting any callable object, including lambdas. So, instead of defining a whole new function or functor, you can pass a lambda function directly to tailor its behavior to your needs.

Let's take an example. Suppose you want to square each element in a vector. Instead of creating a separate function named `square`, you can pass a lambda, as shown in the following code:

```
std::transform(vec.begin(), vec.end(), vec.begin(),
               [](int x) { return x * x; });
```

Lambdas can also capture variables from their surrounding scope, giving you the power to use external data in your custom logic. For instance, if you want to multiply each element in a vector by a dynamic factor, you can capture that factor in a lambda and use it inside:

```
void vectorTransform(std::vector<int> &vec, int factor) {
  std::transform(vec.begin(), vec.end(), vec.begin(),
                 [factor](int x) { return x * factor; });
}
```

Lambda functions in C++ offer a succinct and flexible way to define anonymous, inline functions, greatly simplifying the code, especially for short, one-time-use functions. They enhance readability and maintainability, and when used in conjunction with STL algorithms, they allow for concise and powerful custom behaviors without the need for verbose function or functor definitions.

Mixing patterns with lambdas for ultimate customization

When you combine the power of design patterns with the flexibility of lambda functions, you get a toolset that allows for profound customization of existing algorithms. For instance, you could use the **strategy pattern** to define a family of algorithms and then employ lambda functions to fine-tune the behavior of each strategy. This synergy can lead to highly modular and adaptable code, maximizing code reuse and minimizing redundancy.

Let's look at an example of using lambdas with the strategy pattern:

```
#include <algorithm>
#include <iostream>
#include <vector>
```

```cpp
// Define a Strategy interface
class Strategy {
public:
  virtual void
  execute(const std::vector<int> &data) const = 0;
};

// Define a Concrete Strategy that uses std::for_each and a
// lambda function
class ForEachStrategy : public Strategy {
public:
  void
  execute(const std::vector<int> &data) const override {
    std::for_each(data.begin(), data.end(), [](int value) {
      std::cout << "ForEachStrategy: " << value << "\n";
    });
  }
};

// Define a Concrete Strategy that uses std::transform and
// a lambda function
class TransformStrategy : public Strategy {
public:
  void
  execute(const std::vector<int> &data) const override {
    std::vector<int> transformedData(data.size());
    std::transform(data.begin(), data.end(),
                   transformedData.begin(),
                   [](int value) { return value * 2; });

    for (const auto &value : transformedData) {
      std::cout << "TransformStrategy: " << value << "\n";
    }
  }
};

// Define a Context that uses a Strategy
class Context {
public:
  Context(Strategy *strategy) : strategy(strategy) {}

  void setStrategy(Strategy *newStrategy) {
    strategy = newStrategy;
```

```
  }

  void executeStrategy(const std::vector<int> &data) {
    strategy->execute(data);
  }

private:
  Strategy *strategy;
};

int main() {
  std::vector<int> data = {1, 2, 3, 4, 5};

  ForEachStrategy forEachStrategy;
  TransformStrategy transformStrategy;

  Context context(&forEachStrategy);
  context.executeStrategy(data);
  context.setStrategy(&transformStrategy);
  context.executeStrategy(data);
  return 0;
}
```

Here is the example output:

```
ForEachStrategy: 1
ForEachStrategy: 2
ForEachStrategy: 3
ForEachStrategy: 4
ForEachStrategy: 5
TransformStrategy: 2
TransformStrategy: 4
TransformStrategy: 6
TransformStrategy: 8
TransformStrategy: 10
```

In this example, `Strategy` is an abstract base class that defines a family of algorithms. `ForEachStrategy` and `TransformStrategy` are concrete strategies that implement these algorithms using `std::for_each` and `std::transform`, respectively. Both algorithms use lambda functions to define their behavior. The `Context` class uses `Strategy` to execute an algorithm, and `Strategy` can be changed at runtime. This demonstrates the power of combining design patterns with lambda functions to create highly modular and adaptable code.

Customizing existing algorithms is an art and a science. It requires a deep understanding of the existing STL tools, a dash of creativity, and the discipline to maintain clarity and efficiency. As you venture forward, always prioritize understanding the problem and choosing the right tool for the job. Customize thoughtfully, and the STL will reward you with elegant solutions to even the most intricate problems.

Summary

As we conclude this chapter on creating STL-compatible algorithms, we have learned the essential techniques and concepts for crafting versatile and efficient algorithms in C++. Starting with the fundamentals of type-generic programming, you have learned the art of using function templates, variadic templates, and the subtle yet powerful SFINAE principle. These tools enable you to write algorithms that are adaptable to a multitude of data types, a hallmark of the STL's flexibility and power.

This chapter has also guided you through the intricacies of function overloading, a critical skill for tailoring algorithms to different STL containers and scenarios. You've learned how to navigate the complexities of function resolution and the importance of maintaining clarity and consistency when overloading functions. This knowledge ensures that your algorithms are not only versatile but also intuitive and efficient in their interaction with various STL components.

Looking ahead, the next chapter will uncover the world of type traits and policies, exploring how these tools enhance code adaptability and empower metaprogramming. You'll learn about the benefits of using policies in relation to the STL, how to build modular components, and the potential challenges you may encounter. This chapter will not only deepen your understanding of advanced C++ features but also equip you with practical skills for implementing type traits and policies in your code, ensuring compatibility and flexibility in your programming.

18

Type Traits and Policies

This chapter covers compile-time type information (type traits) and modular, policy-based design in C++. It will showcase how they empower metaprogramming and foster versatile code design when working with the C++ **Standard Template Library** (**STL**) data types and algorithms. It also discusses policies, presenting a strategy to customize the behavior in templated code without altering core logic. Through real-world examples, hands-on implementation techniques, and best practices, you will harness the potential of these powerful C++ tools with the STL, creating adaptable and optimized software components.

This chapter will cover the following:

- Understanding and using type traits
- Utilizing type traits with the STL
- Understanding and using policies in C++
- Using policies with the STL

Technical requirements

The code in this chapter can be found on GitHub:

https://github.com/PacktPublishing/Data-Structures-and-Algorithms-with-the-CPP-STL

Understanding and using type traits

When writing generic code in C++, there's often a need to gather information about types without knowing the specifics of those types in advance. Enter **type traits**—a toolkit for querying and manipulating type information at compile time. Think of them as inspectors that report on the characteristics of types, allowing you to make informed decisions in your code based on those reports.

C++'s STL provides a rich collection of type traits in the `<type_traits>` header. These traits can answer questions such as: Is a particular type a pointer? An integer? Is it arithmetic? Can it be default-constructed? For instance, `std::is_integral<T>::value` will return `true` if T is an integral type or `false` otherwise.

Enhancing code adaptability with type traits

Type traits aren't just a means of introspection; they're enablers of adaptability. By understanding the properties of types, you can design algorithms and data structures that adjust their behavior accordingly.

Consider a generic function that must operate differently for pointers and non-pointer types. With the help of `std::is_pointer<T>::value`, you can conditionally execute code paths using `if constexpr` statements, tailoring the behavior at compile time. This creates cleaner and more intuitive code and results in optimal performance, as the unnecessary code paths are pruned away during compilation.

Another everyday use case is optimizing storage in generic containers. For instance, if a type is trivially destructible (without custom destruction logic), you can safely skip calling its destructor, leading to performance gains. Here, `std::is_trivially_destructible<T>::value` comes to the rescue.

Empowering metaprogramming with type traits

Metaprogramming, the act of writing code that generates or manipulates other code, is a hallmark of advanced C++ programming. Type traits are invaluable tools in this area, enabling richer and more expressive compile-time computations.

A classic metaprogramming problem is factorial calculation at compile time. While this can be achieved through template recursion, the real challenge is to halt the recursion for non-integer types. This is where `std::is_integral<T>::value` proves its worth, ensuring that the computation only progresses for valid types.

Another powerful facet is using type traits with `static_assert` to enforce constraints. If you're writing a template function that should only accept arithmetic types, a simple static assertion with `std::is_arithmetic<T>::value` can ensure the code won't compile for unsuitable types, providing clear and immediate feedback to the developer.

Toward more informed and adaptable code

As you master type traits, remember these tools are not just about querying type properties. They leverage that knowledge to craft more robust, adaptable, and efficient code. Whether you aim for ultimate performance, cleaner interfaces, or just the satisfaction of metaprogramming mastery, type traits are ready to assist.

In the following sections, we'll further explore how type traits synergize with policies and, more importantly, how to craft your own type traits and policies, tailoring them to fit the unique demands of your projects.

Utilizing type traits with the STL

Utilizing type traits with STL data types and algorithms is a powerful technique that enhances the efficiency and correctness of C++ programming. When applied to STL data types, type traits enable a deeper understanding of the characteristics of these types, such as their size, alignment, or whether they are fundamental types. This insight can significantly optimize data storage and access patterns, leading to better memory management and performance.

In the context of STL algorithms, type traits are instrumental in selecting the most appropriate algorithm or optimizing its behavior based on the properties of the types involved. For example, knowing whether a type supports certain operations can allow algorithms to bypass unnecessary checks or use more efficient techniques. This boosts performance and ensures that algorithms with various types behave as expected.

Applying type traits in STL data types and algorithms is essential to advanced C++ programming, enabling developers to write more efficient, robust, and adaptable code. Let's begin to discover the full potential of type traits in the context of the STL's data types and algorithms.

Working with data types

Understanding and utilizing type traits is important for writing robust and adaptable code. Type traits, a part of the STL, allow programmers to query and interact with types at compile time, fostering type safety and efficiency.

Type traits offer the compile-time introspection of types, enabling programmers to write generic and type-safe code. They are particularly useful in template metaprogramming, where operations depend on type properties. By leveraging type traits, developers can ascertain type properties, such as whether a type is an integer, floating-point, or whether it supports certain operations. We can also tailor code behavior based on type characteristics without incurring runtime costs or use them to write more straightforward, more maintainable code that automatically adapts to different types.

Consider a scenario where we need a function template to process numerical data, but the processing differs for integer and floating-point types. Using type traits, we can create a specialized behavior for each type:

```cpp
#include <iostream>
#include <type_traits>

template <typename T> void processNumericalData(T data) {
  if constexpr (std::is_integral_v<T>) {
```

```
      std::cout << "Processing integer: " << data << "\n";
    } else if constexpr (std::is_floating_point_v<T>) {
      std::cout << "Processing float: " << data << "\n";
    } else {
      static_assert(false, "Unsupported type.");
    }
}

int main() {
  processNumericalData(10);
  processNumericalData(10.5f);

  // Error: static_assert failed: 'Unsupported type.':
  // processNumericalData(10.5);
}
```

Here is the example output:

```
Processing integer: 10
Processing float: 10.5
```

In this example, std::is_integral_v and std::is_floating_point_v are type traits that assess whether T is an integer or floating-point type, respectively. The if constexpr construct enables compile-time decision-making, ensuring that only the relevant code block for the type T is compiled. This approach makes the code type safe and optimizes performance by avoiding unnecessary checks at runtime.

Utilizing type traits with STL data types enhances code reliability, efficiency, and maintainability. Next, let's explore more advanced uses of type traits, such as how they can be combined with other template techniques to build sophisticated, type-aware algorithms and data structures.

Working with algorithms

In addition to their indispensable role in crafting adaptable code and enabling metaprogramming, type traits also play a crucial role in conjunction with STL algorithms. This synergy between type traits and algorithms empowers us to write highly versatile and type-aware code.

Type traits for algorithm customization

STL algorithms often operate on generic data structures, ranging from sorting to searching. The ability to customize the behavior of these algorithms based on the properties of the elements they process is essential for writing efficient and flexible code.

Consider the std::sort algorithm, which can sort elements in a container. By employing type traits, we can make it more versatile. For instance, you may want to sort elements in descending order for types that support it (e.g., integers) while leaving the order unchanged for others. Using `std::is_integral<T>::value`, you can conditionally pass a custom comparison function to `std::sort`, tailoring the sorting behavior to the type being sorted as the following code illustrates:

```
template <typename T>
void customSort(std::vector<T> &data) {
  if constexpr (std::is_integral<T>::value) {
    std::sort(data.begin(), data.end(), std::greater<T>());
  } else {
    std::sort(data.begin(), data.end());
  }
}
```

This approach demonstrates how type traits can lead to more efficient code by eliminating unnecessary conditionals at runtime.

Ensuring algorithm compatibility

Consider an algorithm that processes a collection of objects to demonstrate the power of type traits with user-defined types. This algorithm requires that the objects provide a specific interface, for instance, a `serialize` method for converting the object state to a string. By employing type traits, we can ensure that the algorithm is only used with types that conform to this requirement at compile time:

```
#include <iostream>
#include <string>
#include <type_traits>
#include <vector>

// Define a type trait to check for serialize method
template <typename, typename T>
struct has_serialize : std::false_type {};

template <typename T>
struct has_serialize<
    std::void_t<decltype(std::declval<T>().serialize())>,
    T> : std::true_type {};

template <typename T>
inline constexpr bool has_serialize_v =
    has_serialize<void, T>::value;

class Person {
public:
  std::string name;
```

```
    int age{0};
    std::string serialize() const {
      return "Person{name: " + name +
             ", age: " + std::to_string(age) + "}";
    }
};

class Dog {
public:
  std::string name;
  std::string breed;
  // Note: Dog does not have a serialize method
};

template <typename T>
void processCollection(const std::vector<T> &collection) {
  static_assert(has_serialize_v<T>,
                "T must have a serialize() method.");
  for (const auto &item : collection) {
    std::cout << item.serialize() << std::endl;
  }
}

int main() {
  // Valid use, Person has a serialize method
  std::vector<Person> people = {{"Alice", 30},
                                {"Bob", 35}};
  processCollection(people);

  // Compile-time error:
  // std::vector<Dog> dogs = {{"Buddy", "Beagle"}};
  // processCollection(dogs);
}
```

Here is the example output:

```
Person{name: Alice, age: 30}
Person{name: Bob, age: 35}
```

In this example, has_serialize is a custom type trait that checks for the existence of a serialize method. The processCollection function template uses this trait to enforce that it is only used with types that provide this method. The static_assert generates a clear compile-time error message if an incompatible type is used.

Developers can create more robust and self-documenting code by enforcing algorithm compatibility with custom types using type traits. This approach ensures that constraints are clearly defined and checked at compile time, preventing runtime errors and leading to more predictable and reliable software.

Optimizing algorithms for specific types

Efficiency is a critical concern in algorithm design. Type traits can help optimize algorithms for specific types by choosing the most efficient implementation based on type properties.

For example, consider an algorithm that calculates the sum of elements in a container. If the element type is integral, you can use a more efficient integer-based accumulator, while for floating-point types, you may prefer a floating-point accumulator. Type traits such as `std::is_integral<T>::value` can guide your choice of accumulator type, resulting in more efficient calculations.

Type traits combined with STL algorithms enable you to create type-aware and efficient code. You can take full advantage of the STL while crafting robust and high-performance C++ applications by customizing algorithm behavior, ensuring compatibility, and optimizing for specific types.

Understanding and using policies in C++

Policy-based design is a design paradigm in C++ that emphasizes modularity and flexibility without sacrificing performance. It revolves around decomposing a software component's behavior into interchangeable policies. These policies dictate how specific actions are executed. By choosing different policies, the behavior of a component can be modified without changing its fundamental logic.

Benefits with respect to the STL

In the context of the STL, a policy-based design is particularly relevant. The STL is inherently generic and designed to meet a broad spectrum of programming needs. Implementing policies can significantly enhance its versatility, allowing for precise customization to specific use cases. For example, the container memory allocation strategy can be defined as a policy. Whether employing the standard allocator, a pool allocator, or a custom stack-based allocator, you can simply insert the desired policy, and the container adjusts without modifying its primary logic.

Moreover, policies can be tailored for performance in particular contexts. A sorting algorithm could utilize varied comparison strategies depending on the data type. Rather than drafting multiple iterations of the algorithm, one can design a single version and replace the comparison policy as required.

Here's a C++ code example demonstrating this concept:

```
#include <algorithm>
#include <iostream>
#include <vector>

// Define a generic comparison policy for numeric types
```

```cpp
template <typename T> struct NumericComparison {
  bool operator()(const T &a, const T &b) const {
    return (a < b);
  }
};

// Define a specific comparison policy for strings
struct StringComparison {
  bool operator()(const std::string &a,
                  const std::string &b) const {
    return (a.length() < b.length());
  }
};

// Generic sort function using a policy
template <typename Iterator, typename ComparePolicy>
void sortWithPolicy(Iterator begin, Iterator end,
                    ComparePolicy comp) {
  std::sort(begin, end, comp);
}

int main() {
  // Example with numeric data
  std::vector<int> numbers = {3, 1, 4, 1, 5, 9,
                              2, 6, 5, 3, 5};

  sortWithPolicy(numbers.begin(), numbers.end(),
                 NumericComparison<int>());

  for (auto n : numbers) { std::cout << n << " "; }
  std::cout << "\n";

  // Example with string data
  std::vector<std::string> strings = {
      "starfruit", "pear", "banana", "kumquat", "grape"};

  sortWithPolicy(strings.begin(), strings.end(),
                 StringComparison());

  for (auto &s : strings) { std::cout << s << " "; }
  std::cout << "\n";

  return 0;
}
```

Here is the example output:

```
1 1 2 3 3 4 5 5 5 6 9
pear grape banana kumquat starfruit
```

In this example, we have two comparison policies: `NumericComparison` for numeric types and `StringComparison` for strings. The `sortWithPolicy` function is a template that takes a comparison policy as an argument, allowing the same sorting function to be used with different data types and comparison strategies. The numeric data is sorted in ascending order, while the strings are sorted based on their length, demonstrating the flexibility of using policies to tailor sorting behavior.

Building modular components using policies

Consider designing a templated data structure, such as a hash table. Policies can dictate multiple elements of this hash table: the hashing technique, the collision resolution method, or the memory allocation approach. By segregating these as individual, switchable policies, the hash table can be fine-tuned to specific requirements without altering its core functionality.

This modularity also encourages code reusability. A well-crafted policy can be applied across various components, ensuring code consistency and easier maintenance.

Potential challenges

While policy-based design offers numerous advantages, it presents particular challenges. One of the primary concerns is guaranteeing policy compatibility with the main component logic. Although a component might be structured to accommodate diverse policies, each must conform to a predetermined interface or standard.

Documentation also emerges as a challenge. Given the increased flexibility that policies provide, it's essential to meticulously document the expected behaviors, interfaces, and each policy's implications, enabling users to make knowledgeable choices.

The role of policies in modern C++

As C++ progresses, the shift toward more generic and adaptable components becomes evident. Policy-based design is pivotal in this evolution, enabling developers to devise components prioritizing modularity and performance. Gaining proficiency in this design approach will empower you to produce software that not only endures but also efficiently adapts to changing needs.

In the upcoming sections, we'll examine the practical aspects of implementing type traits and policies, laying a robust groundwork for their practical application in your projects.

Using policies with the STL

In exploring policy-based design, we've established how this design paradigm fosters modularity and flexibility in C++ software components. Now, let's get into the specifics of how policies can be effectively employed to enhance the functionality and adaptability of STL data types, contributing to more efficient and customized solutions.

Memory allocation policies

One of the most pertinent applications of policies in the context of STL data types is the management of memory allocation. Consider a scenario where you must optimize memory allocation for a specific container, such as a `std::vector` instance. By introducing memory allocation policies, you can tailor the container's memory management strategy to your requirements.

For instance, you may have a specialized memory allocator optimized for your application's specific use case. Instead of modifying the container's internal logic, you can seamlessly integrate this custom allocator as a policy. This way, the `std::vector` instance can efficiently use your custom allocator without requiring fundamental code changes, as illustrated here:

```
template <typename T,
          typename AllocatorPolicy = std::allocator<T>>
class CustomVector {
  // Implementation using AllocatorPolicy for memory
  // allocation
};
```

This template class accepts a type T and an allocator policy, defaulted to `std::allocator<T>`. The critical point is that such a design allows for seamless integration of custom memory allocation strategies without altering the fundamental code structure of the container.

Sorting policies for versatile algorithms

STL algorithms, including sorting algorithms, often work with various data types. Policies offer an elegant solution when different comparison strategies are needed for sorting. Rather than creating multiple sorting algorithm versions, you can design a single algorithm and introduce a comparison policy as required.

Let's take the example of a sorting algorithm. Using a comparison policy, you can sort elements differently based on the data type. This approach streamlines your code base and avoids code duplication:

```
template <typename T,
          typename ComparisonPolicy = std::less<T>>
void customSort(std::vector<T> &data) {
  // Sorting implementation using ComparisonPolicy for
```

```
    // comparisons
}
```

This example showcases a templated `customSort` function, demonstrating how a default comparison policy can be overridden to tailor the sorting behavior for different data types. This approach exemplifies a powerful strategy for creating versatile, maintainable, and efficient sorting algorithms within the STL framework, showcasing the benefits of policy-based design in C++ programming.

Fine-tuning data structures with policies

When designing custom data structures that mimic STL containers, you can leverage policies to fine-tune their behavior. Imagine building a hash table. Policies can govern critical aspects such as the hashing technique, collision resolution method, or memory allocation approach.

By isolating these functionalities as individual, interchangeable policies, you create a hash table that can be adapted to specific use cases without altering its core logic. This modular approach simplifies maintenance, as you can adjust individual policies as needed, keeping the rest of the structure intact.

Let's look at an example of how custom hash tables can be tailored for enhanced interaction with STL types and algorithms through policy-based design. This approach allows the behavior of the hash table (such as the hashing mechanism, collision resolution strategy, or memory management) to be defined by policies, making the data structure flexible and adaptable to different use cases:

```cpp
#include <functional>
#include <list>
#include <string>
#include <type_traits>
#include <vector>

// Hashing Policy
template <typename Key> struct DefaultHashPolicy {
  std::size_t operator()(const Key &key) const {
    return std::hash<Key>()(key);
  }
};

// Collision Resolution Policy
template <typename Key, typename Value>
struct SeparateChainingPolicy {
  using BucketType = std::list<std::pair<Key, Value>>;
};

// Custom Hash Table
template <typename Key, typename Value,
```

```
            typename HashPolicy = DefaultHashPolicy<Key>,
            typename CollisionPolicy =
                SeparateChainingPolicy<Key, Value>>
class CustomHashTable {
private:
  std::vector<typename CollisionPolicy::BucketType> table;
  HashPolicy hashPolicy;
  // ...

public:
  CustomHashTable(size_t size) : table(size) {}
  // ... Implement methods like insert, find, erase
};

int main() {
  // Instantiate custom hash table with default policies
  CustomHashTable<int, std::string> hashTable(10);
  // ... Usage of hashTable
}
```

`DefaultHashPolicy` and `SeparateChainingPolicy` are default policies for hashing and collision resolution in this example. The `CustomHashTable` template class can be instantiated with different policies as required, making it highly versatile and compatible with various STL types and algorithms. This policy-based design enables fine-grained control over the behavior and characteristics of the hash table.

Policies in C++ offer a powerful toolset to enhance the adaptability and performance of STL data types. Whether it's optimizing memory allocation, customizing sorting strategies, or tailoring data structures to specific needs, policies enable us to modularly extend the capabilities of the STL components while maintaining code consistency and reusability.

Summary

In this chapter, we have covered the intricacies of type traits and policies within the context of the C++ STL. We began by examining type traits, which serve as a toolkit for compile-time type inspection, allowing us to make decisions in our code based on type characteristics. Through exploring various type traits provided in the `<type_traits>` header, we learned how to determine whether a type is a pointer, an integer, arithmetic, default-constructible, and more.

Next, we investigated how type traits enhance code adaptability, enabling us to tailor the behavior of our algorithms and data structures. We saw firsthand how traits such as `std::is_pointer` and `std::is_trivially_destructible` can optimize performance by informing our code to behave differently based on type properties.

We then transitioned to policies, exploring their role in enabling modularity and flexibility in design without compromising performance. We recognized the benefits of policy-based design in STL applications, such as customizing memory allocation and sorting strategies. The modularity of policy-based components was highlighted as a means for fine-tuning behavior and encouraging code reusability.

The utility of this chapter lies in its potential to enhance our coding practices. We can write more robust, adaptable, and efficient code using type traits. At the same time, policies allow us to construct flexible, modular components tailored to various requirements without fundamental changes.

In the next chapter, *Chapter 19*, *Exception Safety*, we will build upon the knowledge acquired here by learning about the guarantees provided by the STL regarding exceptions. We will start by understanding the basics of exception safety, focusing on the pivotal role of program invariants and resource integrity in robust software design. We will examine strong exception safety, exploring how to build STL containers that offer unwavering guarantees. Finally, we'll discuss the impact of `noexcept` on STL operations, further preparing us to write reliable and efficient C++ code that stands resilient in the face of exceptions.

Part 5: STL Data Structures and Algorithms: Under the Hood

We conclude our exploration of STL data structures and algorithms by getting into some of its more advanced usage patterns. We will venture beyond the surface into the mechanics and guarantees that enable robust, concurrent C++ applications. We will start by discovering exception safety, detailing the levels of guarantees provided by STL components and strategies for writing exception-safe code with an emphasis on the impact of noexcept.

We then venture into areas of thread safety and concurrency, dissecting the delicate balance between concurrent execution and the thread safety of STL containers and algorithms. We will gain actionable insights on race conditions, the prudent use of mutexes and locks, and the thread-safe application of STL containers, highlighting specific concerns and detailed insights into their behaviors in multithreaded environments.

Next, we will introduce the interaction of STL with modern C++ features like concepts and coroutines, showcasing how these features refine template usage and enable asynchronous programming with STL.

Finally, we will dive into parallel algorithms, discussing the incorporation of execution policies, the impact of constexpr, and performance considerations when employing parallelism in STL. This part of the book equips readers with the advanced knowledge to exploit the full potential of the STL in concurrent and parallel environments, ensuring their code is efficient, safe, and modern.

This part has the following chapters:

- *Chapter 19: Exception Safety*
- *Chapter 20: Thread Safety and Concurrency with the STL*

19

Exception Safety

This chapter will guide you through the complexities of exception safety. It demystifies the levels of exception safety, distinguishing between basic and strong guarantees, underscoring their significance, and offering proven strategies to achieve them. Mastering these advanced topics allows you to create more resilient, efficient, and adaptable C++ applications and data structures.

In this chapter, we will cover the following topics:

- Basic exception safety
- Strong exception safety
- The effect of `noexcept` on STL containers

Technical requirements

The code in this chapter can be found on GitHub:

```
https://github.com/PacktPublishing/Data-Structures-and-Algorithms-
with-the-CPP-STL
```

Basic exception safety

Basic exception safety, colloquially termed the *guarantee*, pledges that your program won't leak resources when an exception occurs and its invariants are preserved. Simply put, the software won't devolve into chaos. When unforeseen exceptions occur, the operation might fail, but your application continues functioning, and no data gets mangled.

Two real-world examples of unforeseen exceptions that can be effectively managed without causing resource leaks or data corruption include the following:

- **File operation failure during data processing**: Consider an application that processes large data files. During this process, the application might encounter an unexpected exception, such as a failure to read a portion of the file due to disk I/O errors. In this case, basic exception safety ensures the application does not leak resources (such as file handles or memory allocated for data processing). It maintains the integrity of any data structures involved. The application might not complete the intended file processing. Still, it will handle the exception gracefully, freeing up any resources and leaving the application in a stable state to continue functioning.

- **Network communication interruption in a client-server application**: In a client-server application, an unforeseen exception might occur if the network connection is suddenly lost during a critical data exchange. Basic exception safety in this scenario ensures that the application does not end up with partial or corrupted data states. The system might fail to complete the current operation (such as updating a record or retrieving data), but it will effectively manage resources such as network sockets and memory buffers. The application will catch the exception, clean up resources, and ensure its core functionality remains intact and ready for subsequent operations.

The pivotal role of program invariants in the STL

Imagine you're crafting a sophisticated application, and at its heart lies the C++ **Standard Template Library (STL)** containers. Each container, be it `std::vector`, `std::map`, or any other, operates under specific invariants. A `std::vector` container, for instance, guarantees contiguous memory. If any operation disrupts these invariants, the results can range from performance penalties to insidious bugs.

To ensure basic exception safety with the STL, you need to ascertain that operations on these containers either succeed or, if they throw an exception, leave the container in its original state without violating its invariants. For instance, if a `push_back` operation on `std::vector` throws an exception, the vector should remain untouched.

Let's look at an example of how we could use basic exception safety when pushing data into `std::vector`:

```cpp
// Adds an element to the vector, ensuring basic exception
// safety
void safePushBack(std::vector<int> &vec, int value) {
  try {
    // Attempt to add value to the vector
    vec.push_back(value);
  } catch (const std::exception &e) {
    // Handle any exception thrown by push_back
    std::cerr << "Exception caught: " << e.what() << "\n";
    // No additional action needed, vec is already in its
    // original state
  }
}
```

In this example, if an exception occurs (i.e., due to `bad_alloc` if the system runs out of memory), the `catch` block handles it. Importantly, if `push_back` throws an exception, it guarantees that the state of the vector (`vec`) remains unchanged, thus preserving the container's invariants.

Resource integrity – the guardian of robust software

An exception thrown during a memory allocation or other resource-intensive tasks can spell disaster if not managed correctly. The STL, however, offers tools that, when used aptly, ensure that resources remain intact, even when exceptions loom.

STL containers such as `std::vector` and `std::string` handle their memory. If an exception arises during an operation, the container ensures no memory leaks occur. Moreover, the idiom **Resource Acquisition Is Initialization** (**RAII**), a hallmark of C++ design, assures that resources are acquired upon object creation and released when they go out of scope. The RAII principle is a sentinel against resource leaks, particularly during exceptions.

> **Note**
>
> RAII, is a programming idiom used in C++ to manage resource allocation and deallocation. In RAII, resources (such as memory, file handles, and network connections) are acquired and released by objects. When an object is created (initialized), it acquires a resource, and when the object is destroyed (its lifetime ends), it releases the resource. This ensures automatic and exception-safe resource management, preventing resource leaks and ensuring clean resource release even in the face of exceptions. RAII is a fundamental concept in C++ for effective resource management.

Harnessing the STL for basic exception safety

With the STL at your disposal and knowledge of its intricacies, achieving basic exception safety becomes less daunting. Consider the following best practices:

- **Leveraging the copy-and-swap idiom**: When modifying STL containers, a common technique to ensure exception safety is to create a copy of the container, perform the operations on the copy, and then swap the contents with the original. If an exception arises, the original remains unaffected.

- **Resource management with RAII**: Make extensive use of smart pointers and member variable initialization. For instance, both `std::shared_ptr` and `std::unique_ptr` not only manage memory but also guarantee no leaks during exceptions.

- **Guarded operations**: Before any irreversible operation on an STL container, always ensure that any operation that can throw an exception has already been executed.

- **Staying informed with STL documentation**: Familiarize yourself with the exception guarantees of STL functions and methods. Awareness of what exceptions a particular STL function might throw aids in crafting resilient software.

Embracing basic exception safety with the STL sets the stage for more resilient, reliable, and robust software. With this foundational understanding, you're equipped to tackle the intricacies of STL, ensuring that even when the unexpected occurs, your software stands unyielding. But this is just the beginning, as the next level, strong exception safety, beckons, offering even more robust guarantees and strategies to wield the STL with finesse.

Strong exception safety

As you immerse yourself further into the intricate world of C++ and the STL, you'll encounter the term *strong exception safety*. This is not just fancy jargon but also the gold standard in the STL's exception handling. It guarantees developers an assurance like no other – operations will either complete successfully or revert to their previous state without any side effects. It's like having a safety net that ensures, come what may, your application's integrity remains unscathed.

Navigating STL containers with strong guarantees

Remember those dynamic days spent with `std::vector`, `std::map`, and other STL containers? Now, think of adding elements, resizing, or even modifying them. When these operations succeed, it is business as usual. But if they falter and throw an exception, strong exception safety guarantees that the container remains as it was, untouched and unaltered.

Achieving this with STL containers, fortunately, doesn't demand Herculean efforts. Many STL container operations naturally provide strong exception safety. But when they don't, techniques such as the *copy-and-swap* idiom rescue them. By operating on a copy and swapping the contents with the original only when sure of success, you can guarantee no changes to the original container if an exception is thrown.

Crafting custom STL containers with strong guarantees

When venturing into the territory of creating custom STL containers, the responsibility to ensure strong exception safety rests squarely on your shoulders. Key strategies to achieve this include the following practices:

- **Localized commit points**: By delaying any changes that affect the container's state until the very last moment and ensuring that these changes are exception-free once started, you solidify a strong guarantee.

- **RAII to the forefront**: Harnessing the might of RAII, especially with resource management, is pivotal. This ensures that resources are appropriately managed and cleaned up if there are exceptions, leaving the container unchanged.

- **Immutable operations**: Whenever possible, design operations that don't modify the container until they're sure of success.

To illustrate the concept of creating custom STL containers with strong guarantees, let's consider the example of a custom container that manages a dynamic array. The code will demonstrate localized commit points, the RAII idiom, and immutable operations to provide strong exception safety.

First, we are going to create the `CustomArray` class. The `CustomArray` class is a template class designed to manage dynamic arrays of a specified data type, T. It provides essential functionalities for creating, copying, moving, and managing dynamic arrays with a strong exception guarantee. The class uses RAII principles and leverages `std::unique_ptr` for resource management, ensuring efficient and safe memory handling. It supports both copy and move semantics, making it suitable for use in various scenarios, such as dynamic array manipulation and container reallocation. Let's walk through this in sections.

We will break this example up into several sections to discuss here. For the full code example, please refer to the GitHub repository. First, we will look at the constructors:

```
template <typename T> class CustomArray {
public:
  explicit CustomArray(size_t size)
      : size(size), data(std::make_unique<T[]>(size)) {
    // Initialize with default values, assuming T can be
    // default constructed safely std::fill provides strong
    // guarantee
    std::fill(data.get(), data.get() + size, T());
  }

  // Copy constructor
  CustomArray(const CustomArray &other)
      : size(other.size),
        data(std::make_unique<T[]>(other.size)) {
    safeCopy(data.get(), other.data.get(), size);
  }

  // Move constructor - noexcept for strong guarantee
  // during container reallocation
  CustomArray(CustomArray &&other) noexcept
      : size(other.size), data(std::move(other.data)) {
    other.size = 0;
  }

  void safeCopy(T *destination, T *source, size_t size) {
    // std::copy provides strong guarantee
```

```
    std::copy(source, source + size, destination);
}
```

We provided three constructors for our class:

- `explicit CustomArray(size_t size)`: This is the primary constructor of the `CustomArray` class. It allows you to create an instance of the class by specifying the desired size for the dynamic array. It initializes the `size` member variable with the provided size and allocates memory for the dynamic array, using `std::make_unique`. It also initializes the elements of the array with default values (assuming that type T can be safely default-constructed), using `std::fill`. This constructor is marked as `explicit`, meaning it cannot be used for implicit type conversions.

- `CustomArray(const CustomArray &other)`: This is the copy constructor of the `CustomArray` class. It allows you to create a new `CustomArray` object that is a copy of an existing `CustomArray` object, `other`. It initializes the `size` member with the size of `other`, allocates memory for the dynamic array, and then uses the `safeCopy` function to perform a deep copy of the data from `other` to the new object. This constructor is used when you want to create a new copy of an existing object.

- `CustomArray(CustomArray &&other) noexcept`: This is the move constructor of the `CustomArray` class. It enables you to efficiently transfer ownership of the data from one `CustomArray` object (typically `rvalue`) to another. It transfers the ownership of the dynamically allocated array from `other` to the current object using `std::move`, updates the `size` member, and sets `size` of `other` to zero to indicate that it no longer owns the data. This constructor is marked `noexcept` to ensure a strong guarantee during container reallocation, meaning it won't throw exceptions. It's used when you want to move the contents of one object into another, typically for optimization purposes.

Next, let's look at the assignment operator overloads:

```
// Copy assignment operator
CustomArray &operator=(const CustomArray &other) {
  if (this != &other) {
    std::unique_ptr<T[]> newData(
        std::make_unique<T[]>(other.size));
    safeCopy(newData.get(), other.data.get(),
             other.size);
    size = other.size;
    data = std::move(
        newData); // Commit point, only change state here
  }

  return *this;
}
```

```
// Move assignment operator - noexcept for strong
// guarantee during container reallocation
CustomArray &operator=(CustomArray &&other) noexcept {
  if (this != &other) {
    data = std::move(other.data);
    size = other.size;
    other.size = 0;
  }

  return *this;
}
```

Here, we provided two overloads of the assignment operator. These two member functions are assignment operators for the `CustomArray` class:

- `CustomArray &operator=(const CustomArray &other)`: This is the copy assignment operator. It allows you to assign the contents of one `CustomArray` object to another of the same type. It performs a deep copy of the data from `other` to the current object, ensuring that both objects have independent copies of the data. It also updates the `size` member and transfers ownership of the new data using `std::move`. The operator returns a reference to the current object, allowing for chaining assignments.

- `CustomArray &operator=(CustomArray &&other) noexcept`: This is the move assignment operator. It allows you to efficiently transfer ownership of the data from one `CustomArray` object (typically `rvalue`) to another. It moves `std::unique_ptr` containing the data from `other` to the current object, updates the `size` member, and sets `size` of `other` to zero to indicate that it no longer owns the data. This operator is marked `noexcept` to ensure a strong guarantee during container reallocation, meaning it won't throw exceptions. Like the copy assignment operator, it returns a reference to the current object:

```
int main() {
  try {
    // CustomArray managing an array of 5 integers
    CustomArray<int> arr(5);
    // ... Use the array
  } catch (const std::exception &e) {
    std::cerr << "An exception occurred: " << e.what()
              << '\n';
    // CustomArray destructor will clean up resources if an
    // exception occurs
  }

  return 0;
}
```

To summarize this example, the `CustomArray` class demonstrates the following principles:

- **Localized commit points**: The state of the container (the internal array, `data`) is only changed at commit points, such as at the end of the copy assignment operator, after the success of all operations that could potentially throw an exception.

- **RAII to the forefront**: `std::unique_ptr` manages the dynamic array, ensuring that memory is automatically deallocated when the `CustomArray` object goes out of scope or an exception occurs.

- **Immutable operations**: Operations that could throw exceptions, such as memory allocation and copying, are performed on temporary objects. The container's state is modified only when these operations are guaranteed to have succeeded.

This example follows C++ and STL best practices and uses modern C++ features, ensuring a custom container that respects strong exception safety guarantees.

Infusing exception safety into custom STL algorithms

Algorithms dance in harmony with data. In the STL, ensuring that custom algorithms provide strong exception safety guarantees can be the difference between an efficient application and one riddled with unpredictable behaviors.

To ensure this, you should keep the following in mind:

- **Operate on copies**: Wherever feasible, operate on a copy of the data, ensuring the original remains unmodified if exceptions are thrown.

- **Atomic operations**: Design algorithms where operations, once started, are completed successfully or can be rolled back without side effects.

Exception safety is the path to robust applications

Strong exception safety is more than just a tenet – it is a commitment to the reliability and robustness of your application. When wielding the STL, its containers, and its algorithms or venturing into creating your own, this guarantee stands as a bulwark against unforeseen exceptions and unpredictable behaviors.

By ensuring that operations either see through to their successful completion or restore the original state, strong exception safety not only elevates the reliability of applications but also imbues developers with confidence that their software can weather the storms of exceptions, leaving the integrity of their data and resources intact.

With this, we wrap up our exploration of exception safety in the STL. As we explored basic and strong guarantees, the hope is that you're now equipped with the knowledge and tools to craft resilient and dependable C++ applications. And remember that in the dynamic world of software development, it is not just about preventing exceptions but also ensuring we're prepared when they arise. Next, we will examine the use of `noexcept` on STL operations.

The effect of noexcept on STL operations

The C++ STL gives a rich assortment of data structures and algorithms that greatly simplify programming in C++. Exception safety is a critical aspect of robust C++ programming, and the `noexcept` specifier plays a pivotal role in achieving it. This section elucidates the impact of noexcept on STL operations and how its correct application can enhance the reliability and performance of STL-based code.

An introduction to noexcept

Introduced in C++11, `noexcept` is a specifier that can be added to function declarations to indicate that the function is not expected to throw exceptions. When a function is declared with `noexcept`, it enables specific optimizations and guarantees that make exception handling more predictable. For instance, when an exception is thrown from a `noexcept` function, the program calls `std::terminate`, as the function violated its contract of not throwing exceptions. Hence, `noexcept` is a commitment that a function promises to uphold.

Application to STL data types

Using `noexcept` with STL data types primarily affects the move operations – move constructors and move assignment operators. These operations are fundamental to the performance of STL containers, since they allow the transfer of resources from one object to another without costly deep copies. When these operations are `noexcept`, STL containers can safely perform optimizations, such as reallocating buffers more efficiently during resizing operations.

Consider a scenario with `std::vector`, an STL container that dynamically resizes itself as elements are added. Suppose the vector holds objects of a type whose move constructor is `noexcept`. In that case, the vector can reallocate its internal array by moving the objects to the new array without the overhead of handling potential exceptions. If the move constructor is not `noexcept`, the vector must use the copy constructor instead, which is less efficient and might throw exceptions, leading to a potential partial state and loss of strong exception safety.

Application to STL algorithms

The impact of `noexcept` extends beyond data types to algorithms. STL algorithms can offer stronger guarantees and perform better when working with functions that are `noexcept`. For example, `std::sort` can execute more efficiently if its comparison function does not throw exceptions. The algorithm can optimize its implementation, knowing that it does not need to account for the complications that arise from exception handling.

Let's take the `std::for_each` algorithm, which applies a function to a range of elements. If the used function is marked as `noexcept`, `std::for_each` can operate with the understanding that exceptions will not interrupt the iteration. This can lead to better inlining and reduced overhead, as the compiler does not need to generate additional code to handle exceptions.

Consider the following example:

```cpp
std::vector<int> data{1, 2, 3, 4, 5};
std::for_each(data.begin(), data.end(), [](int& value) noexcept {
    value *= 2;
});
```

In this example, the lambda function passed to `std::for_each` is declared `noexcept`. This informs the compiler and the algorithm that the function is guaranteed not to throw any exceptions, allowing potential performance optimizations.

The `noexcept` specifier is a powerful tool for C++ developers, providing performance optimizations and semantic guarantees about exception safety. When applied judiciously to STL operations, `noexcept` enables STL containers and algorithms to operate more efficiently and reliably. Understanding and using `noexcept` appropriately is essential for intermediate-level C++ developers looking to write high-quality, exception-safe code with STL.

Summary

In this chapter, we looked to understand the crucial concept of exception safety with the STL. We explored the different levels of exception safety, namely basic and strong guarantees, and outlined strategies to ensure that your programs are resilient to exceptions. We learned how to maintain program invariants and resource integrity through detailed discussions, mainly focusing on RAII principles and guarded operations to prevent resource leaks and maintain container states during exceptions.

Understanding exception safety is indispensable for writing robust C++ applications. It ensures that, even in the face of errors, your software's integrity remains intact, preventing resource leaks and preserving the validity of data structures. This knowledge is the backbone of reliable and maintainable code, as it allows us to uphold strong guarantees that our applications will behave predictably under exceptional conditions.

In the next chapter, titled *Thread Safety and Concurrency with the STL*, we will build upon the foundation of exception safety to tackle the intricacies of concurrent programming in C++.

20

Thread Safety and Concurrency with the STL

This chapter explores concurrency within the C++ **Standard Template Library** (**STL**). The chapter begins by building a solid foundational understanding of thread safety, race conditions, and their inherent risks. We then shift to the STL, decoding its thread safety guarantees and spotlighting its potential pitfalls. As we proceed, readers will gain insights into the array of synchronization tools available in C++, mastering their application to safeguard STL containers in multi-threaded environments. Upon concluding this chapter, readers can ensure data consistency and stability in concurrent C++ applications.

We will cover the following topics in this chapter:

- Concurrency versus thread safety
- Understanding thread safety
- Race conditions
- Mutexes and locks
- STL containers and thread safety
- Specific container concerns
- Concurrency support within the STL
- Using `std::thread`, `std::async`, `std::future`, and thread-local storage
- Concurrent data structures in the STL

Technical requirements

The code in this chapter can be found on GitHub:

`https://github.com/PacktPublishing/Data-Structures-and-Algorithms-with-the-CPP-STL`

Concurrency versus thread safety

Concurrency is the concept of multiple tasks executing in overlapping periods. These tasks can either run at the same time on different processing units or might interleave on a single processing unit. The main goal of concurrency is to increase the system's responsiveness and throughput. Concurrency is beneficial in various scenarios, such as when designing servers that handle multiple simultaneous client requests or in user interfaces that must remain responsive while processing tasks in the background.

In C++, concurrency can manifest in multiple forms: multi-threading, where separate threads of execution run (potentially) in parallel, or asynchronous programming, in which specific tasks are offloaded to be executed later.

In C++, it's crucial to understand that concurrency and **thread safety** are related but distinct concepts. Concurrency refers to the program's ability to execute multiple sequences of operations simultaneously, which can be achieved through multi-threading or other parallel execution techniques. However, being concurrent does not inherently guarantee thread safety. Thread safety is the property that ensures code functions correctly when accessed by multiple threads concurrently. This involves carefully managing shared resources, synchronizing data access, and avoiding race conditions. Achieving thread safety in a concurrent environment is a challenging aspect of C++ programming. It requires deliberate design choices and the use of specific mechanisms, such as mutexes, locks, and atomic operations, to prevent data corruption and ensure consistent behavior across all threads.

Thread safety – a pillar for stable concurrency

Thread safety refers to the capability of a piece of code to function correctly when accessed by multiple threads concurrently. It ensures that shared data maintain their integrity and that the results remain consistent. Thread safety doesn't inherently mean a function or method is lock-free or lacks performance bottlenecks; instead, it signifies that concurrent access won't lead to unpredictable results or compromise data.

Consider an analogy: If **concurrency** were akin to a busy city intersection, then thread safety would be the traffic signals ensuring that cars (threads) don't crash into each other.

The interplay of concurrency and thread safety

While both concepts are intertwined, they serve different purposes. Concurrency focuses on designing systems to perform multiple tasks in overlapping time frames, aiming for improved performance and responsiveness. Thread safety, on the other hand, is all about correctness. It's about ensuring they don't step on each other's toes when these concurrent tasks interact with shared resources.

Let's consider a simple example: a counter class in C++. Concurrency might involve incrementing the counter's value from multiple threads. However, if the counter's increment operation isn't thread-safe, two threads might read the same value simultaneously, increment it, and then write back the same incremented value. In such a case, despite trying to be faster using concurrency, the counter would end up missing counts, leading to incorrect results.

Challenges and rewards

Introducing concurrency can undoubtedly make applications faster and more responsive. However, it also introduces complexities. Managing multiple threads with issues such as deadlocks and race conditions can be challenging.

But, when done right, the rewards are substantial. Programs become more efficient, potentially utilizing all available processing units fully. Applications can be more responsive, leading to improved user experiences. Concurrent programming is no longer a choice but is necessary for many modern high-performance applications.

Concurrency without thread safety – a recipe for chaos

Imagine a world where every task tries to execute itself as fast as possible without coordination. In such a world, tasks might collide, disrupt each other, and produce nonsensical outcomes. That's what concurrent programming without thread safety looks like. It's a realm where speed is prioritized over correctness, often leading to chaos.

As a C++ developer, the key is to find the right balance. While striving for high concurrency to make applications fast, investing in thread safety mechanisms is equally crucial to ensure correctness.

Understanding the difference between concurrency and thread safety sets the stage for the following sections. We'll be looking at the tools and constructs provided by the STL to achieve high concurrency and ensure thread safety.

Understanding thread safety

Executing multiple simultaneous tasks can lead to boosted performance and responsiveness. Ensuring thread safety, especially when using the STL, becomes paramount. If overlooked, the dream of seamless concurrency can quickly morph into the nightmare of data inconsistency and unpredictable behavior.

Thread safety in STL containers – laying the groundwork

The allure of the STL lies in its rich ensemble of containers, which offer a smooth experience for storing and managing data. But the moment we introduce multiple threads, potential dangers loom.

Thread safety is primarily about ensuring that your code behaves predictably and correctly when accessed by multiple threads, even when those threads overlap. For STL containers, the basic guarantee is simple: simultaneous read-only access to containers is safe. However, once you introduce writes (modifications), things get intricate.

It's critical to understand that while STL containers have thread-safe read operations, write operations don't. If one thread is updating a container, no other thread should be reading or writing to it. Otherwise, we're courting disaster or, in technical jargon, **undefined behavior**.

Grasping the thread-safe nature of STL algorithms

If STL containers are the soul of the library, algorithms are undoubtedly its beating heart. They're responsible for the STL's rich functionality, from searching and sorting to transforming data.

Here's the catch: STL algorithms are functions, and their thread safety isn't determined by the algorithm itself but by the data they operate on. If an algorithm operates on shared data across threads without adequate synchronization, you're setting the stage for race conditions, even if that algorithm only reads data.

Consider the scenario where you're using `std::find` across multiple threads. While the algorithm is inherently safe for concurrent read operations, the results could be skewed if another thread modifies the data during the search.

Race conditions – the ghosts in the machine

Race conditions keep concurrent programmers up at night. A **race condition** occurs when the behavior of your software depends on the relative timing of events, such as the order in which threads are scheduled. The consequences range from benign (slightly incorrect data) to catastrophic (complete data corruption or application crashes).

Using the STL in a multi-threaded environment without the proper precautions can introduce race conditions. For instance, imagine two threads simultaneously pushing elements onto a `std::vector`. Without synchronization, the internal memory of the vector could become corrupted, leading to a host of problems.

Let's look at a simple race condition. In this example, we will use two threads to increment a counter:

```
#include <iostream>
#include <thread>

// Shared variable
int counter = 0;

// Function that increments the counter
void incrementCounter() {
```

```
  for (int i = 0; i < 100000; ++i) {
    ++counter; // Race condition occurs here
  }
}

int main() {
  // Creating two threads that run incrementCounter()
  std::thread thread1(incrementCounter);
  std::thread thread2(incrementCounter);

  // Wait for both threads to finish
  thread1.join();
  thread2.join();

  // Print the final value of counter
  std::cout << "Final value of counter is: " << counter
            << std::endl;

  return 0;
}
```

Here is a possible example output:

```
Final value of counter is: 130750
```

A race condition occurs because both threads access and modify the shared variable counter simultaneously without any synchronization mechanism (such as **mutexes** or **locks**). Due to the lack of synchronization, the two threads may read, increment, and write back the value of the counter in an unpredictable order. This leads to the final value of the counter being unpredictable and usually less than the expected 200,000, as some increments are lost. Running this program multiple times will likely yield different results for the final value of the counter due to the race condition. To resolve this issue, proper synchronization mechanisms, such as mutexes, should be used to ensure that only one thread modifies the shared variable at a time.

Safeguarding concurrency – the way forward

It's evident that merely understanding thread safety is half the battle. As we progress through this chapter, we'll arm you with the tools and techniques to tackle race conditions head-on, master the synchronization mechanisms at your disposal, and ensure that your STL-powered multi-threaded applications stand as bastions of stability and consistency.

Race conditions

A race condition in programming occurs when the behavior of a system depends on the relative timing of multiple threads or processes. In such scenarios, the system's outcome becomes unpredictable because different threads may access and modify shared data concurrently without proper synchronization. This can lead to inconsistent or erroneous results, as the final state of the data depends on the order in which the threads execute, which cannot be determined in advance. Race conditions are a common issue in concurrent programming. They can be particularly challenging to detect and resolve, requiring careful design and synchronization mechanisms to ensure correct and predictable program behavior.

Steering clear of a silent peril – race conditions in the STL

As you journey into concurrent programming, race conditions represent one of the most subtle yet treacherous pitfalls. Though silent in their manifestation, they can cause unexpected and, at times, bewildering results. Recognizing and sidestepping these race conditions, especially within the realm of the STL, is crucial to crafting robust multi-threaded applications.

The anatomy of a race condition in the STL

At its core, a race condition materializes when the behavior of your application hinges on the sequence or timing of uncontrollable events. In the STL context, this typically arises when multiple threads access shared data in an uncoordinated fashion.

Imagine a scenario where two threads, in an unfortunate coincidence, try to insert elements into the same position of `std::vector` concurrently or consider another instance where one thread reads from `std::unordered_map` while another erases an element. What is the outcome? Undefined behavior, which in the world of C++, is the equivalent of opening Pandora's box.

More than meets the eye

Race conditions are especially treacherous due to their unpredictable nature. While a concurrent application may seem to work flawlessly in one run, slight changes in thread execution timings can lead to entirely different results in the next.

Beyond erratic behavior, race conditions with STL containers and algorithms can lead to more sinister problems. Data corruption, memory leaks, and crashes are just the tip of the iceberg. Given their elusive and intermittent appearance, these issues can be challenging to debug.

Anticipating race conditions

Forewarned is forearmed. By familiarizing yourself with common scenarios where race conditions manifest in the STL, you position yourself to tackle them preemptively:

- **Container resizing**: Containers, such as `std::vector` and `std::string`, automatically resize when their capacity is exceeded. If two threads simultaneously trigger a resize, the internal state could be left in turmoil.

- **Iterator invalidation**: Modifying containers often invalidates existing iterators. If one thread traverses using an iterator while another modifies the container, the first thread's iterator can end up in no-man's-land.

- **Algorithm assumptions**: STL algorithms make certain assumptions about the data they operate upon. Concurrent modifications can violate these assumptions, leading to incorrect results or infinite loops.

Safeguarding your code – a proactive stance

Having acquainted ourselves with the potential hotspots, the natural progression is to fortify our code against these hazards. The essence lies in synchronization. We can effectively thwart race conditions by ensuring that only one thread can access shared data or perform certain operations simultaneously.

However, indiscriminate synchronization can lead to performance bottlenecks, rendering the benefits of concurrency moot. The key is to strike a balance, applying synchronization judiciously.

We'll introduce a robust arsenal of tools and techniques as we move further into this chapter. From mutexes to locks, you'll acquire the means to detect and effectively neutralize race conditions, ensuring your STL-driven applications are swift and steadfast.

Are you ready to conquer the challenges of concurrent programming with the STL? Let's navigate this landscape together, ensuring your software remains consistent, reliable, and race condition-free.

Mutexes and locks

A **mutex**, short for **mutual exclusion**, is akin to a digital gatekeeper. It regulates access, ensuring that at any given moment, only a single thread can enter its protected domain, eliminating the chaos of concurrent access. Imagine a high-stakes auction room where only one person can place a bid at any instant, thereby preventing overlap and conflict. That's the function of a mutex in the world of multi-threaded applications.

Within the C++ Standard Library, the header `<mutex>` bestows several types of mutexes upon us. The most commonly used among them is `std::mutex`. This basic mutex is a versatile tool suitable for many synchronization needs. A pair of operations—`lock()` and `unlock()`—provides a straightforward means to guard shared resources.

From manual to automatic – lock guards and unique locks

Manually locking and unlocking mutexes can be error-prone. There's always the lurking danger of forgetting to unlock a mutex, leading to a deadlock. Enter lock guards and unique locks; these simplify mutex management by embracing the **resource acquisition is initialization** (**RAII**) principle.

`std::lock_guard` is a lightweight wrapper that automatically manages the mutex's state. Once a lock guard acquires a mutex, it guarantees its release when the lock guard's scope ends. This eliminates the risk of forgetting to release the mutex.

On the other hand, `std::unique_lock` is a bit more flexible. Besides the automatic lock management that `lock_guard` offers, `unique_lock` provides manual control, deferred locking, and even the ability to transfer ownership of a mutex. This makes it suitable for more complex synchronization scenarios.

Avoiding the stalemate – deadlock prevention

Imagine a scenario where two threads are in a standoff, each expecting the other to relinquish a resource. As a result, both are stuck in a perpetual waiting, leading to a classic deadlock. This situation isn't merely hypothetical, especially when mutexes are involved, as they can inadvertently create such a deadlock if not managed carefully. When multiple mutexes are involved, it is essential to adopt strategies to avoid deadlocks. One common approach is always to acquire the mutexes in the same order, regardless of which thread you are in. But when this isn't feasible, `std::lock` comes to the rescue. It's designed to lock multiple mutexes simultaneously without the risk of causing a deadlock.

Incorporating mutexes with STL containers

With the knowledge of mutexes, lock guards, unique locks, and deadlock prevention techniques, integrating these synchronization tools with STL containers becomes an intuitive exercise.

For instance, protecting `std::vector` from concurrent access might involve placing `std::lock_guard` at every function that modifies or accesses the vector. Similarly, if multiple operations on `std::unordered_map` must be executed atomically, `std::unique_lock` can offer protection and the flexibility to manually control the lock's state when needed.

With the tools of mutexes and locks in hand, threading in the STL no longer feels like treading on thin ice. By ensuring the reasonable and consistent application of these synchronization primitives, you can harness the full power of concurrency while keeping the pitfalls of race conditions and deadlocks at bay.

In the following sections, we'll continue our exploration, specifically focusing on the unique challenges and considerations when threading with specific STL containers.

STL containers and thread safety

When discussing STL containers, assuming a blanket level of thread safety across all of them is tempting. However, such assumptions can be misleading. By default, STL containers are not thread-safe for modifications, meaning if one thread modifies a container, other threads simultaneously accessing it might lead to undefined behavior.

However, some inherent guarantees exist. For instance, it is safe for multiple threads to simultaneously read from an STL container, as long as no thread is modifying it. This is often referred to as **read concurrency**. Yet, the moment even a single thread tries to change the container while others read, we're back in the dangerous territory of race conditions.

When safety needs reinforcements – concurrent modifications

While reading concurrently is safe, modifications bring a different set of challenges. Suppose two or more threads attempt to modify an STL container simultaneously. In that case, the behavior becomes undefined unless synchronization mechanisms (such as those we explored with mutexes and locks) are used.

Take the case of `std::vector`. A race condition emerges if one thread appends an element using `push_back` while another tries to remove one with `pop_back` without a mutex guarding these operations. The vector's size could change mid-operation, or memory could be reallocated, leading to crashes or data inconsistencies.

Container iterators – the fragile bridge

Iterators are fundamental to STL containers, providing a means to traverse and manipulate container elements. However, iterators are fragile when it comes to concurrency. If a thread modifies the container in a way that causes reallocation or restructuring, other threads' iterators might become invalidated. Using invalidated iterators is, yet again, undefined behavior.

For example, in containers such as `std::list` or `std::map`, adding an element won't invalidate the existing iterators. However, with `std::vector`, a reallocation triggered when the vector exceeds its current capacity can invalidate all existing iterators. Being aware of these nuances is crucial when orchestrating multi-threaded operations.

Containers with a built-in shield – concurrent containers

In recognizing the challenges developers face when synchronizing standard STL containers, the library introduced concurrent containers. These containers, such as `std::atomic` and those in the `concurrency` namespace (for some compilers), come with built-in synchronization, offering thread-safe operations at the potential cost of performance.

It's important to note that these containers might not provide the same interface or performance characteristics as their standard STL counterparts. They are specialized tools that are ideal for scenarios where the overhead of manual synchronization might be too significant.

While STL containers bring a world of convenience and efficiency to C++ programming, they come with the responsibility of understanding their threading characteristics. By discerning when and where explicit synchronization is required and leveraging the tools and techniques at our disposal, we can ensure that our multi-threaded applications remain robust, efficient, and free of concurrency-induced bugs.

Specific container concerns

Different STL container types present unique challenges and considerations in a multi-threaded environment. The thread safety of operations on these containers is not inherently guaranteed, making their use in concurrent scenarios a matter of careful planning. For instance, containers such as `std::vector` or `std::map` might behave unpredictably when simultaneously accessed or modified from multiple threads, leading to data corruption or race conditions. In contrast, containers such as `std::atomic` are designed for safe concurrent operations on individual elements, but they don't safeguard the container's structure as a whole. Therefore, understanding the specific threading implications of each STL container type is essential. Developers must implement appropriate locking mechanisms or use thread-safe variants where necessary to ensure data integrity and correct program behavior in a multi-threaded environment.

Behaviors of std::vector in multi-threading

`std::vector` is a widely-used STL container that acts as a dynamic array, adjusting its size as needed. Its contiguous memory allocation provides advantages such as cache locality. However, in multi-threaded scenarios, challenges arise.

For example, when a vector's capacity is surpassed and reallocates memory, all associated iterators, pointers, and references can be invalidated. If one thread iterates the vector while another prompts a reallocation (adding elements beyond its limit), this can lead to issues. To prevent such scenarios, synchronization mechanisms should be implemented during operations that trigger reallocations when multiple threads access the vector.

Characteristics of std::list in concurrency

`std::list`, which is a doubly-linked list, has behaviors that are beneficial in multi-threaded situations but also require caution. A key advantage is that insertions or deletions do not invalidate iterators unless they target the specific removed element, making some operations naturally thread-safe.

However, there's a need for caution. While iterators may remain intact, concurrent modifications can alter the sequence of elements, resulting in inconsistent outcomes.

Considerations with associative containers

Containers such as `std::set`, `std::map`, `std::multiset`, and `std::multimap` order elements based on their keys. This ensures organized data retrieval.

In multi-threaded situations, this trait presents challenges. Concurrent element insertions might result in an unpredictable final sequence. Additionally, concurrent removals can give rise to race conditions.

Concurrency aspects of unordered containers

The unordered versions of associative containers, such as `std::unordered_set` and `std::unordered_map`, do not keep elements in a defined order. However, they are not exempt from multi-threading issues. These containers leverage hashing, and element additions might trigger rehashing to optimize performance.

Rehashing can lead to iterator invalidation. Hence, despite their unordered nature, careful handling is necessary during concurrent operations.

Insights into container adaptors

The STL provides container adaptors such as `std::stack`, `std::queue`, and `std::priority_queue`. These don't possess their storage and instead encapsulate other containers. Their thread safety properties depend on the containers they are based on. For example, an instance of `std::stack` that utilizes `std::vector` would have the same reallocation and iterator invalidation issues.

Being informed about the specific behaviors of each STL container is vital for developing thread-safe C++ programs. While the STL delivers numerous tools with distinct advantages, they also have challenges in multi-threaded contexts.

Concurrency support within the STL

The STL has evolved significantly, transforming from a collection of data structures and algorithms into a comprehensive library incorporating advanced constructs for concurrent programming. This expansion responds to the increasing demand for efficient and robust multi-threaded applications, especially in the era of multi-core processors. Modern software development frequently requires leveraging the power of concurrency to enhance performance and responsiveness. As such, a deep understanding of the STL's concurrency support is beneficial and essential for developers looking to optimize their applications in this multi-threaded landscape.

This section will examine the concurrency features integrated within the STL. This includes a detailed examination of thread management, asynchronous tasks, atomic operations, and challenges with utilizing concurrency.

The STL's offerings in the area of concurrency are not just about facilitating multi-threading but are also about doing it in an effective and manageable way. This section is designed to provide a comprehensive understanding of these tools, enabling you to write high-performance, scalable, and reliable C++ applications in today's computationally demanding world.

Introduction to threads

At the heart of concurrent programming lies the concept of threads. Within the STL, this is represented by `std::thread`. This class offers a straightforward interface for creating and overseeing threads. Initiating a new thread is essentially about defining a function or a callable entity and passing it to the thread constructor. After executing your task, you can join (await its conclusion) or detach (permit its independent execution) the thread. However, here's a word of caution: manually handling threads requires careful attention. It's imperative to ensure all threads are correctly joined or detached to avoid potential issues, including lingering threads.

The advent of asynchronous tasks

Direct thread management provides considerable control, but the STL introduces `std::async` and `std::future` for tasks that don't require such meticulous oversight. These constructs enable developers to delegate tasks for potential parallel execution without the intricacies of direct thread oversight. The function `std::async` initiates a task, and its resultant `std::future` offers a method to fetch the result when it's ready. This fosters more organized code, mainly when the focus is on task-centric parallelism.

Atomic operations

The STL provides a robust solution through atomic operations for inefficient, low-overhead operations, where the locking mechanisms may appear disproportionate. The atomic operations, encapsulated within the `std::atomic` class template, play a pivotal role in concurrent programming by guaranteeing the atomicity of operations in fundamental data types.

`std::atomic` is designed to ensure that operations on basic types, such as integers and pointers, are executed as indivisible units. This atomicity is crucial in multi-threaded environments, as it prevents the potential hazards of interrupted operations, which can lead to inconsistent or corrupt data states. By ensuring that these operations are completed without interruption, `std::atomic` obviates the need for traditional locking mechanisms, such as mutexes, thereby enhancing performance by reducing the overhead associated with lock contention and context switching.

However, it is essential to note that using atomic operations requires careful consideration and an understanding of their characteristics and limitations. While they provide a mechanism for lock-free programming, atomic operations are not a panacea for all concurrency problems. Developers must know the memory order constraints and the potential performance implications on different hardware architectures. In particular, the choice between memory orderings (such as `memory_order_relaxed`, `memory_order_acquire`, `memory_order_release`, etc.) demands a thorough understanding of the synchronization requirements and the trade-offs involved.

Memory orderings, such as `memory_order_relaxed`, `memory_order_acquire`, and `memory_order_release`, dictate how operations on atomic variables are ordered with respect to other memory operations.

Choosing the correct memory ordering is crucial for ensuring the desired level of synchronization while balancing performance. For instance, `memory_order_relaxed` offers minimal synchronization and imposes no ordering constraints on memory operations, leading to higher performance but at the risk of allowing other threads to see operations in a different order. On the other hand, `memory_order_acquire` and `memory_order_release` provide stronger guarantees about the ordering of reads and writes, which is essential for correctly implementing lock-free data structures and algorithms but can come with a performance cost, especially in systems with weak memory models.

The trade-offs involved in these decisions are significant. A more relaxed memory ordering can lead to performance gains but also introduce subtle bugs if the program's correctness relies on certain memory ordering guarantees. Conversely, opting for stronger memory orderings can simplify the reasoning about the correctness of concurrent code but may lead to decreased performance due to additional memory synchronization barriers.

Therefore, developers must be aware of the synchronization requirements of their specific application and understand how their choice of memory ordering will interact with the underlying hardware architecture. This knowledge is critical for writing efficient and correct concurrent programs in C++.

Potential concurrent challenges

Concurrency, though powerful, isn't devoid of challenges. Developers might confront deadlocks, race conditions, and resource contention. Deadlocks transpire when multiple threads indefinitely wait for each other to release resources. Race conditions can give rise to erratic bugs stemming from unforeseen overlaps in thread operations.

False sharing is another notable challenge. It happens when different threads modify data situated in the same cache line. This can hamper performance because even if threads modify distinct data, their memory closeness can trigger redundant cache invalidations. Awareness and prudence can aid in sidestepping these challenges.

Using the STL's concurrency features

The STL provides a range of tools for concurrent programming, spanning from the initiation of threads to the assurance of atomic tasks. These tools cater to a variety of requirements. Nevertheless, it's vital to employ them judiciously.

Concurrency promises enhanced performance and nimble applications but comes with complexities and potential bugs. In concurrency, knowing what tools are available is a necessary starting point, but effectively using them requires ongoing trial and learning.

The following C++ code example illustrates the STL's various concurrency features. This example encompasses thread creation, asynchronous task execution, and atomic operations while highlighting the importance of proper thread management and the potential pitfalls of concurrency:

```cpp
#include <atomic>
#include <future>
#include <iostream>
#include <thread>
#include <vector>

// A simple function that we will run in a separate thread.
void threadTask(int n) {
  std::this_thread::sleep_for(std::chrono::seconds(n));
  std::cout << "Thread " << std::this_thread::get_id()
            << " completed after " << n << " seconds.\n";
}

// A function that performs a task and returns a result.
int performComputation(int value) {
  std::this_thread::sleep_for(std::chrono::seconds(1));
  return (value * value);
}

int main() {
  // Start a thread that runs threadTask with n=2
  std::thread t(threadTask, 2);

  // task management with std::async and std::future
  std::future<int> futureResult = std::async(
      std::launch::async, performComputation, 5);

  // Atomic operation with std::atomic
  std::atomic<int> atomicCounter(0);

  // Demonstrate atomicity in concurrent operations
  std::vector<std::thread> threads;
  for (int i = 0; i < 10; ++i) {
    threads.emplace_back([&atomicCounter]() {
      for (int j = 0; j < 100; ++j) {
        atomicCounter += 1; // Atomic increment
      }
    });
  }
```

```
    // Joining the initial thread to ensure it has finished
    // before main exits
    if (t.joinable()) { t.join(); }

    // Retrieving the result from the future
    int computationResult = futureResult.get();
    std::cout << "The result of the computation is "
              << computationResult << ".\n";

    // Joining all threads to ensure complete execution
    for (auto &th : threads) {
      if (th.joinable()) { th.join(); }
    }

    std::cout << "The final value of the atomic counter is "
              << atomicCounter << ".\n";
    return 0;
}
```

Here is the example output:

```
Thread 32280 completed after 2 seconds.
The result of the computation is 25.
The final value of the atomic counter is 1000.
```

In this example, we did the following:

- Created a thread using `std::thread` that sleeps for a given number of seconds and then prints a message.
- Used `std::async` to perform a computation in a potentially parallel manner, and we used `std::future` to obtain the result once it was ready.
- Demonstrated using `std::atomic` to perform an atomic increment operation within multiple threads.
- Ensured that all threads are correctly joined to avoid dangling threads.

This code is a simple demonstration and serves as a starting point for understanding concurrency in C++. Developers must further explore and handle more complex scenarios, including synchronization, preventing deadlocks, and avoiding race conditions and false sharing for robust concurrent applications.

Using std::thread, std::async, std::future, and thread -local storage

Let's look at four core components of C++'s concurrency toolkit: `std::thread`, `std::async`, `std::future`, and thread-local storage. Each of these elements is vital for facilitating multi-threaded programming in C++. `std::thread` is the foundation, allowing for the creation and management of threads. `std::async` and `std::future` work in tandem to asynchronously execute tasks and retrieve their results in a controlled manner, offering a higher level of abstraction over raw threads. Thread-local storage, on the other hand, provides a unique data instance for each thread. This is crucial for avoiding data conflicts in a concurrent environment. This section aims to comprehensively understand these tools, demonstrating how they can be used effectively to write robust, efficient, and thread-safe C++ applications.

Initiating threads using std::thread

A primary tool in the realm of concurrency within C++ is `std::thread`. This class allows developers to concurrently run procedures by starting distinct threads for execution. To launch a new thread, pass a callable entity (such as a function or a lambda) to the `std::thread` constructor. For instance, to print "Hello, Concurrent World!" from an independent thread, see the following:

```
std::thread my_thread([]{
    std::cout << "Hello, Concurrent World!" << "\n";
});
my_thread.join();
```

Utilizing the `join()` function ensures that the main thread waits until `my_thread` completes. There's also `detach()`, which lets the primary thread progress without delay. However, the careful management of detached threads is crucial to avoid unexpected behavior.

Managing asynchronous operations with std::async and std::future

Though `std::thread` offers significant capabilities, direct thread management can be intricate. The STL presents an elevated abstraction for administering potential parallel operations through `std::async` and `std::future`.

The approach is clear-cut: assign a task to `std::async` and retrieve a `std::future` object that will eventually contain that task's result. This division allows the primary thread to either continue or optionally await the outcome using the `get()` method of `std::future`, as shown in the following code example:

```
auto future_result = std::async([]{
    return "Response from async!";
```

```
    });
    std::cout << future_result.get() << "\n";
```

As you can see, `std::async` and `std::future` are designed to work well together to help manage asynchronous operations.

Preserving data consistency using thread-local storage

Ensuring distinct data storage for each thread to avoid overlap and maintain data consistency in concurrent programming can be challenging. This is addressed by **thread-local storage (TLS)**.

Using the `thread_local` keyword when declaring a variable ensures a unique instance of that variable for each thread. This is instrumental in sustaining data consistency and circumventing the issues associated with shared data access:

```
    thread_local int thread_counter = 0;
```

Here, `thread_counter` is instantiated for each thread, shielding it from inter-thread interference.

Integrating tools for proficient concurrency

With `std::thread`, `std::async`, `std::future`, and TLS, you are prepared to navigate various concurrent programming situations in C++. The STL offers the requisite tools for delegating tasks for parallel execution or adeptly managing thread-specific data.

It's pivotal to note that while initiating threads or tasks is straightforward, ensuring synchronized operations devoid of contention, deadlocks, or data races demands attentiveness and continual refinement.

Retaining the foundational insights from this segment is paramount as we transition to the subsequent sections that review the STL's concurrent data structures. Concurrent programming is an evolving landscape, and mastering each tool and concept augments your capacity to develop efficient and stable concurrent applications.

Let's walk through a code example that illustrates the use of `std::thread`, `std::async`, `std::future`, and TLS to concurrently execute tasks and manage per-thread data:

```
    #include <future>
    #include <iostream>
    #include <thread>
    #include <vector>

    // Function to demonstrate the use of Thread Local Storage
    void incrementThreadCounter() {
      // Unique to each thread
      thread_local int thread_counter = 0;
```

```
    thread_counter++;
    std::cout << "Thread " << std::this_thread::get_id()
              << " counter: " << thread_counter << "\n";
}

int main() {
  // Initiating a new thread using std::thread
  std::thread my_thread([] {
    std::cout << "Hello, Concurrent World!"
              << "\n";
  });

  // Ensure the main thread waits for my_thread to complete
  if (my_thread.joinable()) { my_thread.join(); }

  // Asynchronous operations w/std::async and std::future
  auto future_result =
      std::async([] { return "Response from async!"; });

  // Retrieve the result with std::future::get when ready
  std::cout << future_result.get() << "\n";

  // Demonstrating the use of Thread Local Storage (TLS)
  std::vector<std::thread> threads;
  for (int i = 0; i < 5; ++i) {
    threads.emplace_back(incrementThreadCounter);
  }

  // Join all threads to the main thread
  for (auto &thread : threads) {
    if (thread.joinable()) { thread.join(); }
  }

  return 0;
}
```

Here is the example output:

```
Hello, Concurrent World!
Response from async!
Thread 11672 counter: Thread 1
32816 counter: 1
Thread 7124 counter: 1
Thread 43792 counter: 1
Thread 23932 counter: 1
```

In this code, we did the following:

- Created a thread to print a message to the console using `std::thread`.

- Used `std::async` to perform an asynchronous operation that returns a string. The result is accessed via a `std::future` object.

- Demonstrated the use of TLS with the `thread_local` keyword to maintain a separate counter for each thread.

- Started multiple threads, each incrementing its local counter, to show how TLS variables are instantiated for each thread.

This example encapsulates the essentials of concurrent programming with the STL, from thread creation and synchronization to data isolation with TLS. While these mechanisms simplify parallel execution, we must exercise careful judgment to prevent concurrency-related issues, such as deadlocks and race conditions. The upcoming sections will explore STL's concurrent data structures, which build upon these foundational concepts to enable the creation of robust concurrent programs.

Concurrent data structures in the STL

The STL provides a variety of data structures, but not all are inherently suited for concurrent access. Understanding how to effectively utilize and adapt these data structures for safe and efficient use in a multi-threaded context is crucial. We will examine the thread safety aspects of common STL data structures, discuss the appropriate use cases for each in a concurrent environment, and explore the strategies to ensure safe and effective concurrent access. This section is designed to equip developers with the knowledge to leverage STL data structures to maximize performance while maintaining data integrity in a multi-threaded landscape.

The STL's concurrency-optimized containers

While the STL provides many containers, not all are optimized for concurrent access. However, with the increasing demand for concurrent programming, specific concurrency-friendly containers have made their way into the repertoire of many C++ programmers.

One notable example is `std::shared_timed_mutex` and its sibling `std::shared_mutex` (from C++17 onwards). These synchronization primitives allow multiple threads to read shared data simultaneously while ensuring exclusive access for writing. This is particularly handy when read operations are more frequent than writes, such as in caching scenarios.

Consider a situation where you have `std::map` storing configuration data:

```
std::map<std::string, std::string> config_data;
std::shared_timed_mutex config_mutex;
```

To read from this map, multiple threads can acquire a shared lock:

```
std::shared_lock lock(config_mutex);
auto val = config_data["some_key"];
```

However, for writing, a unique lock ensures exclusive access:

```
std::unique_lock lock(config_mutex);
config_data["some_key"] = "new_value";
```

While not a container, `std::shared_timed_mutex` can protect any STL container, ensuring concurrent read access while serializing writes.

Striving for maximum efficiency in concurrent environments

Concurrency isn't just about making operations thread-safe but is also about achieving better performance. As you've seen, atomic types and concurrency-optimized containers help ensure safety, but there's more to it than that. Fine-tuning performance may involve considering lock contention, avoiding false sharing, and minimizing synchronization overhead.

A few tips for maximizing efficiency include the following:

- **Limit the scope of locks**: While locks are essential for ensuring data consistency, holding them for extended durations can impede performance. Ensure you're only holding locks for the necessary duration.

- **Choose the right data structure**: Containers optimized for concurrency might offer better performance for multi-threaded applications, even if they might be slower in single-threaded scenarios.

- **Consider granularity**: Think about the granularity of your locks. Sometimes, a finer-grained lock (protecting just a part of your data) can perform better than a coarser-grained one (protecting the entire data structure).

Best practices in action

Let's look at a code example demonstrating best practices in using STL containers in a concurrent environment, focusing on performance optimization techniques such as minimizing lock scope, selecting appropriate data structures, and considering lock granularity.

First, we will write a concurrency-optimized container, specifically ConcurrentVector, designed to handle multi-threaded environments effectively. This custom container class, which is templated to hold elements of any type (T), encapsulates a standard std::vector for data storage while employing std::shared_mutex to manage concurrent access (we will break this example up into a few sections. For the complete code, please refer to the book's GitHub repository):

```cpp
// A hypothetical concurrency-optimized container that uses
// fine-grained locking
template <typename T> class ConcurrentVector {
private:
  std::vector<T> data;
  mutable std::shared_mutex mutex;

public:
  // Inserts an element into the container with minimal
  // lock duration
  void insert(const T &value) {
    std::unique_lock<std::shared_mutex> lock(mutex);
    data.push_back(value);
  }

  // Finds an element with read access, demonstrating
  // shared locking
  bool find(const T &value) const {
    std::shared_lock<std::shared_mutex> lock(mutex);
    return std::find(data.begin(), data.end(), value) !=
            data.end();
  }

  // Size accessor that uses shared locking
  size_t size() const {
    std::shared_lock<std::shared_mutex> lock(mutex);
    return data.size();
  }
};
```

Next, we will write the function performConcurrentOperations, which will demonstrate the practical application of our ConcurrentVector class in a multi-threaded context. This function accepts a reference to ConcurrentVector<int> and initiates two parallel operations using C++ standard threads:

```cpp
void performConcurrentOperations(
    ConcurrentVector<int> &concurrentContainer) {
  // Multiple threads perform operations on the container
```

```
std::thread writer([&concurrentContainer]() {
  for (int i = 0; i < 100; ++i) {
    concurrentContainer.insert(i);
  }
});

std::thread reader([&concurrentContainer]() {
  for (int i = 0; i < 100; ++i) {
    if (concurrentContainer.find(i)) {
      std::cerr << "Value " << i
               << " found in the container\n";
    }
  }
});

// Join threads to ensure complete execution
writer.join();
reader.join();

// Output the final size of the container
std::cout << "Final size of the container:"
         << concurrentContainer.size() << "\n";
}
```

Finally, we write main() to drive the program:

```
int main() {
  ConcurrentVector<int> concurrentContainer;
  performConcurrentOperations(concurrentContainer);
  return 0;
}
```

Here is the example output:

```
...
Value 98 found in the container.
Value 99 found in the container.
Final size of the container: 100
```

In total, in the preceding code example, we did the following:

- We have defined a `ConcurrentVector` template class that mimics a concurrency-optimized container, which internally uses `std::shared_mutex` to enable fine-grained control over read and write operations.

- The `insert` method uses a unique lock to ensure exclusive access during write operations, but the lock is held only for the insert duration, minimizing the lock scope.

- The `find` and `size` methods use shared locks, allowing for concurrent reads, demonstrating the use of shared locking to enable higher read throughput.

- A writer thread and a reader thread were created to perform concurrent insertions and searches on the `ConcurrentVector` instance, showcasing the container's ability to handle concurrent operations.

This example illustrates critical considerations for optimizing concurrent performance, such as limiting the duration of locks, choosing appropriate concurrency-friendly data structures, and using fine-grained locking to protect smaller sections of the data. These practices are crucial for intermediate-level C++ developers looking to enhance the performance of multi-threaded applications.

Summary

This chapter discussed the intricacies of thread safety and concurrency within the STL. We started by distinguishing between concurrency and thread safety, underscoring that while related, each serves a distinct purpose. Our journey began with a foundational understanding of thread safety as a pillar for stable concurrency and how the lack thereof can lead to unpredictable software behavior. We examined the interplay between these concepts, addressing the challenges and highlighting the rewards of concurrent programming when thread safety is maintained.

We looked into the thread-safe nature of STL containers and algorithms, dissecting race conditions and the techniques to anticipate and guard against them. The chapter provided detailed insights into the behaviors of various STL containers under multi-threaded scenarios, from `std::vector` to `std::list` and associative to unordered containers. We also uncovered the concurrency aspects of container adaptors, asserting that knowledge is power when writing concurrent applications.

We've been equipped with the core tools: `std::thread`, `std::async`, `std::future`, and TLS. With these, we initiated threads, managed asynchronous operations, and preserved data consistency across threads. These capabilities have prepared us for proficient concurrency about safety and performance.

The chapter examined the STL's atomic types and concurrency-optimized containers, providing tips for maximizing efficiency in concurrent environments. These insights are pivotal for developing high-performance, thread-safe applications using the STL.

The knowledge imparted in this chapter is essential because thread safety and efficient concurrency are critical for modern C++ developers. As multi-core and multi-threaded applications become the norm, it is crucial to understand these principles to be able to leverage the full power of the STL.

In the next chapter, we will dig further into advanced STL usage. We will introduce concepts and robust template features, allowing for more precise type checks at compile-time. We will learn how to refine the constraints in STL algorithms and effectively use these constraints to enhance data structures with explicit requirements. Moreover, we will explore the integration of the STL with coroutines, assessing the potential synergies with ranges and views and preparing for the paradigm shift that awaits in contemporary C++ programming.

21

STL Interaction with Concepts and Coroutines

This chapter will explore the interplay between the STL and two of C++'s advanced features: concepts and coroutines. This chapter is designed to deepen your understanding of how these modern C++ features enhance and interact with the STL.

We begin by learning about concepts, starting with an introduction and progressively exploring their role in refining STL algorithm constraints, enhancing data structures, and developing custom concepts. This section is crucial for grasping how explicit type constraints can lead to more robust and readable code.

Following this, we focus on coroutines, providing a refresher before examining their integration with STL algorithms and data structures. This includes exploring potential synergies with ranges and views, culminating in discussing how coroutines might herald a paradigm shift in C++ programming.

This chapter will provide a comprehensive understanding and practical insights into using these features effectively, highlighting their importance in modern C++ development and their potential challenges.

In this chapter, we will cover the following topics:

- Concepts
- Coroutines

Technical requirements

The code in this chapter can be found on GitHub:

https://github.com/PacktPublishing/Data-Structures-and-Algorithms-with-the-CPP-STL

Concepts

The introduction of concepts in C++20 marked a pivotal step towards safer and more expressive templated programming. With their inherent ability to specify constraints on template arguments, concepts promise to reshape how we interact with and utilize the **Standard Template Library** (**STL**). Let's discover how concepts intertwine with the rich tapestry of STL algorithms and data structures to create a more robust and declarative C++ programming paradigm.

A brief introduction to concepts

Concepts provide a mechanism to specify and check constraints on template arguments. Essentially, they allow developers to assert requirements about the types passed to a template. Concepts aim to make template errors more readable, help avoid common pitfalls, and promote the creation of more generic and reusable code.

Consider the following concept for an arithmetic type:

```
template<typename T>
concept Arithmetic = std::is_arithmetic_v<T>;
```

Using this concept, one can constrain a function only to accept arithmetic types:

```
template<Arithmetic T>
T add(T a, T b) { return (a + b); }
```

Refined constraints in STL algorithms

STL algorithms, historically, have relied on complex, sometimes nebulous requirements for their template parameters. With concepts, these requirements become explicit and understandable. For instance, the `std::sort` algorithm requires random access iterators, which can now be asserted using concepts. This leads to more precise error messages if one mistakenly uses a list (which only provides bidirectional iterators).

Effectively constraining templates

When working with C++ template programming, ensuring that a given type satisfies a specific set of requirements has historically been challenging. Before the introduction of concepts, developers would rely on complex techniques involving **substitution failure is not an error** (**SFINAE**) or specialized trait classes to impose type constraints. These methods were verbose and error-prone, often resulting in convoluted error messages that were difficult to decipher.

Concepts allow developers to define a set of predicates that a type must satisfy, offering a more structured and readable way to constrain templates. Using concepts, you can specify the requirements that template arguments must meet. When a type does not match the constraints defined by a concept, the compiler will reject the template instantiation, producing a more straightforward and more meaningful error message. This enhances the template code's readability, maintainability, and robustness. With concepts, the compiler can quickly ascertain the suitability of a type for a given template, ensuring that only appropriate types are utilized, thereby minimizing the potential for runtime errors or undefined behavior.

Here's a code example that demonstrates the use of concepts and how the same task had to be carried out before the introduction of concepts:

```cpp
#include <iostream>
#include <type_traits>

// Create a class that is not inherently printable.
struct NotPrintable
{
  int foo{0};
  int bar{0};
};

// Concept definition using the 'requires' clause
template <typename T>
concept Printable = requires(T t) {
  // Requires that t can be printed to std::cout
  std::cout << t;
};

// Before C++20:
// A Function template that uses SFINAE to implement a
// "Printable concept"
template <typename T,
          typename = typename std::enable_if<std::is_same<
              decltype(std::cout << std::declval<T>()),
              std::ostream &>::value>::type>
void printValueSFINAE(const T &value) {
  std::cout << "Value: " << value << "\n";
}

// After C++20:
// A Function template that uses the Printable concept
template <Printable T> void printValue(const T &value) {
  std::cout << "Value: " << value << "\n";
}

int main() {
```

```
    const int num = 42;
    const NotPrintable np;
    const std::string str = "Hello, Concepts!";

    // Using the function template with SFINAE
    printValueSFINAE(num);
    // This line would fail to compile:
    // printValueSFINAE(np);
    printValueSFINAE(str);

    // Using the function template with concepts
    printValue(num);
    // This line would fail to compile
    // printValue(np);
    printValue(str);

    return 0;
}
```

Here is the example output:

```
Value: 42
Value: Hello, Concepts!
Value: 42
Value: Hello, Concepts!
```

In this example, we define a concept called `Printable` using the required clause. The `Printable` concept checks if a type can be printed to `std::cout`. We then have two function templates, `printValue`, and `printValueSFINAE`, that print a value if it satisfies the concept or the SFINAE condition, respectively.

When using the `printValue` function template with the `Printable` concept, the compiler will ensure that the type passed to it can be printed, and if not, it will produce a clear error message. This makes the code more readable and provides meaningful error messages.

On the other hand, when using the `printValueSFINAE` function template, we rely on SFINAE to achieve the same task. This approach is more verbose and error-prone, as it involves complex `std::enable_if` constructs and may lead to cryptic error messages when the constraints are unmet.

By comparing these two approaches, you can see how concepts improve the readability, maintainability, and robustness of C++ template code, making it easier to specify and enforce type requirements.

Enhanced data structures with explicit requirements

STL containers, such as std::vector or std::map, often have their requirements for stored types, such as being copy-constructible or assignable. Concepts can articulate these requirements with great clarity.

Imagine a custom container that necessitates its elements to be default constructible. This requirement can be eloquently expressed with concepts, ensuring safer and more predictable container behavior.

Custom concepts and STL interactions

One of the strengths of concepts is that they're not limited to the ones provided by the standard library. Developers can create custom concepts tailored to specific needs, ensuring that STL structures and algorithms can be adapted to unique and complex scenarios without sacrificing type safety.

For instance, if a particular algorithm demands types with a specific interface (such as having a draw() member function), one can design a concept to enforce this, leading to more intuitive and self-documenting code. Let's look at a code example:

```cpp
#include <concepts>
#include <iostream>
#include <vector>

template <typename T>
concept Drawable = requires(T obj) {
  { obj.draw() } -> std::convertible_to<void>;
};

class Circle {
public:
  void draw() const { std::cout << "Drawing a circle.\n"; }
};

class Square {
public:
  // No draw() member function
};

template <Drawable T> void drawShape(const T &shape) {
  shape.draw();
}

int main() {
  Circle circle;
```

```
    Square square;

    drawShape(circle);

    // Uncommenting the line below would result in
    // 'drawShape': no matching overloaded function found:
    // drawShape(square);

    return 0;
}
```

Here is the example output:

Drawing a circle.

In the preceding code example, we do the following:

- We define a custom concept called `Drawable`, which requires a type with a `draw()` member function returning `void`.

- We create two example classes: `Circle`, which satisfies the `Drawable` concept by having a `draw()` member function, and `Square`, which does not satisfy the concept because it lacks the `draw()` member function.

- We define a generic function called `drawShape`, which takes a `Drawable` type as a parameter and calls its `draw()` member function.

- In the `main` function, we create instances of `Circle` and `Square` and demonstrate that `drawShape` can be called with a `Drawable` type (e.g., `Circle`) but not with a type that does not satisfy the `Drawable` concept (e.g., `Square`).

This example illustrates how custom concepts can enforce specific interface requirements, ensuring type safety and making the code more intuitive and self-documenting when working with complex scenarios and algorithms in C++.

Potential challenges and caveats

While concepts are undeniably powerful, there are a few considerations to be made:

- **Complexity**: Designing intricate custom concepts can be challenging and may steepen the learning curve for newcomers

- **Compile times**: As with most template-based features, over-reliance or misuse can increase compilation times

- **Backward compatibility**: Older codebases may require refactoring to leverage or comply fully with new concept-driven constraints

This section provided a window into a powerful feature in C++ that allows us to specify constraints on template parameters. We began with a brief introduction to concepts, understanding their role in enhancing the expressiveness and safety of our code. We then explored how refined constraints can be applied in STL algorithms, leading to more robust and readable code. We also learned how to constrain templates effectively, which is crucial for preventing the misuse of our code and ensuring that it behaves as expected.

However, we also acknowledged the potential challenges and caveats associated with concepts. While they offer many benefits, using them judiciously is important to avoid unnecessary complexity and potential pitfalls.

The knowledge gained from this section is invaluable as it equips us with the tools to write safer, more expressive, and more efficient code using the STL. It also prepares us for the next section, where we will explore another exciting feature of C++: coroutines.

The next section will refresh our understanding of coroutines and discuss their integration with STL algorithms and data structures. We will also explore potential synergies with ranges and views, which can lead to even more efficient and elegant code. Finally, we will look at how coroutines represent a paradigm shift in how we write asynchronous code.

Coroutines

The integration of coroutines into C++20 ushers in a new paradigm for asynchronous programming that's more readable and intuitive. By allowing functions to be suspended and resumed, coroutines offer an alternative to the callback-heavy style often seen in asynchronous C++ code. While transformative in its own right, this evolution also provides fresh, innovative ways to interact with the venerable STL. Examining the interaction of coroutines with STL algorithms and data structures reveals how they simplify asynchronous operations.

Understanding coroutines – a refresher

A **coroutine** is a generalization of a function. While a traditional function runs to completion and then returns, a coroutine can be paused at specific points, returning control to the caller and then later resuming from where it left off. Three primary keywords are vital to understanding coroutines in C++: `co_await`, `co_return`, and `co_yield`:

- `co_await`: Suspends the current coroutine until the awaited expression is ready, at which point the coroutine resumes
- `co_return`: This is used to finish the coroutine, potentially returning a value
- `co_yield`: Produces a value in a generator-like fashion, allowing iteration over a coroutine

STL algorithms and coroutine integration

With coroutines, STL algorithms that previously demanded a more convoluted asynchronous approach can now be elegantly written with direct, linear logic. Consider algorithms that operate on sequences or ranges; they can be combined with coroutines to asynchronously generate values.

For instance, a coroutine could asynchronously produce values and then process them using `std::transform` or `std::for_each`, weaving asynchronous code seamlessly with synchronous STL algorithms.

Coroutines and STL data structures

The magic of coroutines also touches the realm of STL data structures. Coroutines present an intriguing potential for containers such as `std::vector` or `std::list: populating` (asynchronously).

Imagine a scenario where data must be fetched from a network source and stored in `std::vector`. A coroutine can be used to fetch the data asynchronously, yielding values as they arrive, and then these values can be directly inserted into the vector. This blend of asynchronicity with the directness of STL data structures simplifies code and reduces cognitive overhead.

Potential synergies with ranges and views

As the C++ language evolves, other features, such as ranges and views, combined with coroutines, can offer a more expressive way to handle data manipulation and transformation. Coroutines can generate ranges, which can be lazily evaluated, filtered, and transformed using views, resulting in a robust and composable asynchronous programming model.

Let's look at the following code example that involves the following steps:

- **STL data structure**: We will use `std::vector<int>` to store a sequence of numbers.

- **Coroutine**: A generator that asynchronously generates numbers to populate our vector.

- **STL algorithms and ranges**: We will filter the numbers in the vector to keep only even numbers using `std::ranges::copy_if`.

- **Views**: By using `std::views::transform`, we'll multiply each number by two. First, we must create our `generator` class with a special `promise_type` structure that our coroutine will use. The generator class template and its nested `promise_type` structure in this code are key components in implementing a coroutine for generating a sequence of values in C++.

A **generator** is a class template designed to produce a sequence of values of type T, one at a time, upon request. It encapsulates the coroutine's state and provides an interface to control its execution and access the yielded values.

The `promise_type` nested within the generator is the coroutine's lifecycle and state management backbone. It holds the current value to be yielded (value) and defines several key functions:

- `get_return_object`: Returns the generator object associated with this coroutine
- `initial_suspend` and `final_suspend`: Control the coroutine's execution, suspending it initially and after completion
- `unhandled_exception`: Defines behavior for unhandled exceptions, terminating the program
- `return_void`: A placeholder for when the coroutine reaches its end
- `yield_value`: This is called when a value is yielded (co_yield), suspending the coroutine and storing the yielded value

The code example below is broken into several sections (the complete example can be found in the book's GitHub repository):

```cpp
template <typename T> class generator {
public:
  struct promise_type {
    T value;

    auto get_return_object() {
      return generator{handle_type::from_promise(*this)};
    }

    auto initial_suspend() {
      return std::suspend_always{};
    }
    auto final_suspend() noexcept {
      return std::suspend_always{};
    }

    void unhandled_exception() { std::terminate(); }
    void return_void() {}

    auto yield_value(T x) {
      value = x;
      return std::suspend_always{};
    }
  };

  using handle_type = std::coroutine_handle<promise_type>;

  generator(handle_type h) : m_handle(h) {}
```

```
generator(const generator &) = delete;
generator(generator &&o) noexcept
    : m_handle(std::exchange(o.m_handle, {})) {}

~generator() {
  if (m_handle) m_handle.destroy();
}

bool next() {
  m_handle.resume();
  return !m_handle.done();
}

T value() const { return m_handle.promise().value; }

private:
  handle_type m_handle;
};
```

The preceding code defines a generic template class called generator. This class is instantiated as the return type of the generate_numbers function, which creates a sequence of integers from start to end. When called, it initiates a coroutine that iteratively yields integers within the specified range. Each iteration suspends the coroutine, making the current value available to the caller. The generator class provides mechanisms to resume the coroutine (next()) and retrieve the current value (value()). The generator's constructor, move constructor, destructor, and deleted copy constructor manage the coroutine's lifecycle and ensure proper resource management.

That was the hard part. Now, we can get to work building and using our coroutine:

```
generator<int> generate_numbers(int start, int end) {
  for (int i = start; i <= end; ++i) { co_yield i; }
}

int main() {
  std::vector<int> numbers;

  auto gen = generate_numbers(1, 10);
  while (gen.next()) { numbers.push_back(gen.value()); }

  std::vector<int> evenNumbers;
  std::ranges::copy_if(numbers,
                       std::back_inserter(evenNumbers),
                       [](int n) { return n % 2 == 0; });
```

```
const auto transformed =
    evenNumbers |
    std::views::transform([](int n) { return n * 2; });

for (int n : transformed) { std::cout << n << " "; }

return 0;
}
```

Here is the example output:

```
4 8 12 16 20
```

In this example, we did the following:

- We created a `generator` class to represent asynchronous generators.
- We used the coroutine `generate_numbers` to asynchronously generate numbers from 1 to 10.
- With ranges, we filtered only even numbers and stored them in another vector.
- Using views, we transformed these even numbers by multiplying them by two.
- Lastly, we output the transformed sequence.

Looking ahead – a paradigm shift

Coroutines in C++ represent a significant advancement in the domain of asynchronous programming. By introducing a standardized way to handle asynchronous tasks, coroutines facilitate writing nonblocking, efficient, and maintainable code. When used in conjunction with the STL, coroutines have the potential to streamline complex operations, transforming the landscape of C++ programming.

The STL provides a robust framework for data manipulation and algorithm implementation. The introduction of coroutines enhances this framework by offering a concurrency model that is less error-prone and more intuitive than traditional threading mechanisms. This synergy allows for developing sophisticated asynchronous programs to leverage the full power of the STL's containers, iterators, and algorithms without compromising performance.

As coroutines become more integrated within the STL, we anticipate a paradigm shift where high-performance code will not only be characterized by its speed but also by its clarity and modular structure. The adoption of coroutines is poised to expand, driven by their ability to produce scalable and responsive software.

The future iterations of the C++ standard will likely introduce more features that complement the coroutine–STL interface, providing developers with a richer toolkit. This evolution will solidify C++'s role as a premier language for developing high-performance, asynchronous applications. The commitment to continual improvement within the C++ community maintains the language's relevance and efficacy in solving modern programming challenges.

Summary

This chapter uncovered the integration of C++20's concepts and coroutines with the STL. We began by exploring the role of concepts in templated programming. Concepts strengthen code robustness by enforcing type constraints and enhancing the expressivity and safety of template use. They replace error-prone SFINAE techniques with a more readable and declarative syntax. We saw how concepts improve the clarity of algorithms' requirements, leading to more maintainable code.

Next, we examined how coroutines introduce a new level of sophistication to asynchronous programming in C++. We discussed the mechanics of coroutines, emphasizing the use of `co_await`, `co_return`, and `co_yield` for creating nonblocking operations. We looked at how coroutines can interact with STL data structures and algorithms, allowing asynchronous and synchronous code to blend seamlessly.

Understanding the interplay between concepts, coroutines, and the STL is crucial. It enables us to write code that is not just performant but also clear and reliable. This knowledge equips us to tackle complex programming scenarios with confidence and foresight.

Next, we will focus on applying execution policies that enable parallelism in STL algorithms. The chapter will guide us through the nuances of parallel execution policies, the role of `constexpr` in enhancing compile-time optimizations, and the best practices for achieving optimal performance in concurrent environments.

22

Parallel Algorithms with the STL

This chapter covers the topic of C++ parallelism, particularly with the tools and techniques introduced in C++17. Starting with the foundations, the chapter unfolds the power of execution policies that allow developers to harness parallel processing in their C++ **Standard Template Library** (**STL**) algorithms.

We will cover the following topics in this chapter:

- Introduction to execution policies
- Incorporating execution policies
- The impact of `constexpr` on algorithms and containers
- Performance considerations

Technical requirements

The code in this chapter can be found on GitHub:

`https://github.com/PacktPublishing/Data-Structures-and-Algorithms-with-the-CPP-STL`

Introduction to execution policies

Processors have transitioned from focusing on increasing the speed of individual cores to incorporating multiple cores for enhanced performance. For developers, this means the potential to execute multiple instructions concurrently across these cores, improving application efficiency and responsiveness.

This move to multi-core configurations highlights the importance of integrating parallel programming techniques. With the advent of C++17, C++ made notable progress in this domain by introducing the `<execution>` header.

The <execution> header– enabling parallelism in STL algorithms

Before C++17, although the STL provided a comprehensive suite of algorithms, they were executed sequentially. This sequential operation meant that STL algorithms did not fully utilize the capabilities of multi-core processors.

The <execution> header addresses this limitation. Instead of adding new algorithms, it enhances existing ones by incorporating parallelism by introducing execution policies.

Execution policies serve as directives, indicating to the STL algorithms the desired mode of operation: sequential, parallel, or vectorized. With the <execution> header, developers can specify these preferences.

The primary execution policies include the following:

- `std::execution::seq`: Dictates a sequential execution of the algorithm
- `std::execution::par`: Facilitates parallel execution where feasible
- `std::execution::par_unseq`: Supports both parallel and vectorized execution

Implementing parallel execution

Integrating parallelism into STL algorithms is straightforward. Consider the `std::sort` algorithm. Typically, it's used in the following manner:

```
std::sort(begin(vec), end(vec));
```

To employ parallel sorting with the <execution> header, the syntax is as follows:

```
std::sort(std::execution::par, begin(vec), end(vec));
```

This modification equips the `sort` algorithm to leverage multiple cores, potentially enhancing the speed of the sorting process.

Reflecting on the transition to parallel STL

While introducing the <execution> header and its associated execution policies is a notable advancement, it's essential to approach their usage with discernment. Parallelism does introduce overheads, such as thread context-switching and data coordination. These overheads can sometimes negate the benefits of parallelism, especially for tasks with smaller datasets.

However, when used judiciously, the <execution> header can significantly enhance application performance. Subsequent sections will provide a more detailed exploration of execution policies, enabling developers to utilize them effectively.

In summary, C++17's `<execution>` header is a pivotal enhancement. Offering a mechanism to imbue existing STL algorithms with parallel capabilities equips developers with the tools to develop applications optimized for multi-core generation.

Incorporating execution policies

The `<execution>` header, introduced in the C++17 standard, adds a significant layer of depth to C++ programming by furnishing a suite of tools designed for parallel computation. This header, when used in conjunction with the STL algorithms, allows developers to leverage the capabilities of concurrent computing effectively.

Execution policies, a key feature of the `<execution>` header, are instrumental in controlling the manner in which STL algorithms execute. By specifying an execution policy when invoking an STL algorithm, developers can dictate whether the algorithm should run sequentially, in parallel, or in parallel with vectorization. This level of control can lead to substantial performance improvements, particularly in applications that are computationally intensive or that operate on large datasets.

In essence, the `<execution>` header and its associated execution policies represent a powerful toolset for C++ developers. They provide a means to tap into the potential of modern multi-core processors and distributed computing environments, thereby enabling more efficient and faster code execution.

Integrating policies with standard algorithms

Execution policies serve as directives for STL algorithms, indicating the preferred mode of operation. For those familiar with STL algorithms, integrating these policies requires minimal modification to existing code.

Consider `std::for_each`, an algorithm that acts on each element in a collection. By default, it operates sequentially:

```
std::for_each(std::begin(vec), std::end(vec), [](int val) { /*...*/
});
```

For large datasets or computationally demanding operations within the lambda function, parallel execution can be beneficial. This can be achieved by simply introducing an execution policy:

```
std::for_each(std::execution::par, std::begin(vec), std::end(vec), []
(int val) { /*...*/ });
```

With the inclusion of `std::execution::par`, the algorithm is now prepared for parallel execution.

Understanding parallel execution policies

There are two primary parallel execution policies:

- `std::execution::par`: This indicates that an algorithm may be executed in parallel. It allows the implementation to decide on parallelism based on the specific context.

- `std::execution::par_unseq`: This goes further by suggesting parallelism and allowing for vectorization. This means that multiple loop iterations might execute concurrently on a single processor core when supported by the hardware.

For instance, the `std::transform` algorithm, which applies a function to each collection element, can utilize these policies:

```
std::transform(std::execution::par_unseq, std::begin(vec),
std::end(vec), std::begin(output), [](int val) { return val * val; });
```

Each `vec` element is squared, and the result populates the output. The `std::execution::par_unseq` policy indicates the potential parallelization and vectorization of this operation.

Selecting the appropriate execution policy

While execution policies enhance parallel computation capabilities, they must be applied thoughtfully. Not every dataset or algorithm will gain from parallel execution, and sometimes, the overhead might negate the advantages for smaller datasets.

The `std::execution::seq` policy explicitly opts for sequential execution, ensuring the algorithm operates in a single-threaded mode. This is beneficial when parallelism introduces undue overhead or in contexts where parallel execution is not recommended.

It's also vital to be wary of potential issues when utilizing parallel policies with algorithms that possess side effects or necessitate synchronization.

C++17's execution policies facilitate straightforward access to parallelism. Pairing these with traditional STL algorithms allows developers to use multi-core processors optimally. Whether utilizing `std::transform` on a vast dataset, sorting large collections with `std::sort`, or filtering items using `std::remove_if`, execution policies provide an added performance dimension.

However, always validate that parallel execution genuinely augments your application without ushering in unforeseen challenges or bottlenecks. It's imperative to evaluate and test your code continually.

With this foundation, we're poised to consider performance considerations in the upcoming section. Through discerning the application of parallelism, we can develop efficient C++ applications tailored to contemporary computational demands.

The impact of constexpr on algorithms and containers

With the introduction of the constexpr specifier in C++11 and its enhancements in subsequent versions, compile-time computation in C++ has taken a significant leap. The ability for functions and constructors to operate at compile time via constexpr enables optimization and assurance of specific attributes before the code runs. This section examines the integration of constexpr within the STL, particularly concerning algorithms and containers.

Evolution of constexpr

In its infancy during C++11, constexpr was primarily for straightforward computations. The C++14 extension broadened its scope, embracing loops and conditional structures. By C++20, there was further augmentation allowing for constexpr allocations via std::allocator. This made containers such as std::vector and std::string usable with constexpr, though with certain restrictions.

Algorithms and the role of constexpr

Originally, constexpr wasn't widely applicable to STL algorithms due to their generic design and multifaceted requirements. However, with the C++20 standard, more STL algorithms became constexpr-compatible. This means that provided all inputs are constant expressions, it is possible to compute algorithmic outcomes at compile time.

Take, for example, the std::find or std::count functions. When used on static data structures such as arrays or std::array, they can operate during the compilation phase. However, as of C++20, dynamic allocation remains mainly outside the domain of constexpr.

The following code snippet uses std::array to highlight the use of std::find and std::count with constexpr:

```
#include <algorithm>
#include <array>
#include <iostream>

constexpr std::array<int, 6> data = {1, 2, 3, 4, 3, 5};

constexpr bool contains(int value) {
  return std::find(data.begin(), data.end(), value) !=
        data.end();
}

constexpr size_t countOccurrences(int value) {
  return std::count(data.begin(), data.end(), value);
}
```

```cpp
int main() {
  static_assert(contains(3));
  static_assert(countOccurrences(3) == 2);

  std::cout << "Array contains 3: " << contains(3) << "\n";
  std::cout << "Occurrences of 3: " << countOccurrences(3)
            << "\n";

  return 0;
}
```

Here is the example output:

```
Array contains 3: 1
Occurrences of 3: 2
```

The contains and countOccurrences functions in the preceding code are evaluated at compile time because they operate on a constexpr-compatible std::array, and all their inputs are constant expressions.

It's worth noting that parallel algorithms using execution policies such as std::execution::par are not suitable for constexpr contexts due to their inherent reliance on runtime resources.

Containers and constexpr integration

C++20's capability for compile-time allocations enabled specific STL containers to function within a constexpr environment. While std::array was always compatible, even some operations on std::vector and std::string became feasible. Nonetheless, any operation requiring dynamic memory or leading to undefined behavior will result in a compile-time error within a constexpr context.

The trajectory of constexpr indicates an evolving C++ environment where the lines between compile-time and runtime evaluation become increasingly indistinct. We might soon see more advanced algorithms and containers being evaluated entirely during compilation, optimizing performance and code safety.

However, the convergence of constexpr and parallel algorithms remains an uncertain prospect due to the fundamental runtime nature of parallelism.

In summary, constexpr has undeniably reshaped C++ development. As it integrates more deeply into the STL, developers have more avenues to refine and solidify their applications.

Performance considerations

Parallel algorithms are a cornerstone in exploiting the capabilities of multi-core processors, aiming to enhance computational efficiency and performance. However, the journey from sequential to parallel programming is not straightforward. It requires a deep understanding of the inherent complexities and trade-offs. In this section, we will explore the various facets of parallel algorithms, including their potential for performance improvement, the challenges of parallel execution, optimal data sizing for parallelism, synchronization issues, and the subtleties of balancing workloads across threads. This comprehensive overview will provide a deeper insight into the effective utilization of parallel algorithms, underlining the importance of informed decision-making and profiling in achieving optimal performance in a parallel computing environment.

Parallel algorithms present both opportunities and challenges for performance enhancement. While they offer the potential for faster computations in multi-core processing environments, their practical use requires careful consideration and decision-making.

Parallelism overhead

As developers experiment with parallel solutions, it's essential to understand that parallel execution doesn't uniformly benefit all algorithms or scenarios. There can be overheads, such as those associated with initiating multiple threads and data synchronization. For example, for small datasets, the overhead of thread management can surpass the computation time, making parallelism less efficient.

Determining optimal data size

Parallel execution reveals its benefits beyond a specific data size threshold. This threshold is influenced by factors such as the algorithm employed, the computation's nature, and the hardware specifications. A resource-intensive task with a large dataset is typically well-suited for parallelism, whereas smaller datasets might be more efficiently processed sequentially.

Understanding the data and computation type is critical to optimize performance. Profiling becomes invaluable, helping developers evaluate their code's runtime behavior and decide when to employ parallelism.

Data access and synchronization challenges

Concurrency leads to scenarios where multiple threads access the same resources concurrently. Data contention can arise, especially with frequent shared data access. Implementing proper synchronization is vital to prevent data inconsistencies. However, synchronization has its associated overheads.

False sharing – a subtle performance issue

Even if threads access distinct data, false sharing can still occur. This happens when threads on different cores modify variables on the same cache line, leading to cache invalidations and potential performance degradation. It's crucial to be mindful of data layout and aim for cache-optimized code.

Load balancing

Different computational tasks may require varying processing times. If threads finish their tasks at different rates, it can result in resource underutilization. Practical parallel algorithms ensure that workloads are distributed uniformly across threads. Some advanced parallel techniques, such as work stealing, can dynamically reallocate tasks to maintain consistent thread engagement.

The importance of profiling

A consistent theme in performance optimization is the essential role of profiling. Relying solely on assumptions is not advisable. Profiling tools such as `perf` and `gprof` and advanced tools such as Intel® VTune™ can identify performance bottlenecks, thread behaviors, and contention areas. These tools provide concrete data to fine-tune parallel strategies.

Throughout this section, we reviewed the performance considerations when working with parallel algorithms. We learned that while parallel algorithms can significantly enhance computational efficiency, their effective use requires a nuanced understanding of various factors. We discussed the potential overheads associated with parallel execution, such as thread initiation and data synchronization. We also highlighted the importance of determining the optimal data size for parallel execution, emphasizing that parallelism may not be beneficial for all scenarios, particularly those involving small datasets. We further explored the challenges of data access and synchronization in a concurrent environment, including the issue of false sharing. We also touched upon the concept of load balancing, explaining how uneven distribution of computational tasks can lead to resource underutilization. We discussed advanced techniques such as work stealing that can help maintain consistent thread engagement by dynamically reallocating tasks.

The insights gained from this section are invaluable as they equip us with the knowledge to make informed decisions when implementing parallel algorithms. Understanding these performance considerations allows us to exploit the full potential of multi-core processors while avoiding common pitfalls. This knowledge is crucial in today's multi-core processing environment, enabling us to write more efficient and performant code. It also sets the stage for our continued exploration of data structures and algorithms with the C++ STL, as we strive to deepen our understanding and enhance our programming skills.

Summary

This chapter introduced parallel algorithms within the STL. We began by acquainting ourselves with the `<execution>` header introduced in C++17, which has been pivotal in enabling parallelism in STL algorithms. This addition allows us to specify execution policies such as `std::execution::seq`, `std::execution::par`, and `std::execution::par_unseq`, thereby dictating the execution mode of STL algorithms.

We progressed to implementing these execution policies in standard algorithms, demonstrating the simplicity of transitioning from sequential to parallel execution. This was exemplified by adapting algorithms such as `std::sort` and `std::for_each` to run in parallel, thus harnessing the computational power of multiple cores.

The chapter then focused on the `constexpr` specifier and its profound impact on STL algorithms and containers. We explored the evolution of `constexpr` from C++11 through C++20 and its role in enabling compile-time computations for algorithms such as `std::find` and `std::count`.

Performance considerations formed the crux of our final discussion, underscoring the benefits and potential pitfalls of employing parallel algorithms. We addressed the overheads associated with parallelism, the importance of determining optimal data size, and strategies for effective data access and synchronization to avoid issues such as false sharing and load imbalance.

The information imparted in this chapter is invaluable for leveraging the STL's capabilities in a multi-core processing environment. We can write more efficient and responsive code by understanding when and how to apply parallel algorithms. This deepened comprehension of parallel execution policies and the ability to optimize code with `constexpr` equips us to maximize performance and resource utilization.

Index

www.packtpub.com

Subscribe to our online digital library for full access to over 7,000 books and videos, as well as industry leading tools to help you plan your personal development and advance your career. For more information, please visit our website.

Why subscribe?

- Spend less time learning and more time coding with practical eBooks and Videos from over 4,000 industry professionals

- Improve your learning with Skill Plans built especially for you

- Get a free eBook or video every month

- Fully searchable for easy access to vital information

- Copy and paste, print, and bookmark content

Did you know that Packt offers eBook versions of every book published, with PDF and ePub files available? You can upgrade to the eBook version at www.packtpub.com and as a print book customer, you are entitled to a discount on the eBook copy. Get in touch with us at customercare@packtpub.com for more details.

At www.packtpub.com, you can also read a collection of free technical articles, sign up for a range of free newsletters, and receive exclusive discounts and offers on Packt books and eBooks.

Other Books You May Enjoy

If you enjoyed this book, you may be interested in these other books by Packt:

Hands-On Design Patterns with C++ Second Edition

Fedor G. Pikus

ISBN: 978-1-80461-155-5

- Recognize the most common design patterns used in C++
- Understand how to use C++ generic programming to solve common design problems
- Explore the most powerful C++ idioms, their strengths, and their drawbacks
- Rediscover how to use popular C++ idioms with generic programming
- Discover new patterns and idioms made possible by language features of C++17 and C++20
- Understand the impact of design patterns on the program's performance

C++20 STL Cookbook

Bill Weinman

ISBN: 978-1-80324-871-4

- Understand the new language features and the problems they can solve
- Implement generic features of the STL with practical examples
- Understand standard support classes for concurrency and synchronization
- Perform efficient memory management using the STL
- Implement seamless formatting using std::format
- Work with strings the STL way instead of handcrafting C-style code

Packt is searching for authors like you

If you're interested in becoming an author for Packt, please visit authors.packtpub.com and apply today. We have worked with thousands of developers and tech professionals, just like you, to help them share their insight with the global tech community. You can make a general application, apply for a specific hot topic that we are recruiting an author for, or submit your own idea.

Share Your Thoughts

Now you've finished *Data Structures and Algorithms with the C++ STL*, we'd love to hear your thoughts! Scan the QR code below to go straight to the Amazon review page for this book and share your feedback or leave a review on the site that you purchased it from.

https://packt.link/r/1835468551

Your review is important to us and the tech community and will help us make sure we're delivering excellent quality content.

Download a free PDF copy of this book

Thanks for purchasing this book!

Do you like to read on the go but are unable to carry your print books everywhere?

Is your eBook purchase not compatible with the device of your choice?

Don't worry, now with every Packt book you get a DRM-free PDF version of that book at no cost.

Read anywhere, any place, on any device. Search, copy, and paste code from your favorite technical books directly into your application.

The perks don't stop there, you can get exclusive access to discounts, newsletters, and great free content in your inbox daily

Follow these simple steps to get the benefits:

1. Scan the QR code or visit the link below

https://packt.link/free-ebook/978-1-83546-855-5

2. Submit your proof of purchase

3. That's it! We'll send your free PDF and other benefits to your email directly

www.ingramcontent.com/pod-product-compliance
Lightning Source LLC
Chambersburg PA
CBHW060645060326
40690CB00020B/4523